The Watering Holes of Scotland

NATURAL MINERAL WATER

Highland Spring is the United Kingdom's largest Natural Mineral Water producer.

We have achieved this position because of the excellence of our water and a total commitment to quality of service. Both we and our stockists in the hotel and restaurant sectors want you to enjoy the benefits of our unique water when you enjoy their hospitality.

Highland Spring is described as a 'natural mineral water' because it is naturally pure and wholesome and may be bottled in its natural state without treatment. Not all bottled waters are 'natural mineral waters'. Indeed, to qualify for this sought after status stringent European Community and UK Government standards must be strictly observed. Crucially each natural mineral water must come from a specific underground source and be consistently free from pollution and harmful micro-organisms. A natural mineral water must show a consistent analysis within the required quality criteria for a period of two years before its water can be registered as a natural mineral water. Highland Spring has been a registered natural mineral water since 1979. The catchment area for Highland Spring natural mineral water is in the Ochil Hills, Perthshire, Scotland. This wide area is controlled by Highland Spring and is a conservation area where no farming or habitation is permitted and no animal husbandry is allowed. As you can gather, the quality of our product is paramount together with the steps we take to protect it.

Highland Spring is committed to playing an active role in the Scottish community and relishes the association of our natural mineral water with events and people who share our commitment to excellence. The decision to sponsor this book, 'The Watering Holes of Scotland' was made because we recognise that Scotland's hotels and restaurants are now numbered among the leading international exponents of their profession.

What follows is a selection of over 200 watering holes located throughout Scotland. Each has been selected by Kensington West the publishers, who specialise in the production of quality travel books. Naturally it can only be a sampling of Scottish establishments, but I hope that this book encourages readers to visit parts of Scotland they have perhaps not visited for sometime. It is a wonderfully varied and beautiful country with a history and tradition of hospitality. Today we are proud to be part of that tradition through the excellence of our water and our involvement with this excellent book. Both aim to promote your health and happiness.

Robert Gibbons, Chairman, Highland Spring Limited

No poison bubbles at its brink; no
blood stains its limpid glass:
beautiful, pure, blessed and
glorious, forever the same,
sparkling pure water!
Toast to Water, John B Gaugh

Kensington West Productions Ltd

Acknowledgements

The publishers would like to acknowledge the support of the Highland Spring marketing department who have invested so much time in helping to produce this title. We are also extremely grateful to the Scott consultancy, Edinburgh for their efforts in developing the project. We would also like to thank the many hoteliers who so kindly assisted us in our research and compilation particularly those who were able to provide pictures. Finally we were able to acknowledge the help of all those who have helped us to produce an outstanding first edition particularly Rosentiels for providing us with many of the colour illustrations which are included within the pages of the first of what we hope will be many Watering Holes titles.

Kensington West Productions Ltd

5 Cattle Market

Hexham NE46 1NJ

Northumberland

Tel: (0434) 609933, Fax (0434) 600066

Contributing Editors
Ken Anderson, Janet Blair, Eric Blair, Sarah Caisley, Jane Chambers, Simon Cooper, Jaqui Hawthorn, Sarah Mann, Edward Rippeth, Simon Tilley, Julian West, Peter Winter.

Design	**Typesetting**	**Cartography**
Angela Burrows	RTC James, England	Rosemary Coates

Origination and Printing
Emirates Printing Press, United Arab Emirates

Contents

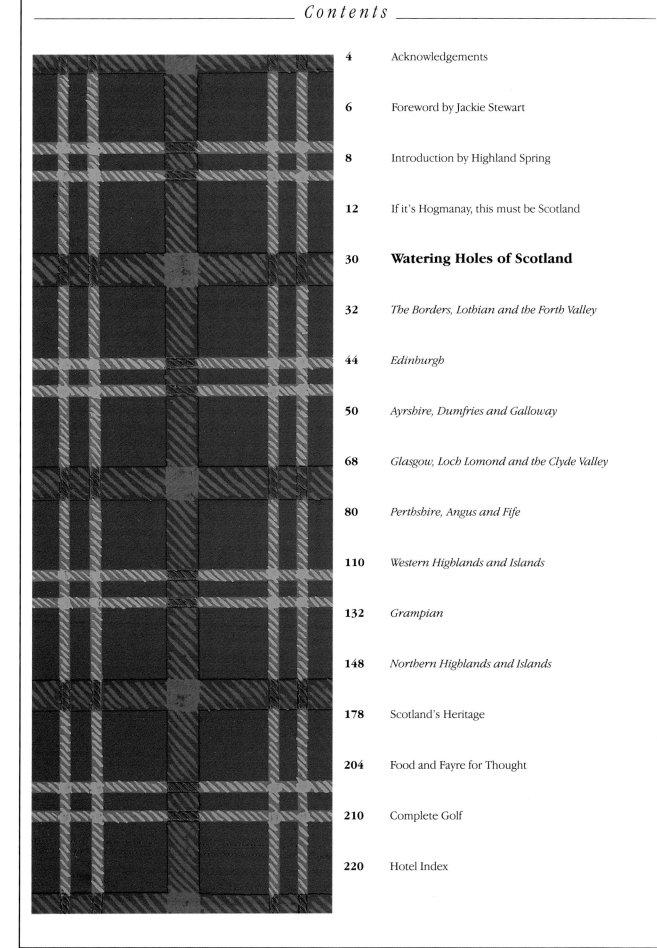

Scotland enjoys a wonderful reputation throughout the world for its hospitality and beauty. Today, more than ever before, open arms are the order of the day.

This book is a selection of some 250 watering holes which can be commended for their food, location or leisure facilities - or perhaps a combination of all three.

In short, whether you travel from lowland or highland through heather and Glen following fairways or burn, I wish you a visit of happiness and fond memories.

Jackie Stewart

Introduction

The expression 'a watering hole' is somewhat misguidedly described in the good old Oxford dictionary as a cavity which captures water. In more common usage it has a more romantic sense. It suggests a welcoming smile, a hearty refreshment and a cheery atmosphere.

In Scotland there are literally thousands of watering holes of infinite variety. We have chosen 250 of the very best. Each and every hotel will have received at one time or another stocks of Highland Spring Natural Mineral Water, hopefully this will be the case when you visit so please do ask. There are many other hotels we could have mentioned many of which also stock Highland Spring Natural Mineral Water, it is however simply impossible to include everybody, no matter how good. Please do let us know if you feel your favourite has been omitted and we will try and rectify this in future editions.

The book essentially follows a simple pattern and we hope you will enjoy its colour, variety and humour. We have greatly enjoyed producing it and we trust you will gain similar entertainment reading it and perhaps more importantly by visiting a watering hole or two.

In short, a brief introduction to the vagaries of Scotland has been penned in a few words by an Englishman with a love of the bonnie land. This is followed by a section devoted to the Watering Holes themselves. We have split Scotland into eight relatively arbitrary areas to ease reference but naturally many readers will wish to cross our notional borders to discover the various delights gathered therein.

Naturally, when it comes to the watering holes themselves there are a broad range of facilities available and in consequence prices charged vary dramatically. They also differ from season to season. Indeed many of the more northerly 'watering holes' take a well earned break for a month or two when winter sets in. Clearly, the best plan is to decide roughly where you want to travel and ask for a few brochures and tariffs to be sent to you which should further whet the appetite and help you make a choice. In order to smooth matters slightly we have given a broad price guide at the back of the book but it has been kept deliberately broad to help ensure accuracy.

In the final chapter we have introduced a range of restaurants, a glossary of golf courses and a list of stately houses and castles that you may wish to visit.

Scotland has a wealth of attractions to offer. Its history is fascinating and its scenery breathtaking. We are extremely grateful to all at Highland Spring for enabling us to produce such a vivid and we hope interesting travel guide. This book, however, provides only a fraction of the story, the richest ingredients are ours to explore and from the many watering holes included in this book we can make those discoveries in style.

The knowledge of man is as the waters, some descending from above, and some springing from beneath, the one informed by the light of nature, the other inspired by divine revelation.

Francis Bacon

Natural Mineral Water

Since man first learned how to express an opinion there does seem to have been a general consensus that water was an important commodity when it came to survival. This and the availability of copious quantities of clean air for the purposes of breathing are about the only two concepts which are universally accepted and understood.

While fame and fortune still awaits the man who can sell us the idea of paying for the air we breathe (watch out for the final demand), the privilege of paying for the rain that falls from the heavens to be packaged and delivered to us is one we have enjoyed for a number of years. In our civilised society we have been conditioned to expect no less.

The quality of the air we breathe may sometimes be questionable, but for the moment we can still rely on nature to manage the atmosphere for us without the need for oxygen reservoirs and filtration plants. With water we have been reduced to the level where it takes a very brave (foolhardy) man to risk quenching his thirst direct from any lake, river or stream.

*You must not pump spring-water unawares
Upon a gracious public full of nerves.*

Elizabeth Barrett Browning - Aurora Leigh

As the old saying goes, you can lead a horse to water but you can't make him drink. The same could be said of the British and bottled waters. Even today, with supermarket shelves literally groaning under the weight of up to 90 different brands, we still do not consume anything remotely approaching the same quantities as our European cousins. It is, however, estimated that a third of the population do take a sip of the bottled stuff from time to time.

While there may be a discernible lack of public awareness there is no denying the trend towards increasing health consciousness and the value of pure and wholesome water has never been questioned. Throughout the 20th century demand for water has grown and grown and though it is now estimated that only three per cent of our domestic water supply is actually consumed as food and drink, it is 'quality' again that has become the key issue in the public

8

mind. Highland Spring recognised the need for 'healthy' water in the 1970s and in 1979 two boreholes were sunk close to Blackford in the Ochil Hills. The emphasis was placed on protecting rather than treating the natural mineral water on its route to the consumer. Natural mineral water in itself is not a health product, but it is a 'healthy' product and the form of water that most matches bodies needs. Tap water is a treated product containing a powerful disinfectant to ensure that it is drinkable without the risk of infection.

Water has become big business and a general increase in the health consciousness of the general public has been a major factor in this boom with a perceivable trend from a 1980s wine bar phenomenon to a 1990s lifestyle staple. The British have always prided themselves on the quality of their tap water and arguably, without European interference we would have remained in blissful ignorance of many of our shortcomings in this respect.

As no water can award itself the designation 'natural mineral water', the consumer is assured that whatever he takes from a bottle bearing this description has come from a rock-based source and has been naturally filtered. This means that the naturally occurring micro-organisms within natural mineral water which are thought beneficial to the digestive system have not been removed by chemical process. As the water filters through the rock strata it also acquires a mineral content by dissolving salts which provide both the distinctive flavour and wholesome character.

Prevailing legislation effectively permits anybody to sell water in a bottle as long as it is free from the same kind of harmful chemicals minerals and bacteria as are removed from our tap water.

There is one exception and this is the classification 'Natural Mineral Water'. Unfortunately, as mineral water has become the generic term for bottled water, the significance of the three words 'natural mineral water' has been somewhat diluted.

What then of the competition, the 'Spring Waters', 'Table Waters' and 'Purified Waters' with all their much vaunted claims to fame?

Like tap water, we can be sure that they are all safe to drink and probably for the same reasons too, in that they will generally have undergone chemical treatment to ensure harmful chemicals, minerals and bacteria have been removed to ensure compliance with strict health regulations. We can also be sure that this will have been at the expense of the beneficial minerals and/or bacteria that give 'natural mineral waters' their distinctive taste and character.

Highland Spring

The story begins some 400 million years ago in the Ochil Hills, as red sandstone, andesite and basalt lavas assumed the geological formations that were to produce a water source. The exceptionally pure quality of the springs in the Blackford area has been a matter of record since records were kept. It is known that in 1488 King James IV paid twelve shillings for a quantity of the celebrated Blackford Ale, the reputation of which owed much to the quality of the local water. By the mid 19th century the issue was more quantity than quality, and in 1876 steps were taken to bring together 19 springs on the hillside above Blackford to form one reliable water source for the surrounding region.

All natural mineral water may start as rain falling freely from the heavens, but in Highland Spring's case it falls as rain from the unpolluted westerly airstream from Greenland and Iceland. The catchment area is Highland Spring's 2000 acres of land near Blackford in the Ochil Hills which are protected so nothing can harm the rainwater. No farming is permitted, so there is no pollution from fertilisers or pesticides. No animal husbandry is allowed or habitation permitted and access is controlled by Highland Spring to limit human impact.

The rainwater filters through the soil and vegetation zone and then slowly down through thousands of minor fissures in layers of sandstone and basalt to the spring itself. It takes an average of 15 years to reach the Highland Spring borehole, during which any toxic micro-organisms die of starvation or lack of oxygen naturally achieving the part played by chemicals in the production of tap water. It is now that the water picks up traces of minerals and elements dissolved from the rocks it passes through which characterise it as natural mineral water.

The public is assured that any bottle bearing the description 'natural mineral water' is of a known quality, from an identified source and is wholesome without treatment.

If it's Hogmanay, this must be Scotland

Highland Cattle – David Dane. Courtesy of Rosentiel's.

Auld Lang Syne traditionally sung at *Hogmanay* to see out the old year and bring in the new. This classic Burns lyric is largely incomprehensible to the uninitiated. It serves then as a suitable introduction to our A-Z of Scotland in which we shall attempt to provide some guidance to this mysterious land, its culture and foreign tongue.

Angus, traditional name which can be found as Christian name or surname or applied to cattle. There are many famous two legged Angus's, but the four legged Aberdeen variety is enjoyed universally.

Andrew, traditional name (see *Angus*) but do not apply to cattle. St Andrew is the patron saint of Scotland and the blue flag with a white X, which visitors to Scotland may encounter from time to time also bears his name.

Arkle, Scottish mountain better known for winning an English horse race over fences called the Gold Cup - not to be confused with the real *Gold Cup* which is run without an obstacle course in Scotland (see *Ayr*).

Ayr, home of the *Gold Cup* and the *National* (see *Foinavon*).

Adam and the *Adam* Architects. The only name in 18th century architecture, the family's work can be seen principally in Edinburgh and Ayrshire. In true artistic tradition their company nearly went bankrupt in the 1760s, but the dynasty survived to influence architecture to the 1790s.

Architecture favourite subject of Welsh Prince Charles as opposed to Scottish Prince Charles (see *Bonnie*).

Bonnie Prince Charles and the stuff of legends. There is unfortunately not ample space here to do full justice to this Scottish hero whose fame derives in the main from an attempt to overthrow the monarchy in England. Although this 18th Century Prince Charles is most dear to Scottish hearts there are those who would claim his 20th Century equivalent is enjoying greater success (see *Architecture*). Penchant for wearing lady's clothing only to be discussed in context (see *Flora*).

Bannockburn, heroic and historic victory (1314) over vastly superior English forces, leading ultimately to Scottish independence (1320). Similar endeavours of the Bonnie Prince became heroic failure (see *Culloden*).

Borders, scene of many famous bloody conflicts, a tradition maintained in the Rugby Strongholds of Kelso, Gala, Selkirk, Jedforest and the home of `7s', Melrose, whose sons still sally forth against the English on a regular basis.

Berwick on the border where the English soccer team plays in the Scottish football league.

Brigadoon which isn't anywhere except in the imagination of Hollywood film producers (thankfully).

Bagpipes (thankfully?) the national musical instrument which when played properly produces a stirring sound that is forever Scottish. Otherwise the term `drone' can be applied in reference to the single drone from which today's triple drone instrument developed.

Ben, a song by the much misunderstood Michael Jackson and often wrongly attributed as dedicated to a rat instead of a Scottish mountain.

Ben Nevis, highest mountain in Scotland and just one of a number of Bens that might have been worthy of Mr. Jackson's affections.

Burns - Scottish streams.

B is really for **Burns** as in Robert Burns, Scotland's national poet in whose honour Burns night suppers are held (all over the world) on the 25th January. It is unlikely that one song about a Scottish mountain will earn Mr. Jackson equal recognition for posterity but in the main his words are easier on the untrained English ear. For those anxious to learn more bout the man who gave us *Auld Lang Syne*, Dumfries is the place to visit with its *Burns House, Burns Mausoleum* and *Burns Centre*.

Bruce, popular with Australians, this Scottish King was inspired by a spider to defeat the English at Bannockburn.

Battle, term generally used to describe social encounters between the English and Scottish - it is very rare for the term to be used in conjunction with other visitors, though there were some initial misgivings about Scandinavian visitors from across the North Sea (see *Viking*). These stemmed in the main from the bad press given all foreigners after earlier attempts by Italian tourists (see *Roman*) to influence the host nation's lifestyle and culture. History, alas, fails to reveal whether the custom of reserving territory with a towel while on foreign soil began with the *Huns, Goths* and *Vandals* on their brief sorties north to Scotland.

Beaches, as may be expected (given the geography of Scotland) there are a lot of these expanses of sand. On the West Coast where the Gulf Stream flows, palm trees and other such exotic tropical fauna can be found in the proximity of beaches. Temperatures do not, however, always match the Caribbean or even the Mediterranean and modern day *Huns, Vikings* and *Romans* no longer visit primarily to improve their sun tans.

Blackwatch famous Scottish regiment held in esteem despite allied association with English regiments.

Coldstream (see *Blackwatch*) a border town from whence came the guards and which is nearly in England anyway.

Chevy Chase, battle named after ancient American comic actor.

Charlie as in *Bonnie Prince Charlie* (see *Bonnie*) (see also *Prince*) just in case importance of this figure is being underestimated.

Culloden where the gallant Jacobite rising of 1745 inspired by the Prince was doomed to heroic failure at the hands of the infamous Butcher, the Duke of Cumberland (see *Sausage*) in 1746. Although the Duke's forces ranged against Prince Charles' Jacobites included Scottish Loyalists, atrocities perpetrated by the Duke's forces have never been forgotten (see *Murrayfield*).

Clan, during lulls in disputes with the English it was not uncommon for *Clans* to practise amongst themselves. Historically a *Clan* member had to be Scottish and actually live in Scotland, the rules have been somewhat changed nowadays to accommodate the nation's economy (see *Tartan*). *Clans* generally consisted of people of the same family and it was not untypical for *Clans* to enter into disputes over such trivialities as a stolen sheep which then developed into lifelong feuds and even promoted kinship with the English if it would serve a purpose (see *Culloden*).

Celtic, adjective used to describe essentially Gaelic (see *Gaelic*) heritage culture etc as opposed to Scottish. However, the followers of Glasgow Celtic Football Club have fought to keep the spirit of Clan warfare alive in fine Scottish tradition and with the full co-operation of like-minded supporters of Glasgow Rangers. This rivalry chiefly manifests itself in the wearing of different colours (see *Tartan*), singing different songs, and worshipping at different venues (*Ibrox* and *Parkhead*). Nowadays the two Clans meet on a minimum of four occasions between August and May and visitors to Glasgow are advised to check these days out in advance before planning their schedule.

Celt not a *Celtic* Clan member specifically, though related over the centuries as indigenous warrior race.

Claymore from the *Gaelic* `Claidheamhor' meaning 'great sword' and presumably carried for ceremonial purposes only.

Caddie from the French 'Cadet' used since Mary Queen of Scots' time to denote a carrier of things and specifically golf clubs (see *Golf*), not to be confused with *Caddy* from the Malay 'Kati' used to denote a receptacle containing tea.

Caber which is tossed during Highland games, the *caber* being a large heavy telegraph pole which is not as much tossed as allowed to topple forwards in a straight line. Marks being awarded for presentation and style rather than distance. A bit like ski-jumping really.

Curling, a winter sport invented by Neanderthal Scots when the Ice Age froze over the bowling greens.

Cattle; there are a number of famous breeds of Scottish cattle though not all have had human beings named after them (see *Angus*). The beauty of these beasts when on display and in competition inspired the terms 'cattlemarket' and 'beefmarket' for *homo sapiens* equivalents.

Ceilidh; when not throwing things or judging cattle, the Scots can be found singing, dancing and playing musical instruments at gatherings known as the *Ceilidh*. These can be tremendous fun and should be attended if the invitation is extended. Those visitors of an easily embarrassed or self-conscious nature are advised to partake heavily before and during (see *Dram, Whisky, Rab. C. Nesbitt*).

Chaser (see *Whisky*).

Castles built to host *Ceilidhs* originally, hence the unbelievable concentration of castles in this country. These constructions were to come in useful when the peace-loving Scots entertained the English.

Cake as in 'take with a piece of' (see *Castles*). *Dundee* is famous for *Cake*.

Carnegie. Dunfermline's loss and America's gain (see also *McEnroe*), though *Andrew Carnegie* never forgot his roots. After his family emigrated in 1848 to settle near Pittsburg, the 13 year old Andrew Carnegie benefited initially from Scottish connections to gain employment in the cotton industry. Upon his retirement in 1901 he was reputed to own the largest private fortune in the world, made in the main from iron and steel. One of life's great and few true philanthropists he was to give it all away before he died and his legacy continues to benefit us to this day on both sides of the 'pond'.

Donald, those born with this name should note that the question `Donald, where's your trousers?' is rhetorical. The song from which the lyric is taken did not form part of *Andrew Carnegie's* legacy.

Dancing of which art form only Scottish Dancing is recognised in this context, with an apology that again there is insufficient space to fully explore the intricacies of the eightsome reel or adequately analyse the basic skip change of step.

Dirk, a dagger worn like a *Claymore* only for decoration but more useful at *Ceilidhs* when slipped into the sock as deterrent during the more boisterous phases of the dancing.

Fishing in Calm Waters – George Cammidge. Courtesy of Rosentiel's.

D is for

Dram generally used in conjunction with the adjective *Wee*. As a rule of thumb should the words `Wee Dram' be followed by `of whisky', then the conventional association of *Wee* with small may be forgotten.

Partaking in *Wee Drams* has been recommended to certain parties visiting *Ceilidhs* for the first time, though care must be taken not to consume quantities that encourage use of the *Dirk*.

Distillery where the whisky is distilled. There are a lot of distilleries in Scotland and their importance to the national economy is such that a special trail has been laid to ensure none of them get lost.

Dogs of which like *Cattle* there are a number of famous Scottish Breeds mainly of the `Terrier' variety e.g. Border, Highland, Cairn. The phrase *Scottie dog* is, however, best applied only in reference to the white stuffed variety with tartan collars seen nodding sagely in rear windows of cars (see *Lassie*).

E is for

Edward (see *Flower of Scotland*) unfortunate King of England whose army suffered ignominious defeat at *Bannockburn* and returned to England to ponder the error of their ways.

England which in a perfect world would be populated purely by the descendants of defeated English armies.

English acknowledged as language in widespread use though often unrecognisable when spoken (see *Rab C Nesbitt*) or sometimes in its written form (see *Burns*). Otherwise the actual word has negative connotations and should be used sparingly. N.B. People native to *England* are rarely referred to as *English* and upon application any Scot will divulge the terms in more common usage (usually without even being offered an inducement (see *Whisky*).

Edinburgh where there is a famous Zoo.

F is for

Festivals of which there are many but the most popular is held in Edinburgh where numbers are swelled by those visiting the zoo.

Fringe, the Edinburgh festival is not to be missed because of its Fringe which really isn't part of the Festival, more part of the zoo. Many famous funny people's careers have begun at the fringe. *Chevy Chase* has never appeared at the fringe as it is the scene of a battle.

Football, a game with two codes generally played on grass, which grows in fields which can be battlefields when the games are played against the English.

Flower and as the perceptive reader may have guessed by now bears no association to colourful fauna whatsoever. *Flower of Scotland* describes victorious Scottish army and name of song sung to inspire similar feats when playing games, especially against the English (see *Football, Murrayfield*).

Flour, there is another flour of Scotland often seen in lorries travelling up the A1. Do not confuse in conversation with *Flower*.

Fishing (see *Sea, Rivers, Loch*).

Feuds (see *Clans*) of which the most notorious is perhaps the feud between the Campbells and MacGregors as featured in 'Rob Roy' by Sir Walter Scott.

Foinavon another Scottish mountain (see *Arkle*), best known for winning by process of elimination a barbaric English horse race known as the *Grand National* not to be confused with the real *National* (see *Ayr*).

Flora which is spread on bread in memory of *Flora MacDonald* who helped *Bonnie Prince Charlie* escape the clutches of the English. Those interested in the history of transvestitism through the ages may care to enquire further.

Flings which, though synonymous with 'throws', may not be used to describe tossing the caber at Highland Games meetings. Anyone found performing a fling during the Games will actually be *Dancing* (see *Dancing* and begin to appreciate how much space would be needed).

Gay, adjective commonly used to describe *Gordons* when *Dancing*. (see *Dancing, Flings*, no further comment).

Gordon (see *Gay*) (see *Highlander*). A useful tip when meeting your first *Gordon* is to avoid calling him gay in the interests of provoking a reaction that will shed more light on this subject. This advice applies especially if the *Gordon* is also a *Highlander*.

Greyfriars Bobby and the phrase 'let sleeping dogs lie' (see *Gay, Gordons*). *Greyfriars Bobby* was a terrier whose grave can be found in Edinburgh next to her shepherd master's. The dog watched over her master's grave for 16 years from 1858-1872 and was adopted by the people of Edinburgh. The story epitomises the loyal and tenacious nature of Scottish breeds of Terrier, traits of character that apply equally to the Scots themselves.

Gaelic, the native language of the *Gael*. For our purposes a Gael may be construed as a general sort of *Pict* or *Celt* whose descendants are spread around Scotland, Ireland and the Isle of Man and consequently there are three Gaelic dialects though written Gaelic is fairly standard. Scottish Gaelic is spoken by less than 2% of the total population but it is in widespread use throughout the North West Highlands, the Hebrides and the Isle of Skye. There is also a notable clique of Gaelic speakers in Glasgow, though this figure is often mistakenly exaggerated by those with an untrained ear (see *English, Rab C. Nesbitt*).

Glen from the Gaelic 'Gleann' meaning a narrow valley with a stream running through. Idyllic, romantic images conjured up are often rudely shattered by tales of massacres. (see *Glencoe*).

Glencoe (see *Glen*).

Gretna Green, as per *Glen* place where romantic image may belie reality .

Graverobbers and their contribution to medical research in Edinburgh.

Golf, a game probably not invented by the Chinese.

Golf, a game almost definitely not invented by the Dutch.

Golf, a game that must have been invented by the Scots as it involves hitting something with a big club on a grassy surface. A national pastime that has its origins in hitting somebody with a big stick on a grassy surface known as a battlefield. In its present format the game consists of a challenge to knock the ball into 18 small holes, in the right order, and using less blows to the ball than an opponent/or opponents, a scoring system that hearkens back to the traditions of the Highland Games and the development of man as an efficient fighting machine (see *Games*). The ultimate definitive challenge can be found at St. Andrews, the home of golf, where holes that are not to be played consecutively are actually quite close together; a hole being anything from 4½ inches to hundreds of yards. The Royal and Ancient Golf Club of St. Andrews have been trying to get the rules of this game sorted out for years and have a new go every 12 months. Lots of Scots are authorities on the game of golf and will gladly spend hours explaining the intricacies of the game, if required, in the context of their own experiences.

Games of which there are only one type namely *Highland*, though the *Games* are to be found not only in *Highland* (see *Highland*) but throughout Scotland. Over the years the nature of the games has been somewhat tempered and the combative origins which extolled the skills of warriors have been all but lost. The Olympic movement's debt of gratitude to the *Highland Games* format cannot be quantified, and is celebrated in opening and closing ceremonies inspired by the displays of dancing, piping and massed bands to be found at the *Highland Games*.

Highland, area of Scotland and term used in preference to Scottish to describe things that really are Scottish.

Highlander almost by definition a soldier or warrior. Also in finest Hollywood tradition (see *Brigadoon*) a film about warrior blessed/cursed to live for eternity (see *Brigadoon*). Also in fine Hollywood tradition the Scottish actor Sean Connery appears in the film but not as the *Highlander*, this role being played by a Frenchman.

Hollywood named by Scot with a speech impediment after palace in Edinburgh. This suburb of *Los Angeles, California* is the last bastion of Scottish folklore (see *Brigadoon, Highlander*) and the tradition of warring clans is reputed to have spread throughout the city, inspired by either love or hatred of Billy Connolly.

Holyrood or *Holyrood House* a palace in Edinburgh famous

for its association with the romantic legend of *Mary, Queen Of Scots*. (see *Mary*).

Hampden, a palace in Glasgow famous for its association with *Football* (see *Football*).

Hadrian, a Roman Emperor more famous for building a wall than a palace. Conventional wisdom has it that the purpose of the wall was to protect the 'English' from the rampaging Celtic tribes (often referred to as barbarians). In the light of the subsequent frequency of aggressive intrusions perpetrated by the English this explanation seems somewhat dubious.

Hess who with great regard for the peace loving traditions of the Scots flew to Scotland in an apparent attempt to bring the Second World War to a peaceful conclusion. Strangely his mission was not an unqualified success.

Artist: **John Trickett**   *FISHING THE LOCH* — *Courtesy of Sally Mitchell Fine Arts*

H is for

Harris not as in *Bomber Harris* (see *Hess*) but as in *Harris Tweed* which is nearly as famous as *Tartan* (see *Tartan*).

Haggis which everybody knows does not consist of minced sheeps' liver, heart etc boiled up with suet and oatmeal. For details as to when Haggis are in Season and their breeding grounds apply to local Tourist Board.

Heather, popular as a girls name. Heather can be very pretty or pretty unpleasant when found on a golf course.

Horseracing (see *Ayr*).

Hogmanay, a Scottish concept (see *Auld Lang Syne*) with traditions and origins that curiously may not be either pagan or Gaelic. Whatever the case there is no finer place to witness the passing of the last day (*Hogmanay*) of the old year and welcome in the new. There are also no finer people to celebrate with (see *Shand*) and while we are on the subject of fine things....
Highland Springs Mineral Water.

I is for

Islands of which there are many.

J is for

Jocky who does not ride a horse but became a World champion in time honoured Scottish tradition by throwing sharp pointed things known as darts.

Jock, 'jocular' name for the Scots.

Jimmy from the *Gaelic* 'Sceahughjimi' meaning hello, goodbye, watch out or anything at all depending on context (see *Rab. C. Nesbitt*).

James I of England and VI of Scotland, son of *Mary, Queen Of Scots*, whose accession to the crown unified the two

kingdoms in 1603. The term 'unified' is to be understood in its broadest possible context, or treated with utmost suspicion.

Jacobites who failed to understand concept of unification and had to resit the exam twice in the 18th century, without achieving any success other than being in the same company as *Bonnie Prince Charlie* second time around (see *Mole*).

John O'groats which is to Scotland what Land's End is to England.

K is for

Kilt which is to man what skirt is to woman, and has its origins at the beginning of the 17th Century replacing the *Leincroich* which was too difficult to pronounce.

Kintyre which has a *Mull* (see *Mull*) that is world famous thanks to a 'Song' by an Englishman with a Scottish surname who comes from Liverpool, an English city immortalised in

song by *Jimmy Osmond*. It is a subject of much debate as to which location has suffered most.

King Arthur's Seat which is an extinct volcano and has nothing to do with the legend of King Arthur which is jealously guarded by the people of *Cornwall*.

L is for

Lorna Doon who sounds Scottish but was really from *Cornwall*.

Lassie, used in Scotland as affectionate term for female of species (see *Heather*). However, in international use as a good name for four legged friend (see *Dog*) courtesy of Hollywood. When in Scotland it is very important not to mix these two concepts.

Leinechroich, a saffron shirt stretching to the knees like a cassock which was a popular fashion till the Union of the Crowns in 1603 when it became too hard for the English to pronounce (see *Kilt*).

Loch which the English could pronounce as it is very similar to *Lake* and means exactly the same (well nearly). Scottish *Lochs* are spectacular, teeming with fish, and surrounded by history (see *Monster*). English Lakes are dull, grey affairs in overcrowded tourist areas where even the poets preferred to write about daffodils.

Law which is spelt and just about pronounced the same in England and in Scotland, but differs greatly. Scottish Law s not enshrined in stone tablets, it has evolved to accommodate the 'not Proven' verdict which is akin to a second serve in tennis.

Moonwalk, a dance generally performed in tennis shoes or trainers by aforementioned Burns aspirant Michael Jackson. The steps bear absolutely no relation to Scottish Dance steps and further underline Jackson's failure to emulate the great man.

Mac - generally 'Big' and eaten between slices of bread, taking name of much smaller trouserless predecessor called 'Donald'.

Macbeth and whose name should not have been pronounced by those whose lips move when they read. Behind every great man, they say, is a woman and in the Shakespearean legend no man had greater support in his ascent to the throne of Scotland.

McEnroe, there are no records in Scotland of this clan which was probably expelled for _Caber_ abuse (see _Games_).

Murrayfield from the Gaelic 'Muhrae' meaning 'bloody battle.' Location in Edinburgh. (see _Football, Flower_).

Mary, Queen Of Scots, a character from a 16th Century Jackie Collins novel bubbling with sex and violence from start to finish. Real life intrigues and murders dogged the footsteps of this reputedly beautiful Queen on both a personal scale and in her attempts to win greater tolerance

for the Roman Catholic faith. At 26 she was forced to flee to England and her cousin Queen Elizabeth in order to escape Protestant forces. There are those who claim the English Queen promptly imprisoned her for being too beautiful and for no other reason, but a prisoner she remained until her execution in 1587.

Mole an animal which had more success than _Mary_ against the Protestants, it being a molehill upon which William of Orange's horse stumbled throwing the King to his death. Favourite animal of the Jacobites, who were also _Catholic_ as was you know who.

Mull(see _Kintyre_).

Music (see _Bagpipes_)(see _Shand_) do not bother with _Kintyre_.

Monster supposed to reside in Scottish _Loch_ (see _Ness_). Though various expeditions have been launched with the latest in high technology to track down the monster there is as yet no proof of its existence. Much credibility is given to eye witness accounts from normal, well-balanced people living in the vicinity of the _Loch_. The awareness of these people to the commercial realities of life (see also _Tartan_) is further proof of their sanity.

Ness, deepest _Loch_ in Scotland as yet never completely explored, in which a monster is supposed to reside or at the very least species as yet unknown to man.

Nationalist, while all Scots are nationalists by inclination, this is not reflected in support for the _Scottish Nationalist Party_ in General Elections. (Avoid discussing politics in public/pubs).

Nesbitt, Rab. C. (avoid at all costs). Glaswegian anti-hero, achieved legendary cult following for his T.V. series in England by rabbiting on in a drunk and incoherent fashion while wearing a string vest, thus enabling the English to reaffirm all their worst fears about the Scottish on a regular

basis for half an hour every week. A pleasure denied them since Billy Connolly went commercial (see _Hollywood_).

Nip (see _Dram_).

Neep, turnip traditionally served mashed with _Haggis_.

Northern Lights seen in Aberdeen which city also lays claim to being the Flower of Scotland but as we already know this is a song. Aberdeen is also called the _Granite City_, as well as being Scotland's answer to Dallas with its link to the oil industry. The city also lends its name to a breed of cattle and a chain of restaurants but is not as famous for cake as Dundee.

Oil (see _Northern_) to be found in the North Sea, or more accurately the Scottish part of the North Sea.

Orange (see _Mole_) a colour associated with the Protestant religion thanks to King William who originated from Holland.

The Scotch Gamekeeper – Richard Ansdell. Courtesy of Rosenstiel's

P is for

Prince (see *Bonnie*) (see *Charlie*).

Princes, Street in Edinburgh with lots of shops.

Princess, sister of the Welsh Prince Charles, Princess Anne is popular not just for her fine work with children and charities but for her support of the Scottish Rugby Union Football team, and her enthusiasm for Scottish dancing.

Pubs which are almost as popular in Scotland as the *Princess*.

Proscription which was nearly as bad as the American Prohibition period, when all clan activities were outlawed in the wake of Culloden.

Poaching which despite tradition remains illegal. Form of fishing and is useless for cooking eggs.

Picts (see *Celt*) another type of indigenous warrior race.

Porridge traditional Scottish breakfast dish made from oatmeal, which traditionalists eat with salt. The English have been known to pour milk and sugar on porridge.

Powderhall where professional sprinters race for less money than amateur Olympians.

Ponies of which the most famous is the Shetland (from the Islands).

R is for

Reels (see *Dancing*).

Rugby (see *Football, Murrayfield*).

Rangers (see *Celtic*) and note that though they play in blue, orange would be a more appropriate colour for the strip. Avoid religion when discussing football unless sure of which side is which.

Romans who once they had fulfilled contractual obligation to construct wall to keep the English out, were invited to tour Scotland. Regrettably bad habits learnt from association with the English were to get the better of them and the usual violence and mayhem ensued. The *Romans* never fully came to terms with the Scots despite trying to pin their most ardent adversaries behind another wall from the Forth to he Clyde, and eventually they retreated south of Hadrian's Wall.

Rebellion, art form at which the Scots excel.

Reiver, a raider traditionally from the Borders who would practise his trade on the English in preference to other clans.

River a place to fish.

S is for

Scotch, name used when referring to or ordering whisky e.g. 'a large Scotch please', this is equivalent to a wee dram or nip of the hard stuff (see *Whisky*). Do not refer to anybody who is Scottish or anything else north of Hadrian's wall other than Whisky as *Scotch*. This is unforgivable and can lead to immediate expulsion (see *McEnroe*).

Sassenach from the Gaelic 'peasant', complimentary term for an Englishman.

Spider, national insect of Scotland (see *Bruce*).

Sporran, thought of by many as a kind of purse worn over the kilt to compensate for lack of pockets. Sporrans in everyday wear may be of leather, but preferably should be the head of a fox, badger or other such animal if a *Sassenach* is not available.

Sir Walter Scott, not just a novelist telling tales of 'derring do' against the dramatic backdrop of the Highlands, but a champion of Scotland and things Scottish who did much to restore the pride of Scotland after *Proscription* with some degree of poetic license. As with *Burns* there is a whole tourist industry devoted to Scott but the truth lies somewhere in the *Borders*.

Stevenson, Robert Louis another Scottish novelist whose works include *Kidnapped* and *Treasure Island*, and who single handedly is responsible for ensuring no pirate received any credibility until he had lost at least one limb, one eye, and adopted a parrot. The custom of blackballing prospective new members of clubs (especially Golf clubs) may have its origins in the 'Black Spot'. Equally Stevenson may have been inspired by the introduction of this custom at his local club.

Shand, another famous Scottish entertainer who with his band used to annually entertain the English at Hogmanay until TV censorship was introduced.

Smokie, pop group who had numerous hits in the 1970s and are still very popular in Germany. But not as popular as the *Arbroth Smokie*, a salted and smoked haddock, traditionally eaten for breakfast. It will remain a mystery as to which Smokie would have induced *Hess* to forsake Germany for Scotland in the 1990s.

Shetland, islands where ponies (see *Ponies*) come from.

Artist Wendy Reeves   HIGHLAND RIVER   Courtesy of Rosenstiel

Skye, another island and the one to which the *Prince* escaped in a boat rowed by *Flora Macdonald*.

Song, there is a song about this escapade which in its own way evokes the same passions as the one about flowers. Confusingly, the lyric refers to the boat as 'bonnie' rather than the Prince who is a mere lad born to be King. The words may therefore have been penned by a forefather of Mr. Jackson, alternatively the repetition of 'over the Sea to Skye' has its parallels in the *Mull Of Kintyre* song where the technique is used by the Scouse with the Scottish name to ultimate effect.

Stuart originally *Stewart* a Scottish regal dynasty comprising a lot of *King James* and two *Queen Marys* only one of whom was a Stuart.

Salmon and no visit to Scotland would be complete without either catching or eating one. Do not attempt *Poaching* (see *McEnroe, Scotch*).

Sausage, but not Cumberland Sausage which has unfortunate connotations that have nothing to do with EC directives.

Tartan, a modern day industry thrives in the wake of Sir Walter Scott's romantic revival of the Clan Spirit. The association of *Tartan* to *Clan* goes deeper than may be suspected with dress codes determining the wearing of 'clan' and 'district' tartans, 'dress' tartans, 'hunting' tartans etc., as well as accessories such as the *Sporran*. None of this concerns the weavers or the wool industry and *Tartans* can now be made to order or invented to suit anybody from anywhere.

Tattoo which rhymes with *Zoo* and therefore is easily recognisable as an attraction in Edinburgh of an essentially militaristic nature, though it is not as painful as being tattooed which is something totally different, while beating a

tattoo has no effect whatsoever on the tattoo.

Tweed, (see *Tartan*)(see *Harris*)(see *River*)

Terriers (see *Dogs*)(*Greyfriars Bobby*).

Thistle, national emblem and flower not to be confused with the Flower of Scotland. Like Heather very pretty but unpleasant if not handled correctly.

Twelfth as in glorious. A day (and night) in August which marks he opening of the grouse season.

Trout (see *Salmon*).

Underwear, the dress codes applicable to *Tartan* are not specific as to what should be worn under the kilt. Rumour

has it that nothing is worn but visitors are urged to adopt caution when pursing their enquiries (see *Gordon*).

Victoria who fell in love with Scotland and left us *Balmoral*.

Vikings who fell in love with Scotland and left many people

dead as they began their quest through the ages for cheap alcohol.

War, ongoing state of affairs applicable to relations with the English, and the friendly rivalry between *Rangers* and *Celtic* fans.

Wallet, rumours abound to the effect that the Scots have very deep pockets (when not wearing kilts) and that carrying a *Wallet* does not necessarily mean it will be opened. These rumours have no basis in fact and are maliciously spread by the English who have grown fat on the profits from Scottish oil and whisky. Bearing in mind the national emblem (see

Thistle) It is not, however, recommended that the casual visitor should rely on the generosity of his hosts too much (see *Gordon*).

Wee, which means small except when used to describe a measure of Whisky.

Wee, which does mean small when used in conjunction with whisky e.g. 'a large Scotch and a wee drop of water.' If entertaining a Scottish guest who inquires after a 'wee dram with a wee drop' be sure to get the proportions correct.

Water, (see *Wee*)(?)

Wool, material from sheep employed in the production of clothing. The Scottish Borders are renowned for production of quality knitwear, most of which is worn by one English golfer.

Whisky, the lifeblood of the nation, Scotland's biggest export and a major source of revenue for the English. Scotch whisky is the real thing, whiskey with an 'e' is Irish. There are many ways to drink whisky; as a chaser with beer, neat with water, with ice and water and on and on, including pollution with Coke. There are blended whiskies and single malts and a whole variety of processes and ingredients to discover and there is no better place to start than the Whisky Trail in Speyside.

Day's Dying Glow - Joseph Farquharson. Courtesy of Rosentiel's.

D.F.Dane

Watering Holes

Crofter's Cottage – David Dane. Courtesy of Rosentiel's.

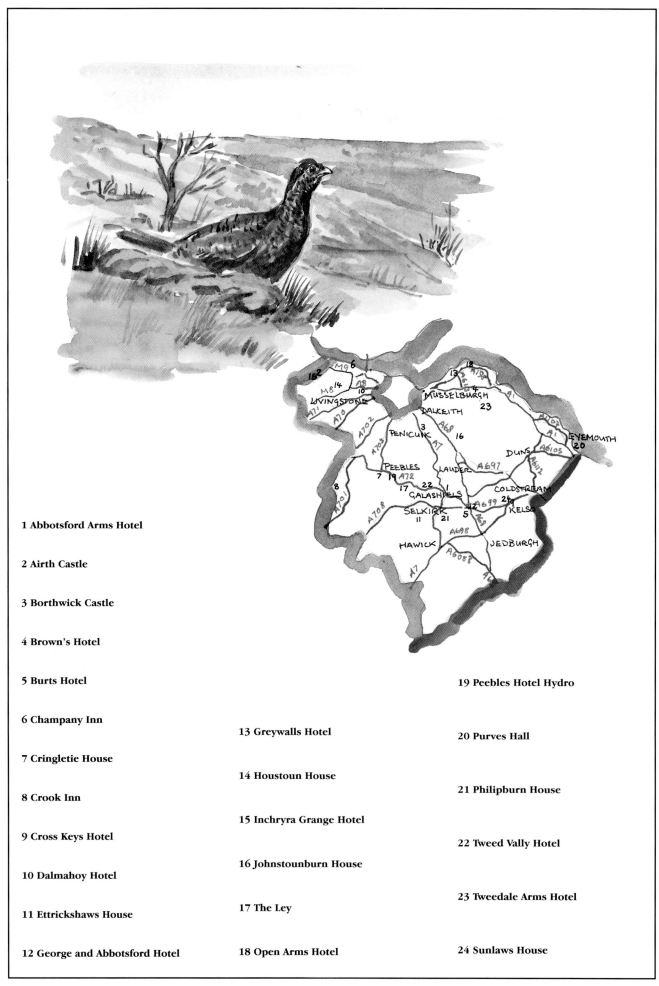

1 Abbotsford Arms Hotel

2 Airth Castle

3 Borthwick Castle

4 Brown's Hotel

5 Burts Hotel

6 Champany Inn

7 Cringletie House

8 Crook Inn

9 Cross Keys Hotel

10 Dalmahoy Hotel

11 Ettrickshaws House

12 George and Abbotsford Hotel

13 Greywalls Hotel

14 Houstoun House

15 Inchryra Grange Hotel

16 Johnstounburn House

17 The Ley

18 Open Arms Hotel

19 Peebles Hotel Hydro

20 Purves Hall

21 Philipburn House

22 Tweed Vally Hotel

23 Tweedale Arms Hotel

24 Sunlaws House

The marvelously loyal Scots who inhabit the border country are a welcoming group of natives. To feel the warmth of this once traditionally hostile area, just visit Kelso races where the action is always superb and in the bars a mixture of whisky and hearty chatter is entertainment itself. Mind you, sassenachs stopping for refreshment on the long drive back to England after a day at Murrayfield have been known to be less appreciative of border banter.

This essentially rural region is speckled with a variety of border towns each offering various attractions to the visitor. The many castles and fortified houses in the region are a stark reminder of centuries of border skirmishing that shaped the border between Scotland and neighbouring Northumberland. Looting and pillaging were common place and standing as monuments to those turbulent times are the great abbeys of Melrose, Kelso, Jedburgh and Dryburgh which were uncompromisingly ravaged by the English. These magnificent buildings remain, at least in part, as a reminder to the locals of times when relations with neighbouring England were not quite so friendly.

The borders of today are far more peaceful and any journey through this countryside should be taken at a leisurely pace. Local traditions are held dear, particularly those which serve as a reminder of the brutality that once held sway. The Selkirk Common Riding is a particularly moving ceremony in which the town remembers the single Selkirk soldier who returned after the Battle of Flodden. More delightful local events include agricultural shows, pipe band displays and many sheep dog and horse trials.

Country houses, boasting elegant interiors and impressive facades are plentiful, and each has its own fascinating history; Abbotsford, once home to the distinguished author Sir Walter Scott, Bowhill, with its celebrated art treasures, Manderston with its renowned gardens, and Floors castle, an imposing house in an idyllic setting beside the river Tweed. Another of note is the fascinating Traquair, the oldest continually inhabited house in Scotland. Dating from 1107 it has provided shelter to many a royal visitor including the feted and ill-fated Mary Queen of Scots.

The Borders are also alive to many opportunities for outdoor pursuits with fishing on the Tweed, golf on some seventeen courses and riding, walking and cycling a plenty. The Borders woollen trail is famous and its tartan and tweeds renowned the world over.

East Lothian and the Forth valley present a somewhat different scene but they too have their fair share of attractions. Golf is surely one of East Lothian's greatest treasures. Links courses such as Muirfield, Dunbar and North Berwick are revered amongst golfers of all nationalities. These fairways have ardently stood the test of time (and the odd hacking rabbit) for some four centuries. In Gullane, there are five courses in the village itself, including the Open Championship links of Muirfield, but it is not merely the golfer who is well catered for here. Typically, the history of this area is both colourful and bloody. Tantallon Castle, once the home of the notorious Black Douglas family, enjoys an imposing site perched atop the cliffs overlooking North Berwick. Contrast this with the infinitely more romantic Dirleton Castle with its magnificent garden and bowling green.

The attractive and gentle countryside of the Forth Valley will seem a million miles from the hustle and bustle of the Royal Mile. Here more stately homes, gardens, lochs and rivers can be found amidst a mixture of small towns, farmlands and winding roads which head relentlessly north.

No visit to the area would, however, be complete without a trip to Culross, a delightfully unspoilt 17th century town which time passed by, and Inchcolm, the tiny island in the middle of the River Forth where King Alexander I founded an abbey in the 12th century. South of the Forth, the Royal Burgh of Linlithgow has much of interest, the Royal Palace, where Mary Queen of Scots was born in 1542 is now ruined but still spectacular. Torched in 1746 by the Duke of Cumberland, the palace still retains its magnificence overlooking Linlithgow Loch.

West of the Forth more sights to savour include the Antonine Wall which dates from the 2nd century. The best preserved remains can be seen at Kinneil Estate, Bo'ness and Tamfourhill. Roughcastle is the best preserved fort on the Wall.

You must remember as you speed along your tarmac motorway that the country through which you pass was formerly marshland and as your imagination wanders over unforgiving treacherous landscapes, spare a thought for the Roman Legions and the defeated armies of Bannockburn and the '45 rebellion. These were tough times, hard times and forbidding times, but today the welcome is hearty and genuine from the Borders to the lands where the Highlands Spring. This is countryside in which to take your time and enjoy the variety and peace that now pervades.

Sunlaws House

33

The Abbotsford Arms Hotel

The Abbotsford Arms Hotel is a beautiful, modernised family run establishment set in the busy Border Town of Galashiels, 32 miles south of Edinburgh.

The attractive new Beef Tub Restaurant seats 40 and a la carte menus offer a high standard of interesting cuisine. Jamaican grapefruit baked with rum and brown sugar, Border trout Cleopatra with prawns and caper butter and breast of duck sauteed with lardons of bacon have all featured. A varied wine list is available.

The Normandy Bar and Conservatory caters for weddings and dinner dances and seats 150.

The tastefully decorated Lounge Bar serves lunches and suppers, and there is a comfortable residents' TV lounge.

Most of the 13 bedrooms have en suite bathrooms, all are centrally heated with colour TV and tea/coffee making facilities.

63 Stirling Street, Galashiels Tel: (0896) 2517

Airth Castle Hotel

Airth Castle, standing on a small hill and looking out over the lush grazing of the Forth Valley, has been part of Scotland's history since the 14th century. In the 15th century it passed by marriage from the Erth family to the Bruce family and in the 16th to the Elphinstones.

The earliest part of the castle, the west wing, was a simple stone tower or keep which was later incorporated into a much larger and more comfortable residence comprising the west wing and south front, built on the Z-plan characteristic of Scottish fortified houses in the 16th and 17th centuries. The windows of the south front were enlarged in 1690 and the north front, which is now the main entrance, was added in 1803.

The whole castle has been carefully restored so that today's guest can enjoy all the atmosphere of the castle's long history but in comfort that previous occupants could only have dreamed of.

The elegant public rooms boast ornate ceilings, traditional furniture and fine views over the surrounding countryside. Each of the 74 bedrooms are equipped with every modern facility.

The Conference Centre and Country Club complex is the newest addition to the castle.

The fine cobbled courtyard leads through the original coachhouse and stables to three conference and function suites, a cocktail bar, a magnificent swimming pool, a sauna, gymnasium and sun-beds.

Situated as it is on the edge of the central belt of Scotland, equally accessible by motorway from Edinburgh and Glasgow airports, Airth Castle is ideally situated for both business and pleasure. The castle's weathered stone walls and the 12 acres of mature woodland which surround them provide a wonderfully tranquil haven in which to work and relax.

Airth, by Falkirk, Stirlingshire FK9 8JF, Tel: (0324) 831411, Fax: (0324) 831419

If thou would'st view fair Melrose aright,

Go visit it by the pale moonlight;

For the gay beams of lightsome day

Gild, but to flout, the ruins grey.

The Lay of the Last Minstrel Sir Walter Scott

This historic castle was built in 1430 by the warring Borthwick family and is steeped in history. Mary Queen of Scots and her lover, the Earl of Bothwell took refuge here in 1567 and in 1650 Oliver Cromwell beseiged it. The medieval atmosphere and grandeur of the castle have been perfectly preserved from those turbulent days. Guests dine by candlelight and logfire in the remarkable stone-vaulted Great Hall with its magnificent forty foot Gothic Arch, Minstrel's Gallery and hooded fireplace. A bar and lounge, with leather sofas, are also situated here, as is the window from which the hapless Scottish queen escaped.

The delicious Scottish cuisine on offer uses the best of fresh local produce such as fresh salmon, Aberdeen Angus beef, Scotch lamb and game. The ten bedchambers are tastefully furnished in period style and have central heating, showers and toilet en suite. The very bedchambers used by Bothwell and Mary are available and come complete with four poster beds. There is so much to explore. There are spiral staircases, fourteen feet walls, twin towers, battlements and dungeons.

The castle is situated at the summit of a knoll, at the fringe of the beautiful border country which Sir Walter Scott immortalised. It lies less than a mile from the little village of North Middleton, and just twelve miles south of Edinburgh. It is therefore conveniently located to allow visits to this great city with its numerous attractions.

Borthwick Castle, North Middleton, Nr Gorebridge, Lothian EH23 4QY, Tel: (0875) 20514, Fax: (0875) 21702

Browns is a distinctive Georgian house built in the early 18th century. It provides uninterrupted views of the beautiful Lammermuir Hills. It is just one mile away from the county town of Haddington and is easily accessible from Edinburgh. The surrounding area is real golfing country and there are 16 courses within easy reach. Other activities available nearby include sailing, swimming, nature trails, bird watching and fishing. The history 'buff' is in his element here, with a large number of museums and historic houses in the vicinity. Haddington was built a royal burgh in the 12th century to promote trade in this rich agricultural area. It was more than once razed to the ground and yet the basic layout has stayed the same. Most of its houses date from the 18th century. Look out for the old lanterns, monuments and signs which give clues to the town's fascinating past.

The hotel prides itself in being small, intimate and friendly. There are four double bedrooms and one single, all with en suite bathroom, colour television and telephone. Guests can relax in the elegant but cosy Drawing Room.

Traditional and high quality dinners are served in the graceful dining room and guests can choose from the fine selection of wines.

Browns is also ideal for the small wedding reception, business seminar or party luncheon.

West Road, Haddington, East Lothian EH41 3RD, Tel: (062) 082 2254

Burts Hotel

Life need not always be hectic, is the philosophy you'll find encapsulated in the atmosphere of Burts Hotel in Melrose which stands almost in the shadow of the three peaks of the Eildon Hills in the very heart of historic Border country.

Burts, in the picturesque 18th century setting of Melrose Market Square, was built in 1722 and reflects much of the period charm of that time. A listed building due to its architectural significance, Burts offers all you would expect of a first class hotel.

Managed personally by Graham and Anne Henderson in the best tradition of Scots hospitality, Burts provides each guest with every modern comfort and the ultimate in service.

The elegant restaurant offers a choice of Scottish and international cuisine. Special emphasis is laid on local game, fish and poultry dishes with all produce being prepared fresh by expert hands.

Vegetarian dishes are also available together with the very best in French haute cuisine.

Alternatively, an extensive lunch and supper menu is on offer in the lounge bar which is a popular local meeting place.

The 21 bedrooms are equipped with en suite facilities of the highest standard.

Colour TV, radio, telephone, tea/coffee making facilities and hairdryers are tastefully blended with the decor.

Ideally situated for a whole range of outdoor activities - including horse-riding and salmon fishing - Burts has a secluded garden where, summer weather permitting, you can choose simply to relax.

Market Square, Melrose, Roxburghshire TD6 9PN, Tel: (0896 82) 2285, Fax: (0896 82) 2870

Champany Inn

This outstanding restaurant is run by Clive and Anne Davidson. The Inn dates from the 16th century and has a marvellous character. Mary Queen Of Scots was born at Linlithgow just two miles away and after her return to Scotland in 1561 she used to ride out from Linlithgow Palace. She would invite friends to join her a la campagne and it is believed that this is how the Champany Inn got its name.

The Inn is one of the 'finest restaurants in the world' according to Lord Litchfield's 'Book Of The Best'. Specialising in Aberdeen Angus beef, the Champany has held the good food Guide award for the best steak in Britain for the last five years. Besides steak, the Inn offers many examples of the best in Scottish produce. There is lamb as well as Shetland salmon, lobster, crayfish and oysters from their sea water pool.

It is not only the food which deserves a mention. In 1988 the Inn received the award for 'Egon Ronay Wine Cellar of the Year' for Great Britain is one of many accolades.

They specialise in Burgundy and Bordeaux wines with celebrated vineyards and growers listed . The Champany also offer over 100 single malt whiskies and over 50 cognacs and 100 Armagnacs. The choice here in food, wine and after dinner drinks makes dining at the Champany a real pleasure.

Champany, Linthigow, West Lothian EH49 7LU, Tel: (0506) 834532

Cringletie House Hotel

Set in 28 acres of gardens, three miles north of Peebles and just off the Edinburgh - Peebles road, Cringletie House Hotel offers real tranquillity. There are antiques, flowers from the garden, and open fires all of which seem just right in this large red sandstone house. Food is a particular pride of the proprietors and many of the products used in the cooking come from the hotel's own gardens and provide very special results. There are 13 comfortable bedrooms, all with private bathrooms. Apart from croquet and putting in the hotel's gardens, further afield there are the attractions of many golf courses, including the 18 hole course in Peebles. In addition there are the other attractions of the Borders and the advantage of the proximity of the capital. Many of the municipal buildings in Peebles were paid for by the famed businessman and philanthropist, Andrew Carnegie, and are worth a glimpse. Closed from January to mid-March.

Cringletie House Hotel, Peebles, Lothian EH45 8FL,
Tel: (072 13) 233, Fax: (072 13) 244

The Crook Inn

One of the oldest licensed inns in Scotland, the Crook Inn is situated in the centre of the beautiful Tweed Valley. Formerly a coaching inn, this is now a comfortable hotel.

The Inn has seven bedrooms, all with en suite facilities. There are open fires in the bar and lounge for guests to enjoy and there is an extensive bar menu on offer as well as the restaurant menu. The dishes are produced using fresh local produce and the wine list also includes wines produced in Scotland.

The Crook Inn is steeped in history. In the 17th century it was a meeting place for Covenantors and one of them was hidden from the Dragoons in a peat stack by Jeanie o'the Crook. Rabbie Burns dropped in for a drink in the old kitchen which now serves as the bar and Sir Walter Scott was inspired by the history and scenery of the local area.

For walkers and climbers the countryside around the Inn is ideal.

Broad Haw, the second highest summit in southern Scotland is just five miles away.

There are three golf courses in the vicinity and nearby fishing is superb. As well as 30 miles on the Tweed there is fishing on the Talla, Fruid and Meggat reservoirs.

The new Tweedsmuir Craft Centre is attached to the hotel and guests can watch the glassmaker at work.

The Crook Inn is a delightful place to stay and guests can be certain of a warm welcome and friendly service.

Tweedsmuir, Peebleshire ML12 6QN, Tel: (08997) 272

The Cross Keys Hotel

The Cross Keys Hotel is a majestic sight in the unique French- style square of the picturesque border town of Kelso. The hotel is one of Scotland's oldest coaching inns and has now been thoroughly and tastefully modernised. Situated on the banks of the rivers Teviot and Tweed, Kelso is renowned for its all year round sporting facilities. Guests can indulge themselves fishing, riding and in the winter sport of curling, all of which the hotel is only too happy to organise. The Tweed and its tributaries provide excellent game fishing, or the more ambitious may wish to venture to the coast and try a spot of seafishing.

The hotel offers an ideal combination of intimate and comfortable accommodation and practical, modern facilities to satisfy every possible need. The attractively appointed bedrooms include private bathrooms, satellite television, telephone, central heating and tea/coffee facilities. The function and banqueting suite provide privacy and a capacity for party groups of up to 300. The hotel also features a fully equipped gym with relaxing sauna and solarium. The intimate restaurant offers cuisine which is both traditional and international, with a range of dishes from the Border Country.

The Square, Kelso, Roxburghshire TD5 7HL, Tel: (0573) 223303, Fax: (0573) 225792

Dalmahoy Golf and Country Club

You will certainly be impressed with Dalmahoy. This Georgian mansion is something of a masterpiece. Set in beautiful acres of wooded countryside at the foot of the Pentland Hills it is surrounded by magical lakes and streams. Although you feel you are miles from anywhere such is the air of tranquillity, you are in fact only 7 miles from Edinburgh, Scotland's historic capital city.

If you are looking for a truly outstanding leisure resort with some of the best golfing in Scotland you need look no further. Dalmahoy has two 18 hole courses set in lovely woodlands with a number of lakes and streams. But you certainly do not have to spend every day golfing when there are so many other leisure activities to enjoy such as tennis, squash and snooker and outdoor activities like clay pigeon shooting and off-road driving.

The bedrooms have all been beautifully designed some with a period theme, they all have en-suite bathrooms trouser press and colour televisions. From many of the rooms you can see the impressive golf courses and surrounding countryside.

Dining in the Pentland restaurant is an experience in itself, set in lovely surroundings you can savour the finest Scottish produce. There is a terrace restaurant overlooking the pool and a choice of bars provides you with relaxing venues for a more informal meal or drink.

Dalmahoy also has very impressive conference facilities which also have splendid views across the golf course and even as far as Edinburgh Castle. With its magnificent surroundings and wonderful leisure facilities Dalmahoy is definitely a place to visit time and time again.

Kirknewton, Mid Lothian EH27 8EB, Tel: 031 333 4105, Fax: 031 333 3203

Ettrickshaws Country House Hotel

This fascinating house dates back to 1891, when Thomas Scott Anderson started the building on a recently acquired plot of thirty acres. The steel lattice access bridge across Ettrick Water still stands, marking the start of the quarter-mile drive to the house. The house nestles in the shelter of Shaws Hill which rises to 1500 feet and is surrounded by spectacular scenery. The area is ideal for birdwatching and hill-walking. The Ettrick River, a 'leisurely few yards' stroll down the drive, provides excellent trout and salmon fishing for guests. The local countryside is scattered with ruined abbeys, castles and historic homes, including Sir Walter Scott's home at Abbotsford and Traquair house (a fortified mansion which has been inhabited for the past nine hundred years and where the guest list has included Mary Queen of Scots and Bonnie Prince Charlie). The delightful village of Ettrickbridge is nearby and the town pottery offers tuition in that fine art. There are also tweed and woollen mills at Selkirk, Galashiels and Hawick, complete with mill shops. Hawick has its newly built Teviotdale Centre, a sports centre and swimming pool and there are famous glassworks at Lindean Mill and Selkirk.

The classic country house, Ettrickshaws not only provides some fine views but features an attractively furnished Drawing Room, Bar and Restaurant which have open fires; an ideal place for private house parties.

The cuisine served in the dining room is of first class quality and is mainly made of fresh local produce. The proprietors, David and Barbara White, are only too pleased to be of assistance and take great pride in the warm and relaxing atmosphere at Ettrickshaws.

Ettrickbridge, Selkirkshire TD7 5HW, Tel: (0750) 52229

George & Abbotsford Hotel

Situated in the heart of the Scottish Borders, the George & Abbotsford is an ideal base for visitors to the area whether on business or pleasure.

The spacious lounge bar, with its range of malt whiskies and draught beers, features open fireplaces while its home-cooked bar meals are appreciated by residents and locals alike.

The Waverley Restaurant offers a choice of a la carte and table d'hote menus, as well as a famous children's menu.

Once a haunt of Sir Walter Scott, this 18th century coaching inn is furnished in period style with wood-panelled rooms, glass-shaded brass chandeliers and plush red upholstery. The facilities, however, belong very much to the 1990s.

The Borders of Scotland feature a wealth of stately homes and places of interest.

The border towns are renowned for their woollen goods and there are all manner of sporting opportunities available too.

Whether you are looking for a break away, or merely a break en route, the George and Abbotsford is well situated and extremely welcoming.

High Street, Melrose, Roxburghshire TD6 9PD, Tel: (089682) 2308, Fax: (089682) 3363

Greywalls

Greywalls was designed in 1901 by the renowned Edwardian architect Sir Edwin Lutyens with the gardens attributed to his imaginative partner, Gertrude Jekyll. The proprietors, Giles and Ros Weaver, are the third generation of the family to live here and although run as a hotel since 1948, Greywalls still retains the feel of a much loved country home.

The lightwood panelled Library features a grand piano and open fire and boasts spectacular views of both the Firth of Forth to the north and the gardens to the south. Edwardian elegance pervades every room in the house, yet no modern comfort has been spared.

All 23 rooms have private facilities and little personal touches like books and portable radios help guests make themselves feel at home.

Chef Paul Baron's daily changing menus make every meal a special occasion. Everything from bread to petits fours is home-made. Such interesting choices as breast of wood pigeon served on rosti potato with a port and truffle sauce, roast quail with grapes, and iced Drambuie parfait are complemented by an exceptional wine list.

For the golfer Greywalls is paradise with many courses within 5 miles. The house itself looks out over the immaculate 9th and 18th greens of Muirfield.

Within the grounds, a hard tennis court and croquet lawn are available to non-golfers or for golfers wanting a change of scenery!

Edinburgh is only half an hour's drive away and the Border country is easily accessible. Closer to hand are East Lothian's glorious sandy beaches, a haven for seabirds.

Greywalls offers a comfortable, unpretentious home with excellent food and needless to say many guests return year after year.

Muirfield, Gullane, East Lothian EH31 2EG, Tel: (0620) 842144,

Houston House Hotel

The Houston Hotel comprises three different elements all steeped in history. The Old Tower of Houstoun was built back in the early 17th century by Sir John Shairp, formerly an advocate to Mary Queen of Scots and was lived in by the Shairp family for 350 years. It is adjoined to the 16th century Woman House by a stone-flagged courtyard. The final part, the Steading, was formerly an estate factor's house and offices.

All the hotel's rooms look out over Houstoun's historic gardens which were laid out in the 18th century with the yew hedge being planted in 1722. The great cedar is even older.

The three dining rooms are set in the old Drawing Room, Library and Great Hall respectively. All are clad with 17th and 18th century wood panelling, adorned with fine mouldings and furnished with elegant paintings and antiques. The menu offers an enticing choice of both traditional Scottish and international cuisine and there is an excellent range of wines and malt whiskies.

The thirty bedrooms are spacious and vary in style, some being very contemporary and others traditional, including some with four-poster beds; all are well equipped with en suite bathrooms. The lounges and function rooms are similarly varied in style.

The hotel is located at the heart of things in central Scotland Edinburgh and Glasgow are within an hour's drive and the historic attractions of Linlithgow Palace, Hopetoun House and the village of Dalmeny are close by. Uphall Golf Course is directly adjacent to Houstoun, and rounds can be arranged for guests by the hotel. The 26-acre garden with its marquee offers an ideal place for garden parties and balls in the summer months.

Uphall, West Lothian EH52 6JS, Tel: (0506) 853831, Fax: (0506) 854220

Inchyra Grange Hotel

The Inchyra Grange Hotel is a fine-looking Scottish country house set in 44 acres of private grounds. Situated at the hub of central Scotland, with Glasgow, Perth and Edinburgh all within easy reach, the Grange is the ideal venue for conference meetings, private parties or as a base for touring the scenic countryside and many places of interest in this fascinating region. Stirling Castle, Linlithgow Palace and several famous golf courses, such as St Andrews and Carnoustie, are but a short drive away, as is the stunning scenery of the Trossachs and the idyllic Loch Lomond. The new Pelican Leisure Club provides a host of facilities for the guests. There is a leisure pool, fitness suite, beauty therapist, spa bath, sauna and steam room.

Comfort and friendliness are bywords at this hotel. The 43 elegantly furnished bedrooms and suites are fully equipped with en suite bathroom, colour television, telephone, hair dryer, mini bar and tea/coffee facilities. The immaculate restaurant serves a range of carefully and imaginatively selected dishes from its a la carte and table d'hote menus, while light meals and snacks are also available at the Pelican Club and in the cosy Earl Lounge. The Menteith Suite, which is able to hold 200 people, is a stylish venue for the big events such as wedding receptions and business conferences.

Grange Road, Polmont, Falkirk FK2 0YB, Tel: (0324) 711911, Fax: (0324) 716134

Johnstounburn House

Dating from 1625, Johnstounburn House stands at the foot of the Lammermuir Hills just 15 miles south of the city of Edinburgh. Set amid lawns and parklands in a private estate, its grounds feature imposing yew hedges, an orchard, a patio rose garden and herbacous walled garden. Upon entering the house, guests will immediately appreciate the Scottish heritage preserved here. Refurbishments have enhanced the original features whilst enabling guests to enjoy modern comforts.

Of the 20 well appointed bedrooms, 11 are in the house and 9 in the tastefully converted coach house. There is a spacious cedar panelled lounge where an open fire will warm you on chilly days. In the 18th century pine panelled dining room, chef Bryan Thom prepares sumptuous fare from the finest Scottish produce. The wine list has been carefully compiled to satisfy all our visitors and our selection of malt whisky will suit every palate.

Johnstounburn is an ideal centre from which to tour. Within 30 minutes drive are Edinburgh city centre, the championship links golf courses of East Lothian and the picturesque border region with its many historic houses, castles and gardens.

Humbie, East Lothian EH36 5PL, Tel: (087533) 696, Fax: (087533) 626

The Ley

This distinctive hotel is set in thirty acres of woods and gardens amid the peace and quiet of the Border countryside. Built in 1861, it is an ideal retreat for visitors looking to relax in an elegant, spacious setting with a warm, friendly atmosphere. The rooms are attractively furnished and well-equipped and the proprietors, Doreen and Willie McVicar, take great pride in the quality of food on offer. A full Scottish Breakfast is available and is brought to the guest's room if required. Dinner is a set four-course menu which changes each day but is invariably tasty and imaginative. Alternatives can be provided for vegetarians and those on special diets if notice is given. The meal can be accompanied by wine from the Ley's extensive collection.

The Scottish Borders are a delight to the eye and offer a rich historical heritage to explore.

Within short driving distances are the Border Abbeys and Castles, Traquair House, Abbotsford, Mellerstain and other great houses.

At the foot of the Ley's drive is a nine hole golf course and the local hills provide picturesque walking country. Edinburgh is a pleasant forty minute drive away should the lure of the city prove irresistible.

Innerleithen, Peeblesshire EH44 6NL, Tel/Fax: (0896) 830 240

The Open Arms

Arthur Neil is a host par excellence and The Open Arms a much loved market inn set in the charming East Lothian coastal village of Dirleton, overlooking the 13th century castle and the village green.

Whether visiting on business, enjoying a holiday or coming in for lunch or dinner, you will find the lounge an ideal place to relax. The friendly cocktail bar is popular with both locals and visitors, and there is a comprehensive range of aperitifs, spirits, wines, beers and liqueurs.

Both a la carte and table d'hote menus take full advantage of excellent seafood and agricultural produce fresh from local markets and food is prepared and presented with the panache only to be expected from a successful operation which has been in the same family's hands for over forty years. The wine list provides a natural compliment to the originality of the cuisine with a pleasing choice of thoughtfully selected vintages.

The hotel specialises in hosting small meetings, dinner parties and weddings in the dining room, which can seat up to 80 people in comfort.

With only seven bedrooms, The Open Arms has an intimate and friendly atmosphere. All bedrooms are en suite with a choice of bath or shower. Every bedroom has recently been tastefully redecorated and individually furnished in the classic style, featuring co-ordinated fabrics and wallpaper. All have colour TV, direct dial telephones, radio, hairdryer and tea/coffee making facilities.

The Lothians offer a wide range of holiday pursuits. Golf can never be far away, and historic castles, country houses and gardens abound. The scenic countryside and wide sandy beaches are much favoured by naturalist or pleasure-seeker alike

Dirleton, Nr North Berwick, East Lothian EH39 5EG, Tel: (062085) 241, Fax: (062085) 570

Peebles Hotel Hydro

Peebles Hotel Hydro is an imposing building set in the Borders half an hour's drive away from Edinburgh. It is privately owned and is run in conjunction with the adjacent Park Hotel. The latter is a smaller, quieter hotel but the many facilities of the Hydro are available to guests who are staying at either place. The facilities of the Peebles Hydro include many indoor and outdoor recreations; squash, table tennis, badminton, snooker and a luxurious leisure complex with heated swimming pool, sauna, solaria, steam bath and gymnasium. In the 30 acres of hotel grounds there are; tennis, croquet, putting and pony trekking. Many golf courses are nearby, including the 18 hole course at Peebles.

All 137 bedrooms have the expected facilities. Suites and superior twin rooms with balconies are available. The hotel dining room offers haute-cuisine and traditional Scottish dishes prepared from fresh local produce. Enquire about weekend parties and the many special breaks which are available. Conferences and functions can also be arranged.

Peebles Hydro, Peebles EH45 8LX, Tel: (0721) 720602, Fax: (0721) 722999

The Philipburn House Hotel

Philipburn, formerly the Dowager House to Philiphaugh Estate, was built in 1751 and overlooks the Border market town of Selkirk. It is 45 minutes drive from Edinburgh and less than 90 from Glasgow.

Owned and run since 1972 by Jim and Anne Hill, former Olympic swimmers, Philipburn House Hotel is run as a country hotel where all are welcome including children and the disabled.

The Poolside and Garden Restaurants are outstanding and both enjoy views of the hotel pool, the gardens and the heather hills beyond. The menus feature local game and Border lamb as well as salmon caught in the nearby rivers of Tweed, Teviot and Ettrick. An international wine list features many European and New World wines.

Assistance will be given in the arrangement of many activities, including shooting, fishing, walking, golf, climbing and canoeing. In the autumn, Philipburn hosts musical nights, theme dinners and wine tastings. In winter, spring and autumn, midweek and weekend breaks are available. There are special three day breaks at Easter, Christmas and New Year. Business entertainment and facilities can be arranged.

Selkirk TD7 5LS, Tel:(0750) 20747, Fax: (0750) 21690

Tweed Valley Hotel and Restaurant

This attractive Edwardian house was originally built in 1906 as a wedding present from Henry Ballantyne to his son. It retains much of its original character with its oak panelling, carvings and the ornate dining room ceiling and enjoys an idyllic setting overlooking the River Tweed and the heather-clad hills.

This quiet and unspoilt part of Scotland is steeped in history dating back to the Border Raids. The area is dotted with famous mansions and castles, including Floors, Bowhill and Traquair, abbeys and parklands. The valley is particularly well-known for its woollens, cashmere and tweed cloth. There are a number of mill shops at some of which hotel guests can enjoy special discounts. There are also craft and antique shops. The beautiful countryside is ideal for golf, fishing, shooting, walking, riding, archaeology and birdwatching and the hotel is only too keen to help arrange a visitor's (or perhaps a business party's) holiday to incorporate such activities.

The hotel prides itself on its cosy and relaxed atmosphere and the comfortable lounge with its log fire quickly makes a guest feel at home. The Edwardian Restaurant serves delightful food, including home smoked products, using the freshest local produce, including vegetables and herbs from the walled kitchen garden. The fifteen well-appointed bedrooms are well-equipped. There is also a solarium, sauna and mini-gym. The hotel provides a bottle of sparkling wine, flowers and chocolate on arrival for guests celebrating a honeymoon, anniversary or other special event.

Walkerburn, Peeblesshire EH43 6AA, Tel: (089) 687636, Fax: (089) 687639

Tweedale Arms Hotel

In a title deed of 1687 the Tweedale Arms is referred to as "the Great Inn at Gifford". It stands in the mainly 18th century High Street, looking across the village green to a 300 year old avenue of lime trees leading to the gates of Yester House, formerly the home of the Marquesses of Tweedale.

The hotel is personally managed by the proprietor and the service is friendly and efficient. Traditional hospitality goes side by side with modern facilities. There is a comfortable and restful lounge with an open log fire. All bedrooms have bathroom en suite and colour TV, clock-radio, direct-dial telephone, trouser press and tea/coffee making facilities.

The lounge-bar, recently modernised, provides a wide range of refreshments including bar lunches. A more local flavour may be found in the public bar to which a games room is attached.

The restaurant offers table d'hote menus at all times. The a la carte menu in the evening, provides a wide choice of British and continental cuisine and features traditional Scottish dishes in season.

There is excellent accommodation for functions with catering requirements for up to 80 people and the hotel has a wide reputation for wedding receptions and similar parties. The village, widely recognised as one of the most attractive in Scotland, is ideally situated - close to Edinburgh yet deep enough in the glorious countryside of East Lothian to give access to the beautiful coastline.

Many of Scotland's best known golf courses are within easy reach, and Gifford itself has a delightful nine-hole course.

High Street, Gifford, East Lothian EH41 4QU, Tel: (062 081) 240, Fax: (062 081) 488

Purves Hall is a fine country house built in 1908, with historic connections going back to the 1670's. It is set in 10 acres of wooded parkland, with superb views south to the Cheviot Hills. There are secluded gardens in which to relax, and walks through the woods or surrounding country lanes for those who enjoy walking. For family leisure activities, Purves Hall has a tennis court, heated outdoor swimming pool, croquet lawn, and putting green. Stables are available for those who wish to bring horses.

The resident proprietors, Wing Commander and Mrs B.D. Everett, and their staff personally prepare all meals and seek to ensure that your stay at Purves is comfortable and enjoyable. The Hall with its log fires is also centrally heated throughout. The en-suite bedrooms have full tea making facilities and colour TV's with video system and telephone. The Cheviot Restaurant offers a varied menu and fine wines. Coffee is served in the elegant main lounge adjoining the cocktail bar where a wide selection of liqueurs is available.

The area has many fine golf courses and good river fishing. Shooting can be arranged (in season) with sufficient advance notice. Bird watching on the East Coast at St Abb's and the Farne Islands. Chillingham Castle, home of the white wild cattle, who are descendants from prehistoric herds of the Great Caledonian Forests, all await the visitor in pursuit pleasure and relaxation.

Purves Hall is situated in the centre of the Scottish Borders Region and all its historic towns, castles and stately homes, most places of interest being less than one hours drive. Peebles, Selkirk, Melrose, Kelso, Jedburgh, Berwick, Duns, Coldstream and St Abb's are but a few well worth visiting. The East Coasts of Berwickshire and Northumberland can easily be reached through quiet country roads and Edinburgh is less than one hour away.

Greenlaw, Berwickshire TD10 6UJ, Tel: (089084) 558

Sunlaws House stands in the heart of Scotland's beautiful Border country, in 200 acres of gardens and mature parkland along the banks of the Teviot, three miles from the historic town of Kelso.There has been a house on the same site at Sunlaws for nearly 500 years and from its beginnings it has always been a Scottish family house – and that, to all intents and purposes, is how it will stay!

Sunlaws has a place in history, from the faint echoes of ancient strife when English armies of the 15th and 16th centuries came marauding through Roxburghshire and the Borders, to the Jacobite rebellion of 1745. Indeed Prince Charles Edward Stuart is reputed to have stayed on November 5th 1745 and to have planted a white rose bush in the grounds.

Sunlaws hope that their guests will find that in the intervening year there have been some welcome changes. Its owner, the Duke of Roxburghe, has carefully converted Sunlaws into the small, welcoming but unpretentious hotel of comfort and character that it is.

There are 22 bedrooms, which include the splendid Bowmont Suite and six delightful rooms in the stable courtyard, all furnished with care to His Graces' own taste and all with private bathroom or shower, colour television, radio and direct-dial telephone. Disabled guests too are provided with the amenities they need.

The spacious public rooms are furnished with the same care and elegance, which adds to the overall atmosphere of warmth and welcome with log fires burning in the main and inner hall, drawing room, library bar and dining room, throughout the winter and on cold summer evenings.

Flowers and plants, from the gardens and the conservatory, will be found all over the house; herbs too are grown for the kitchen and will be found in many of the traditional dishes that are prepared for the dining room. Not only is Sunlaws right in the heart of Scotland's beautiful Border Country, it is also the perfect centre for a host of holiday activities. Sporting and cultural interests are well served, too.

Salmon and trout fishing, and a complete range of shooting are available at the Hotel, with golf, horse-riding, racing and fox hunting all nearby.

Sunlaws is the perfect location for touring the Borders, with great country houses including Abbotsford, the home of Sir Walter Scott, and a number of abbeys and museums all within easy reach.

Kelso, Roxburghshire Tel: 05735 331 Fax: 05735 611

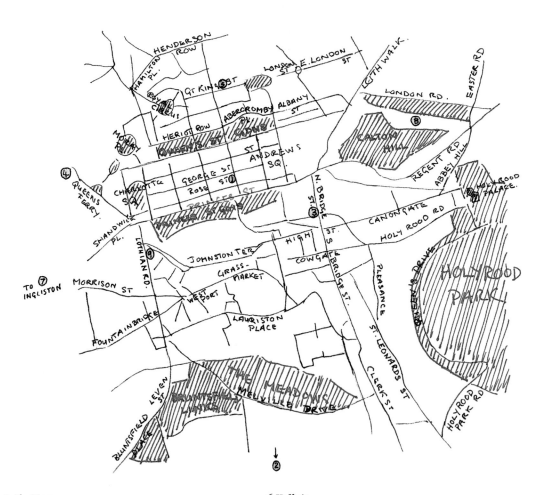

1 Alp-Horn	6 Kelly's
2 Braid Hills Hotel	7 Norton House
3 Carlton Highland	8 Royal Terrace Hotel
4 Channings	9 Edinburgh Sheraton Hotel
5 Howard Hotel	

Of all the capital cities in the world, Edinburgh must rank as one of the most beautiful. Beneath the imposing skyline of castle and crag, cobbled streets and broad avenues part to reveal a staggering array of shops, elegant town houses, hotels and restaurants catering for all tastes and budgets and servicing a truly global clientele.

The old town has its roots in medieval times, with narrow lanes and steep winding streets a prominent feature. The new town, which dates predominantly from the 18th century, follows a more classical pattern of architecture with fine squares and crescents graciously threaded together. This curious cocktail leaves a delightful impression upon the visitor who, thanks to the relatively small compass of the city, can explore much in a day and still find the time to venture slightly further afield and enjoy the delights of Leith's waterfront setting or Duddingston Loch's fine houses and tiny Norman church.

The heritage of the city, epitomised by the lofty castle, can be combined with a stroll along the Royal Mile and Princes Street, famous for shopping. Here, eye catching arrangements of tartan, tweed, wool and cashmere promise sartorial elegance to those not transfixed by the vast array of whisky, shortbread and other such fayre on display.

The parks and gardens below the castle add floral colour and verdant variety to a fascinating city whose Botanical gardens and Zoo already enjoy universal acclaim.

Edinburgh is a festival city. The renowned International Festival is a celebration of classic culture which provides some of the best entertainment in the world. The Festival Fringe is famed for originality and many respected entertainers have made their debut on the Edinburgh Fringe stage.

While festivals may come and go, some centres of excellence for art enjoy a more permanent footing: the Victorian Royal Lyceum and The Kings, feature repertory productions of new plays and the classics while The Playhouse offers a variety of opera, ballet and pop. Also worth a visit are the elegant Queens Hall and the National Gallery of Modern Art.

Sport is also well represented both inside and beyond the city's confines.

The National Stadia of Meadowbank and Murrayfield contrast dramatically with the oft tranquil links of Muirfield, Gullane, North Berwick and Longniddry to name but a few of the 'local' golf courses that need no introduction to the itinerant golfer.

From the towering rock atopped by the castle to the bustle of the Royal Mile, the real flavour of Edinburgh can be found and enjoyed in the many small restaurants, bistros and bars nestling amidst the historical and commercial diversions.

Edinburgh truly has something for everyone, be it the visitor combining a night at the Tattoo with a day's shopping and sightseeing, the connoisseur whose horizons extend no further than the Scotch Whisky Heritage Centre or those seeking to immerse themselves in the castle, palaces and museums overflowing with Scottish history. Edinburgh, with its mix of old and new, has it all.

Edinburgh

Alp-Horn

This attractive Swiss restaurant is ideally placed in the centre of Edinburgh to kick off an evening out in the great city. The pine-clad columns and ceiling, alpine landscape scenes and cowbells all lend an authentic Alpine air to a lively restaurant which seats up to 62 diners. A whole range of Swiss dishes are on offer - cheese and beef fondues (served for two or more), air dried Swiss beef and ham, veal sausage (kalbsbratwurst), venison with apple and cranberry sauce and spatzli, and perhaps homemade apple strudel with ice cream for dessert.

The wine list features an unusual range of Swiss wines which are well worth sampling. At lunch the restaurant offers a generously priced 'square deal' two to three course meal and a shortened a la carte menu.

167 Rose Street, Edinburgh, Lothian EH2 4LS, Tel: 031 225 4787

Braid Hills Hotel

The Braid Hills is magnificently situated, with panoramic views across Edinburgh to the Pentland Hills, the Firth of Forth and the Fife hills beyond. This impressive building was built in 1886 to accommodate golfers visiting the nearby Braid Hills golf course and it remains to this day a popular base for a golfing break with many of the country's top courses nearby. It is also ideally placed for access to the sights and sounds of Edinburgh - the Castle, museums, galleries, theatres and concert halls - and for major events such as the Edinburgh Festival and the Royal Highland Show. There are tennis courts and a riding school nearby and Europe's longest artificial ski-slope, at Hill-end, is just a mile away.

The hotel takes great pride in its 68 individually and attractively furnished bedrooms, which are equipped with private bath, colour television, telephone, radio and a myriad of other facilities to make the visitor's stay as comfortable as possible. The hotel restaurant is elegantly decorated and offers superb views of the city. The table d'hote and a la carte menus feature a number of uniquely Scottish dishes and the carefully selected wine list offers a wide range, including a number of classic vintage. The cocktail lounge is famous for its award-winning whisky-based cocktails, while a more traditional 'pub' atmosphere can be found at the hotel's Buckstone Lodge. Dinner dances, parties and functions are held in the large Function Suite. The hotel offers a series of packages for honeymooners and golfers and its noted Champagne Interlude is ideal for short holiday breaks.

134 Braid Road, Edinburgh EH10 6JD, Tel: 031 447 8888, Fax: 031 452 8477

Carlton Highland Hotel

The Carlton Highland Hotel, overlooking Princes Street in the heart of Scotland's capital, enjoys an international reputation for excellence. An imposing staircase leads from the sophisticated reception foyer to the comfort of the lounges and cocktail bar. On the floor above, all of the 197 individually styled luxury bedrooms have an impressive array of facilities to ensure guests enjoy a comfortable stay. One floor below, guests can dance the night away in the hotel's own exclusive nightclub.

With its well deserved reputation for excellent food, fine wines and efficient service the Carlton Highland offers a choice of three dining rooms. Carlyle's Patisserie serves light meals and mouthwatering French pastries throughout the day. The Carlton Court Carvery and the more formal Quills Restaurant serve impeccably prepared Scottish dishes and international cuisine from an a la carte menu.

To counteract the inevitable over indulgence, guests may take advantage of the impressive facilities in the Carlton Club, the hotel's sports and leisure centre. Qualified instructors are on hand in the fully equipped gymnasium, squash courts and aerobics and dance studios. For the less energetic, the sauna, solarium, steam rooms or heated swimming pool may hold more appeal, or perhaps a frame of snooker on one of the four full sized tables.

Extensive conference facilities are available for up to 360 delegates. For banquets and receptions, 280 guests can dine in the elegant Highland suite. For business or pleasure, the Carlton Highland lives up to its reputation.

North Bridge, Edinburgh EH1 1SD, Tel: 031 556 7277, Fax: 031 556 2691

Walk through the quiet cobbled streets of Edinburgh's city centre, just a little way from the castle and push open the door of a row of five beautifully maintained Edwardian townhouses. These, together, make up Channings, a privately owned hotel with cosy, old-fashioned clublike atmosphere right in heart of historic Edinburgh. The style of Channings is rarely found today; a feeling of classic care from the peaceful, fire-lit lounges to any of the 45 individually designed guest rooms, several of which offer wonderful panoramic views over the Firth of Forth to the hills of Fife.

The Brasserie is one of the popular haunts of the city. A restaurant that prides itself on honest food and personable service. After dinner, the bar welcomes you with an interesting and highly tempting range of malt whiskies and the odd game of chess. In the warmer months, take your lunch outside where the hotel's terraced garden captures the heat of the sun.

The quiet, classical feel of the hotel makes it the ideal venue for a corporate dinner or small conference but it is more than homely enough for any private meeting too. Any such gathering can be held in one of seven different rooms, including the oak-panelled Library and the Kingsleigh Suite.

For a rewarding afternoon's browsing through local and not-so-local history, the hotel has an absorbing collection of antique prints, furniture, object d'art, periodicals and books, or wander through the streets of the Edinburgh itself and soak up the atmosphere and culture of this beautiful city.

Take a short trip into the surrounding countryside to the famous golf clubs of Scotland. It was at nearby Muirfield where the Honourable Company of Edinburgh Golfers was founded in 1744, on the southern tip of the Firth of Forth, the oldest golf club in history.

South Learmonth Gardens, Edinburgh EH4 1EZ, Tel: 031 315 2226, Fax: 031 332 9631

The George Intercontinental

To describe the entrance of the George as a reception would be a masterly piece of understatement. The George sits in George Street, the earliest and principle street of the new Town laid out by James Craig in the eighteenth century. The hotel's facade is suitably Georgian, neo-classical. The entrance itself opens up with brightly polished marble floors and fluted Corinthian columns.

There is even a raised seated area where guests can relax after a busy shopping expedition on nearby Princess Street and watch the world go by.

If expectations are raised by the entrance the 195 rooms will not disappoint. The rooms are of two styles, the original rooms in the west wing tend to be more traditional, while those in the modern east wing are a little smaller but no less luxurious. The rooms are well furnished, mostly with free standing yew furniture, a settee or armchairs, a small refreshments cabinet and colour televisions. Craig purposefully laid out the New Town to make the most of Edinburgh's cityscape, and many of the rooms benefit with superb views.

The popular Gathering of the Clans bar is decked with the crests of the highland clans and curios from the whisky industry.

The George boasts two fine restaurants. The Carvers Table serves traditional roasts whilst Le Chambertin specialises in French and Taste of Scotland cuisine.

19 George Street, Edinburgh EH2 2PB, Tel: 031 225 1251, Fax: 031 226 5644

The Howard

The Howard is an elegant Georgian town house situated in seclusion amongst the quiet Georgian terraces in Edinburgh's new town yet within easy reach of Princes Street and a pleasant walk from the castle. The exterior, designed by James Craig (1766), exhibits a wealth of architectural splendour. The Howard is certainly a hotel like no other and you may be mistaken for thinking it is someone's home. It has been completely renovated to its original town house character.

Careful research went into all the fabrics and furnishings which are chosen to reflect the style and grace of the Georgian period. The colour schemes of green, blue and the purple of heather create an outstanding effect.

The Drawing Room with its heavy brocade curtains looks out onto the cobbles stones of King Street. It is a comfortable room with deep sofas and armchairs inviting you to relax after a busy day savouring the wonderful sites of Edinburgh. Although the Howard does not have a bar, guests may order what they wish from the waiter.

The bedrooms have ample style and comfort, with individual colour schemes making the best use of irregular room shapes. The en suite bathrooms echo the period without detracting from the comforts provided. For added comfort there is a television, VHS player, radio and telephone. The rooms rather unusually are identified by famous street names rather than numbers .

The splendour of the Howard continues in the restaurant, Number 36, which has its own entrance on Great King Street.

With the same elegant style as the rest of the Howard it creates a wonderful atmosphere that is club-like and intimate. The cuisine is to the highest international standards and is described by the chef as a blend of classical and Scottish. The wine list provides you with plenty of good quality and good value wines.

With its perfect location and sumptuous surroundings, The Howard is the ideal place to stay when savouring the delights of Edinburgh and those of many surrounding attractions.

36 Great King Street, Edinburgh, Lothian EH3 6QH, Tel: 031 557 3500, Fax: 031 557 6515

Norton House Hotel

Norton House is a luxuriant Victorian mansion situated just 15 minutes away from the centre of Edinburgh and is also fairly close to the airport. It is ideally placed to explore one of the most lively and exciting cities in Europe, with its renowned summer festival for the arts, and magnificent physical and architectural features. The surrounding countryside is classically Scottish - rolling hills, mountains, glens and lochs and offers scope for a huge range of activities.

The hotel, set amid extensive and picturesque grounds, remains an island of tranquillity. Its magnificent foyer is flanked by marble columns and features an oak staircase, a carved oak fireplace and a gallery. There is also a delightful little pub in the old stables called the Norton Taverns, which has a barbecue area, walled garden and a children's play area.

There are 47 bedrooms including the 30 oak-furnished executive rooms, and each comes complete with colour television, bathroom, radio and complementary newspaper. The dining room is spacious and elegant, and a wide range of succulent dishes is on offer, much of it made with the finest local produce.

Ingliston, Nr Edinburgh, Lothian, EH28 8LX, Tel: 031 333 1275, Fax: 031 333 5305

The Roxburghe

The New Town's finest achievement is Robert Adam's Charlotte Square, one of Europe's architectural masterpieces. The Roxburghe's neighbours include Bute House, the Secretary of State for Scotland's official residence; West Register House with a permanent exhibition and the National Trust for Scotland, who have restored The Georgian House as a home of the Georgian period.

The Roxburghe itself has as its hallmark a tradition of fine food and accommodation for the past 150 years. Guests can enjoy the atmosphere of a private house on comfort and style. Its 57 rooms all have en suite facilities with colour televisions.

The hotel has an a la carte restaurant which serves Scottish and international whilst a bistro serves snacks and light meals all day.

18 Royal Terrace, Edinburgh Lothian EH7 5AQ, Tel: 031 557 3222 Fax: (031) 557 5334

Royal Terrace Hotel

The Royal Terrace in Edinburgh was built in 1822 to celebrate and commemorate the visit to the city of George IV, two years after his succession to the throne. The Royal Terrace Hotel is a magnificent affair made up of six neighbouring houses in the Terrace. People who decide to linger in Scotland's capital will find a stay in the Royal Terrace Hotel a memorable experience. It is sumptuously furnished and carpeted and has elegant curtains which are a feature of all the reception and residents' lounge areas. There are chandeliers and altogether much finery. There are 95 well furnished bedrooms which vary considerably in size and choice of view so that you are advised to specify your requirements when booking.

All the rooms have every modern facility but some of the bathrooms have the addition of a slightly unexpected impulse shower. There are attractively landscaped gardens at the back of the hotel. There is an excellent leisure complex which has an indoor swimming pool, spa bath, solarium, sauna and a good gymnasium. Beauty and hair salons are available on the premises. There are conference rooms for up to 40 people. Enquiries about the facilities should be made to the hotel.

There is much to see and to enjoy in and around Edinburgh although this obviously varies with the time of year. If a visit to the Festival is intended, early booking is recommended. Sport of all kinds is available in the environs of Edinburgh, particularly golf. There are good books to help you find what courses would be available to you but the hotel will always advise you. In Scotland's beautiful capital itself there is the magic of the whole place, including the Castle, the Cathedral, the Royal Mile, the old part of the city known as Auld Reekie and Holyrood House.

18 Royal Terrace, Edinburgh Lothian EH7 5AQ, Tel: 031 557 3222 Fax: (031) 557 5334

Sheraton Grand Hotel Edinburgh

Edinburgh is one of the most historic places in the world and to visit it is to bring tales of Auld Reekie, of Arthur's Seat, of St. Margaret's Chapel in the Castle and Holyrood to reality. Within sight of the Castle, the Sheraton Edinburgh Hotel is situated right in the heart of the city and has recently expanded into Festival Square creating two new restaurants. The Terrace Restaurant offers Special Nights with different menus and a wide range of food and wines. The Grill Room is smaller and serves the best of Scottish foods in highly imaginative menus. A children's menu is available.

Refurbishment of all the hotel bedrooms is under way and reflects the designs and colours of Scotland. Conference facilities are comprehensive and will shortly accommodate 600 delegates in the Edinburgh Suite and up to 90 in the Melville Suite.

The Banqueting foyer has been extended whilst there is also a Boardroom and three private meeting rooms. A leisure centre provides pool, sauna and gymnasium.

A pianist plays in the new Lobby Bar. Special weekend rates are available.

1 Festival Square, Lothian Road, Edinburgh EH3 9SR, Tel: 031 229 9131, Fax: 031 229 6254

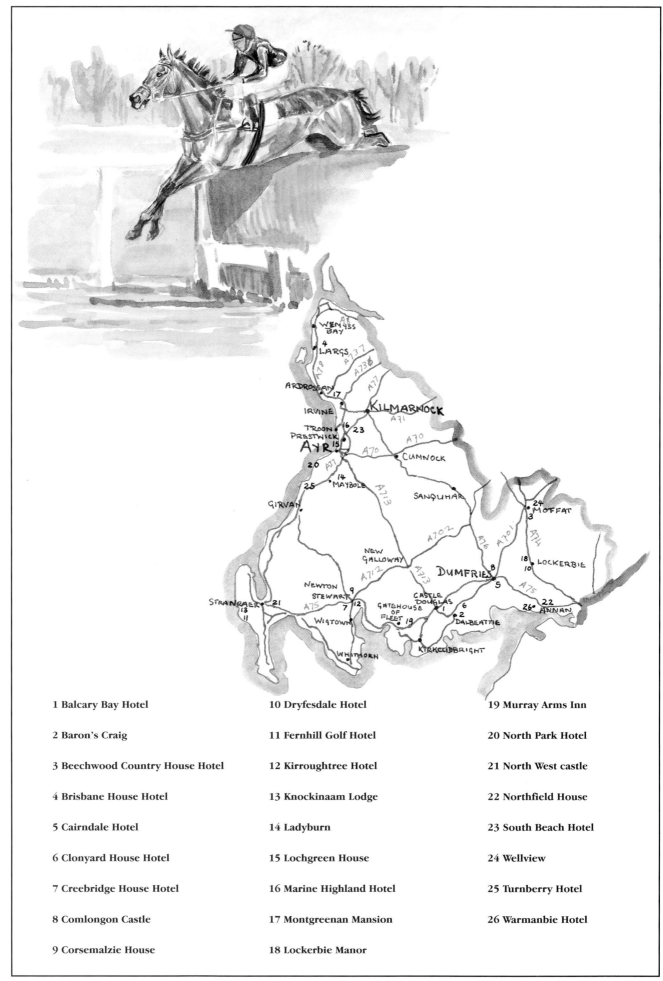

1 Balcary Bay Hotel

2 Baron's Craig

3 Beechwood Country House Hotel

4 Brisbane House Hotel

5 Cairndale Hotel

6 Clonyard House Hotel

7 Creebridge House Hotel

8 Comlongon Castle

9 Corsemalzie House

10 Dryfesdale Hotel

11 Fernhill Golf Hotel

12 Kirroughtree Hotel

13 Knockinaam Lodge

14 Ladyburn

15 Lochgreen House

16 Marine Highland Hotel

17 Montgreenan Mansion

18 Lockerbie Manor

19 Murray Arms Inn

20 North Park Hotel

21 North West castle

22 Northfield House

23 South Beach Hotel

24 Wellview

25 Turnberry Hotel

26 Warmanbie Hotel

The Land O' Burns where today the visitor will find the very best in hotel accommodation and facilities. Golf, fishing, castles and gardens and a coastline which boasts many unspoilt beaches. Here all manner of activities can be enjoyed. The Great Western Meeting at Ayr races is one sporting event to consider but there are many more. Golf courses are everywhere and with Prestwick, Troon and Turnberry to name but three, the lover of links courses will indeed be spoilt for choice - that is assuming the weather stays fine. There are numerous less prestigious courses which welcome all standards of player and provide a less demanding but no less enjoyable round.

Ayrshire's most celebrated son is Scotland's national bard; Robert Burns. The poet was born in Alloway and spent most of his short life in the district. Today, visitors follow in the poet's footsteps from his cottage or 'auld clay biggin' onwards. In the grounds of the cottage is the Burns Museum and also close by is the Land of Burns Centre.

Alloway Kirk features in Burn's epic poem Tam O'Shanter as well as the Auld Brig O'Doon. In Tarbolton the debating society known as the 'Bachelor's Club' was founded by Burns and his brother Gilbert. In 1785, after a brief spell in Irvine, Burns became a tenant at Mossgiel Farm. Three years later he married his childhood sweetheart Jean Armour and set up home in Mauchline. Tragically, the bard lived only another eight years, dying prematurely at the age of 37 in 1796.

For those looking to discover the more scenic delights of Ayrshire, Girvan, with its busy harbour, is a popular stopping off place and a good staging post on the way to Culzean Castle. Perched on a rocky outcrop in one of the most beautiful locations on the Ayrshire coast it is a splendid example of the work of Robert Adam, most notably for the magnificent oval staircase and round drawing room.

South east of Ayr a number of industrial heritage centres, which reconstruct the age of iron smelting, steam and coal, can be found in the Doon Valley, once an industrial heartland, and now a haven for hill walkers and lovers of spectacular scenery.

This solitude can be exchanged for a more lively atmosphere in the town of Ayr, altogether a more lively place. There are a number of attractions for the visitor here from the local races to fun parks and watering holes a plenty.

North of Ayr, Troon offers not just a celebrated golf course and sandy beaches but also nearby Dundonald Castle, the ancient seat of the Kyle Stewarts. Its first occupant, Walter Stewart, was the son in law of Robert Bruce and father of the first Stewart monarch.

Another edifice on which to feast the eyes is Dean Castle. A leisurely exploration of the castle itself and the Country Park grounds will reveal a whole host of attractions for young and old alike. An attraction of a different kind is likely to draw the visitor on to Kilmarnock and Scotland's most famous export, Johnny Walker whisky. Ideal with a drop of Highland Spring.

The Irvine Valley carries many a reminder of the textile industry which once flourished in this area and, at its head, Irvine Harbour houses the Scottish Maritime Museum which is well worth a visit.

To the south of the region, we find an area once infamous for smuggling. Indeed, the muddy creeks on the northern shore of the Solway Firth were a haven to smugglers of contraband into Scotland.

Nowadays the only furtive visitor is likely to be the motorist putting the miles between himself and England as rapidly as possible en route to the Highlands and Heartlands. To do so is to miss some of the most stimulating scenery Scotland has to offer.

Here are the flat marshlands where flocks of geese, swans and other waterfowl spend their winters, and windswept headlands where only the ghosts of more violent times watch out from deserted battlements and ancient ruins. This is an agricultural area famed for its dairy produce and yet at its heart lies the great wilderness of the Galloway Forest Park.

Dumfries and Galloway saw more than its fair share of Scotland's turbulent history, having attracted 'tourists' since time immemorial. It was here, hiding in the magnificent solitude of a damp cave, that Robert Bruce found the inspiration to defeat the English.

Not all visitors, however, came to make war, especially those eloping lovers drawn across the border to Gretna Green, a name forever to be linked with the romance of Scotland.

Turnberry Hotel

This lovely country-house hotel, which dates back to 1625, has a secluded and enchanting situation on the edge of Balcary Bay facing the Solway coast and the Cumbrian Hills beyond. In the foreground of this delightful panorama is Heston Isle, the infamous smugglers' haunt. Standing in over three acres of garden, two miles from Auchencairn, the house was purchased in 1645 by a firm of shippers who used it as headquarters for smuggling.

The present day owners, Ronald and Joan Lamb - along with their son Graeme - have ensured that the hotel retains much of its old character and charm whilst being thoroughly modernised, tastefully decorated and centrally heated throughout. All of the 17 bedrooms have en suite facilities, colour TV, telephone, hairdryer and tea/coffee making facilities.

There is a cocktail bar with patio overlooking the bay, and two comfortable lounges, one with log fire. The cuisine in the dining room is excellent. It is based on the imaginative preparation of local delicacies, including Galloway beef and lamb, Heston Isle lobsters and - of course - Balcary Bay salmon. The wine list is equally impressive.

Robert Burns, Sir Walter Scott and John Buchan are among many authors who have found inspiration in romantic Galloway.

The unspoilt countryside has a rich variety of scenery from sandy bays to lochs, forest and moorland and with the benefit of the Gulf Stream enjoys a mild and long holiday season.

Balcary is an excellent base for walking and touring. Several golf courses are within 15 to 30 minutes drive and there is plenty of choice for anglers and birdwatchers.

Good hospitality in a family atmosphere that is efficient but friendly and a superb setting make Balcary Bay an ideal holiday hotel.

Auchencairn, Nr Castle Douglas, Kirkcudbrightshire DG7 1QZ, Tel: (055) 664 217/311, Fax: (055) 664 272

Encircled by twelve acres of thickly wooded grounds, Baron's Craig Hotel is an imposing late 19th century granite mansion. Although extended to provide modern comforts and amenities its character has been retained. The well-appointed lounge is spacious and airy, whilst the pretty pink and green restaurant overlooks the wide expanse of the Solway and Rough Firth. Most of the twenty-seven bedrooms have private bathrooms and all are tastefully and comfortably furnished.

Under the personal supervision of the owner and his friendly staff, the restaurant offers tempting and interesting menus combining the best of traditional and Continental cooking.

Solway salmon baked in filo pastry and served with basil essence is one of many excellent dishes. There is a good wine list and a convivial cocktail bar for pre-dinner drinks.

The grounds provide a suitable setting with lush green lawns and a blaze of colour in spring and early summer from the masses of rhododendrons. Just three minutes walk from the hotel, in the little village of Rockliffe, there is excellent bathing from the beach which is particularly safe for children. About a mile away at Kippford sailing is available and local lochs and rivers provide trout and coarse fishing. For the golfing enthusiast there are both nine and eighteen-hole courses nearby.

Rockliffe, by Dalbeattie, Kirkudbrightshire DG5 4QF ,Tel: (055 663) 225

Beechwood is a gracious country house set in a charming garden against twelve acres of beech trees. It overlooks the Annan valley and the little town of Moffat tucked away in the peaceful south west corner of Scotland.

The Victorian house was originally a private boarding school for young ladies. Today Jeff and Lynda Rogers offer a less formal welcome. All public rooms have views of the gardens. The bedrooms all have en suite bathrooms and are well equipped with extras - colour television, clock/radio, hair dryer, mending box, tea/coffee facilities, direct dial telephone etc. There are two comfortable lounges - one with a small cocktail bar - where aperitifs, malt whiskies and liqueurs are served. Guests may relax with the newspapers, make use of the library or even play chess while log fires burn brightly on chilly evenings.

Fine, fresh food including the best available local produce is offered on the Table d'Hote menu.

There is an imaginative vegetarian selection and a selection of fine wines. Lovely walks and drives are within easy reach of Beechwood and gourmet packed lunches are available to order for your picnic. There is a challenging 18-hole golf course near at hand and excellent tennis courts a few minutes away. Fishing, riding and pony trekking can all be arranged.

If you are feeling less energetic you can stroll in the beech wood or simply relax in the garden. Visit Beechwood in any season and enjoy the shifting beauty of the trees, fresh green in spring and mellow gold in Autumn.

Moffat, Dumfriesshire DG10 9RS, Tel: (0683) 20210, Fax: (0683) 20889

Brisbane House Hotel is the perfect place to escape the pressures of everyday life, yet is within a half hour's drive from Glasgow. Set amidst the spectacular beauty of the hills and islands of the Firth of Clyde, many of the rooms offer unsurpassed views south to the Isles of Arran and the Cumbraes and north to the Romatic Kyles of Bute.

From the moment one sets foot in the exquisite marble Entrance Hall with its twin staircase, the scene is set. The twenty-three beautifully appointed bedrooms, each with custom-made cherry wood or mahogany furniture and tasteful fabrics, will satisfy the needs of the discerning guest.

The elegant Dining Room, with its crisp linen and lovely china, glass and silver will satisfy the discerning palate from the extensive Table d'Hote and A la Carte menus, matched by a comprehensive wine list. In fact, any one of the fishing boats out on the Firth may be landing your lunch as you study the menu in the comfort of the Lounge Cocktail Bar, which also serves meals and delicious cream teas.

The Dining Room is also ideal for receptions and functions of all kinds, seating 150 people in comfort. For conferences and seminars the well-equipped Glen Room accommodates 30 delegates.

The picturesque seaside town of Largs has much to offer in the way of recreation and is a perfect base for exploring the area. There are two golf courses with views over the bay and the tennis, badminton or squash enthusiast is well catered for. The protected waters of the bay provide sailing and all types of water sports.

Largs KA30 8NF, Tel: (0475) 687 200 Fax: (0475) 67629

Situated some 10 miles from Dumfries and 14 from Gretna this ancient castle was built by the Murrays and played its part in Border warfare. The present castle dates from 1450 and it has one of the most massive Keeps in Scotland with walls 13 feet (4 metres) thick. Adjoining the castle is a fine mansion of Scottish Baronial style built by the Earls of Mansfield.

The magnificent Great Hall is oak panelled with displays of weapons and armour. Bedrooms are en suite, some with whirlpool baths and 4 poster beds, including our 2 Bridal Chambers.

Surrounding the castle are 50 acres of gardens, woodlands and park. Currently new water gardens and a walled medieval herb garden are under renovation.

Each evening guests are given a unique candle-lit tour of the medieval Keep visiting vaulted cellars, Laird's chamber, dungeon with Pit and much more. The history of the castle is graphically told together with the story of our Ghost, the Green Lady who fell from the battlements in 1560.

After the tour guests may enjoy a dinner by candle light with a wide choice of Scottish fayre served in the oak panelled dining room.

Over the centuries many marriages have taken place in the castle as recorded by the many carved coats of arms or 'wedding stones'. The tradition has been revived since religious ceremonies are frequently conducted in the Laird's Chamber by a Minister of the Church of Scotland. Full details are given in our wedding brochure.

Clarencefield, Dumfries DG1 4NA, Tel: (038787) 283, Fax : (038787) 266

Corsemalzie House Hotel, a secluded country mansion is set in the heart of the picturesque countryside of the Machars (moors) of Wigtownshire, away from the rigours of city life. Relax in a setting which is hard to beat, the only noise to upset the tranquillity are the cries of the whaup (curlew) and the babbling burn. The seasonal changes create a different backdrop for the hotel, making Corsemalzie a delight to stay at whatever time of year is your preference.

The gastronome will find Corsemalzie has a great deal to offer, with dishes created using only the finest ingredients carefully and enthusiastically supervised by the proprietor Mr Peter McDougall. Fresh and local produce is used whenever possible.

This attention to detail is carried throughout the hotel with Mr and Mrs McDougall ensuring that your stay will not only be memorable for the cuisine but also for the little things that make the difference between a good hotel and a great hotel.

If you can drag yourself away from this comfort, the surrounding area has much to offer, with riding pony trekking and walking, some superb golf on your doorstep, a whole host of 9 hole courses, with 18 hole courses at Portpatrick, Glenluce where the hotel pays half your green fees, Stranraer and a little further afield at the famous Turnberry Links course.

For the game sportsmen, shooting and fishing are here in an abundance, Mr McDougall will personally organise and assist you shooting for pheasant, grouse, partridge, duck geese, snipe woodcock, rabbits and hares in the hotel grounds and neighbouring estates amounting to some 8,000 acres. The hotel has exclusive salmon and trout fishing rights on four and a half miles of the River Bladnoch and five miles on the River Tarff. Fishing can also be organised in the Mazie Burn. A gillie is available for most of the season to advise and assist wherever needed.

Port William, Newton Stuart, Wigtownshire DG8 9RL, Tel: (098 886) 254, Fax: (098 886) 213

Cairndale Hotel

Privately owned and managed by the Wallace family, this well established hotel offers all the comforts expected from one of the region's leading three star hotels.

Situated close to the centre of the market town of Dumfries in South West Scotland, the Cairndale Hotel is ideally located for touring the Borders, Burns Country and the beautiful Solway Coast.

Originally three Victorian town houses, the Cairndale now has a total of 76 bedrooms. All rooms have private facilities, colour television, radio, direct dial telephone, hairdryer and hospitality trays as standard, while new Executive rooms and suites have Queen size double beds, mini-bars, trouser presses and jacuzzi spa baths.

The Hotel Dining Room, which is open to non-residents, serves both table d'hote and a la carte menus. Sawney Bean's Bar and Grill offers traditional hot roasts, pies and casseroles from the Carvery. The Forum Cafe Bar, overlooking the Swimming Pool, is also open throughout the day, serving light meals, snacks and beverages in a Continental Cafe Bar environment.

A dinner dance is held in the hotel every Saturday night from the beginning of April until the end of November, while the extremely popular Cairndale Ceilidh and Taste of Scotland Dinner is arranged every Sunday over the summer months from May until the end of October.

The hotel's Barracuda Club offers residents free use of the heated indoor swimming pool, steam room, hot spa bath and gymnasium. And you'll be on 'Cloud Nine' after a visit to the fully equipped Health and Beauty salon of the same name.

English Street, Dumfries DG1 2DF, Tel: (0387) 54111, Fax: (0387) 50555

Clonyard House Hotel

This attractive Victorian country house hotel is situated in seven acres of secluded wooded ground on the Solway Coast. The area is aptly named the 'quiet country'. It is as yet undiscovered by the many tourists often found elsewhere in Scotland and yet is startling in its beauty - with high cliffs, sheltered creeks, sandy beaches, lochs and forested hills, and miles of rolling farm and moorland. There are numerous sites of interest to visit - abbeys, museums, castles, and the local towns and villages are steeped in history. There are four golf courses within ten miles, coarse fishing is available on nearby lochs, salmon and trout fishing on the river Urr and sailing and sea trips can be organised for budding sailors.

The hotel is small and friendly and has a lively atmosphere in the evening as the cocktail bar and restaurant are popular with the local community. The 15 rooms are of two types - traditional, well-furnished and very spacious in the mainhouse, or the Garden Wing rooms which are modern and comfortable, with a small patio, and facing south to catch the sun. One of these is specially fitted for disabled guests. All are centrally heated, with private bath or shower, tea making facilities and telephone. Children are particularly welcome, and will safely enjoy playing in the grounds with its 'enchanted tree'. Dinner is served in the 19th century dining room, using mainly fresh local produce such as Kirkcudbrightshire scallops, Solway salmon and Galloway beef and lamb and a mouthwatering selection of home-made sweets.

Colvend, Dalbeattie, Dumfriesshire DG5 4QW, Tel: (055) 663 372, Fax: (055) 663 422

Creebridge House Hotel

The Creebridge House Hotel was once the home of the Earl of Galloway and takes its name from the nearby River Cree. It is situated in three acres of idyllic gardens and woodlands at the edge of the Penninghame and Kirroughtree Forests. This distinguished looking house has retained all of its original character and is ideal for anybody looking for a peaceful sojourn in the beautiful south-west of Scotland and yet is located just three minutes walk from the centre of the vibrant town of Newton Stewart. There are a number of leisure pursuits which can be done locally such as golf in Newtown Stewart, pony trekking, fishing on the rivers Bladnoch, Minnoch and Cree (tuition is available from the hotel Ghillie and fishing parties, with equipment, can be arranged with the hotel) or walking in the scenic Galloway hills. Ayr racecourse is an hour's drive away, and the hotel also organises special racing weekends which incorporate trips to Ayr's major race meetings.

The hotel is spacious and comfortable throughout. The drawing room features a spectacular period mahogany fireplace and the individually appointed bedrooms each offer private bathroom, colour television, tea/coffee tray and telephone. The main restaurant offers a la carte and table d'hote menus and uses only fresh local produce for its dishes which are imaginative and varied - such as Venison Parcels and Pan Fried Medallions of Beef Fillet. More informal meals can be bought in the lively surroundings of the Bar and there is an extensive range of real ales and malt whiskies available to the connoisseur.

Newtown Stewart, Wigtownshire DG8 6NP, Tel: (0671) 2121

The Dryfesdale Hotel

A former manse, this 18th Century bulding is situated on the outskirts of the busy town of Lockerbie. It is within easy access of the main Scottish/English link road (A74) and Lockerbie railway station is part of the Intercity link between London and Glasgow.

With 5 acres of magnificent grounds and breathtaking views of the Scottish countryside the Dryfesdale Hotel offers a tranquil resting place.

There are 15 beautifully furnished bedrooms, all with private en suite facilities. They all have tea and coffee making facilities, colour television, radio and direct dial telephone. Of the 6 ground floor double/twin rooms, one is specifically designed for wheel chair use.

The restaurant has an excellent reputation for its high standard of cuisine. Guests and patrons may choose from either the extensive a la carte menu, or the table d'hote menu which changes daily. After the meal you can tempt yourself with one of the eighty single malt whiskies on offer in the bar.

The nearby town of Lockerbie provides shopping, curling and a cinema. Hotel guests have free access to the Squash Club.

Some of the finest fishing rivers and lochs in the country are in this locality and Hotel guests can book day and week permits for much of the local fishing. There are several fine golf courses in the area and local shooting includes pheasant grouse and deer stalking. In fact the outdoor enthusiast is well and truly catered for with a national tennis club at Moffat, nature reserves, national parks, sailing, castles and archaeological sites.

Lockerbie, Dumfriesshire DG11 2SF, Tel:(05762) 2427, Fax:(05762) 4187

Fernhill Hotel

Spectacularly situated above the village of Portpatrick, Fernhill Hotel looks down on a snug-set harbour of yachts and fishing craft and to the Irish Sea beyond. The Gulf Stream brings spring early to Galloway, and the seacoast ranges from rugged cliffs and unfrequented coves to family-safe beaches.

Fernhill is set in its own secluded grounds and Anne and Hugh Harvey have regularly improved and updated it to maintain high standards throughout. There are 21 bedrooms, including six executive rooms with magnificent sea views. Three of the bedrooms have patio doors with balconies. All bedrooms are centrally heated, and most are double glazed with colour television, hairdryer and direct dial telephone. There are trouser presses in Superior and Executive rooms, and most rooms have private facilities.

The Cocktail Bar is stylish and the Bar Lounge comfortable, while the Conservatory - with its panoramic view of Portpatrick and the sea - is an especially attractive area for a la carte and bar meals.

The restaurant offers a fine selection of food and wine and the regular patronage of local people bears testament to the high quality of the cuisine.

Fernhill is justifiably proud of its reputation as a golfer's paradise. A five minute stroll from the hotel leads to the first tee of the cliff-top Dunskey Course. Autumn evenings are long, and the light still holds for that final putt when down south the car lights are going on. Special rates are available for inclusive golf holidays, and 'The Garden House', sleeping up to eight, is perfect for small golfing parties. Ideal for family holidays too!

Heugh Road, Portpatrick, Wigtownshire DG9 8TD, Tel: (0776) 81 220, Fax: (0776) 81 596

Kirroughtree is a striking eighteenth-century mansion, elevated amidst the unspoilt beauty of Galloway, where guests can experience gracious living in luxurious surroundings. The hotel nestles in the foothills of the Cairnsmore of Fleet, on the edge of the Galloway Forest Park, in an area rich in fascinating history and dramatic unspoilt scenery, which remains largely undiscovered. The Heron family built this house in 1719 and the emphasis is firmly upon comfort and relaxation. French doors lead to the croquet lawn and terrace, with superb views over the surrounding hills. From the lounge rises the original staircase, from which Robert Burns recited his poems to the Heron family and guests.

Each bedroom at Kirroughtree is individually decorated and lavishly furnished, with coloured bathroom suites, central heating and direct-dial telephone.

However, many guests are attracted to Kirroughtree solely through its reputation for excellent food. The chefs are highly trained professionals, bringing to Kirroughtree's special cuisine their own experience in some of the finest restaurant in Europe.

Only the best local produce is used in creating meals of great originality and finesse. These sophisticated creations are enjoyed in the elegant surroundigs of the intimate dining rooms, and to complement the food, the wine list is long and varied to satisfy all tastes and price ranges. Meanwhile the charming cocktail bar provides the perfect environment for aperitifs.

Whether you are planning a long or short stay, Kirroughtree offers peace and tranquility in magnificent surroundings. For the golfer, free golf can be arranged for residents on two local courses, one of which was designed by James Braid, who designed Gleneagles and Carnoustie. Golf clubs can be hired from the hotel if necessary. Fishing can also be arranged on the rivers Cree and Bladnoch, as well as rough shooting, deer-stalking and clay-pigeon shooting in the hotel grounds.

Kirroughtree Hotel is easily accessible, being only half a mile from A75, less that two hour's drive from the M6. The friendly and courteous management will ensure that your stay is totally pleasurable and relaxing.

Wigtownshire DG8 6AN, Tel: (0671) 2141

Knockinaam was built as a holiday house for Lady Hunter Blair in 1869 and enlarged in 1901. The house stands in a secluded enclave at the foot of a deep and thickly wooded glen, surrounded on three sides by sheltering cliffs and looking out to sea. A beautiful garden with wide lawns runs down to a private sandy beach where guests can enjoy magnificent views of the distant Irish coastline, the changing moods of sea and sky, and stupendous sunsets. Indeed, such is the timeless tranquility of this extraordinary place, that Sir Winston Churchill chose it during the Second World War for a secret meeting with General Eisenhower and their Chiefs of Staff.

The house was converted into a 'restaurant avec chambres' and quickly established a reputation for the finest cooking in the south of Scotland. This reputation has been assiduously maintained and today, you can sit in the attractive dining room with the sea breaking over the rocks at the end of the lawn and dine on the tender Galloway beef – surely the best in the world? – fresh lobsters, scallops, scampi and many other locally produced delicacies, including home grown vegetables. In cooler weather, log fires burn in the public rooms and there is full central heating throughout the house. Small business meetings can be accommodated during the autumn.

Knockinaam is an ideal base for exploring this little known and unspoiled corner of Scotland. Quaint villages, early Christian sites, ruined and still inhabited castles, standing stones dot an undulating green landscape, dissected by rough, dry stone walls and twisting single track roads. The unusually mild climate engendered by the Gulf Stream can support almost every species of tropical plant and there are many famous gardens within easy reach. There are two excellent golf courses close to the hotel, and world famous Turnberry is less than an hour's drive. Further inland, forests of spruce and larch lead into vast racts of wild country, easily accessible by car or on foot, where a wonderful variety of wild game abounds amongst lochs, rivers and tawny hills.

Knockinaam offers its visitors the chance to escape from the pressures of the outside world, to shed cares and restore neglected values. The passage of time has left the holiday house atmosphere intact, and those romantic qualities that Sir Winston Churchill appreciated, remain unchanged.

The resident owners, Marcel and Corina Frichot and their attentive young staff, look forward to welcoming you to this unique and unforgettable place.

Portpatrick, Wigtownshire DG9 9AD, Tel: (077681) 471, Fax: (077681) 435

Ladyburn, the home of David and Jane Hepburn, lies in the heart of 'the most beautiful valley in Ayrshire' on the edge of the magnificent estate of Kilkerran surrounded by the most intriguing pattern of woods and fields. Ladyburn was acquired in the late 17th century by the Fergussons of Kilkerran and remained in their hands until the death of Francis, widow of Sir James Fergusson.

Visitors are welcomed to Ladyburn by the friendly atmosphere of gracious living enjoyed by former generations of Hepburns. The house is furnished with antiques inherited by the family. All the bedrooms are different, each with its own character and style of furniture and furnishings. The cuisine is traditional using only local fresh produce, much of which is grown in the gardens, and is prepared by Jane.

For those who are 'Following the Fairways', Ladyburn is situated only a short drive from the world famous Turnberry courses and within 45 minutes drive are the excellent and equally renowned courses of Royal Troon and Prestwick.

Ladyburn is situated only 12 miles from Ayr, site of Scotland's premier race course with over 30 fixtures organised usually incorporating a full programme for both the Flat and National Hunt.

Staying at Ladyburn is being a guest in a beautiful country house where the welcome and attention given by David and Jane Hepburn is reminiscent of a bygone era.

Maybole, Ayrshire KA19 7SG, Tel: (06554) 585, Fax: (06554) 580

Lochgreen House Hotel

Lochgreen House Hotel is owned and run by Bill and Catherine Costley. It is in Southwood, near Troon, in the heart of Robbie Burns country and is a fine mansion which was built in 1905 for stockbroker George Morton. It is situated in 15 acres of land and is adjacent to the Royal Troon Open Championship course. The Managing Director is Charles Price.

The hotel is furnished with imagination as to decor and with thoughtfulness as to comfort. It is the owner's intention that modern facilities are offered alongside the traditions of an historic house. But, after dealing with the comfort of their guests, food is a top priority and the chef patron Bill Costley was coach to the Scottish team in the last 'Food Olympics' and in fact won Scotland's first gold medal. He states that fine wines and fresh produce are the essential elements of Lochgreen cuisine.

All the bedrooms at the hotel have excellent private facilities.

There is no shortage of things to do in the area. You could follow in the path of Robbie Burns who was born a few miles away in a cottage at Alloway. You could play golf at any number of the world's top courses. You could take advantage of the first class yachting and sailing facilities. You could pitch and putt or play tennis near at hand and arrangements can be made for fishing and for pony trekking. Consult William or Catherine Costley for details of whatever interest you wish to pursue.

Reaching Lochgreen House Hotel is a simple matter whatever form of transport you choose. You can get there by rail and a short taxi journey, or by road - both are easy journeys from Glasgow.

Prestwick International Airport is only a mile south, while Scotland's main air terminal at Glasgow is 30 miles to the north. There are local ferries which link the Ayrshire mainland with Arran and Bute.

Monktonhill Road, Southwood, Troon KA10 7EN, Tel: (0292) 313343, Fax: (0292) 318661

Marine Highland Hotel

An air of quiet sophistication and timeless elegance is immediately apparent on entering the handsome Victorian structure of the Marine Highland Hotel. Traditional service, unobtrusive but attentive staff and superb facilities combine to make the hotel worthy of its well deserved reputation at home and abroad.

All of the seventy two rooms have private bathrooms, telephone, hairdryer, trouser press, satellite television, toiletries and a complimentary welcome tray with tea and coffee. There are several deluxe suites which also have a private sitting room and mini-bar.

The Arran lounge overlooks the 18th fairway of Royal Troon Championship Golf Course and has a breathtaking view across the Firth of Clyde to the Isle of Arran, providing a relaxing atmosphere in which to enjoy a traditional afternoon tea or one of a fine range of malt whiskies available.

A superb choice of Scottish and international cuisine - all prepared with the finest fresh produce - is presented daily in the Fairways restaurant. A more informal atmosphere prevails in Crosbie's Brasserie where hot and cold meals and snacks accompanied with a good range of teas, coffees and drinks, are served all day.

The exclusive Marine Club has an extensive range of sport and leisure facilities, including gymnasium, heated pool and squash courts, and the Ayrshire coastline offers many challenging courses for the golfer - Royal Troon, Turnberry, Barassie, Prestwick, Gailes and many more.

The Marine Highland is a very special hotel which has admirably blended style and tradition with outstanding modern facilities, creating a perfect balance which nowadays is so rare to find.

Troon, Ayrshire KA10 6HE, Tel: (0292) 314444, Fax: (0292) 316922

Montgreenan Mansion House

The Mansion House at Montgreenan was built by Dr Robert Glasgow in 1817 and has always been a family home, with a tranquil, peaceful atmosphere very different from the modern purpose-built hotel. 18th century features including marble and brass fireplaces and decorative plasterwork have been retained, lending the mansion a distinctly Georgian feel.

Bedrooms are furnished with reproduction pieces or antiques and all 21 have en suite facilities, writing desk, colour TV, radio, direct dial telephone, hairdryer, trouser press, tea/coffee making facilities and minibar. A spa in the bathroom is available by request. There are three suites.

An outstanding cellar boasts over 200 bins and is designed to complement the tempting cuisine inspired by a wealth of local produce. The elegant restaurant has a deserved reputation for delicious individually prepared dishes.

As well as being within 40 minutes of 30 championship golf courses Montgreenan has its own practice course, putting green, tennis court, lawn croquet and billiard room.

Set in 50 acres of garden and woodland it is the perfect place to get away from the hustle and bustle yet within easy reach of Glasgow, Kilmarnock, Ayr and Irvine and only twenty minutes from two motorways and airports - Glasgow and Prestwick.

Montgreenan has a growing reputation as a centre for executive conferences. The six syndicate rooms are each as individual as they are grand, with panoramic views of the Ailsa Craig and the peaks of Arran.

Montgreenan is the perfect setting for a conference or function of any kind.

Montgreenan Estate, Kilwinning, Ayrshire KA13 7QZ, Tel: (0294) 57733/4, Fax: (0294) 85397

Set amidst 78 acres of tranquil park and woodland, Lockerbie Country Manor is a haven of peace and relaxation, yet it is situated only a mile off the A74. Built in 1814 for Sir William Douglas and Dame Grace Johnstone, whose great-grandson, the Marquis of Queensbury, formulated the present day boxing rules, it became the smart country hotel it is today in 1920.

Guests can enjoy the traditions of a bygone era at Lockerbie Manor. The long tree-lined driveway gives a taste of the luxury that lies ahead. Both of the public lounges are furnished in authentic period style with an Adam fireplace amidst period furniture and walls lined with oil paintings. The atmosphere exudes warmth and hospitality; a home away from home for the traveller.

All the 29 bedrooms are individually decorated with private bathrooms, colour T.V. and every comfort. There are three four-poster bedded suites, with front-facing views over the fields and surrounding countryside. The Queensbury Dining Room, with its wood panelled wall, ornate chandeliers and magnificent views, is the ideal setting for a delectable meal. The cuisine is of an international nature, where Eastern flavours and cooking subtly blend with Western recipes.

Golfers will love the courses in the area, offering challenges of varying degrees of difficulty. Lockerbie, Dumfries, Lochmaben, Powfoot and Moffat are all near by. If shooting is more your scene, there are numerous large estates around Lockerbie offering facilities. For the fisherman, the Rivers Annan, Milk, Cree, Blanock and Penkiln all beckon. Within the space of a short drive you can visit the beautiful Galloway coast, Drumlanrigg Castle, Maxwellton House in Monaive, Threave Gardens and Castle near Castle Douglas, and Thomas Carlyle's birthplace at Ecclefechan.

Boreland Road, Lockerbie, Dumfries and Galloway DG11 2RG, Tel: (05762) 2610, Fax: (05762) 3046

The Murray Arms Hotel

The Murray Arms is a hotel with a long and fascinating history. The Arms' Coffee House existed before 1642, when it was referred to as the 'Gait House' - from which the surrounding village derived its name. The Murray Arms itself was built in 1760 and was a well-known refreshment halt for the Dumfries to Stranraer stage coach. Cotton mills, tanneries, a wine company and quarrying subsequently arrived at Gatehouse and the town grew up around the hotel.

The hotel has been carefully modernised but retains its Georgian character and the traditional white-washed walls distinctive of the area. Its twelve bedrooms are fully equipped and have en suite bathrooms. The three dining rooms serve a variety of dishes with the emphasis on local fare such as Galloway Beef and Smoked River Cree Salmon. The Lunky Hole is open all day and offers the widest range of meals and snacks. Visitors can while away the evening in the lively atmosphere of the cocktail bar, the lounge bar, or one of the three public rooms (including the Burns Room where the great Scottish bard wrote 'Scots Wha Hae').

The surrounding area is famed for its picturesque landscapes and rich heritage.

There are many historical buildings and sites of interest within a short walk of the hotel, such as Cardoness Castle at the mouth of the River Fleet and the Mill on the Fleet. Gatehouse is in a National Trust for Scotland Conservation Area and Fleet Bay and the Fleet valley are habitats to a wide variety of flora and fauna. Fleet Bay, with its wide sandy expanses, is ideal for swimming, dinghy yachting, wind surfing, water-skiing or sunbathing.

There are a number of golf courses a short drive away, such as Turnberry and Portpatrick. There are also a tennis court and a bowling green in the town. The area with its hills, valleys, lochs, rivers and the coast makes for ideal walking, cycling and fishing. The hotel will be keen to help arrange any of these activities.

Anne Street, Gatehouse of Fleet, Dumfries & Galloway DG7 2HY, Tel: (0557) 814207, Fax: (0557) 814370

Northpark House Hotel

Northpark was built in 1720 as a farmhouse for the Belleisle Estate and is now home to two magnificent 18-hole golf courses. Indeed, a total of ten championship golf courses lie within twenty minutes of the hotel.

Northpark is situated in the historic village of Alloway, which was the birthplace of Scottish National Bard Robbie Burns and Burns Cottage can still be visited. Culzen Castle, a National Trust Centre and Country Park, is nearby, while the Ayrshire coast offers an ideal place to relax during warm summer days.

The house has been fully and sympathetically restored to retain its Georgian character. The bedrooms feature captivating views of the Golf Course and Gardens and they are attractively furnished, with remote control television, telephone and hair dryers. There is full room service.

The elegant restaurant offers a fine range of dishes, many using fresh local produce and it also caters for vegetarians.

The cuisine is accompanied by a fine range of wines and spirits as well as a full Bar.

The Northpark rooms are ideal for small executive conferences, meetings and exhibitions.

2 Alloway, Ayr KA7 4NL, Tel: (0292) 42336, Fax: (0292) 45572

The North West Castle Hotel

Built in 1820, and the former home of explorer John Ross, the North West Castle Hotel stands in its own grounds opposite the busy ferry port at Stranraer.

Accommodation includes 80 de luxe bedrooms, many with views over Loch Ryan, two suites and a four poster bedroom. All bedrooms are en suite with colour television, direct dial telephone, radio alarm, hairdryer, trouser press plus many other little extras to help make your stay enjoyable.

An atmosphere of spaciousness and elegance prevails in the widely acclaimed Regency Dining Room. The owners search for the freshest produce and an extensive wine list is offered. A professional and friendly staff willingly caters for your every need. Order dinner while you sip an aperitif in Captain Ross's Lounge and during dinner, pianists will be delighted to play your requests. On Saturdays (except in June, July and August) dinner is followed by dancing to one of the popular local bands.

Gentlemen are requested to wear jacket and tie in the Regency Dining Room.

North West Castle was the first hotel in the world to have its own indoor curling rink and attracts curlers from all over the globe to play the roarin' game.

There is also a heated swimming pool with jacuzzi, saunas, sunbeds and multi-gym. The large games room offers short carpet bowling, snooker, pool and table tennis.

Owner Hammy McMillan and his family are proud to welcome guests to this magnificent hotel and are dedicated to ensuring them absolute enjoyment and comfort.

Portrodie, Stranraer DG9 8EH, Tel: (0776) 4413, Fax: (0776) 2646

Northfield House

The delightful, award-winning Northfield House is situated in a secluded and scenic twelve acre ground overlooking the River Annan and is about a mile away from the village of Annan. The Dumfriesshire countryside is among the prettiest and most tranquil in Scotland and is ideal for getting away from it all at any time of the year. The landscape is dotted with castles, ruins, attractive little villages and small lochs. There are excellent opportunities for fishing, golf and bird-watching. The hotel has private fishing on a stretch of the Annan and a limited number of rods are available for use by the guests.

The owners, James and Mary Airey, go out of their way to make their guests feel welcome and to cater for their every need.

The three en suite bedrooms are attractively furnished and all have a colour television, electric blanket and tea/coffee tray. The drawing room features a log fire providing a warm and relaxing atmosphere on even the coldest of days. The elegant dining room is a fitting venue for Northfield's wonderful cuisine with a carefully selected menu using the best of local produce. Specialities include Poached Solway Sea-trout and Breast of Pigeon. Packed lunches can be made up if required. There is also a Garden Suite suitable for families.

Northfield House, Eaglesfield Road, Annan, Dumfriesshire DG12 5LL, Tel: (0461) 202851

The South Beach Hotel

The South Beach Hotel is situated on the edge of Troon, looking out into the magnificent Firth of Clyde and the beautiful islands of Arran and Ailsa Craig. Troon is renowned throughout the world as a golfer's paradise, with no fewer than five courses within the burgh, including the classic links course, Royal Troon. In addition 15 more courses lie within a 20-mile radius, including Prestwick and Turnberry.

The hotel is owned by the Watts family, who take pride in its ambience - here, visitors are treated as friends. Every need is catered for - the 27 bedrooms are en suite and include television, radio, tea/coffee making facilities and telephone; the hotel has its own fully equipped leisure and health suite, complete with jacuzzi, sauna, solarium, gymnasium and beauticians. The commodious dining room is of quite unique design, opening into the hotel gardens and guests are treated to four course meals featuring the finest Scottish food. Guests have the option of retiring to the delightful Sun Lounge with its splendid sea views, or the Residents Lounge. The magnificent Paton Suite is scene for frequent dances and other social functions, while the bars provide a further facility for the mid-day or evening sojourn.

The hotel provides an ideal base for taking off to pursue a whole range of activities, as well as golf - including swimming, tennis, riding, sailing and bowling. Just 15 minutes drive along the coast is the Magnum Leisure Centre, one of the finest sports centres in Western Europe. The Ayrshire coast is among Britain's most attractive, and in nearby Ardrossan there is a regular ferry to Arran.

Troon, Ayrshire, Tel: (0292) 312033/314282, Fax: (0292) 318438

Well View Hotel

Set in half an acre of garden, Well View nestles at the foot of hills overlooking Moffat, which is half a mile away.

This small and charming hotel is owned and run by Janet and John Schuckardt. Both former teachers, Mr and Mrs Schuckardt took over Well View in 1984. The house was built for two brother shoemakers in 1864 and was named after one of several sulphurous wells which led to Moffat's growth as a Victorian spa town.

All seven bedrooms are furnished to an excellent standard and supplied with fresh fruit, home-made biscuits and sherry.

Well View has two lounges and there are no better surroundings for unwinding after a day out touring Scotland's lovely Border country. The large lounge provides a quiet haven, whether for reading or for taking an aperitif and hors d'oevres before dinner. After dinner, relaxation is the keynote as you are served coffee and Well View's own home-made sweetmeats with perhaps, a liqueur or a malt whisky.

The lounge features a display of Border knitwear, wool and fashion yarns.

Janet Schuckhardt and her culinary team have created a respected and widely known reputation, not only for the high quality of their ingredients but also for the imaginative range of dishes. The presentation of their dishes is particularly widely admired. There is an extensive wine list to complement your meal. Special dinners at the Well View include The Winter Dinner, Christmas Day Lunch, the Hogmanay Dinner, the Celebration of Fish and Game and the Welcome Spring Dinner.

Janet and John have cultivated a restful ambience amid traditional furnishings. Their aim has always been to encourage guests to treat Well View as their own home during their stay.

Ballplay Road, Moffat, Dumfriesshire DG10 9JU, Tel: (0683) 20184

Highland Sheep– *Basil Bradley. Courtesy of Rosentiel's.*

Voted Britain's 5 Star Hotel of the Year in 1990, and perhaps best known for its two championship links golf courses, Turnberry is located on the west coast of Scotland, set in 360 acres overlooking the islands of Arran and Ailsa Craig.

The two golf courses, owned and managed by the hotel, make it a year round Mecca for golfers and the Ailsa Course will again host the British Open in 1994. A superb new Clubhouse will open in Spring 1993.

The new Turnberry Spa and Leisure is an additional amenity for our guests. The leisure facilities include a 20 metre deck level pool, poolside spa bath and bio-sauna, 2 squash courts, cardiovascular and muscular gymnasium and planned aqua and floor aerobics. The nine treatment rooms offer a complete range of treatments, including aromatherapy and hydro-therapy.

Nearby are riding stables, and fishing, rough shooting, clay pigeon shooting can be arranged. Culzean Castle, Robert Burns country and the Burrell Collection are also of interest in the area.

The hotel was built at the turn of the century and the tradition of elegance and comfort is retained in the bedrooms. At Turnberry, living is indeed comfortable and relaxed; every bedroom has its individual character.

The Turnberry Restaurant, under the direction of Executive Chef, Stewart Cameron, specialises in an alliance of traditional Scottish and French cooking. Entertainment is provided each evening by resident musicians and the atmosphere is very much that of the grand Country House.

The Bay at Turnberry Restaurant enjoys spectacular views of Turnberry Bay towards Arran and Ailsa Craig. The focus is on a lighter style of cooking both at lunch and dinner, in an informal setting.

Whilst staying at Turnberry, guests will enjoy warm hospitality, the constant concern and those little formalities and gracious touches that make all the difference. Perhaps it is because of this that so many guests and their families choose to return year after year.

Turnberry, Ayrshire KA26 9LT, Tel: (0655) 31000, Fax: (0655) 31706, Telex: 777779

Warmanbie, a Georgian Country House Hotel and Restaurant, set in 40 acres of secluded woodland grounds overlooking the River Annan, has been owned by the Duncan family since 1953. It has many interesting architectural and decorative features and is tastefully furnished with a combination of the Duncan family's antiques and more contemporary furniture. Rod Duncan, who converted it into a hotel in 1983, still runs Warmanbie for the family. He looks on Warmanbie as the family home and won't do anything that will spoil it.

Fishing for salmon, sea-trout and brown trout is free on the hotel's private stretch of the River Annan (except from 9/9 to 15/11 when there is a charge of £8.00 a day). In addition the hotel has access to numerous other stretches of water on the Annan (booking rods on two stretches in advance to make sure they are available) and to fishing on both the River Eden, near Carlisle, and the River Nith, near Dumfries. They can arrange for a ghillie to help and advise you or give you tuition, and the hotel has a supply of rods/tackle for sale/hire, a large freezer and drying facilities. Meal times are of course completely flexible to suit your fishing.

All the bedrooms have a private bathroom, colour television, tea / coffee making facilities and direct-dial telephone to ensure your complete comfort, as well as many thoughtful extra little touches such as fresh flowers, iced water and sweets. The Master bedroom is delightfully furnished with a solid mahogany four-poster bed and deep Victorian tub bath. The hotel is awarded four crowns, commended by the Scottish Tourist Board, and is recommended by Egon Ronay and the Cadogan Guide.

Here is somewhere where you can relax and unwind from the pressures of everyday life and enjoy service which, although relaxed and friendly, is still of the highest standard.

Dinners are a mixture of the creative and traditional. You'll enjoy the large steaks (using local beef) and fresh mussels, or you can try one of the hotel's more creative dishes such as pork fillet in pastry with a mushroom, cointreau and orange stuffing, or avocado and smoked salmon salad. The Scottish breakfast which the hotel serves can only be described as huge. How about porridge with Drambuie, or a champagne breakfast with smoked salmon and scrambled eggs. The cosy bar has an excellent selection of malt whiskies for you to savour while discussing the day's catch.

You'll find wildfowling, golf, tennis, squash, curling and various water sports all nearby. Clay pigeon shooting can be arranged with prior notice. Warmanbie is also an ideal base for beachcombing on the Solway Coast and exploring the picturesque countryside of South West Scotland, the Borders and Lake District.

Annan,F/F Dumfriesshire, DG12 5LLL, Tel: (0461) 204015

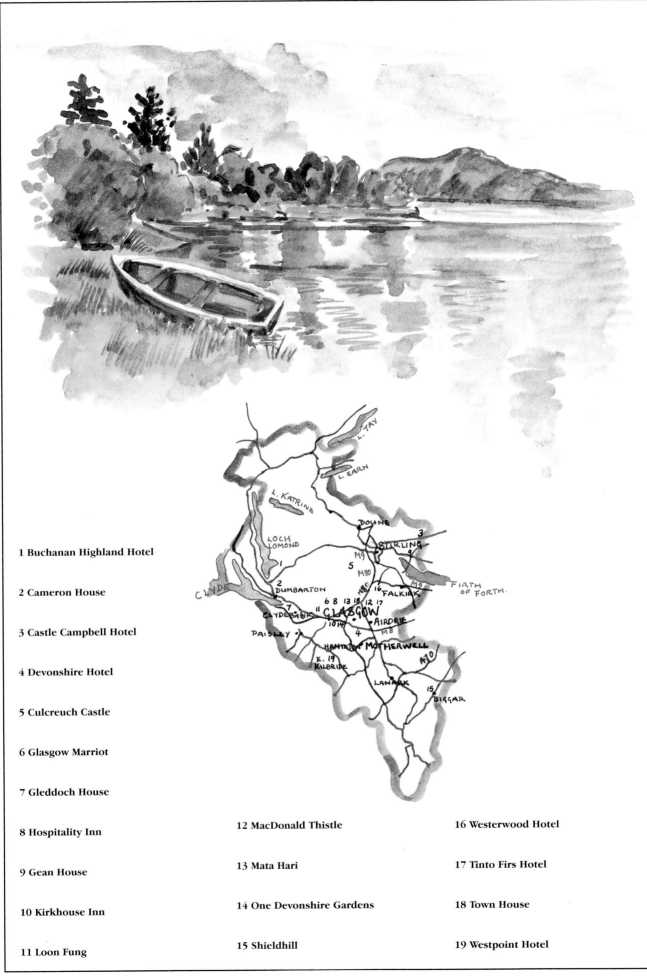

1 Buchanan Highland Hotel

2 Cameron House

3 Castle Campbell Hotel

4 Devonshire Hotel

5 Culcreuch Castle

6 Glasgow Marriot

7 Gleddoch House

8 Hospitality Inn

9 Gean House

10 Kirkhouse Inn

11 Loon Fung

12 MacDonald Thistle

13 Mata Hari

14 One Devonshire Gardens

15 Shieldhill

16 Westerwood Hotel

17 Tinto Firs Hotel

18 Town House

19 Westpoint Hotel

This is an area which represents the very soul of Scotland, an area of contrasts - the excitement and atmosphere of Glasgow contrasting with the tranquillity and beauty of Loch Lomond, the magnificence of the Victorian, modern and post-modern architecture of Glasgow's city centre against the stunning Trossachs mountains. This area encapsulates everything that is Scotland - fascinating culture, mountains, glens and lochs, historic buildings and castles, remote villages and bustling market towns.

Glasgow is a city which literally never sleeps - there is always something going on, whatever the time of the year there are events that will suit everyone from the smallest child to the most demanding connoisseur of the arts. The Scottish Opera, Scottish Ballet and Royal Scottish Orchestra are all based here. In the summer there are several major festivals, such as the Mayfest and the Glasgow International Jazz Festival, as well as more traditionally Scottish events such as the World Pipe Band championships held in August.

The city is renowned for its visual arts and its excellent museums and galleries, such as the award-winning Burrell Collection, the museum of Transport and the brand new St Mungo's Museum of Comparative Religions. The city's architecture is among the most spectacular in Europe, and covers a broad spectrum - from the 12th century cathedral, to the opulent Victorian City Chambers and finally, the Art Nouveau buildings of Charles Rennie Mackintosh.

It is truly a wonderful setting for the best shopping, wining and dining one could wish for - from the chic sophistication of Princes Square, the busy excitement of St Enoch Shopping and entertainment Centre, to the traditional local flavour of Glasgow's famous Barras Street Market. And away from all the bustle are over 70 parks and gardens, ideal for a picnic or walk, or perhaps to rest those weary legs.

Outside the city the stunning beauty of the countryside is plain to see, low, rolling meadows, gentle streams and woods in the Clyde Valley, shimmering lochs, glens and the awe-inspiring mountains of Lomond and the Trossachs. Nowhere is the latter more perfectly illustrated than at Breadalbane in the Trossachs, with its high mountain tops looking down on serene lochs, a land that inspired the writing of Sir Walter Scott, and was the haunt of the legendary Scottish outlaw, Rob Roy MacGregor. The beautiful Queen Elizabeth Forest Park stretches from the 'bonny banks' of Loch Lomond to the heart of this spectacular region, and there plenty of trails, walks and cycleways.

Loch Lomond in its splendour is a sight to behold, and the ideal place to indulge in some aquatic activity, such as sailing, fishing, and pleasure boating, while the surrounding country features beautiful villages, craft centres, golf courses and castles to visit. The neighbouring sea lochs of Gare loch and loch Long provide perfect sailing waters and regularly attract colourful yachts.

The stunning university town of Stirling is the setting for a magnificent hill-top castle, power base for the Stuart dynasty in turbulent days gone by, and many battles were fought in the vicinity, notably Bannockburn. The gorgeous little spa town of Bridge of Allan lies just beyond.

On the edge of the Trossachs lies the 'hillfoot' villages of the 'Wee County' of Clackmannan, a series of delightful little villages built around the streams and waterfalls of the area. This was ideal territory for textile mills and the woollen and tartan industry thrive to this day.

The Clyde Valley, with its meadows and streams, is famous for its flora, and the numerous gardens make for a very colourful part of Scotland indeed. The breathtaking Falls of Clyde at New Lanark inspired the painter Turner and several of Britain's greatest writers, such as Wordsworth, Coleridge and Scott.

The Valley is steeped in history, with numerous historic buildings, such as Craignethan Castle, which is rumoured to be haunted by Mary, Queen of Scots and the unusual Hamilton mausoleum, which has the longest echo of any building in Europe. New Lanark, founded by the textile entrepreneur, David Dales, once had one of the biggest mills in the world and that great age can be revisited in the Annie MacLeod Experience Museum. Ballantyre was birthplace to the great explorer, David Livingstone and a museum of his life can be found here.

Four more museums can be found at the famous village of Biggar (as the saying goes, London is big but Biggar's Biggar) and in the secluded Lowther Hills, there's not only gold to be found but the highest Scottish settlements, namely Leadhills and Wanlockhead.

Glasgow and the surrounding regions cannot be fully appreciated on a brief acquaintance - there is too much to see and experience, with one of Europe's most exciting cities, some of Europe's most picturesque landscapes and a rich cultural heritage to boot.

Freud's theory was that when a joke opens a window
and all those bats and bogeymen fly out,
you get a marvellous feeling of relief and elation.
The trouble with Freud is that
he never had to play the old Glasgow Empire
on a Saturday night after Rangers and Celtic
had both lost.

Ken Dodd

A warm, traditional atmosphere is the hallmark of this well established former coaching inn, situated only a few miles from picturesque Loch Lomond and the Trossachs. Tastefully decorated throughout, in a style which complements the original architecture of the building and its surroundings, the hotel provides care, service and attention of the highest standards.

The Endrick Lounge has open fires, comfortable sofas and deep armchairs, while the adjoining Garden Room provides a bright, spacious area for drinks or coffee.

Bedrooms have every facility to ensure a comfortable stay - private bathroom, telephone, hairdryer, trouser press, satellite TV, toiletries and complimentary welcome tray with a selection of tea and coffee.

Tapestries Restaurant enjoys a superb reputation for good food, matched with an excellent wine selection. The best fresh produce, fruit and vegetables, are incorporated into a menu of traditional Scottish and international dishes.

The Granary Restaurant offers more informal surroundings with a tempting choice of hot and cold meals, snacks and drinks available all day.

The Highland Buchanan Sport and Leisure club is fully equipped with sauna, jacuzzi, solarium, gymnasium, heated swimming pool and squash courts. A wide range of outdoor activities including golf, sailing and windsurfing can be arranged.

The Buchanan Highland Hotel is an ideal base for touring. Loch Lomond and the many activities available there is only a short drive away, historical Stirling is only 20 minutes away, and Glasgow can be reached in only 25 minutes.

The Buchanan Highland Hotel has long been synonymous with a warm welcome, and well-trained, friendly staff take pleasure in looking after guests and ensuring that your stay, be it holiday or business, is enjoyable and relaxing.

Drymen, Loch Lomond, Stirlingshire G63 0BQ, Tel: (0360) 60588, Fax: (0360) 60943

Situated on the banks of Loch Lomond in its own 108 acre estate, lies the luxurious Cameron House Hotel.

A building has stood on this site since the 14th century and cameron House has been lovingly restored to its former baronial glory.

Every one of the bedrooms provides a world of elegance, comfort and relaxation. They are equipped with every facility and there are special touches such as sherry and fresh flowers to make your stay unique.

Cameron House has the charm and character of a much loved country house. Wander through the magnificent panelled rooms and enjoy the restful atmosphere. Relax in front of the fire in the oak panelled Library as you decide which of the three restaurants is your choice for dinner. The Georgian Room offers a wide selection of imaginative dishes whilst the more informal Grill Room places its emphasis on fresh Scottish produce; salmon, trout and Aberdeen Angus beef. The Brasserie offers everything from freshly baked croissants to a delicious three course meal.

The hotel has an extensive range of leisure facilities. Indoors, these include two swimming pools, squash and badminton courts, a gymnasium, aerobics studio, sauna, jacuzzi, steam room and health and beauty facilities. Outdoors are first class tennis courts and a nine hole golf course. The hotel has its own marina and clubhouse with sailing, cruising and windsurfing on Loch Lomond.

Loch Lomond, Alexandria, Dunbartonshire, G83 8QZ, Tel: (0389) 55565

Castle Campbell Hotel

The beguiling Castle Campbell Hotel is situated on the high street of the attractive Clackmannanshire town of Dollar, next to the bridge over Dollar Burn. For tourism or business alike, it is superbly located, being within half an hour's drive of Stirling, Falkirk and Grangemouth and less than an hour away from Glasgow, Edinburgh, Dundee and the beautiful Trossachs mountains. There are over 35 quality golf courses within an hour's drive, including Gleneagles and St Andrews and golf packages can be arranged through the hotel. Loch and river fishing, clay pigeon shooting and rough shooting are other possible sporting activities.

The hotel is rapidly acquiring a fine reputation for its fine food and cosy accommodation. The tastefully decorated rooms are either twin or single and have been recently refurbished. They have en suite facilities, central heating, colour television and tea/coffee facilities. The attractive Restaurant offers an extensive and varied a la carte menu as well as a set price dinner. Visitors may also wish to try the lunches and suppers which are served in the Lounge Bar along with a large selection of alcoholic beverages. A function suite which seats 75 is also available for weddings, conferences and dinner parties.

11 Bridge Street, Dollar FK14 7DE, Tel: (0259) 42519

The Devonshire Hotel

The Devonshire Hotel of Glasgow can be found on the corner of a tree-lined Victorian terrace only minutes away from the city. This impeccably restored Hotel offers excellence without compromise.

The hotel has many interesting features such as the majestic central staircase which has been restored to the carved glory of days gone by and the charming conservatory in which the highlight is the original stain glass window. You can also appreciate the countless collection of original paintings which reflect the status of The Devonshire Hotel.

Guests will marvel at the traditional grand country style hospitality which is certainly very easy to become accustomed to especially in such sumptuous surroundings.

The intimate atmosphere of the dinning room is complemented by the high standard of cuisine with interesting menus and a well chosen wine list.

The bedrooms have all been tastefully and individually furnished to a very high standard retaining the charm of the bygone era whilst still providing modern, luxurious comforts.

The en suite bathrooms are very elegant and reflect the same attention to design and detail as the rest of The Devonshire.

You will certainly enjoy staying in this rather splendid hotel where personal service and attention to detail are the keystones.

5 Devonshire Gardens, Glasgow G12 0UX, Tel: 041 2339 7878, Fax: 041 339 3980

Fifteen men on the dead man's chest
Yo-ho-ho, and a bottle of rum!
Drink and the devil had done for the rest -
Yo-ho-ho and a bottle of rum

Robert Louis Stevenson (1850-1894)

Culcreuch Castle, the home of the Barons of Culcreuch since 1699 and before this the ancestral fortalice of the Galbraiths and indeed Clan Castle of the Galbraith chiefs for over three centuries (1320 to 1630), has now been restored and converted by its present owners into a most comfortable family-run country house hotel, intimately blending the elegance of bygone days with modern comforts and personal service in an atmosphere of friendly informal hospitality. The eight individually decorated and furnished bedrooms all have en suite facilities, colour television and tea and coffee making facilities. Most command uninterrupted and quite unsurpassed views over the 1600 acre parkland grounds, described by the National Trust for Scotland as a 'gem of outstanding beauty', and beyond a kaleidoscope of spectacular scenery of hills, moorlands, lochs, burns and woods comprising the Endrick valley and the Campsie Fells above.

All the public rooms are decorated in period style and furnished with antiques giving the aura and grace of a bygone age. Log fires create warmth and intimacy and the candlelit evening meals in the panelled dining room make for most romantic occasions, well complemented by freshly prepared local produce and a carefully selected wine cellar.

The Loch Lomond, Stirling & Trossachs area offers the visitor a wide and varied range of country activities, including golf, fishing, shooting, water sports, nature study and bird watching, historical research, or simply walking and exploring in stunningly beautiful countryside.

With over 40 golf courses within a 25 mile radius of the Castle, Culcreuch is a golfer's paradise. A special Golfing Brochure is available on request which gives details of the packages available at a large number of these venues.

Culcreuch is best known, however, for its extensive fishing packages, covering a wide area of the Loch Lomond area including fishing on Loch Lomond itself. The angling season is as follows: Salmon and Sea Trout: 11th February to 31st October, Brown Trout: 15th March to 6th October (Sunday Fishing is strictly prohibited)

Packages are available on the following waters. Salmon and Sea Trout - Loch Lomond, River Leven, River Fruin, Luss Water (except Arden Estate Water), The Gareloch (part) and the River Endrick (major part, - The River Endrick flows through the Culcreuch Estate). Full details, including maps of each water showing pools and other important information, are available in our Fishing Brochure available on request.

Whether for either business or pleasure, Culcreuch is a most convenient, centrally positioned base for visiting Edinburgh (55 minutes by motorway), Glasgow (35 minutes) and Stirling (25 minutes). For business clients there is no comparable venue for entertaining and the Castle specialises in offering its unique facilities for small meetings.

From Autumn to Spring, reduced terms for off-season breaks are offered, together with House Parties over the Christmas and New Year Holidays; and during these cooler months the log fires offer a cheerful welcome on your return from a day out in the Trossachs.

The location of Culcreuch is rural but not isolated, and with the fresh air of the countryside, the space, grace, comfort, good wholesome food and that unique warmth of friendship and hospitality offered from a family run home from home, a stay here is most conducive to shedding the cares and pressures of modern day life and utterly relaxing. We look forward to your company. — The Haslam Family

Frintry, Stirlingshire G63 0LW, Tel: (036 086) 228, Fax: (0532) 390093

The Gean House is one of the finest and most welcoming hotels in Central Scotland. The house was built in 1910 by Alexander Forrester-Paton, a local industrialist, as a wedding gift for his eldest son.

Luxuriously furnished, this architecturally important house has been thoughtfully restored by resident manager John Taylor to retain the grandeur of its halcyon days.

With a log fire burning in the inglenook fireplace, the elegant reception hall offers relaxing surroundings from which to enjoy the fine views of the nearby Ochil Hills.

In the walnut-panelled dining room overlooking the rose garden guests savour the stylish, creative cuisine prepared by award winning chef Antony Milsud.

The beautifully appointed guest bedrooms retain an air of individuality with room service available at all times.

There is much to enjoy locally including hillwalking, horse riding, fishing and golf, St. Andrews and Gleneagles are both nearby.

Gean Park, Tullibody Road, Alloa, Clackmanshire FK10 2HS, Tel: (0259) 219275, Fax: (0259) 213827

Glasgow Marriott

As the former Holiday Inn, this hotel has been a focal point in the social and commercial life of Glasgow for several years. The new Marriott offers even higher standards and continues a tradition of constant improvement.

All 298 spacious guest rooms feature a lounge area in which to work or just relax with individually controlled air-conditioning, mini-bar, remote control colour TV with satellite and video channels, trouser press, hairdryer, tea and coffee tray and direct-dial telephone. Room service is available 24 hours a day.

The Glasgow Marriott has 13 meeting rooms of varying sizes and can accommodate anything from a small boardroom style meeting to an exhibition, or major conference for up to 720 delegates.

Banquets, wedding receptions and dinner-dances for up to 650 guests can be catered for in the stylish Britannia Suite.

The Glasgow Marriott offers the choice of two restaurants; The Terrace where you can make your selection from the produce of the day and L'Academie with its superb a la carte menu and wine list to match.

The Cafe Rendezvous offers snacks and light meals throughout the day and is the ideal venue to relax before, or after your meal.

The hotel features an extensive Leisure Area. Splash out in the large, heated pool; challenge a colleague to a game of squash, keep fit on the exercise equipment or just take it easy in the whirlpool, sauna or solarium.

There is a gift shop within the hotel and the Guest Relations Officer will be pleased to advise you on sightseeing, theatre bookings and car hire.

Argyle Street, Glasgow G3 8RR, Tel: 041 226 5577, Fax: 041 221 9202

Gleddoch House

Gleddoch House is beautifully situated in 360 acres overlooking the River Clyde and Loch Lomond Hills. It was once the home of Glasgow shipping Baron, Sir James Lithgow. Offering all the advantages of gracious living and warm hospitality Gleddoch would be the ideal base from which to explore Scotland's famous sites and attractions.

The bedrooms are designed with very individual characteristics and there are picturesque views of the gardens and surrounding estate. They all have en suite facilities and are very comfortable indeed.

The high standards at Gleddoch are certainly followed in the restaurant which has an excellent reputation for miles around and has achieved international recognition for its high standards of cuisine prepared by the award winning chef. You can enjoy the magnificent views over the Clyde Estuary and Gleddoch estate from the Morning Room and Conservatory which are perfect rooms in which to relax and enjoy the tranquillity of the surroundings.

Gleddoch House has excellent conference facilities and is ideally situated just ten minutes from Glasgow airport. It is also an excellent venue for a wedding.

Whatever your reason for visiting Gleddoch the attention to detail and personal service will ensure you have a wonderful and memorable time.

Langbank, Strathclyde PA14 6YE, Tel: 047 554 711 Fax: 047 554 201

Hospitality Inn

Set on the River Irvine, on the West Coast of Scotland, the Hospitality Inn has a Moorish theme. Eastern delight and Casablanca nights offer not just a relaxing atmosphere but an escape into another world - the secret paradise of Tangiers in the 1930's with all the convenience of a modern day hotel!

There are spectacular lagoon-side suites with palm festooned pathways, wooden bridges and a myriad of plants and rocks.

Guests can bathe to the gentle sound of waterfalls, enjoy the Jacuzzi and the water slide in a constant air temperature of 78 degrees, or simply relax by the lagoon side, soaking up the atmosphere being waited on by the pleasantly attentive staff.

All rooms have private bathroom and shower, colour television, in-house movies, direct dial telephone, double glazing, blackout and temperature controlled atmosphere, writing desk, tea and coffee making facilities, heated trouser presses and built in hairdryers.

The a la carte restaurant offers a fine selection of wines and food, skilfully prepared in one of the most up to date and widely acclaimed kitchens in Scotland.

The Hospitality Inn offers a most comprehensive range of facilities to cater for between 10 to 200 delegates. Membership of the Guaranteed Venue Scheme ensures a full range of well maintained audio visual equipment is always available with trained operators on hand.

The Irvine Hotel is designed to make luxury a pleasure and hospitality a password to relaxation.

Annick Road, Irvine KA11 4LD, Tel: (0294) 74272, Fax: (0294) 77287

Kirkhouse Inn

The village of Strathblane is situated 10 miles north of Glasgow and is therefore readily accessible by air as well as by road and rail.

Kirkhouse Inn caters for the businessman with its well equipped conference room for up to 20 people and excellent general facilities. Golf, fishing, distillery visits and the like can be arranged if required. The Inn is also ideally situated for touring the Clyde coast and Loch Lomond area, where sailing, fishing and wind surfing are available. Walkers will find the Inn convenient for visiting the Trossachs and the Campsie Fells or for tackling other famous challenges including Ben Lomond.

Kirkhouse Inn has recently been refurbished and has 15 bedrooms with en suite bathrooms and the usual modern facilities. The hotel offers weekend and two day breaks and occasional adventure weekends. It specialises in serving Scottish dishes and vegetarian food when required and caters for children with a special menu.

Strathblane, Glasgow G63 9AA, Tel:(0360) 70621, Fax:(0360) 70896

Loon Fung

The Loon Fung is one of Glasgow's premier Chinese Restaurants and offers a full range of delicious Cantonese cuisine. The restaurant is split into two floors and there is ample space to seat up to two hundred diners as this is one of the largest Chinese restaurants in Scotland. Its popularity among Scots, tourists and the Chinese community produces a unique and friendly atmosphere. Added to this is the attractive decoration - notably the colourful carvings depicting the dragon and the phoenix.

Loon Fung is open all day, with a set lunch and dim sum dishes served before seven. The restaurant's evening specialities include sliced abalone with oyster sauce, crunchy stuffed duck and sizzling platters of Cantonese-style fillet steak. A set dinner is also available for vegetarians, while parties and banquets for six or more can be booked in advance.

417 Sauchiehall Street, Glasgow, Strathclyde G2 3JD

The Macdonald Thistle Hotel

Situated in a quiet residential area on the outskirts of the great city, the MacDonald offers a prime location for visitors. The once maligned Glasgow is packed with museums and places of interest, including the world famous Burrell Collection. Just a short drive away is some beautiful countryside - Burns Country, the Clyde coast and Loch Lomond. There are several excellent golf courses nearby, while next door to the hotel is a 50-acre park with swimming pool and theatre, while the hotel itself possesses a sauna and solarium.

The hotel features 57 bedrooms, each attractively furnished, with bathroom en suite, remote control television and with a choice of in- room films, radio, telephone, tea/coffee facilities and hairdryer. 24-hour room service is also available. There are also four sumptuous and elegant suites.

Oscar's is the hotel restaurant and this combines luxuriant surroundings with excellent cuisine, ranging from classical French to traditional Scottish specialities. After dinner, guests can relax over a pint or a glass of malt in one of several hotel bars, including the colonial theme bar,

Eastwood Toll, Giffnock, Glasgow G46 6RA, Tel: (041) 638 2225, Fax: (041) 638 6231

Mata Hari

The Mata Hari is Glasgow's first and only Malaysian restaurant and comes very highly recommended by the likes of the Glasgow Herald, the latest Egon Ronay Guides and the Glasgow Evening Times.

The food is served in a basement restaurant with a non-smoking section and the friendly and enthusiastic staff contribute to a beguiling and relaxed atmosphere.

As Malay is not a language understood by every Scotsman or tourist the menu is supplied with English translation and the choice on offer is great with the staff only too keen to help the uninitiated. The restaurant prides itself on its satay dishes (chicken, prawn, beef and even mushroom for vegetarians) kari udang (a spicy prawn dish) and assam manis ikan (a sweet and sour fish dish) amongst others. An excellent bargain value set meal is served weekdays at lunch time. The Mata Hari is ideally placed in Glasgow's Charing Cross/St George's Cross area to form the focus for an evening out in Scotland's largest city.

17 West Princes Street, St George's Cross, Glasgow G4 9BS, Tel: 041 332 9789

One Devonshire Gardens

There is so much of interest in the city of Glasgow that it attracts many visitors.

Only a few minutes from the city centre, but in a much quieter place and surrounded by other Victorian mansions, you can find One Devonshire Gardens.

This is an hotel of distinction which has been converted from three townhouses and is of such a high standard that it has been voted 'Best City Hotel' by the Scottish Hotel Guide. There are 27 magnificently furnished bedrooms each with the additional comfort of charmingly upholstered sofas.

The decor is outstanding and varies considerably from room to room. There are always fresh flowers and magazines in the rooms and the sumptuous bathrooms are mainly of marble and have such extra luxuries as robes for the use of guests.

There is a residents' dining room and bar and an excellent restaurant which is open to the public. Conferences for up to 50 people can be arranged and there are banqueting facilities for up to 30 or so people.

The food in both restaurant and dining room is designed to vary with the seasons and there is an interesting wine list.

While staying at the hotel take in the world famous Pollock House and Burrell Collection in Glasgow's Pollock Park. The Collection genuinely has to be seen to be believed. It includes Chinese ceramics and much European fine art with an emphasis on French and Dutch work of the 19th and early 20th centuries.

1 Devonshire Gardens, Glasgow G12 0UX, Tel: 041 339 2001, Fax: 041 337 1663

Shieldhill Hotel

Three and a half miles outside Biggar, nestled amongst the rich farmlands and rolling hills of the Clyde valley, stands the stately 'Old Keep' of Shieldhill. A glimpse of the turreted roof through the trees evokes images of Scotland's turbulent past, and whether along the garden pathways or on the secret stairs, the presence of the 'Grey Lady' is still to be felt today.

You will find nothing ghostly in your welcome to the Baronial house of the Chancellor Family these days. Built in 1199, the house only became a hotel eight centuries later. The present owners, Jack Greenwald and Christine Dunstan, offer the same brand of Californian hospitality to be found in Santa Barbara's Cheshire Cat Inn, which they also own. The welcome is warm rather than royal, though with its crested carpeting, grand open fires and deep sofas, Shieldhill exudes comfort and elegance.

There are ten spacious bedrooms and a Honeymoon suite, each uniquely decorated with a King, Queen or Four-poster bed and individually designed and developed in the theme of Scottish battles such as 'Culloden', 'Glencoe' and 'Bannockburn'. The restful tones of Laura Ashley prints adorn the drapes. All rooms have private bathrooms, some with added extras such as fireplaces and jacuzzis.

Shieldhill has a no smoking policy in the bedrooms and also in the Dining Room where there is a choice of either a set-menu or a sensibly short a la carte. The style is modern and sometimes includes such unusual dishes as a soup of lightly curried apples. Scottish produce is well represented by the likes of Aberdeen Angus beef and West Coast salmon, or even Perthshire pigeon.

Shieldhill has excellent facilities for small executive conferences.

Four challenging golf courses are within 15 minutes drive and shooting and salmon fishing on the River Tweed can be arranged with advance notice. The hotel is surrounded by beautiful lawns, and croquet can be played in the grounds.

Quothquan, Biggar, Lanarkshire ML12 6NA, Tel: (0899) 20035, Fax: (0899) 21092

Tinto Firs Thistle Hotel

The Tinto Firs is set in a quiet residential area just four miles out of Glasgow's city centre. It is a short drive from the international airport and is ideally suited for the executive or holiday visitor wishing to see the great and historic city of Glasgow wishing to venture further afield into the lochs and glens.

The hotel exudes luxury and has an attractively furnished Foyer Bar and Lounge with plush red decor, lavish plant displays and external terracing. In contrast the Traders Lounge Bar offers a lighter and more informal atmosphere.

Each of the 27 bedrooms comes equipped to the nines, including en suite bathroom, remote control television with choice of in-room feature films, radio, telephone and tea/coffee facilities, as well as 24-hour room service. Two luxury suites are also available. The elegant terrace restaurant offers a top class cuisine and provides a perfect setting for business lunches or intimate tete a tete meals. A range of stylish facilities is available for business meetings, seminars, exhibitions, private dinner parties and celebrations.

Kilmarnock Road, Glasgow GB43 2BB, Tel: 041 637 2353, Fax: 041 633 1340

The Town House

This elegant hotel in the centre of Glasgow provides a peaceful atmosphere in contrast to the bustle of Glasgow city centre. The staff are courteous and professional, providing a high standard of service.

There are a variety of suites available, whether for a large conference or smaller meeting. The Town House has the facilities to suit all requirements in tasteful and comfortable surroundings. Weddings can be catered for here and there is a private dining room on the first floor which is available for parties or a business lunch.

The 34 bedrooms and suites each have a unique style. They are spacious and individually decorated, all have en suite facilities. Room service is available for everything ranging from a champagne dinner to a cup of tea.

Dining at The Town House is a pleasure.

The Music Room Restaurant exudes calm with the gentle splash of the fountain a charming accompaniment to your meal. The Head Chef chooses only the freshest of ingredients making extensive use of local produce; Tay salmon and Highland lamb. The wine list is one of the finest in the city and as such can provide the perfect complement to your meal.

West George Street, Glasgow G2 ING, Tel: 041 332 3320, Fax: 041 332 9756

Westpoint Hotel

Just twenty minutes from Glasgow, yet quietly secluded in its own landscaped grounds stands the Westpoint hotel.

The 72 well-equipped bedrooms and two executive suites combine luxury with hospitality. In keeping with the philosophy that little things matter, there are the subtleties of fresh flowers and fruit, and a welcoming decanter of sherry in each of the stylishly decorated rooms. As you'd expect, there are also a TV, radio, tea and coffee making facilities, hairdryer, trouser press and stationery.

No effort is spared by the Master Chef and his team to provide the highest standards of presentation and service. The two restaurants offer an excellent and varied range of menus designed to cater for all tastes. Simpsons, with its impeccable ambience, traditional menu and first class wine list, is the perfect place to impress. For less formal occasions, the relaxed atmosphere and stylish surroundings of the Point Grill are ideal. For pre-dinner drinks or simply an informal get together, the Point Grill Bar provides the ideal meeting place.

The Leisure club at Westpoint will literally take your breath away with squash, aerobics and a well-equipped gymnasium. For those with a more relaxed approach there is a solarium, sauna, steam room, spa, indoor pool, snooker and lounge bar.

With unparalleled conference facilities, Westpoint has been thoughtfully designed to provide the perfect backdrop for both business and pleasure and also offers the very best of Scottish hospitality.

Stewartfield Way, East Kilbride G74 5LA, Tel: (03552) 36300, Fax: (03552) 33552

Westerwood Hotel, Golf and Country Club is located in Cumbernauld 13 miles from Glasgow City Centre. Its location on the A80 makes Westerwood within easy access of the key road networks and both Glasgow and Edinburgh Airports.

The hotel has 47 bedrooms, comprising of standard and executive rooms and both one and two bedroomed suites. All rooms are furnished in a traditional style with modern fabrics, many of which have scenic views over the golf course to the Campsie Hills.

Dining at Westerwood offers a choice of a light snack, an informal meal in our Club House overlooking the course or an a la carte menu in the Old Masters Restaurant where a pianist plays nightly.

Set in ideal golfing country the 18 hole par 73 course designed by Seve Ballesteros and Dave Thomas offers an exciting challenge to all golfers. The most spectacular hole is the 15th aptly named the Waterfall, set against a 40 foot rock face.

Each hole meanders through the silver birches, firs, heaths and heathers which are natural to this area of countryside, each offering a different and exciting challenge to every class of golfer.

Standing on the first tee, the player sees the fairway sweep away to the left and two very well struck shots will be required to reach the well guarded green tucked away amongst the trees. This sets the scene for the round and before the majestic 18th is reached there are another 16 golfing delights to savour. These include the difficult 4th with its two water hazards. Seve's trap, the 6th with Seve's cunningly placed bunker in front of the green, the tantalising 9th with its small undulating green, the 15th aptly named the waterfall - a fabulous par 3 and finally the 18th, possibly one of the finest finishing holes in golf.

The round is over, but not the memories. These will linger with you for many a day and entice you back to once again tackle this superb test of golf.

Westerwood is one of a group of three courses, the other two are Murrayshall and Fernfell. Murrayshall is at Scone, Perth and boasts a Country House Hotel with award winning cuisine. Fernfell Golf and Country Club is located just out of Cranleigh, 8 miles from Guildford, Surrey. For details of these courses please refer to their entries in this guide. Corporate golf packages are offered at all three courses with the opportunity to place your company name and logo on a tee, and reserve the course for your company golf day. Golf societies and Green Fee Players are welcome.

St Andrews Drive, Cumbenauld, Glasgow G68 0EW, Tel: (0236) 457171, Fax: (0236) 738478

Highland River – *Wendy Reeves. Courtesy of Rosentiel's.*

The Last Drive, St Andrews– *Robert Wade. Courtesy of Rosentiel's.*

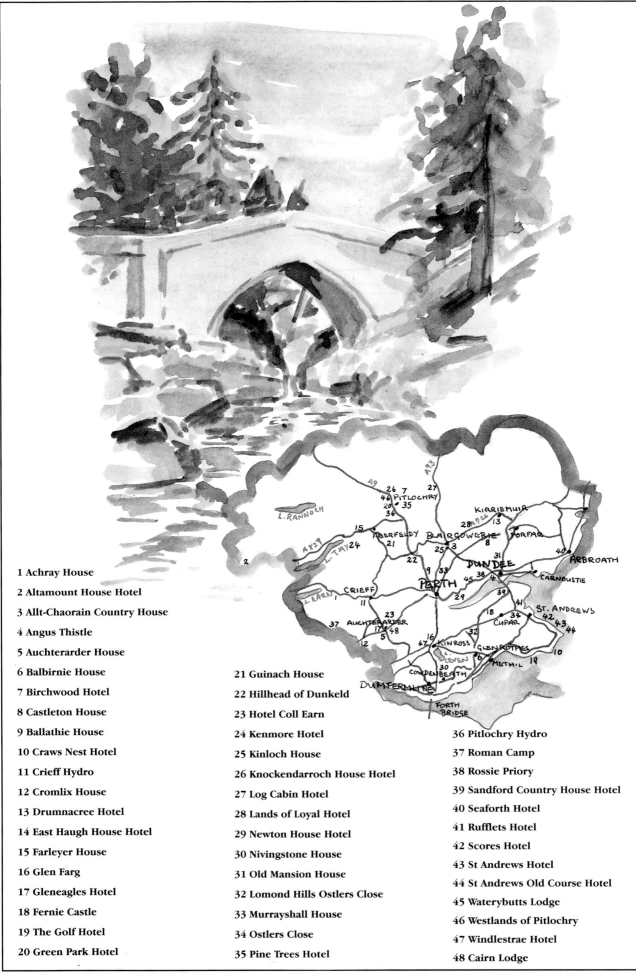

1 Achray House

2 Altamount House Hotel

3 Allt-Chaorain Country House

4 Angus Thistle

5 Auchterarder House

6 Balbirnie House

7 Birchwood Hotel

8 Castleton House

9 Ballathie House

10 Craws Nest Hotel

11 Crieff Hydro

12 Cromlix House

13 Drumnacree Hotel

14 East Haugh House Hotel

15 Farleyer House

16 Glen Farg

17 Gleneagles Hotel

18 Fernie Castle

19 The Golf Hotel

20 Green Park Hotel

21 Guinach House

22 Hillhead of Dunkeld

23 Hotel Coll Earn

24 Kenmore Hotel

25 Kinloch House

26 Knockendarroch House Hotel

27 Log Cabin Hotel

28 Lands of Loyal Hotel

29 Newton House Hotel

30 Nivingstone House

31 Old Mansion House

32 Lomond Hills Ostlers Close

33 Murrayshall House

34 Ostlers Close

35 Pine Trees Hotel

36 Pitlochry Hydro

37 Roman Camp

38 Rossie Priory

39 Sandford Country House Hotel

40 Seaforth Hotel

41 Rufflets Hotel

42 Scores Hotel

43 St Andrews Hotel

44 St Andrews Old Course Hotel

45 Waterybutts Lodge

46 Westlands of Pitlochry

47 Windlestrae Hotel

48 Cairn Lodge

Perthshire lies at the very heart of Scotland and in consequence, for generations it has been the crossroads of this colourful nation. Country roads wind through misty glens with scenic and often historic views aplenty. Blairgowrie, Aberfeldy, Crief, Dunkeld, Pitlochry, Auchterarder and many more such small towns and villages all have their own particular attractions, with a staggering variety of watering holes in which to whet your whistle.

Castles, gardens, local craft and antique shops abound and there can be very few places in Britain where the local heritage is so lovingly preserved and openly displayed. Sporting enthusiasts will also be in their element. Trout and salmon fishing is particularly good, with the River Tay, King of Scottish salmon rivers, being just one of several excellent waters upon which to cast your fly. Golf courses are also in abundance and there are championship fairways at Gleneagles. More significantly perhaps, there are many other less intimidating but no less beautiful courses throughout the area. This is an ideal destination for the most complete holiday. (Editor's note - It was in Perthshire at the age of nine where I struck my first golf ball and caught my first trout.)

Perth and Pitlochry both have theatres of note and there are a number of enchanting crafts and working museums which will also interest the casual visitor. A number of whisky distilleries open their doors to those in search of a dram and the local fayre is second to none. Perthshire claims to offer all of Scotland and after repeated visits I, for one, understand why.

If Perthshire wins the hearts of all lovers of Scotland, golf fanatics will be in heaven in the neighbouring Kingdom of Fife. St Andrews, the home of golf, is a golfing mecca. The Old Course is famed the world over but there are several other courses in St Andrews, while nearby Crail, Elie and Lundin Links offer further tests. St Andrews, however, is not merely a golfing town. It offers history, a variety of recreation and all manner of bars and restaurants that befit a busy tourist and university town.

In contrast to the relatively busy streets of St Andrews, the East Neuk offers an unhurried, peaceful lifestyle. 'Neuk', the old Scots word for corner, is the piece of land which runs from Crail to Anstruther, Pittenweem, St Monans, Elie and Earlsferry, Lower and Upper Largo to Lundin Links. Each port of call has its own individual characteristics with a common seafaring theme.

Small white-washed buildings with red pantiled roofs crowd into small winding streets and paint a picture postcard scene with an ambience akin to true relaxation. Inland, through farmland, the visitor will absorb the splendour of the Lomond Hills a popular area for ramblers and walkers alike. This unspoilt area has been known for centuries as the 'Howe of Fife'.

North of the Howe, the coastline and villages hugging the Tay estuary provide more places to explore, museums, castles, the Scottish Deer Centre and of course, more golf courses.

In contrast to the village atmosphere of Fife, Dundee is a bustling city. Visitors can enjoy castles, gardens and a wealth of industrial heritage here as well as the amenities of a 20th century metropolis. Discovery Point, the new visitor centre for the city's flagship, Captain Scott's 'Discovery' occupies a prime position on the waterfront.

Here, the variety of pursuits and the easy pace of life are surely two of the greatest attractions of Scotland.

In Angus we find a near continuous collage of heather clad hills, running water and clean fresh air. The distinctive character of the Glens is a joy to experience and a wide variety of activities can be enjoyed here, from a quiet streamside picnic in summer to a more rigorous climbing holiday in autumn or skiing in winter.

From Perthshire, through Fife and Angus, the visitor finds fabled castles, renowned golf courses and all manner of watering holes. You may be a beach lover or a sun worshipper but if you wish to free the spirit, come to the very heart of Scotland, it will put spring in your stride.

Crieff Hydro

Achray House

Set in the peaceful village of St. Fillans, on the shore of Loch Earn, Achray House lies at the heart of the southern central Highlands. Only seventy-five minutes from the cities of Glasgow and Edinburgh and within easy reach of a host of major tourist attractions, Achray House is an ideal base from which to discover the splendour of the real Scotland.

An evening stroll by the gardens of St. Fillans, or along the shore of the loch, will reveal the outstanding natural beauty of the locale. The hotel has its own foreshore and jetty and a number of watersports are available, including trout fishing, sailing and windsurfing. There are fourteen golf courses within an hour's drive of the hotel, although St. Fillan's own course is one of the most scenic.

Tony and Jane Ross have owned and run Achray House for more than ten years. The atmosphere is more than welcoming and the hotel has attractions enough to bring people back year after year. All of the ten bedrooms are comfortably furnished with tea and coffee making facilities,

colour television and direct-dial telephone. Most have a loch view and all but three have private facilities. The more traditional rooms boast some of the best views.

Achray House is renowned for its fine food, generous portions and value for money. Lunch and supper can be ordered from the bar menu, which features a wide range of traditional fare and a good vegetarian selection. A la carte and table d'hote menus are available in the restaurant, offering a choice fit to grace the tables of a far larger hotel - pheasant, grouse, steaks, salmon, venison, trout, lamb, pork and seafood.

The speciality of the house, though, is Jane Ross's unique selection of freshly prepared home-made desserts - Ecclefechan tart, tropical island meringue and whisky syllabub, to name but a few. After the meal those with the inclination can sample one or two of the forty malt whiskies on offer in the bar before retiring for a peaceful night's sleep.

Loch Earn, St. Fillans, Perthshire PH6 2NF, Tel: (0764) 685231, Fax: (0764) 685320

Altamount House Hotel

Strolling through the grounds of the Altamount House Hotel it is hard to believe that it is just minutes from the centre of one of Perthshire's busiest tourist towns.

A relaxed atmosphere pervades this fine Georgian country house. Built as a private residence in 1806, the house has six acres of grounds which include extensive lawns, rose gardens and mature woodland.

The rose pink sandstone house has many fine features including a Adam fireplaces, corniced ceilings and beautiful pine doors and panelling. By day, the Terrace Room Restaurant with its elegant furnishings enjoys excellent views of the grounds. By night, subdued lighting and candles

change the mood completely. Since opening in 1980 the restaurant has earned an enviable reputation for its fine Scottish cooking. In the kitchen, great emphasis is placed on quality and freshness, concentrating on home made soups, pates and simple main dishes in which the finest fish, beef poultry and game is used. In the coffee lounge, the inviting aroma of fresh coffee and home baking is enticing.

The Altamount House Hotel has seven bedrooms, all with private facilities and the usual comforts to be expected in a top class hotel. Electric blankets are a thoughtful extra, making this one of the most comfortable and hospitable country house hotels in Scotland.

Blairgowrie, Perthshire PH10 6JN, Tel: (0250) 873512

Allt-Chaorain House Hotel

Allt-Chaorain House is a small residential hotel affording guests the amenities, comfort and atmosphere of their own home. The lounge has a log fire burning throughout the year, a Trust Bar and an adjoining Sunroom which offers a picturesque view of Ben More dominating the Highland landscape.

Situated in an elevated position 500 yards from the roadside between Crianlarich and Tyndrum on the A82, Allt-Chaorain offers the perfect touring centre whether you wish to visit towns, castles, places of interest or simply experience the scenic beauty of the Central Highlands.

All of the comfortable Bedrooms have private facilities and double or twin beds. There are also two family rooms. The wood panelled Dining Room caters for six persons to a table, allowing the most reserved guests the chance of exchanging their day's experience with others.

Keen Ramblers can tackle the West Highland Way which passes close by and for the more intrepid walker a great concentration of Munroes beckon, including such mountains as Ben Lawers, Ben More and Ben Lui.

There is ample opportunity for fishing in the numerous lochs or rivers for trout and salmon.

Boats are available for hire nearby. For the golfer a variety of courses are available at either Killin, Kenmore, Crieff or Callander.

Roger McDonald is proud of the reputation his hotel has earned for good home cooking made from fresh local produce and welcomes you to his home.

Crianlarich, Perthshire FK20 8RU, Tel: (08383) 283, Fax: (08383) 238

The Angus Thistle Hotel

The plush and modern Angus is situated in the heart of the thriving city of Dundee and is ideal for both executive and visitor alike. The 53 bedrooms are tastefully decorated and equipped to the highest standard, with en suite bathroom, remote control television and in-room feature films, radio, tea/coffee making facilities, telephone, trouser press and hair dryer and many rooms offer a spectacular view of the Tay Estuary and the picturesque county of Fife; 24-hour room service is available and there are five luxurious suites. Scott's restaurant, with a Carvery, offers an excellent and varied choice of both Scottish and continental cuisine and the adjoining Cocktail Bar has a range of aperitifs and liquers.

The hotel also possesses extensive facilities for private meetings, conferences, seminars, dinner dances and wedding receptions.

The Angus offers an ideal base to enjoy Dundee, a city best known for its seaport and university, but also set amid some of Scotland's most breathtaking scenery with great opportunities for the outdoor enthusiast - walking, climbing, fishing and even ski-ing in the winter months. The area is, of course, golfing country and there are a number of other sites of historic interest, such as the castles of Blair, Glamis and Balmoral and the numerous attractions of towns such as Pitlochry, Braemar and Glenshee.

Marketgait, Dundee DD1 1QU, Tel: (0382) 26874, Fax: (0382) 22564

Auchterarder House

Auchterarder House combines the essence of Scottish baronialism with the comfort and convenience expected of a modern luxury hotel. This magnificent Victorian family mansion, built some 165 years ago, nestles amid the rolling hills and glens of Perthshire.

Great care has been taken to refurbish the public rooms with style and elegance whilst maintaining the atmosphere of a family home. The grand Dining Room, set with pretty rose-patterned china, has an intimate ambience. Here, diners enjoy Scottish food presented with the finesse of French cuisine. The elegant Drawing Room has views across the grounds and the Old Billiard Room with its splendid vaulted ceiling, leads out onto a croquet lawn. Guests will be able to relax in the panelled Library and the stunning marble Conservatory is a lovely spot to linger a while.

The bedrooms are in keeping with the character of this fine country house and are tastefully furnished to pamper guests with every possible comfort including some thoughtful personal touches fresh fruit and flowers and a decanter of sherry. Rooms in the main wing have splendid mountain views whilst those in the Turret Wing look out over the 17 acres of immaculate grounds.

A putting green, croquet lawn and magnificent gardens provide opportunities for the gentle pursuit of sport and the challenging Gleneagles Golf Course is nearby for the more ambitious. Private shooting and fishing can be arranged in season.

Shopping in the village of Auchterarder is a delight with its antique shops and fine woollens and cashmere.

The historic Scone Palace, Stirling Castle and Drummond Castle and gardens are only a few miles from this very special hotel.

Auchterarder, Perthshire PH3 1DZ, Tel: (0764) 63646, Fax: (0764) 62939

Balbirnie House

Balbirnie House, near Markinch village in the heart of the Kingdom of Fife, is one of Scotland's finest country house hotels. Built in 1777 and extended in 1815, this Grecian-style classical mansion house was for generations the family home of the influential Balfours of Balbirnie. In 1989 it was restored as a luxury hotel. Under the personal supervision of Alan, Elizabeth and Nicholas Russell, this wonderful Georgian mansion maintains the warmth and friendliness of its old days combined with the needs of today's house guests.

The elegant Long Gallery is one of the finest rooms in the house and gives access to the graciously proportioned Drawing Room and the original Library, now an attractive cocktail bar. The 30 guest rooms and suites are individually designed, exquisitely decorated and have every modern comfort. The Garden Room and Ballingal Suite are two of five rooms available for private occasions, meetings and conferences.

Executive Chef, George Mackay, creates imaginative menus with the focus on good quality produce prepared and presented with skill and complemented by fine wines from an extensive cellar.

The House itself is the centrepiece of Balbirnie Park, 416 acres of landscaped woodlands with one of Scotland's best collections of rhododendrons and overlooks the fairways of Balbirnie Park golf course.

Balbirnie is also within easy reach of the famous links of St. Andrews, Carnoustie and a host of other courses.

A perfect base from which to explore the rich heritage and scenic beauty of Fife.

16 Rothsay Mews, Markinch, by Glenrothes, Fife KY7 6NE, Tel: (0592) 610066, Fax: (0592) 610529

Birchwood Hotel

The elegant Birchwood Hotel is situated in the attractive highland town of Pitlochry and lies amid four acres of beautiful gardens and woodland, just five minutes from the town centre. The town is famous for its Victorian architecture and the 'salmon leap' at the Loch Faskally Dam and is ideally located in the heart of Scotland, guarded by the Ben y Vrackie, Criagower and the Fonab hills which create a valley setting of great natural beauty.

The Castles of Blair, Scone and Glamis, Queen's View, Loch Rannoch and Killiecrankie are all just a short drive away whilst for the more active, there are a range of sporting activities to indulge in; golf, bowling, fishing, boating and pony trekking. After dinner, Pitlochry is setting for a range of Scottish entertainments and the town's famous Festival Theatre is just a short walk from the hotel. The hotel is attractively furnished and spacious throughout. All the bedrooms are centrally heated and equipped with colour television, courtesy tray, fresh fruit and electric blankets. There are also larger rooms available for families and all have a view of the glorious Perthshire hills. Adjoining the hotel is a very attractive bungalow, complete with five bedrooms, each centrally heated with shower and toilet and quality furnishing.

The restaurant, which overlooks the gardens, offers a high quality cuisine made from fresh local produce, with a four course meal and a mouth-watering sweet trolley for dinner and a full range of wines to choose from. The elegantly furnished lounge provides an impressive venue for socialising or relaxing against the stunning backdrop of Tummel Valley.

2 East Moulin Road, Pitlochry, Perthshire PH16 5DW, Tel: (0796) 472477, Fax: (0796) 473951

The Cairn Lodge

Known to generations of local people as the Jubilee Cairn, the ancient and imposing structure standing at the main entrance of this attractive Country House lends the hotel its name. Built in 1909 and set in its own landscaped gardens, the Cairn Lodge was converted into an hotel in 1984.

Whether staying for a meal or just stopping off for a drink, the Cocktail Bar offers an ideal place to meet friends. Luxurious furnishing and friendly service make a perfect match, and there are elegant views of the patio and garden.

The mood in the restaurant is quiet and leisurely. The cuisine is of the highest quality and complemented by a good selection of wines and malt whiskies. After your meal it's worth taking the time to linger over coffee and liqueurs in the genial lounge.

Each of the five comfortable bedrooms have en suite bathroom, colour television, central heating and telephone.

Auchterarder is rich in a variety of leisure activities. Gleneagles is nearby, so there are unequalled golfing facilities.

Fishing, hill walking and horse riding are all readily available in the surrounding countryside and a 45 minute drive will lead you to watersports on Lochearnhead.

Ochil Road, Auchterarder, Perthshire PH3 1LX Tel: (0764) 662634/662431

Comrie Royal Hotel

Established in 1765 the Royal still retains that wonderful old fashioned charm that made it a favourite haunt of Queen Victoria, John Brown, Lloyd George and Sarah Bernhardt to name but a few of its more famous guests.

Nigel and Hazel Matheson along with their excellent staff welcome you to The Royal. The hotel is located in an area renowned for its scenic beauty where most types of shooting and stalking can be arranged.

The hotel has two bars, the Cocktail with tartan walls and giant blackboards to tempt you with the chef's delights, and the village bar, hub of local activity.

A range of real ales are served here and if you want to know which are the best pools to fish and which flies are taking this is the place to ask.

Nigel travels all over Scotland to find the best produce for the kitchen. Whether it's kippers from Mallaig, oysters for Loch Fyne, mussels from Glenuig or Venison from Lawers he will find it, ready for serving in the attractive panelled restaurant. Meals are also served in both bars and in the beer garden (weather permitting!), fresh fish and game being the specialties of the house.

The comfortable rooms are all en suite with the facilities expected of fine hotel, including colour televisions.

Fresh imaginative food, a beautiful location and fine accommodation make the Royal a memorable stay.

Melville Square, Comrie, Perthshire PH6 2DN. Tel: (0764) 670200, Fax: (0764) 670479

For my part,
I travel not to go anywhere,
but to go.
I travel for travel's sake.
The great affair is to move.

Robert Louis Stevenson

Ballathie House Hotel

Standing within its own estate by the banks of the River Tay - famous for its salmon fishing - Ballathie is ideally located for the major tourist and sporting attractions of the locale. Built in 1850, this impressive baronial mansion remained a private residence until 1971. Its subsequent conversion to an hotel was sympathetic to the original grandeur of the building and Ballathie retains the essential atmosphere of an elegant country house. More recently the hotel has been extensively refurbished and all the rooms - both public and private - are superbly comfortable.

Each of the 27 bedrooms within the main house is unique. All have views over the surrounding countryside and some overlook the river.

The quality of furnishing is high and features extensive use of antique and reproduction furniture. All rooms have private bath and/or shower. Standard features include colour TV, direct dial telephone, hairdryer, trouser press, radio alarm, tea and coffee tray and fresh fruit. The River Suite and two further bedrooms on the ground floor are equipped for disabled guests and have direct access from cars and to the grounds. The Sporting Lodge, next to the main house, has rooms finished in a simpler style but of a similar high standard.

David Assenti's staff are highly trained and motivated and the service is polite and attentive. Housekeeping is of the highest standard. Head Chef Stephen Robertson and his staff use only the best of local produce and offer daily changing menus complementing traditional Scottish dishes with imaginative modern cuisine for the discerning palate.

Everyone will enjoy a stay in this delightful country house.

Kinclaven, by Stanely, Perthshire PH1 4QN, Tel: (0250) 883268, Fax: (0250) 883396

Craws Nest Hotel

Originally an old manse set in two and a half acres of ground, with crows nestling in the trees and craw step gables, this house was converted into a holiday hotel by the late Mr Eddie Clarke in 1965. Since then the hotel has gone from strength to strength and is now managed by Mr Clarke's wife and family.

Over the years it has seen many extensions and improvements and now has accommodation for up to 100 people. Guests have their own residents lounge, a choice of two bars and the use of the games room. The dining room, which enjoys an excellent reputation, offers a choice of a la carte or table d'hote menus and a superb wine list.

All rooms and suites have en suite facilities, television, telephone, radio and tea/coffee making facilities.

The Eddie Clarke Wing, comprising 19 luxurious bedrooms, was opened in 1985. All the rooms are to the same high standard as the others in the hotel with two specially designed to cater for disabled guests. From this wing there are spectacular views over the River Forth to the Isle of May and the Bass Rock.

Most Saturday nights there is a dinner dance in the function suite to the music of the resident band. In the games room there are electronic games and a pool table and behind the hotel is a beautiful garden.

Anstruther was once the main fishing port in the East Neuk and The Craws Nest overlooks the harbour. You can relax watching the boats come and go or, if something more energetic is called for, there are golf courses nearby as well as swimming, sailing, windsurfing, tennis, riding, bowling, country and coastal walks.

Bankwell Road, Anstruther, Fife KY10 3DA, Tel: (0333) 310691, Fax: (0333) 312216

With its Greek motto proclaiming 'Water is best', Crieff's famous Hydro hotel, set on the edge of the Highlands, is one of Scotland's original watering holes. Established in 1868 and having its own supply, the Hydro founder, the great grand uncle of today's Managing Director, believed implicitly in the moral and physical benefits of putting the guests into water and the water into his guests!

125 years later, under the same family management, the Hydro has become one of Scotland's major conference centres and its leading resort hotel. So much so that it has recently been adjudged by Egon Ronay Guides as the U.K's 'Family Hotel of the Year'.

Water still plays an important part in the Hydro's attraction. Not only do they serve Highland Spring, but at the core of the hotel's unrivalled leisure facilities is the Lagoon swimming complex with its 20 metre heated pool, separate children's pool, spa bath, sauna, steam room, fitness suite and sun beds.

A new golfing centre with magnificent views over the hills offers its own licensed clubhouse, 9 hole course and driving range. A BRS approved riding school, tennis courts, children's adventure playground, all-weather bowling green, croquet lawn, football pitch, jogging and nature trails add to the choice.

For indoor pursuits there is a purpose-built sports hall for a host of team games plus badminton, squash, and table tennis.

Other indoor facilities and entertainments include snooker, pool, a 96-seat cinema, ballroom and Scottish country dancing, a children's hostess, nursery, fashion boutique and gift shop, hairdressing and beauty salon and a news stall.

With almost 200 family bedrooms, suites and single rooms, all with private facilities, and spacious studio suites, secluded self-catering chalets and luxurious cottages, there is a wide choice of accommodation for all tastes and budgets.

Crieff Hydro Hotel, Crieff, Perthshire PH7 3LQ, Tel: 0764 655555 Fax: 0764 653087

Castleton House Hotel is set in it's own wooded grounds 3 miles from Glamis Castle in the heart of the Angus countryside.

This family run Country House Hotel is an ideal base for touring the Glens or just relaxing in beautiful accommodation. Six en suite bedrooms all with Colour Television, Direct Dial Telephone, Radio and Tea and Coffee facilities have all been individually furnished to a high standard for your comfort and relaxation.

After a day touring or golfing return and enjoy a first class meal in our small intimate Restaurant. The menu changes daily and full use is made of fresh local ingredients many from our own walled garden.

For the golfer fine local courses such as Alyth, Forfar, Kirriemuir and Rosemount are only 15 minutes away with St. Andrews, Gleneagles and Carnoustie less than 1 hours drive away. Fishing, shooting and stalking can also be arranged for our guests.

By Glamis, Forfar, Angus DD8 1SJ, Tel: (030784) 340, Fax: (030784) 506

The history of East Haugh House dates back some 300 years to its origins as part of the Atholl Estate. Its life as a hotel began only recently in 1989 with such care taken in its conversion that many of its original, interesting features have been lovingly retained. From the outside it is a beautiful turreted stone house, situated off the old A9 road and set in two acres of lush gardens. Inside, the owners worked hard to create a personal atmosphere and, indeed, the feel is often more that of a house-party than a hotel. In keeping with this ideal, each of the six bedrooms were individually designed, two of them having magnificent four-poster beds. One of those rooms is in antique pine and has its own fireplace - the perfect place for romance on a cold winter's night. All rooms have private bathrooms, colour televisions, tea and coffee making facilities and direct dial telephones.

For the sportsman the surrounding area is a natural paradise with many superb 18-hole golf courses nearby. The owners' personal interest in fishing, shooting and stalking enable them to offer varied pursuits and detailed advice. For the fisherman East Haugh House is particularly impressive with its leasing arrangements on a variety of beats on the Tummel, Garry, Tilt and Shee Rivers, all of which have special arrangements for guests. Situated, as it is, in the heart of the picturesque Highlands the area promises fascinating days out, with ancient castles, distilleries, woollen mills, exhilarating hill walking, pony trekking and much more.

The hotel is well used to guests with hearty appetites and prides itself on preparing dishes only from fresh local produce, specialising, in the summer months, in delicious seafood from the Western Isles; Lobster, Mussels, Surf Clams, Dover Sole, and, when in season, plenty of local game; Wild Duck, Venison, Partridge, Grouse, Pheasant; more than likely shot by Chef / Proprietor Neil McGown.

For something a little less energetic in the evenings, the Pitlochry Festival Theatre, situated on the banks of the river Tummel, produces some wonderful plays every year. Tickets can be easily arranged for guests and Pre or After Theatre Dinners are served until late into the night.

East Haugh, by Pitlochry, Perthshire PH16 5JS, Tel: (0796) 473121, Fax: (0796) 472473

Visiting Cromlix is like stepping into another world. The hustle and bustle of life is replaced by silence and fresh country air. This magnificent estate surrounded by the beauty of Perthshire countryside extends to 3,000 acres and has descended in unbroken family ownership for more than 500 years which makes it extremely special.

The house was built in 1874 as a family residence and has its own small chapel which is the perfect setting for romantic weddings. Much of Cromlix House retains many of its original Edwardian features which add to its charm and originality. You can enjoy the fine prints and paintings, porcelain, silver, beautiful embroideries, family tapestries, drums and bagpipes, some of which date back to the 18th century.

The guest rooms are all individually designed with en suite facilities and some have private sitting rooms. They create a relaxing, luxurious but homely atmosphere.

An experience in itself is dining at Cromlix House. With fresh produce from the estate including; trout, pheasant, grouse, pigeon, woodcock, lamb, vegetables and fruits, you will not be disappointed. Inventive menu's are presented by the chef. Fine wines and whiskies are equally important at Cromlix and indeed you will recognise many celebrated names.

Cromlix is the ideal location for small conferences and intimate functions. It offers with superb cuisine and stylish meeting rooms. The extensive sports and leisure facilities are a great attraction. There are three lochs well populated by wild brown trout and salmon fishing can be arranged on several local rivers. Pheasant and grouse shooting is available in season and rough shooting provides an exciting days sport. Horse riding, tennis and croquet are also available.

Cromlix with its blend of old and new makes it quite simply a wonderful place to retreat to.

Kinbuck, Dunblane FK15 9JT, Tel: (0786) 822125, Fax: (0786) 825450

Drumnacree House Hotel

Converted from a small country house in 1986, Drumnacree House Hotel is situated at the foot of Glenisla in the old market town of Alyth. The climate is surprisingly warm, and you could be forgiven for mistaking the surrounding raspberry fields for vineyards.

Aylth is an ideal centre for touring. At hand are Royal Deeside, the Highlands, the Northeast fishing villages, numerous historical castles and many places of interest. For the sports enthusiast there is golfing, fishing, shooting, pony trekking and hill walking and in winter, downhill skiing at nearby Glenshee and cross country skiing at Glensila.

After a day enjoying any of these pastimes it is time to relax in the comfortable lounge with pre-dinner drinks and snacks.

Allan and Eleanor Cull personally manage their hotel. Eleanor looks after the front of the house while Allan is chef. Having spent 20 years in the oil industry, Allan has travelled extensively and sampled cuisine worldwide. His menus are both imaginative and of an international flavour, gaining him an excellent reputuation. Organic vegetables and herbs

from the kitchen garden are used together with only the best of local fresh produce reflecting the changing of the seasons.

To ensure that such a high standard of cuisine is achieved, much effort goes into the curing of fish and game, preserving of fruit and vegetables, the making of chocolate truffles, bread, ice-creams and sorbets.

Allan is always interested in catering for special dietary requirements, favourite dishes or maybe a special packed lunch.

Eleanor ensures that these high standards are maintained throughout the hotel and that clients are welcomed more as house guests. Nothing is too much trouble whether it is a request for an early call or an emergency button to be sewn on.

After dinner, retire once again to the lounge for a fresh brewed cafetiere of coffee and delicious homemade truffles with perhaps an after dinner liqueur.

The five comfortable bedrooms all have en suite bathrooms, tea/coffee making facilities and television.

St Ninians Road, Alyth, Perthshire PH11 8AP, Tel: (082 83) 2194

Farleyer House

Situated some two miles west of Aberfeldy, this 16th century mansion stands among 70 acres of park and woodland in the scenic Tay Valley. Close by is Castle Menzies and the house and surrounding ares are steeped in clan history.

The house is furnished to the highest standards in the style of a Highland mansion. Fresh flowers and antiques are found in both the public rooms and the bedrooms and all rooms are hung with fine prints and paintings. A true Highland welcome is offered by the owners who have created a delightful ambience of comfort, elegance and tradition. The bedrooms all have modern comforts but at the same time retain the unique character of the house.

Dining at Farleyer is sheer indulgence. The restaurant offers a host of culinary delights on its daily changing menu. Here is a truly unique restaurant which takes full advantage of locally available game, fish and beef. Imagination is used in offering a varied and exciting menu. Alternatively, guests may choose to dine in the more informal Scottish bistro which offers various light meals and is open every lunchtime and evening.

For the outdoor enthusiast there is a 6 hole practice golf course.

Set in a central position, Farleyer provides the ideal base for touring both the Highlands and Lowlands.

Aberfeldy, Perthshire PH15 2JE, Tel: (0887) 20332, Fax: (0887) 29430

The Glenfarg Hotel

Set amidst some of Scotland's finest scenery, close to the Ochil Hills, this fine Victorian hotel was originally built in 1896 to accommodate passengers on the old railway which once wound its way through this peaceful glen, from Edinburgh to Perth.

Tastefully renovated to create a blend of modern comfort and traditional elegance, the hotel provides the perfect setting for a restful holiday, short break or business trip.

The restaurant offers a delicious variety of fresh local produce. Cream of cauliflower and Stilton soup, Harbour Creole, a selection of seafood brought together in a mild curry and ginger sauce and casserole of pheasant 'Auld Reekie' have featured on the imaginative a la carte menus. There is an excellent selection of fine wines to complement your meal.

A good range of bar meals supplements the dining room

menus, real ale is on tap and there is a beer garden beside the small stream behind the hotel.

The hotel has an attractive function room ideally suited for meetings, weddings and parties.

Each of the 15 bedrooms is individually furnished and all have en suite bathroom, colour television and tea/coffee making facilities.

For keen golfers, the surrounding area boasts several of Scotland's famous championship courses including; Carnoustie, Gleneagles and the Home of Golf, St Andrews. There are some 30 equally challenging courses lying within a 30-minute drive of the hotel.

For those of you planning a more leisurely stay, there are plenty of fascinating historic places to visit and the spectacular beauty of the Scottish countryside is a discovery in itself.

Main Street, Glenfarg, Perthshire PH2 9NU, Tel: (0577) 830241

The Gleneagles Hotel

A magnificent baronial-style mansion, set in rolling Perthshire countryside and with an exceptional range of leisure and sporting facilities, the Gleneagles Hotel has an international reputation.

Built in 1924 by the Old Caledonian Railway Company, the hotel became a Mecca for the rich and famous, attracting Royalty, Heads of State, film stars and giants of commerce and industry.

In 1981 the hotel transferred to the private sector and is now owned by Guinness plc.

All 236 rooms have private facilities and are graded according to size and outlook. All are individually decorated to the same high standards from the smallest single room to any of the 20 full suites.

In each of the four restaurants, the best of local produce is used to create dishes wish a uniquely Scottish flavour, cooked and presented to standards of international excellence.

The name Gleneagles is synonymous with golf. There are

three 18-hole championship courses and the nine-hole Par 3 'Wee Course'.

In addition to this, Gleneagles has many other leisure facilities. It would be fair to say, in fact, that Gleneagles has almost everything; Country Club, Health Spa, The Mark Phillips Equestrian Centre, The Jackie Stewart Shooting School, The British School of Falconry, four all-weather tennis courts, one grass court, two salmon and sea trout fishing beats on the river Tay plus lochs for brown trout fishing, lawn bowling, croquet, putting, pitch and putt and - last but not least - with 830 acres of estate - ample facilities for jogging!

If you feel the need to leave the hotel grounds, Gleneagles' position in the very centre of Scotland makes it a marvellous base from which to explore.

With more staff than guests, standards of service are kept extremely high and few will leave Gleneagles without memories of a superb holiday or conference and a desire to return sometime soon to 'The Palace of the Glens'.

Auchterarder, Perthshire PH3 1NF, Tel: (0764) 662231, Fax: (0764) 662134

The Golf Hotel

This fine old Scottish Baronial-style mansion is situated in the heartland of the Kingdom of Fife.

The Golf Hotel combines the friendliness and charm of a country house with the comfort and facilities of a modern hotel. The owner and manager, Campbell Macintyre, has had many years of Scottish Hotel experience and he and the Golf Hotel staff offer you friendly and personal attention and the warmest of welcomes.

Each of the well-appointed bedrooms is centrally heated; has television, radio, telephone and tea/coffee making facilities. All have private bathroom/shower.

The hotel cuisine is based on fresh local produce; Scottish beef, lamb and poultry, fish and shellfish from the nearby port of Pittenweem, and the freshest of vegetables and soft fruits from the Kingdom of Fife.

The Golf Hotel has an extensive wine cellar and a fine variety of blended and malt Scotch whiskies, and the 'Pewter Pot', which serves bar lunches, makes the perfect '19th hole'!

Since early Victorian times, Elie with neighbouring Earlsferry, has been one of Fife's favourite holiday resorts. It enjoys a temperate climate, with generous quantities of sunshine and a modest rainfall. It offers long stretches of golden sand, safe bathing, a sheltered harbour, traditional buildings with pantiled roofs, and crow-stepped gables, antiques and craft shops and of course, golf galore.

Elie, Fife KY9 1EF, Tel: (0333) 330209, Fax: (0333) 330381

The Green Park Hotel

The Green Park is a Victorian country house hotel enjoying a beautiful situation overlooking Loch Faskally.

Since acquiring the hotel over twenty-five years ago, Graham and Anne Brown have continued with their aim of improving comfort and facilities for their guests. You can be assured of a warm welcome, a relaxed atmosphere and good food with a Scottish flavour.

The gardens, leading to the banks of Loch Faskally, are well laid out with flowers and shrubs. Chairs and tables are set out around the gardens, enabling you to have coffee or lunch in restful surroundings amongst the hills.

All 37 bedrooms have private bath or shower, colour television, direct-dial telephone, television and tea/coffee making facilities. They feature elegant Japanese elm furniture.

A varied table d'hote dinner is served in the bright spacious dining-room. Once a week a full 'Taste of Scotland' dinner is served, giving a true flavour of Scotland. Saturday dinner at The Green Park has become famous for its highly acclaimed hors-d'oeuvres table.

Bar lunches are served in the lounge where a splendid view across the loch has proved to be a major attraction. The friendly cocktail bar also serves bar lunches and suppers in the evening.

Amenities include putting, table tennis, bar billiards, fishing from the hotel banks, sailing, sail boarding and a childrens play area.

Pitlochry, being in the heart of Scotland, makes an ideal spot from which to explore the surrounding areas. Golf courses abound and beautiful walks, pony trekking, fishing, bowling and sailing are but a few of the outdoor activities available. The famous Pitlochry Festival Theatre offers a wide variety of entertainment from May until October.

Pitlochry PH16 5JY, Tel: (0796) 473248, Fax: (0796) 473520

Guinach House

Guinach House was built in the early part of this century as a private country house and it stands in three acres of grounds near Aberfeldy in Perthshire. The hotel itself is secluded but it is an easy walk to the centre of Aberfeldy which is the geographical Heart of Scotland.

Owned and run by Bert and Marian Mackay, the hotel has seven bedrooms all en suite and tastefully furnished to a high standard. The rooms all have garden views and one double room is at ground level to enable elderly or disabled guests to have ease of access to the Lounge, Dining Room and garden. The Lounge has a log fire in front of which guests can relax and unwind before dinner.

Bert Mackay is an International Master Chef and the dishes he prepares are varied and delicious as well as being visually impressive. He makes full use of local produce and is happy to prepare dishes for special diets by prior arrangement.

The countryside surrounding the hotel is beautiful and here, in the upper reaches of the Tay, wildlife abounds.

The peaks of Ben Lawers and Schiehallion are a magnificent backdrop for the photographer or a climbing challenge for the more adventurous.

For sportsmen, arrangements can be made for fishing and shooting although advance notice must be given for this. There is also a choice of nine and eighteen hole golf courses as well as horseriding and water sports.

The surroundings, cuisine and friendly atmosphere of this attractive hotel make it the perfect place for those wishing to get away from it all.

'By the Birks', Urlar Road, Aberfeldy PH15 2ET, Tel: (0877) 820251

High above Dunkeld, the ancient capital of Scotland, Hillhead looks out to the south west over white buildings with slate roofs. The cathedral, the river Tay, wooded parklands and distant mountains complete the scene.

Here, in the heart of Macbeth country and enjoying one of Scotland's finest views, this 1830's stone built house stands in six acres, surrounded by terraced lawns, tall trees and colourful flowerbeds.

Beautifully decorated throughout, the hotel features fine china, glassware and napery. The six principal en suite bedrooms, one of which has a single connecting bedroom, have all the usual facilities to be expected of a hotel of high standing. The Lodge also has two further double bedrooms in the annexe.

A private library is available to residents and there is a snooker room, hard tennis court and croquet lawn.

The restaurant is a favourite place for visitors and locals alike.

A bar lunch menu offers daily roasts and traditional Saturday and Sunday luncheons, as well as more unusual delicacies such as baked avocado wrapped in a puff pastry trellis. In the evening, four course table d'hote dinners and full a la carte menu are available. Meals can be made to order and vegetarian tastes are well catered for.

Whether you wish to spend a restful holiday, tour daily through some of the best scenery in Scotland, play the numerous surrounding golf courses, enjoy that special meal or function, or just break your north/south journey on the A9, a visit to Hillhead of Dunkeld will be a delightful experience at any time of the year.

Hillhead of Dunkeld, Brae Street, Dunkeld, Perthshire PH8 0BA Tel: (0350) 728996 Fax: (0350) 728705

Hotel Coll Earn

Staying at the Coll Earn is a thoroughly enjoyable experience. Once a family house built in 1870, the present owners have lovingly restored and improved it without sacrificing any of its Victorian grandeur. Rich wood panelling and carving, mellow colour schemes and the inviting crackle of log fires provide a warm and welcoming atmosphere. The views from the public rooms across the peaceful, well-kept grounds are almost eclipsed by the windows themselves, such is the extent and originality of the magnificent stained glass by Cottier.

The intimate Dining Room, with its handsome fireplace offers a constantly changing menu relying heavily on fresh seasonal produce. Whether traditional Scottish or European, the food is always a sheer delight. A visit to the Cocktail Bar may help the final choice between dishes!

The eight bedrooms have en suite bathrooms and are furnished to a high standard. The efficient staff are both friendly and courteous, as one might expect in a family run hotel.

The village of Auchterarder is an ideal place from which to explore the many places of historic interest nearby, or simply to enjoy some of Scotland's loveliest countryside. Perth, Scotland's ancient capital, is also within easy driving distance and has much to commend it.

Auchterarder, Perthshire PH3 1DF, Tel: (0764) 663553, Fax: (0764) 662376

In the highlands, in the country places,
Where the old plain men have rosy faces
And the young fair maidens
Quiet eyes.

Robert Louis Stevenson

'Tight Lines!' Each year the Kenmore Hotel opens the river Tay Salmon Fishing Season on January 15th, Sunday excepted, with the now familiar toast. Gathered from near and far, the hardy Anglers don their apparel and gather in the Village Square at Kenmore. After an opening speech of welcome and a few drams to give them stamina they march with the Piper round to the river where a further ceremony takes place - the launching of the first boat.

Set amid the splendour of Perthshire, the mighty river Tay meanders through the unspoilt tranquillity of the Taymouth Estate. On either bank for two miles down stream the Kenmore Hotel has its own private pools. The Dairy, The Ladies, Chinese, Castle and Battery are names reminiscent of times when the Campbells of Breadalbane ruled these lands and are now used by the modern day angler who can imagine their former glory.

There is also fishing on Loch Tay, take one of the hotel boats and motor up into the Loch for fly fishing or harling.

The Kenmore Hotel, Scotland's oldest Inn, was built in 1572 and offers the fisherman all the modern comforts when they return from the river. All 38 bedrooms have en suite facilities, direct dial telephone, tea and coffee making facilities and colour television.

The restaurant offers local produce as well as European fayre and the cellar is well stocked to complement the cuisine.

Spring fishing at Kenmore produces not only the hardy Angler but the strongest and cleanest of Salmon. Sea-lice fish are common in the beat, giving the angler a fight before the priest whilst in September and October the fish are not so sprightly but still command the full attention of the angler.

The Kenmore Hotel, Kenmore, Perthshire PH15 2NU, Tel: (0887) 830205, Fax: (0887) 830262

Kinloch House was built in 1840, extended in 1911 and has been in the same ownership of David and Sarah Shentall since 1981. Set in 25 acres of wooded parkland, grazed by Highland Cattle with views over Loch Marlee to the Sidlaw Hills beyond, the house is a fine example of a Scottish country house with oak panelled hall and first floor galleries.

There are 21 bedrooms, including two suites. Most of the double and twin bedded rooms have a southerly aspect and all have private facilities. The rooms are traditionally furnished to the very highest standards, some with four poster or half tester beds

The reception rooms - resident's lounge, lounge, cocktail bar, conservatory and dining room - echo the ambience best desribed as warm and relaxed.

Dinner is regarded as the signature to what has, hopefully, been an enjoyable day.

The comprehensive wine list complements the menu which changes daily, offering an extensive choice of dishes created from Sottish produce: beef and lamb, fish and shellfish,, wildfowl and game, all skilfully prepared.

The area abounds with every form of recreation: golf, walking, shooting, fishing and sightseeing.

The Sportsman's room, having its own entrance, is probably the most complete of any in Scotland - unlimited drying facilities, boot dryer, gun cupboard, deep freeze, game larder, dog bowls - in fact evrything has been thought of for those returning from outdoor pursuits.

by Blairgowrie, Tayside PH10 6SG, Tel: (0250) 884237, Fax: (0250) 884333

Knockendarroch House

This fine Victorian mansion was built in 1880 on a hill above Pitlochry. It commands outstanding views to the south over the Tummel Valley and to the north Ben Vrackie is visible.

The hotel has 11 bedrooms which are attractively furnished. All rooms have either a private bath or shower en suite, colour television and other facilities.

As a family run hotel, the Knockendarroch provides guests with personal attention and the hotel runs almost as a country house. This is particularly true of the restaurant where only the very best local produce is used to create traditional Scottish fayre.

This is a picturesque area with hills and river valleys. The hills provide excellent walking whether on gentle National Trust trails or on more strenuous treks. At Blair Castle, pony trekking is available and is an excellent way to explore the local surroundings.

The hotel provides an ideal base for those wishing to play golf on the many local courses. The famous courses of St Andrews, Gleneagles, Rosemount and Carnoustie are all within easy reach. The Tummel provides excellent fishing for the enthusiast as both salmon and trout abound in these waters.

The Knockendarroch Hotel provides comfort for those wanting simply to relax in these beautiful surroundings or an ideal base from which to explore the heart of Scotland. (Guests should note that this is now a non-smoking hotel)

Higher Oakfield, Pitlochry, Perthshire PH16 5HT, Tel: (0796) 3473

The Log Cabin Hotel

The Log Cabin Hotel is equidistant from Blairgowrie and Pitlochry, just off the A924 in Kirkmichael in Tayside and is built exclusively from whole Norwegian pine logs. The hotel is on one level only which must add to its appeal for the elderly or for the disabled.

The hotel has the simplest of landscaped gardens and as it stands 900 feet above sea level its views are magnificent. It is an independent family run hotel with 13 rooms, all with en suite facilities. The Resident Proprietors of The Log Cabin, Alan F. Finch and Daphne Kirk, pride themselves on their cuisine. In the Edelweiss Restaurant with views by day of Strathardle and by night at candle lit tables, the menus are very special indeed. They are changed daily and invariably fresh food is used with concentration on the best of local produce, particularly game when it is in season.

Those who have not yet visited the area would find The Log Cabin a charming place from which to tour Perthshire and the neighbouring counties of Angus and Fife.

There are many walks in the immediate vicinity and some twenty golf courses are within an hour's drive.

The hotel will advise on all available leisure opportunities including ski-ing at nearby Glenshee. The Glen, of course, is full of wild life and one can ride, go pony trekking or trout fishing on the hotel's loch, undertake stalking, game or clay pigeon shooting on the many acres of a private grouse moor.

Kirkmichael, by Blairgowrie, Perthshire PH10 7NB, Tel: (0250) 881288, Fax: (0250) 881402

Located in the heart of the historic Kingdom of Fife, Fernie Castle Hotel is the ideal base for a golfing holiday. With more than 30 Championship courses within 25 miles of the hotel, there can't be many places which offer such a choice.

The golfer's mecca - St Andrews - is within 30 minutes drive, and the famous courses at Carnoustie and Gleneagles are within easy striking distance. Ladybank, used as an Open Championship Qualifying Course, and loved by all who play it, is only 2 miles away. Complete golf holiday packages can be arranged and staff at the hotel will be delighted to discuss your requirements.

Fernie Castle is a small luxury hotel specialising in the care of its guests and the quality of food offered. Steeped in history, the Castle was first recorded in 1353 when it belonged to the Earl of Fife. By the fifteenth century, Fernie was held by a family known as Fernie of that Ilk, and then, in the sixteenth century by the Arnotts who kept it for a century. In 1680 the Balfours of Burleigh became the owners and their descendants

retained the tenure until 1965. In 1967 the house was converted into a hotel and entered the 'family' of Scottish Country Castle Hotels which have emerged, offering a balance of historic antiquity with modern comfort.

All the bedrooms are equipped with television, telephone, tea and coffee making facilities, private bath or shower and central heating. Guests can relax in the historic Keep Bar or enjoy coffee in the comfortable drawing room. The dining room, with its crystal glass, candlelight and elegance can only add to your delight in your visit. Menus which change daily use only the best fresh produce including mussels from Orkney and salmon from Shetland.

The grounds surrounding the Castle are comprised of formal lawns, mature woodlands, paddocks and a small loch with swans and ducks.

Totally committed to the guests' enjoyment of this splendid part of Scotland, Fernie Castle Hotel will delight and surprise.

Letham, near Cupar, Fife KY7 7RU ,Tel: (033781) 381, Fax: (033781) 422

Set on a hillside overlooking the Vale of Strathmore to the Sidlaw Hills beyond, are 10 acres of tiered and rambling gardens, at the heart of which lies the 'Lands of Loyal'.

This impressive Victorian Mansion was built in the 1830s, commissioned by Sir William Ogilvy, who, on his return from Waterloo, chose Loyal Hill as the site for this magnificent home.

The Lands of Loyal was subsequently owned by a succession of families until being converted into a Hotel in 1945.

It has since been very prominent in the area, holding fond memories for the oldest generations. It is also highly regarded as a second home to country sportsmen who have remained loyal for many years. More recently, an extensive refurbishment programme, carried out in the public rooms, has further enhanced the unique atmosphere of this much respected country house hotel.

A highly acclaimed restaurant in its own right, our style of cuisine is traditional and imaginative, making full use of local fish and game.

An extensive wine list, featuring several wines and madeiras, some over 150 years old, is available to complement your meal.

The Lands of Loyal makes an ideal base for the ambitious golfer. Perthshire has 30 golf courses in total with remarkable variety. All courses are within an hour's drive of the hotel with some of the most famous and desirable spots only a few minutes away.

As fundamentally a sportsman's hotel, The Lands of Loyal appreciates the needs of the golfer. Very early breakfasts and unusually flexible dining arrangements, quality packed lunches etc., are offered courteously. Private rooms for parties can be requested in advance.

The Hotel management are delighted to arrange a complete itinerary for the golfer, whether an individual or a group. Tee times can be arranged and green fees paid. Any correspondence with golf clubs will gladly be undertaken by us.

The Lands of Loyal provides a complete and competitive golfing package. A full colour brochure and tariff is available on request.

Alyth, Perthshire, Scotland PH11 8JQ, Tel: (08283) 3151, Fax: (08283) 3313

Set deep in the heart of the picturesque county of Fife, the Lomond Hills Hotel nestles comfortably in the scenic village of Freuchie, a place to which once courtiers from the nearby Falkland Palace were once banished. Hence the derisory expression `awa tae Freuchie and eat mice'. The beautiful Fife countryside is noted for its forests and hills, and is ideal walking country. The area is also ideal for the sportsman, with thirty golf courses, and several lochs, rivers and reservoirs within easy reach. Other available pursuits include sailing, gliding and pony trekking. Freuchie is also very close to cities such as Edinburgh, St Andrews, Perth and Dundee. The hotel boasts a fine leisure centre with a helpful and knowledgeable staff. The centre includes a swimming pool, jacuzzi, sauna, skittle alley and a range of exercise equipment, such as jogging treadmills, low impact climbers and rowing machines

The hotel has twenty-five well-appointed bedrooms, with en suite bathroom, central heating, telephone, colour television, radio, hair drier and tea/coffee facilities. The two delightful honeymoon suites feature lace trimmed four-poster beds.

The lounge is an ideal place to have a relaxing drink, and features copper and Blue Delft furnishing. The stunning dining room provides an intimate, candlelit atmosphere and its a la carte menu offers a tasty combination of traditional Scottish specialities and French flambe dishes; complemented by a fine choice of wines, sherries and liquers.

Freuchie, Fife, Tel: (0337) 57329

The Murrayshall Country House Hotel and Golf Course is only 4 miles from Perth, set in 300 acres of parkland. Deer stroll the wooded hillside, pheasants and peacocks call from the greens. The natural beauty and splashes of colour in the garden are complemented by the mellow stone of the main house with its crow stepped gables.

The hotel, completely refurbished, is elegantly furnished in a traditional style but with the use of the wonderful fabric designs available today. The bedrooms all have en suite facilities, self dial telephone and colour television.

The aptly named Old Masters Restaurant has walls hung with Dutch Masters and table settings befitting the artistry of master chef, Bruce Sangster. The restaurant has received various culinary accolades. Vegetables and herbs from the hotels walled garden and an abundance of local produce form the basis of the menus which have a Scottish flavour with a hint of modern French cuisine. A well balanced wine list is complemented by the finest of rare malt whiskies.

The 6420 yard, 18 hole, par 73 course is interspersed with magnificent specimen trees lining the fairways, water hazards and white sanded bunkers to offer a challenge to all golfers. Buggies and sets of clubs are available for hire. Neil Mackintosh, our resident professional, is pleased to give tuition, from half an hour to a weeks course. Perth is ideally situated for Scotland's courses. Golfers can relax in the newly refurbished club house which overlooks the course and provides informal dining.

Other sporting activities include tennis, croquet and bowls. However, situated only a few miles from the famous Salmon Waters of the River Tay, even closer to Perth Race Course, Murrayshall is uniquely placed to make it an attractive venue for whatever might bring you to this area of Scotland.

Private dining and conference facilities are available in both the hotel and club house. Conference organisers, requiring the best of service and attention for their senior delegates, will find Murrayshall the ideal conference haven.

Murrayshall is one of three group golf courses, the other two are Westerwood and Fernfell. Westerwood Golf Course was designed by Seve Ballesteros and Dave Thomas and is located at Cumbernauld, near Glasgow. Fernfell Golf and Country Club is located just out of Cranleigh, 8 miles from Guildford in Surrey. Corporate golf packages are offered at all three courses with the opportunity to place your company name and logo on a tee and to reserve the course for your company golf day. Golf Societies and Green Fee Payers are welcome.

Scone, Perthshire PH2 7PH, Tel: (0738) 51171, Fax: (0738) 52595

Newton House Hotel

The Newton House was built circa 1840 as a Dower House and nestles cosily in its one and a half acres of gardens. The surrounding area contains some dramatic scenery with the River Tay and Sidlaw Hills close by and there are numerous local places of interest such as Glamis Castle and Scone Palace. The sportsman will certainly appreciate the location, with over forty golf courses in the vicinity, including Carnoustie and St Andrews. Perth, an attractive town which was Scotland's capital many centuries ago, is just four miles away and Dundee thirteen.

The Newton House prides itself on 'good, old fashioned hospitality' and has ten individually and tastefully decorated bedrooms, and all of these are en suite, with television, telephone, tea/coffee trays and a window overlooking the house gardens.

In the warmth of Cawley's Lounge, with its log fire, visitors can enjoy a drink or a meal from the varied selection of food on offer.

The spacious and ornate Country House Restaurant offers a mouth-watering and varied selection of food, with a particular emphasis on providing a 'Taste of Scotland', and fresh local produce is used where possible.

Glencarse, Nr Perth PH2 7LX, Tel: (073) 886250, Fax: (073) 886717

Nivingston House

Nivingston House, formerly a farm house with parts dating back to 1725, is set in 12 acres of landscaped gardens at the foot of the Cleish Hills. In the grounds, which offer pleasant walks, are two croquet lawns, a putting green and a golf driving net. The historic village of Cleish is a short stroll away and the busy town of Kinross only three miles distant.

The Library and Lounge offer a choice of peaceful havens in which to relax in front a log fire and perhaps sample the home-made shortbread.

Light lunches as well as a comprehensive range of drinks including over 50 malt whiskies are available in the Lounge Bar.

All 17 bedrooms have been individually furnished with co-ordinating fabrics and wallpapers. All have en suite bath or shower rooms. Each room has colour TV, radio, telephone, hairdryer and tea/coffee making facilities. The 'Gairney Room' comes complete with sitting-area and whirl bath.

Lunch and Dinner menus change daily and include only the best of local produce. They are complemented by a balanced wine list with over 100 wines.

Nivingston House is ideally located for a host of sporting and leisure facilities. There are over 22 golf courses within an hour's drive - including St. Andrews.

The famous trout of nearby Loch Leven are a special attraction for anglers and salmon fishing can be arranged. Riding and clay-pigeon shooting are available, or you can even try your hand at Motor Racing at the nearby Knockhill Circuit.

Cleish Hills, Kinross-shire KY13 7LS, Tel: (05775) 216, Fax: (05775) 238

The Old Mansion House Hotel

This 16th century baronial mansion still retains much of its majestic grace of centuries gone. It is steeped in Scottish history, having passed through the hands of several notable families, such as the Strathmores and the Earls of Buchan. Improvements through the years reflect this - such as the stunningly ornate 17th-century plasterwork and open Jacobean fire in the drawing room.

The proprieters take great pride in running a very friendly and relaxed hotel, where guests feel thoroughly at home. The six bedrooms are attractively furnished, two are family suites with a children's bedroom, and all have private bathrooms, television and central heating. The restaurant serves a wide selection of food from its a la carte menu, including a number of local specialities - vegetarians have their own menu too and the wine cellar contains an outstanding range to satisfy any connoisseur.

The house is situated amid ten acres of grounds, where guests will find an outdoor heated swimming pool, squash court, croquet and tennis lawns and beautiful gardens to enjoy. The scenic village of Auchterhouse is nearby and Dundee is just seven miles away on the B954. The surrounding farmlands of Angus offer much scope for shooting and fishing, while the Championship golf courses of Carnoustie and St Andrews are a short drive away. The ski slopes of Glenshee are also within easy reach, for the more adventurous guests in the winter months.

Auchterhouse, Dundee DD3 0QN, Tel: (082) 626 366

Ostlers Close Restaurant

Hidden down a small lane off the main street in Cupar, this small restaurant is intimate and entirely unpretentious.
Ostlers Close has been owned and run by Jimmy and Amanda Graham for the past 12 years. In that time they have established themselves as one of Scotland's top restaurants. Small a la carte menus, offered at both lunch and dinner, are prepared imaginatively by chef/proprietor Jimmy Graham.

Everything is homemade from the bread to the popular Honey, Drambuie and Oatmeal Ice cream and a strong emphasis is placed on local produce. Fresh local salmon, lobster and prawns figure prominently. Herbs and vegetables are grown in season in the restaurant's own garden and wild mushrooms are gathered from nearby forests by the Grahams themselves.

25 Bonnygate, Cupar, Fife KY15 4BU, Tel: (0334) 55574

The Pine Trees Hotel

The Pine Trees is a distinctive Victorian mansion, built in 1892 and set among 14 acres of splendid woodland and garden. It is located in Pitlochry, at the heart of the beautiful county of Perthshire, within easy reach of a number of quality golf courses, such as Pitlochry, Rosemount and Taymouth Castle. The hotel garden accommodates a 9 hole putting green for those eager to get some early practice. Pitlochry itself boasts a number of famous attractions, such as the fish ladder of Loch Faskally and the Festival Theatre. The wonderful countryside, with its mountains, lochs, glens and spectacular wildlife, is waiting to be discovered on numerous walks and hikes and there are plenty of historic attractions to see: castles, sites and objects of interest dating from the Dark Ages to the present day. Fishing and shooting

parties can be arranged by the hotel, although it is advisable to book early for this.
With its warm and friendly atmosphere, the Pine Trees offers an excellent venue to get away from it all for some peace and relaxation. The twenty bedrooms are elegantly furnished, with private bath or shower room, colour televisions, radio, telephone, tea and coffee facilities and heating throughout. The lounges are spacious and tastefully furnished and the drawing room provides an ideal venue for a discreet dinner party or special business meeting, with total privacy and confidentiality assured. Scottish cooking, using only fresh produce such as Tay salmon and Scottish beef and lamb is served in the dining room and there is a range of fine wines and Scottish malts to boot.

Strathview Terrace, Pitlochry, Perthshire PH16 5QR, Tel: (0796) 472121, Fax: (0796) 472460

Pitlochry Hydro Hotel

The hotel stands in its own mature, well tended grounds, overlooking Pitlochry town. Known as the 'Gateway to the Highlands' Pitlochry is the ideal place from which to tour some of Scotland's most rugged and scenic countryside.
Public areas have been refurbished to complement the exterior of the hotel, resulting in a perfect combination of traditional elegance and modern comfort. Spacious lounges, an excellent restaurant, comfortable bedrooms, conference facilities and a new health club combine to make Pitlochry Hydro the perfect destination for the tourist or business person.
All 62 tastefully decorated bedrooms and suites have private bathroom, direct dial telephone, colour TV, free video system and tea/coffee making facilities.
Attractive lounges, overlooking the gardens and a friendly cocktail bar provide a welcoming atmosphere and the ideal

place to relax with an aperitif, or after dinner liqueur.
The restaurant menu features the best in fresh Scottish produce as well as international cuisine and an excellent wine list
A superb heated indoor swimming pool and adjoining spa bath is the focal point of the recently completed leisure club. The club also has male and female saunas, solarium, gymnasium - fully equipped for fitness testing - and a snooker room.
As the geographical centre of Scotland, Pitlochry is the ideal base for touring. Locally there are many interests and activities available includes the famous Pitlochry Festival Theatre, trout and salmon fishing, and an excellent 18 hole golf course.
The Pitlochry Hydro offers you ample opportunity to explore Scotland, follow sporting pursuits, relax or even get fit!

Pitlochry, Perthshire PH16 5JH, Tel: (0796) 472666, Fax: (0796) 472238

The Roman Camp Hotel sits on the North Bank of the River Tieth amongst twenty acres of mature and secluded gardens, which nestle by the picturesque village of Callandar, the Gateway to the Trossachs and the Highlands of Scotland.

The House was originally built as a Hunting Lodge for the Dukes of Perth in 1625 and was given its name from the conspicuous earth mounds, believed to be the site of a Roman Fort, which are visible across the meadow to the east of the walled garden.

The building has grown over many years as each consecutive family has added their own embellishments to this lovely home. The most obvious of these are the towers, one of which contains a tiny Chapel.

Today under the guidance of Eric and Marion Brown the traditional country house atmosphere still evokes its alluring charm. As you enter you will notice the abundance of freshly cut flowers, their scent lingering in the air, and be greeted to this peaceful retreat by great log fires.

Our Library and Drawing Room are of grand proportions, with an atmosphere of warmth and relaxation and are places to enjoy and reflect on the days sport, especially after dinner in the company of friends and a fine malt.

The tapestry hung Dining Room is crowned by a richly painted 16th century style ceiling. Here dinner is served at candle lit tables, laid with fine silver and crystal, while you choose from menus of local game and fish, prepared by our chef and accompanied by vegetables and herbs from our own gardens.

Each of our bedrooms has its own distinctive style and character, and is equipped with all the little thoughtful extras to make your stay as comfortable as possible.

At the Roman Camp Country House you are within easy reach of many Championship and picturesque Golf Courses, and we are able to arrange and book tee times at the local course, only two minutes walk from the hotel.

We have three-quarters of a mile of river running through our gardens, enabling guests to fish complementary for Wild Brown Trout and Salmon on our private beat. There is also the opportunity for the hotel to arrange fishing on the many lochs and other private beats surrounding Callander.

We hope that you will be able to make the Roman Camp your favourite country retreat.

Callander FK17 8BG, Tel: (0877) 30003 Fax: (0877) 31533

St Andrews certainly needs no introduction as a golfing mecca. This is a town where records show that the game was played as long ago as 1547. The people of St Andrews have always enjoyed welcoming visitors in the warm and friendly manner that has been part of the true Scottish hospitality for generations, and Rufflets Hotel is one of the finest upholders of this tradition.

Built in 1924, and designed by the Dundee architect Donald Mills, this turreted mansion house, set in ten acres of award-winning gardens, has been privately owned and personally managed by the same family since 1952. Under the personal supervision of owner Ann Russell and general manager Peter Aretz, the excellent reputation of Rufflets has grown both nationally and internationally. Welcoming open fires in winter, friendly and personal service and excellent home cooking, make it an idyllic retreat, just one hour's drive north from Edinburgh.

Spacious and attractively furnished in contemporary country house style, the hotel has twenty-one tastefully and individually decorated bedrooms with ensuite bathrooms, colour television, direct dial telephone, and tea and coffee making facilities. The Garden Restaurant has gained an AA Rosette and an RAC merit award for the past two years; cooking is light with an emphasis on fresh Scottish produce, and many of the vegetables, fruits and herbs are chosen from the hotel's own flourishing kitchen garden.

Guests to Rufflets will find much to enjoy in the historic town of St Andrews, its combination of Medieval, Victorian and Edwardian streets forming one of the most attractive towns in Britain. The Castle, Cathedral, University and Harbour, theatres, museums, art galleries, the fun of the Lammas Fair, the traditions of the Highland Games ... and golf of course.

At Rufflets, guests can enjoy the rich blend that St Andrews has to offer, and a warm welcome second to none.

Strathkinness Low Road, St Andrews, Fife KY16 9TX, Tel: (0334) 72594, Fax: (0334) 78703

Rossie Priory

This spectacular Gothic building was completed in 1807 by Charles, the eighth Lord Kinnaird and rests at the foot of the Sidlaw Hills, facing south over the magnificent Firth of Tay and Fife's rolling hills. It offers a perfect base for touring the beautiful, unspoilt countryside of Perthshire and Angus. Places of interest nearby include Scone Palace, Glamis Castle and the House of Dun. The shopping and cultural centres of Perth and Dundee are both a short drive away. The area boasts numerous golf courses as well as the famed Carnoustie and St Andrews. There are attractive beaches on the Tayside and Fife coasts. Sporting activities such as shooting, fishing and riding can be easily arranged, while the Priory possesses its own heated swimming pool and tennis court.

The Priory is set amid charming woodland grounds, with secluded pathways through the trees and rhododendrons. Eventually, the guest will stumble upon the famed Water Garden, bordered by shrubs at the foot of Rossie Hill. The Priory interior is spacious and wonderfully furnished. In the Chapel, Library, Great Hall and reception rooms there are numerous treasures, most notably the owner's (Mr Robert Spencer, grandson of the Earl Spencer) collection of oriental art.

The bedrooms are large, strikingly furnished and complete with private bathroom facilities and feature glorious views of the surrounding countryside.

Dinner is served in the elegant dining room where the food is of the highest class.

Inchture, Perthshire PH14 9SG, Tel: (0828) 86028, Fax: (0764) 3276

The Sandford Country House Hotel

This picturesque, listed country house hotel provides an ideal venue for those wishing to play golf in the Kingdom of Fife. Conveniently located near to St. Andrews (7 miles) with 34 other golf courses within a comfortable drive, including Scotscraig, Ladybank and Carnoustie.

Set in seven acres of private grounds, the sixteen en suite bedroom Sandford Hotel, is renowned for its traditional style and warm friendly service. Fine Scottish and European cuisine is the hallmark of Head Chef Steven Johnstone and in the oak-beamed restaurant, open-air courtyard and wine Gallery, a wide variety of dishes, malt whiskies and wines can be enjoyed.

STB Four Crown Highly Commended, member of 'A Taste of Scotland' and 'Where to eat in Scotland'.

Newton Mill, Wormit, Nr Dundee, Fife DD6 8RG. Tel: 0382 541802, Fax: 0382 542136

Hotel Seaforth

The Seaforth is a distinctive hotel which occupies a prominent position on Arbroath southern sea-front, overlooking the sandy beach. It is a short walk from the town's picturesque fishing harbour, historic abbey and the award-winning Signal Tower Museum which contains information and artifacts telling the fascinating history of this east coast fishing town. The east coast of Scotland has many miles of unspoilt coastline, with sweeping sandy beaches and ancient castles, while a short drive inland leads to the spectacular glens of Angus and the start of the Central Highlands. The area is very much golfing country, with Carnoustie and St Andrews both a short drive away. You may also wish to try fishing in one of the local rivers or perhaps the sea.

Dundee Road, Arbroath DD11 1QF, Tel: (0241) 72232, Fax: (0241) 77473

Occupying two fashionable town houses dating from 1880, The Scores Hotel's 30 bedrooms are all en suite and facilities include radio, television and direct dial telephone. Many rooms have panoramic sea views, whilst others enjoy an outlook over the hotel's own small garden.

The hotel is privately owned and is a member of Best Western, one of Britain's leading consortium of independent and individually run hotels. With the emphasis on the attentive and friendly service which is the hallmark of traditional Scottish hospitality you are assured of every comfort.

St Andrews is traditionally the Home of Golf. Situated only yards from the 1st Tee of the world famous Old Course, the hotel commands magnificent views of St Andrews Bay. Savour the view whilst enjoying an aperitif in the Scorecards Bar which features a collection of scorecards from championships played over the Old Course by some of the game's legends. Follow with dinner in Alexanders Restaurant where in a relaxed Regency ambience, menus feature the fresh local seafood for which the East Neuk of Fife is renowned, and an extensive selection of Scottish and International dishes. Scores Coffee Shop is open throughout the day and Chariots Bar boasts a photographic gallery of famous Scots who have made their mark in the fields of medicine, literature, industry and commerce.

Scores Hotel is the ideal choice for business meetings, conferences, presentations and exhibitions as well as dinner/dances, wedding receptions and all manner of private functions. The Garden Suite overlooking the hotel's attractive private garden can cater for functions up to 120 guests, whilst other suites are suitable for the smaller or more intimate event.

St Andrews, Fife KY16 9BB, Tel: (0334) 72451, Fax: (0334) 7394

*A page of my Journal
is like a cake of portable soup.
A little may be diffused into a
considerable portion.*

Journal of a Tour to the Hebrides, James Boswell

St. Andrews Golf Hotel is a tastefully modernised Victorian House situated on the cliffs above St. Andrews Bay, some 200 yards from the 18th tee of the 'Old Course'.

There are 23 bedrooms all with private bath and shower, and all furnished individually to a high degree of comfort, with telephone, radio, T.V., tea/coffee maker, trouser press and hair-dryer. A nice touch is the fresh flowers and welcoming fruit basket.

There is a quiet front lounge for residents and a most interesting golfer's cocktail bar featuring pictures and photographs of Open Champions past and present. This gives onto a small south facing patio garden.

With a separate entrance is 'Ma Bell's' Bar and day time restaurant, popular with students and visitors alike. Tasty food, hot and cold and reasonably priced is served from noon to 6.00 pm. A main attraction is the selection of more than 80 bottled beers from all over the world, and no fewer than 14 on draught, including cask-conditioned ales.

The central feature of the hotel is the candle-lit oak-panelled restaurant with its magnificent sea view. A la carte and table d'hote menus both feature the best of local produce – fish, shell-fish, beef, lamb, game and vegetables – conjured into delightful dishes by chef Adam Harrow. The food is well complemented by an interesting and comprehensive list of wines selected personally by owner, Brian Hughes.

Golf of course, is the speciality of the hotel, and you can find either prepared golf packages and golf weeks or have something tailored to your particular requirements, using any of the thirty or so courses within 45 minutes of St. Andrews.

40 The Scores, St Andrews KY16 9AS, Tel: (0334) 72611, Fax: (0334) 72188

If you are a golfer, then welcome home, for St Andrews is known to every Golfer Worldwide quite simply as 'The home of Golf' and it is certainly the ambition of every player to play here at least once, as a pinnacle to their career, whether they be amateur or professional.

The St Andrew's Old Course hotel, formerly the Old Course Golf and Country Club, is adjacent to the famous 17th 'Road Hole' on the Old Course.

Although being seen as the Mecca for Golf by many, the hotel is now very much a luxury resort offering guests a whole host of alternative activities and facilities to make your stay everlasting memorable.

Each bedroom or suite offers luxurious en-suite marble bathrooms many with balconies which look out over the Old Course, the town and St Andrews Bay.

Stewards will arrange your golf outings, organising your transportation, club rental or club storage, and for those who need a quick reminder, the hotel has a golf professional who is available for lessons.

For the sport minded you can also organise shooting, with a clay pigeon shoot just 15 minutes away 'atop' a hill overlooking the sea and the mountains. Fly fishing for salmon on the Tay can also be included in a package, but prior notification is recommended.

For the golfing widow or for those who are just here to relax, the spa at St Andrews offers guests the opportunity to pamper both 'body and soul'. From the invigorating whirlpool, the lap pool, the latest technology in the fitness room, steam rooms and sunbeds, to a whole variety of massages, hairdressing, facials and body treatments all carried out by a team of fully qualified therapists.

St Andrews is situated amidst some marvellous countryside. For the historically minded, Glamis Castle, Scone Palace and Stirling Castle are all within easy reach. St Andrew's town is in itself well worth spending a couple of hours walking around, being Scotland's oldest University town it is reminiscent in many ways to Oxford and Cambridge.

The evenings can be spent in the magnificent luxury of the hotel with marvellous cuisine in the restaurant supplied by Chef Billy Campbell who was inspired by the world renowned Anton Mosimann.

St Andrews is also a superb location to organise banquets and corporate events. Whatever your reason for travelling to St Andrews, it will be permanently etched in your memories.

St Andrews, Tel: (0334) 74371, Fax: (0334) 77668

The beautiful Georgian lodge has seven double/twin bedrooms all with their own facilities, extremely fine grounds, glorious shrubs and trees and a unique herb garden, set in the gentle climactic region of the Carse of Gowrie.

The original building was a 15th century friary attached to Coupar Angus Abbey, though the lectern style Doocot and small turreted stone stairwell is all that remains. The main Georgian building was erected in 1802 and later added to in the Victorian era.

The atmosphere at Waterybutts is distinctly 'House Party'; guests may play croquet, badminton, bowls, flight a few arrows or maybe just stroll in the grounds, then wine and dine in the splendid dining room.

The 16 foot Charles I refectory table, chandelier, interesting conversation, varied wine list and superb traditional food such as fresh trout pate, moules marinieres, haunch of roe venison, Tay salmon and game in season create an ambience of yesteryear.

Transport can be provided by Mercedes cars whether driven or hired, with collection from airports available. Well behaved dogs are very welcome and shooting, fishing and golf can all be arranged.

A speciality of the house is the attention given to guests whether being driven in the pony and trap or taken on scenic tours by limousine, or off-road by Landrover. Whatever your pleasure or pursuit Rachel and Barry will give every effort to make your visit unforgettable.

Grange by Errol, Perthshire PH2 7SZ, Tel: (0821) 642894, Fax (0821) 642523

Windlestrae has long been recognised for its superior accommodation, quality cuisine, attentive service and friendly relaxed atmosphere. Now, with an impressive range of new purpose-built facilities, the hotel has even more to offer, while still retaining the essential qualities for which it is widely admired.

There were just four bedrooms here when the Doyles arrived ten years ago, now there are 45, all equipped with every modern facility. The latest extension has been carefully designed to complement the existing building. Largely hidden from passing view, it was built to the rear of the original hotel leaving the secluded landscaped gardens untouched.

The new Windlestrae Leisure Club has a turbo-swimming pool, jacuzzi, solarium, sauna, steam room, toning salon, beauty therapy, multi-station gym, snooker and its own Bistro.

The spacious Business and Function Centre offers 240 square metres of undivided floor space and is designed to accommodate up to 250 people in considerable comfort.

At Windlestrae the quiet unhurried pace of life sets the mood for you to relax in luxurious, well appointed accommodation. You can enjoy fine cuisine in the acclaimed Restaurant or take your choice from the imaginative menu in the Pampas Lounge.

There are two 18-hole golf courses beside the hotel and over 50 others within easy reach. There is a fine choice of trout and salmon fishing, hill walking, historical sites such as Loch Leven Castle and Falkland Palace, the RSPB Reserve at Vane Farm and a wide range of other attractions nearby.

The Muirs, Kinross, Tayside KY13 7AS, Tel: (0577) 63217, Fax: (0577) 64733

Westlands is situated in the centre of the highland town of Pitlochry and yet still enjoys some stunning views of the Vale of Atholl and surrounding mountains. Pitlochry is the ideal base for the full highland experience. The hotel can arrange for salmon and trout fishing on the river Tummel and local hill lochs.

There are several excellent golf courses within easy reach, such as Kenmore, St Andrews and Gleneagles, not to mention the town's own fine course. Hiking, boating and walking are other activities the visitor may wish to indulge in. Pitlochry is famed for its local attractions, such as the Festival Theatre and the Salmon Ladder and the hotel runs several special seasonal and theatre short breaks.

The hotel has been totally refurbished to the highest standard of late without losing its traditional friendly atmosphere and the management aim to please in every aspect. The fifteen well-appointed bedrooms are en suite, with colour television, radio, tea/coffee tray, telephone and central heating. The six bedrooms in the new wing are extra large. The elegant and intimate cocktail bar is ideal for a bar meal or a relaxing drink after a day out. The brand new Garden Room Restaurant is tastefully decorated and the chef is noted for his seafood, game and meat dishes and for using only fresh produce.

The exciting menu ranges from traditional 'Taste of Scotland' fare to delicious international dishes. The restaurant also has its own dance floor and enjoys remarkable views of the Highland hills.

160 Atholl Road, Pitlochry, Perthshire PH16 5AR, Tel: (0796) 472266, Fax: (0796) 473994

And the wind shall say "Here were decent godless people:
Their only monument the asphalt road
And a thousand lost golf balls".

T.S. Eliot

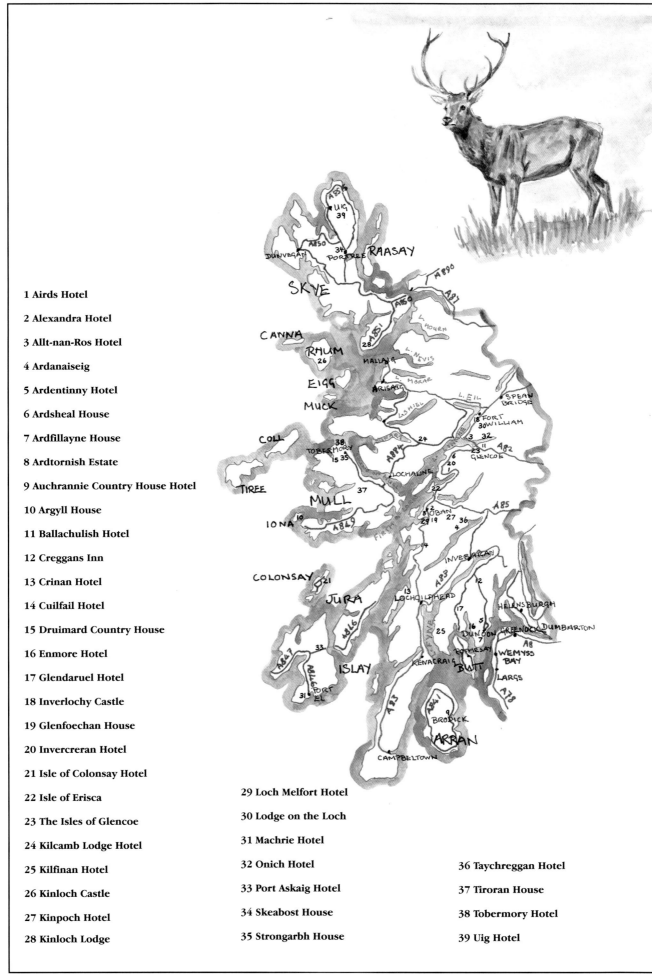

1 Airds Hotel

2 Alexandra Hotel

3 Allt-nan-Ros Hotel

4 Ardanaiseig

5 Ardentinny Hotel

6 Ardsheal House

7 Ardfillayne House

8 Ardtornish Estate

9 Auchrannie Country House Hotel

10 Argyll House

11 Ballachulish Hotel

12 Creggans Inn

13 Crinan Hotel

14 Cuilfail Hotel

15 Druimard Country House

16 Enmore Hotel

17 Glendaruel Hotel

18 Inverlochy Castle

19 Glenfoechan House

20 Invercreran Hotel

21 Isle of Colonsay Hotel

22 Isle of Erisca

23 The Isles of Glencoe

24 Kilcamb Lodge Hotel

25 Kilfinan Hotel

26 Kinloch Castle

27 Kinpoch Hotel

28 Kinloch Lodge

29 Loch Melfort Hotel

30 Lodge on the Loch

31 Machrie Hotel

32 Onich Hotel

33 Port Askaig Hotel

34 Skeabost House

35 Strongarbh House

36 Taychreggan Hotel

37 Tiroran House

38 Tobermory Hotel

39 Uig Hotel

The historic heartland of Celtic Scotland stretches from the Mull Of Kintyre, northwards to the Isle of Skye. Here, the Gaelic tongue, used to recite the many stories of yesteryear, adds a curious mystery to this haunting yet beautiful area of Scotland. The majesty of the mountainous terrain blends with a staggering variety of coastline, ley and loch. The countryside is a rich tapestry of colour changing with the seasons and the weather as dramatically as the history it has witnessed. This is the heart that pumped fire into the 1545 Jacobite Rebellions and even today can fuel the imagination with the sights and sounds of bloody conflict. A day's drive will inevitably take you through some breathtaking scenery, to Campbeltown in the far south, for instance, a busy sailing centre which enjoys a delightful setting providing a gateway to the peninsula's southern tip, the celebrated Mull of Kintyre. Or to Tarbert, a popular touring stop over, choosing the Atlantic or the Firth of Clyde route as a scenic backdrop. But beware. The mountain pass named the 'Rest and be Thankful' gives you some idea of the contours and geography of the area.

Inverary, which boasts the ancestral home of the Dukes of Argyll, is the gateway to Argyll and the Western Islands. Its castle, the headquarters of the Campbell clan, together with Inverary Jail are sights to behold. Crinan and the sailing waters of the West Highlands are also vistas to savour. Watering holes of infinite variety are dotted throughout the region and boast some of the finest seafood available in Scotland.

On a more historic note, Dunadd, the former fortress capital of the ancient Celtic Kingdom, once housed the Stone of Destiny which now resides peacefully within the confines of Westminster Abbey.

The Islands of Islay and Jura are a haven of tranquillity with only the birdlife (or an occasional errant golf ball, to disturb the visitor at peace with his whisky and water. This spirit can be found aplenty in the many distilleries dotted around the islands and touring them is as big an attraction as the equally abundant standing stones, burial chambers and ruined castles. Bowmore reveals the noted 'round church' designed to ensure that there are no corners in which another kind of spirit may lurk. Free spirits will also be content, the walking country is quite beautiful and one celebrated route takes you past the cottage in which George Orwell wrote his masterpiece, 1984.

The Atlantic coast reveals a multitude of small islands of interest. None more so than Iona. This Isle is the burial place of forty-eight Scottish kings and the birthplace of Scottish Christianity from the time of St Columba. The tranquillity of St Oran's chapel, dating from 1080, contrasts with the ragged and windswept west coast.

Nearby, Staffa plunges beneath the ocean, an awesome volcanic island where the seabirds circle the celebrated Fingal's Cave, which has been glorified for ever in the music of Mendelssohn.

Mull, which is separated from the mainland by a forty minute sail from Oban, is well established as a place of interest and water sports, hill walking and fishing occupy the restless while wildlife such as otter, deer and seals can be seen at work and play on this charming isle.

Tobermory adds a variety with panoramas of tumbling rivers and sandy coves. In the bay, a Spanish galleon which sank in 1588, rudely defies all attempts at salvage. The ocean guards its secret well and she still hold this Spanish treasure.

Twisting Ardnamurchan offers some of Britain's most unpopulated and unspoilt lands. Beauty is everywhere and the mystic ruins of Castle Tioram is a special sight to behold. Oban is a splendid crossroads, a focal point of many a West Highland holiday. A plethora of hotels and guesthouses can be found, each with its own vantage point. The coast of Lorne is a joy in itself, numerous castles and a naturally crafted landscape, man and nature competing to create a perfect picture postcard view. Kilchurn Castle on Loch Awe stands proudly amid the mountains and is a striking example of such a scene. This is an inspiring territory, a land of infinite variety and a joy through which to travel.

Northwards from Loch Awe, we find Ballachulish and the formidable scenery that epitomises murderous, ominous Glencoe, where the treacherous MacDonald murders surely cross the mind of every visitor.

How the mind runs free in such a place, but this is a land to be enjoyed, be it in isolated splendour on Rannoch Moor or in the company of the many walkers and skiers drawn to the area.

Loch Leven is one of many fine lochs for water sports and fishing in the region. Coastwards, Castle Stalker is another bold edifice standing proudly on its own island in Loch Laich. And still the tales of bloodshed and intrigue abound. Legends encapsulated by Robert Louis Stevenson's Kidnapped, a tale of brutal slayings, clan revenge and miscarried justice.

Although peace now prevails, the gruesome Well of Seven Heads and the ruins of Glengarry Castle bear testimony to Lochaber's more stormy past. Fort William, which lies in the shadow of Ben Nevis, is a magnet for walkers and climbers and all manner of watering holes can be found in which to refresh oneself.

The Isle of Skye is another magnificent jewel to be appreciated in this somewhat overladen crown, if the visitor can ever be persuaded to leave the mainland ports of embarkation. Glenfinnan at the head of Loch Shiel was the place where the Young Pretender, Charles Edward Stuart, rallied the Jacobite troops to his ill-fated 1745 cause. Mallaig, a busy fishing port and ferry terminal for Skye is another favoured destination. To the north of the town, small villages with lochside settings delight many a passerby. South of Kyle, Glenelg is another hidden gem of a glen, the setting for the delightful tale a Ring of Bright Water. Skye itself, with its wild coastlines and configurations such as the Old Man of Storr, is the perfect setting for legends. Eagles soar, waterfalls cascade and life is peaceful. Dunvegan Castle, home to the Chiefs of MacLeod is just one of many sights to savour. The Isles of the Western Highlands and Argyll, from Arran to Skye, offer some of the most breathtaking scenery you could imagine. Travellers from far and wide are constantly taken aback by each new delight as horizons change. It is said that today's so called 'civilised being' fails to explore his homeland, seeking sights from further afield. Not everybody will discover this area of Britain and perhaps that is a very good thing, but for those who do it is an experience they will treasure.

The Airds Hotel

The Airds Hotel Restaurant is numbered among the best to be found anywhere in Scotland. The philosophy is simplicity; the best of local produce cooked to perfection, complemented by a carefully chosen wine list ranging from modest house wines to the classic Chateaux of France.

Originally a ferry inn for travellers to the island of Lismore, the Airds Hotel has been thoughtfully converted with the modern traveller in mind and provides every possible comfort. Drinks are served by roaring log fires in the two cosy lounges filled with books and magazines or in the flower-filled conservatory on warm summer evenings.

The twelve exceptionally pretty bedrooms are beautifully furnished and provided with everything to ensure a pleasant and comfortable stay. Some have spectacular views over the loch and mountains beyond.

The village of Port Appin, with its quiet lanes and loch-side walks has changed little since Robert Louis Stevenson chose this romantic and beautiful area of Argyll as the setting for his novel 'Kidnapped'. Indeed, one of the pleasures of a stay at the Airds Hotel lies in the journey itself, by the bonnie banks of Loch Lomand or the lovely Loch Earn; north from Glasgow via the majestic peaks of Glen Coe and the southern shores of Loch Linnhe the traveller will not be disappointed.

Port Appin, Argyll PA38 4DF, Tel: (063 173), Fax: (063 173) 535

Alexandra Hotel

A fine example of mid-Victorian architecture, the Alexandra Hotel stands on the Esplanade overlooking a picturesque bay and the islands of Mull and Kerrera. It is ideally situated to watch the gloriously colourful sunsets and is but a stone's throw away from Oban's town centre and harbour, from where ferries leave for the Inner and Outer Hebrides. The hotel has its own motor cruiser, upon which trips to places such as Tobermory or Fort William can be arranged and also runs a coach tour of Iona during the summer months. Oban possesses a fine collection of shops and sporting facilities including a swimming pool, leisure and fitness centre, tennis courts and bowling green. Boat trips and pony trekking are also available locally. The town is set in Whisky country and the hotel offers weekends during winter where you may sample several of its wide range of malts.

The hotel prides itself on a tradition of good food and hospitality - its 54 bedrooms are tastefully decorated and most overlook Oban Bay.

Each room has its own private bath, television, telephone, radio, individually controlled heating and tea/coffee making facilities. The restaurant is spacious and affords a magnificent view of the isles of the Firth of Lorn. The finest of local produce is available on table d'hote and a la carte menus. Entertainment with a Scottish flavour is provided in the Lounge Bar and there is also a lounge with satellite television. There is a lift to all floors and all the public rooms are on the ground floor with the same breathtaking views of the Bay.

Corran Esplanade, Oban, Strathclyde PA54 5AA, Tel: (0631) 62381, Fax: (0631) 64497

Alt-Nan-Ros Hotel

Spectacularly situated on the North Shore of Loch Linnhe, Allt-Nan-Ros Hotel has truly exceptional panoramic views across spectacular mountain scenery and along the Loch, beyond Appin towards the Isle of Mull.

The Hotels name is Gaelic for 'Burn of the Roses' and is derived from the cascading stream which passed through the landscaped gardens and on into Loch Leven and Loch Linnhe.

Originally built as a Victorian shooting lodge, the house has been tastefully upgraded to its present elegant style by the resident proprietors, the MacLeod family.

All public rooms and bedrooms overlook the Loch and gardens and take full advantage of the hotel's southerly aspect. Each bedroom has its own private bathroom, shower, central heating, colour television, radio, electric blankets and tea/coffee making facilities. The lounge, foyer and dining room are richly furnished in traditional style where fresh flowers abound.

Gastronomic delights are provided by the Hotel's highly commended chef. The cuisine is influenced by modern and French styles but also adapts traditional Scottish recipes and West Highland flavours to today's tastes. A list of 100 wines complement your meal and a range of 70 malt whiskies, spirits, liqueurs and beers are available from the bar.

This area is a fisherman's paradise and James MacLeod, the manager of the hotel, has a wealth of information and advice on all aspects.

All forms of watersports are available locally and there are 18 and 9 hole golf courses in nearby Fort William. Situated between Ben Nevis and Glencoe the hotel offers an ideal base for the best and most exciting skiing from beginners to advanced.

For those requiring a more relaxing stay there are boat cruises to Mull viewing seals, otters, eagles and seabirds along the way or perhaps a trip on the steam trains on the most beautiful line in Britain.

Onich, By Fort William PH33 6RY, Tel: (08553) 210, Fax: (08553) 462

This elegant baronial mansion is set against a beautiful backdrop of the mighty Ben Cruachan and the usually serene Loch Awe. Its celebrated gardens of rhododendron and azalea add to the stunning effect.

The area is ideal for a peaceful break and ambling through the magnificent scenery. There is a small fishing boat for use on the loch and the hotel has a tennis court and a snooker table.

The fourteen bedrooms are of differing dimensions and each has a distinctive character with furnishing that includes quality fabrics and antiques. The rooms are also equipped with colour television and telephone. The most spectacular part of the building is undoubtedly the palatial lounge and panelled library bar, which offer magnificent views of the surrounding countryside. Dinner is served in the red dining room and the menu is imaginative and deliciously executed, with dishes such as Pan Fried Monkfish and Fillet of Salmon with Oban Mussels and Fennel.

Kilchrenan By Taynuilt, Argyll PA35 1JG, Tel: (086) 63 333, Fax: (086) 63 222

A warm welcome awaits you at one of the West coast of Scotland's most enchanting old droving inns dating back to the early 1700's.

Ardentinny hotel lies in its attractive small gardens which form a promontory in Loch Long and it is surrounded by the mountainous Argyll Forest park. Many guests come just to relish the peace and quite, abandoning their cars and walking along the shores or in gently sloping, traffic free, 50 miles of forest roads.

There are eleven bedrooms, all with private facilities, central heating, electric blankets, television, direct dial telephone and coffee making facilities. The chefs prepare delightful dinners to a very high standard and all diets are catered for. Taste of Scotland dishes feature every day on the daily changing menus.

The cellar has about 50 bins of mainly French and New World wines and the two bars are busy with residents and Clyde yachtsman, who pick up the hotel moorings, to eat and drink in the hotel or gardens.

The hotel is a good centre for touring the South West Highlands and nearby Benmore Botanical Gardens, Inverary Castle and Hail can be visited amongst many other attractions. There is a nine hole golf course ten minutes away and the Cowal championship course twenty minutes down the road.

Rowing boats can be hired from the hotel with or without engines and guests can fish for cod or mackerel. The Echaig river has good runs of sea trout and salmon and fishing can generally be arranged in advance for the hotel. Mountain Bikes can be hired.

Ardentinny, Loch Long, Argyll PA23 8TR, Tel: (036981) 209, Fax: (036981) 345

An historic old manor with a warm country house atmosphere, Ardsheal House is set in 900 acres and situated on the shores of Loch Linnhe. Some 17 miles south of Fort William and 30 miles north of Oban, it provides an ideal location for exploring the Highlands.

Ardsheal House dates from the early 1500s when it was built as one the manor houses of the stewards of Appin. It plays an important role in Robert Louis Stevenson's 'Kidnapped', for it was only a mile or two away from the house where the infamous Appin murder took place.

The house has oak panelling, open fires and is furnished with family antiques. There are thirteen comfortable bedrooms, all with private bathrooms. Each room is different and has been individually furnished by Robert and Jane Taylor, the resident proprietors.

The dining room conservatory offers an excellent menu. Dishes are prepared using only the freshest local produce; wild salmon, prawns, oysters, trout and vegetables, herbs and fruits come from the hotel's two acre garden. The freshest ingredients result in truly memorable meals. There is an excellent selection of wines and a wide choice of malt whiskies and spirits. The House has its own tennis court and riding, boating and fishing are available nearby. There are idyllic and scenic walks among graceful larches, immense rhododendrons, ancient sycamores and along the shores and borders of Loch Linnhe.

Kentallen of Appin, Highland PA38 4BX Tel: (063174) 227, Fax: (063 174) 342

Ardtornish Estate

The Ardtornish Estate covers approximately 60 square miles of the south-west corner of the beautiful Movern peninsula. Encompassing hills, woodland, rivers, lochs and a 20 mile stretch of coastline on the Sound of Mull and Loch Linne the area is noted for its marvellous abundance of wildlife, indeed part of the estate is protected by the Scottish Wildlife Trust. Primarily the estate is a haven for the fisherman. Salmon and sea trout fishing is available on the River Aline, Loch Arienas and Loch Doire nam Mart. Loch Tearnait and other hill lochs provide fine sport with indigenous brown trout, and fly fishing from the banks of these lochs are included in the rent. Sea fishing is also available and the area is noted for record catches of Common Skate and other deep sea fish; safe mooring and launching facilities are available if you wish to bring your own boat.

The self-catering accommodation available ranges from the spaciousness of the principle Mansion House flats and the Former Factor's House (Achranich) to the comfort and charm of the five estate cottages. Modern amenities such as bathrooms, WCs, electric cookers, fridges, water heating, open fires and stoves have all been added without disturbing the original character; indeed the conservation of much of the decoration and furnishings in the Mansion House has earned a Grade A listing from the Historic Buildings Council. The surrounding area offers the perfect escape from the 20th century. For a change, or for the non-fishing partner, the area abounds in possibilities for all lovers of the great outdoors. The walking is superb, along with bathing, boating, wildlife spotting and fascinating visits to some of the ancient ruins that decorate this country.

Morvern, by Oban, Argyll PA34 5AX, Tel: (0967) 421288

Auchrannie Country House Hotel

Auchrannie Country House Hotel is a delightful Scottish Mansion house ideally located in 6 acres of mature wooded and landscaped gardens just one mile from the ferry terminal at Brodick and within 5 minutes walk of the village and golf course.

Once the home of the Dowager Duchess of Hamilton this fine country house has been tastefully refurbished and extended without losing the character and charm of the original red sandstone building. Now incorporating a magnificent indoor swimming pool and leisure centre - including turbo spa, sauna, turkish bath, fitness suite solaria, snooker room, beauty salon and boutique - the Auchrannie combines comfort and elegance whilst offering a new concept in relaxation and hospitality on Arran.

All 28 luxury bedrooms have private facilities, colour television, telephone, tea and coffee, mini-bar, personal safe, hair dryer, baby-listening and radio.

The popular Brambles Bistro offers a superb menu throughout the day and the Cocktail Lounge, Sun Lounge and Loggia offer the ideal atmosphere to relax and peruse the menus and wine list while enjoying a pre-dinner drink. The renowned Garden Restaurant is open to non-residents and offers a la carte and table d'hote menus using the best of fresh local produce. Gently poached fillet of salmon set on fresh dill cream sauce, prime Scottish fillet steak naped with Arran mustard and whiskey cream sauce and wafer thin crepe filled with mushrooms, hazelnuts and spinach in a nutmeg flavoured cream sauce have all been featured.

Auchrannie Road, Brodick, Isle of Arran KA27 8BZ, Tel: (0770) 302234, Fax: (0770) 302812

Nestling in what is arguably the most beautiful and unexploited area of Scotland, Ardfillayne is a rare find in today's world. Built in 1835 and commanding an enviable view over the Firth of Clyde from its own 16 acres of natural wooded gardens, it retains the charm and warmth of an era now all but lost. There is an almost ethereal quality of the past here, a captivating period charm enhanced by the informal elegance of its eminently Victorian atmosphere.

The drawing rooms reflect this gentler peace, with fine furniture objects d'art and a veritable treasure-trove of antiques perfectly complementing the affluent antiquity of such a house.

Carefully modernised, the seven intimate bedrooms are unique peaceful havens; all en suite, they are designed with your comfort in mind.

The fin de siecle ambience of Ardfillayne's Mackintosh inspired dining room provides the magical setting for the famous Beverley's Restaurant. An atmosphere of sophistication pervades, subtly aided by fresh flowers, candlelight, lace and crystal, and further enhancing the experience of such exceptional food. Classic cuisine and traditional Scottish dishes are exquisitely prepared from the finest of fresh, local produce; game and fish caught from nearby land, loch and sea. All complemented by superb wines from one of Scotland's most exclusive cellars, and perfectly completed by old brandies, malts and vintage ports.

Ardfillayne is the example in this area that seems to have missed the march of time; nearby can still be found lochside hostelries, antiquated Drovers' Inns, and quiet walks through the peace and tranquillity that is uniquely the Forest Park of Argyll.

West Bay, Dunoon, Argyll PA23 7QJ, Tel: (0369) 2267, Fax: (0369) 2501

The beautiful island of Iona with its brilliant waters, white sands and clear light has inspired poets, painters and pilgrims for centuries. The Argyll Hotel, facing the sea with its lawn running down to the shore, is also designed to inspire its guests.

Built as an Inn in 1868, the hotel now has nineteen bedrooms, and a spacious dining room looking over the Sound of Iona to the hills of Mull and Erraid. The very special atmosphere is created by unrivalled hospitality and comfort. Original paintings, etchings and antique furniture are part of the ambience - even a 19th century landscape mural above the fireplace - in payment for the artist's hotel bill!

The hotel serves real home cooking, freshly prepared and using its own organically grown vegetables. Dishes include local produce such as wild Mull salmon, venison, Scottish lamb, Tobermory smoked trout and cheeses. Early morning teas, lunches and home baked afternoon teas are available upon request.

Only a quarter of a mile from the famous Iona Abbey which dates back to the eleventh century, the Argyll Hotel is an ideal place in which to enjoy the natural beauty and tranquillity of this sacred and remarkable island.

Isle of Iona, Argyll, Tel: (06817) 334

The Ballachulish Hotel

One of Scotland's oldest and best known hotels nestles at the base of rugged mountains above the enchanting Loch Linnhe, and commands some inspiring views. For centuries, the hotel has been a welcoming and comfortable stop for travellers and adventurers in this wild and beautiful country. The hotel is ideally placed to see the Highlands, with Glencoe, Fort William, Loch Ness and a number of Munroes, including Ben Nevis, a short drive away. Guests on the other hand may wish to try fishing in one of the nearby lochs or rivers. Those looking for a little exercise are entitled to use the fine Leisure Centre and swimming pool facility at the nearby Isles of Glencoe Hotel.

The hotel has been fully refurbished and skilfully blends traditional style with the highest modern standards. Gracious baronial lounges lead to the elegant Cocktail Bar and the Loch View Restaurant.

Here, a range of mouthwatering and original dishes is available. Use is made of local produce from the sea and hills, such as salmon, scallops, lobster, venison, lamb and grouse. There is also the option of 'Dining around the Loch' - at the nearby Lodge on the Loch and the Isles of Glencoe. Guests can retire to the spacious lounge with its log fire, or join friends and locals in one of the famous 'ferry bars'. The thirty bedrooms are luxuriantly furnished with sturdy pine and each has its own television, telephone and tea/coffee facilities.

Ballachulish, Argyll PA39 4JY, Tel: (08552) 606, Fax: (08552) 629

Creggans Inn

This attractive hotel is set amongst magnificent scenery. Standing on a headland looking out over Loch Fyne, the mountains rise majestically behind.

This is an old Highland inn with a tradition of hospitality and comfort. The bedrooms are prettily decorated and have en suite facilities. The hotel's sitting room is peaceful with a view over the loch. The bars both have log fires to give them a warm welcoming feel.

Dinner is served in a Victorian style restaurant and also enjoys a lovely view of the loch. Lady Maclean has written several cookery books and the dishes created in the kitchens are unique with a mixture of Scottish country house cooking and French cuisine. Local ingredients are used extensively and include Loch Fyne oysters and freshly caught langoustines.

Sir Fitzroy Maclean oversees the cellar with its excellent choice of wines and a wide range of malt whiskies. These include one of their own; Old MacPhunn.

This is an ideal centre for touring with many places to visit. Glasgow is only an hour away and Kilmartin is close by.

This was the heartland of Celtic Dalriada and there are druidic remains to be seen here.

There is also Ellens Isle, made famous in the Lady of the Lake. Gleneagles is not far away and there are more local golf courses too. There is both sea and fresh water fishing and salmon and trout abound in these waters.

Creggans Inn is an ideal place for a holiday for those who want to relax and unwind in the tranquillity of the Western Highlands.

Strachur, Argyll, Tel: (036 986) 279, Fax: (036 986) 637

Crinan Hotel

The Crinan Hotel in this tiny fishing village is very much the heart of the community and has been for over 200 years. With a population of just 58 Crinan, lies at the north end of the Crinan Canal, connecting Loch Fyne to the Atlantic. It is a most welcoming hotel for all types of guest from Hebridean bound yachtsmen, fisherman and itinerant visitors enjoying the beautiful scenery and countryside.

Crinan is very easy to find and is an excellent base being only 24 miles from West Loch Talbert, the terminal for ferries to the islands Islay, Jura and Gigha and 37 miles from Oban, the main base for the ferries to the Inner Hebrides.

The Hotel boasts several unusual features. On the roof you will find the roof bar and seafood restaurant. Lock 16 so named because the last Loch in the Crinan Canal is Lock 15!

The restaurant overlooks the Sound of Jura, Scarba, the Gulf of Corryvreckan and beyond in the distance, the hills of Mull. Here you will sample the most delicious types of seafood ranging from jumbo prawns, clams, lobsters, mussels and oysters. These are caught in the deep water to the west of the Corryvreckan by the boats which are based at Crinan so you can be assured of their absolute freshness.

Crinan has a restaurant on the ground floor. This also has magnificent views and serves all the best local produce. One of the unrivalled specialities includes Loch Fyne kippers.

The bedrooms have private bathrooms and are tastefully designed. All have breathtaking views. This family run hotel is very friendly and offers all the comforts you require to make sure your stay is enjoyable.

Crinan, Argyll PA31 8SR, Tel:(054683) 261, Fax:(054683) 292

Cuilfail Hotel

Originally an old drovers inn, this ivy-clad hotel nestles at the foot of rolling hills close to the shores of Loch Melfort.

Since being taken over by the Birrell family, the Cuilfail has been totally refurbished. The interior has been decorated and furnished to reflect the hotel's Victorian past, creating a relaxed, cosy atmosphere.

The hotel bar, 'family room' and bistro room serve a choice of delicious meals. For residents and non-residents who wish to enjoy a drink or meal in quieter surroundings there is the 'Whisky Lounge' with over 700 whisky miniatures on display. Outside there is the hotel's garden where drinks and meals are also served.

The Cuilfail's 12 bedrooms all have en suite facilities with wash-hand basin, shower or bath, individually controlled central heating, tea and coffee making facilities and colour television. There is a choice of double or twin bedrooms and there are two family suites both with a separate adjoining childrens' room. Favourable rates are often available for longer stays and weekend breaks.

Open to residents and non-residents the Cuilfail dining room offers a different daily menu with freshly cooked to order dishes with the emphasis on locally caught seafood (the area is renowned for its large Sound of Jura prawns and oysters and local West Coast salmon - always a favourite!). There is also a carvery each evening and a selection of vegetarian dishes. Pastry dishes are a speciality and there is a good selection of sweets.

Its gaelic name means 'sheltered corner', and the Cuilfail Hotel has a long tradition of offering highland hospitality to visitors to this beautiful part of Argyll. The Cuilfail is an ideal base from which to tour or explore the Firth of Lorn and it is well known to hill-walkers, anglers and sailors.

Kimelford, Argyll PA34 4XA, Tel: (08522) 274, Fax: (08522) 264

Druimard Country House

The Druimard Country House is situated at the north side of the Isle Of Mull. It stands on a peaceful hillside above the pretty village of Derek, at the head of Loch Cuin. The house itself is Victorian and has been beautifully restored to offer guests every comfort.

This is a family-run hotel with a friendly and relaxed atmosphere. There is accommodation for 14 guests although not all rooms have en suite facilities. The second floor of the hotel contains a family suite which has two double rooms, a sitting room and bathroom. All rooms have colour television, tea/coffee making facilities and direct dial telephone.

The restaurant has recently been awarded the AA red rosette for excellence. It is open to non-residents as well as guests and the quality of food and standard of service is high. The proprietors concentrate on using fresh local produce which is cooked and served by themselves with the help of local staff. The menu is varied and changes each day.

Within the hotel grounds is the 'Mull Little Theatre' which has gained world renown over the years. There are performances between April and October but as there are only 43 seats it is advisable to book in advance. The Druimard provides a pre-theatre dinner.

The Druimard Country House is ideally situated for those wanting peace and quiet in this delightful part of the country.

Dervaig, Isle Of Mull, Tel: (06884) 345

Enmore Hotel

Enmore Hotel is a charming Georgian country house hotel situated on the seafront between Dunoon and Hunters Quay. Originally built as a summer house for a wealthy cotton merchant, it is now cared for by Angela and David Wilson who will ensure that your stay with them is memorable.

When you travel through Scotland's magnificent Cowal Peninsular you cannot fail to be impressed with the views of the Holy Loch and the Firth of Clyde. Enmore is the ideal base hotel at the gateway to the Western Highlands.

All 15 bedrooms are tastefully furnished and either face the sea, mountains or delightful garden. All the bedrooms have bathrooms some with jacuzzi or whirlpool and there is even a waterbed.

You will delight in some of the personal touches Enmore offers, from the fresh flowers, fruit and chocolates to the luxurious fluffy robes in each of the bedrooms. In the homely reception rooms you can enjoy the views using the binoculars on the window- sill, giving further evidence of your hosts delight in surprising their guests with unexpected pleasures.

This elegant hotel is well known for the excellent inventive cuisine prepared by the patron, using produce from the hotel garden and specialising in many traditional five course Scottish dishes.

The wine list is imaginative and carefully chosen to complement your meal.

There are many historic sites and places of outstanding beauty to visit when you are staying at Enmore and for the more energetic there is pony trekking in the hills , fishing, swimming, golfing and the rare pleasure of uncrowded beaches

If you enjoy squash, Enmore has two international standard squash courts, one with video playback facilities.

Whatever you decide to do you can be assured you will be looked after to the highest standards at the Enmore Hotel.

Marine Parade, Kirn PA23 8HH, Tel:(0369) 2230, Fax:(0369) 2148

In AD 1110, Meckau, son of Magnus Barefoot, King of Norway, met the Scots on the banks of the river that flows through this glen. The fighting Scots won the ensuing battle and the bodies of their slaughtered enemies were thrown into the water, turning it red with blood. The river passed into history as `Ruail' and the Glen as `Glen-da-ruail', the `Glen of red blood'. Over the years the name became anglicised to the modern Glendarue.

Despite its violent beginnings, the river now provides a somewhat more pleasing pastime - fishing. The hotel offers private salmon and trout fishing to its guests on the Ruel, which flows directly behind it. In addition there are arrangements with local angling clubs to fish many other waters including the hiring of boats to fish larger lochs and sea.

The hotel itself is small, friendly and family-run. It offers the best in Scottish hospitality with delicious home-cooking. Naturally the private rooms offer the usual range of modern facilities, including colour television, and most have en suite bathrooms.

For a fascinating break from fishing, the surrounding area offers a wealth of open opportunities. Deer stalking is available, as is golf on three courses. Hillwalking provides a rare opportunity to experience first-hand the splendour of

the Highland countryside and the possibility of seeing some of the roaming wildlife, including the red and roe deer, buzzards and golden eagles. All of this and not to mention the wealth of history that surrounds the local area.

Clachan of Glendaruel, Argyll PA22 3AA, Tel: (036982) 274, Fax: (036982) 317

Inverlochy was built by the first Lord Arbinger in 1863, near the site of the original 13th century fortress, against a backdrop of some of the most magnificent scenery in the West Highlands. Queen Victoria spent a week there in 1873 and in her diaries wrote 'I never saw a lovelier or more romantic spot'.

Greta Hobbs owns the castle now and Michael Leonard - resident manager and an aimiable host - personally welcomes each guest to what is more a country house than a hotel.

The beautifully frescoed ceiling of the Great Hall, with its crystal chandeliers and handsome staircase and fine decorations throughout befit the Victorian proportions of the rooms and reflect the atmosphere of a former era. There are 16 apartments, all with private bathrooms, colour

television and telephone.

Standing amongst the foothills of Ben Nevis, in its own grounds of 500 acres and surrounded by rhododendrons and landscaped gardens, Inverlochy offers its guests a warm welcome, peace and seclusion, with cuisine and wine cellar of the highest standard.

The dining room has a pair of heavily-carved sideboards, immaculate table settings with silver cutlery, and boasts a magnificent view across Loch Marak to the mountains beyond. Chef Simon Haigh uses only the finest ingredients to create international dishes with a Highland flair.

There is loch fishing and tennis in the grounds and a wealth of beautiful scenery and countryside a short drive away. Inverlochy Castle has a well deserved reputation for being one of the finest hotels in Scotland.

Torlundy, Fort William PH33 6SN, Tel: (0397) 702177, Fax: (0397) 702953

Isle of Colonsay Hotel

Colonsay is one of the most remote of the islands of Argyll. Northwards it looks across 15 miles of sea to Mull and south to Donegal. To the east, 25 miles away, the mainland of Argyll lies hidden beyond the spectacular skyline of the islands of Jura and Islay. Westwards is the Atlantic. Only Du Hirteach Lighthouse stands between Colonsay and Canada but Colonsay is not a bleak and uniform island - far from it.

The Colonsay Hotel stands above the harbour where the car ferries to and from Oban berth. It provides double, single and family rooms. All bedrooms, except single rooms, have private facilities en suite and there is central heating throughout the hotel.

Menus change daily and make imaginative use of fresh local produce. The atmosphere is relaxed and friendly and

children are welcome.

Within five miles of the hotel are golden eagles, peregrine falcons, a major seal colony, wild goats and otters. Two portions of the ancient Caledonian forest survive on the island, and Colonsay House Gardens are known to rhododendron lovers everywhere.

The hotel provides a hub of social activity for the island and will arrange fishing on the lochs, golf on the 18 hole course, sea fishing and boat trips. Bicycles are provided to adults free of charge and the courtesy car not only meets guests on arrival but is available to ferry family parties to picnic sites.

Visitors are very much encouraged to come to Colonsay and enjoy all it has to offer. At the hotel every effort is made to ensure that guests enjoy their holiday to the full.

Isle of Colonsay, Colonsay, Argyll PA61 7YP, Tel: (09512) 316, Fax: (09512) 353

Ilse of Eriska

Robin and Sheena Buchanan-Smith invite guests to share in the peace, comfort and relaxation that abounds in their baronial mansion on the island sanctuary of Eriska. The setting is idyllic, with outstanding views from the house itself. Wildlife abounds. Seals, herons and deer are frequently seen and you may catch a glimpse of a golden eagle or an otter.

The Big House was built in 1884 by a branch of the Stewarts of Appin. Once the home of the Blair/Clark Hutchinsons, the island was purchased by the Buchanan-Smiths in 1974.

With its bay window to the south and its chintz covered furniture, the Drawing Room invites a feeling of relaxation and in the Lounge, delicious afternoon tea is spread before guests who may help themselves. The Library Bar has doors to the grounds where there is a putting green and croquet lawn.

The attractive, recently re-carpeted Dining Room is the

venue for some enjoyable cuisine. From breakfast offered from hot plates under silver covers to the more formal candle-lit setting for dinner, with the sparkle of crystal glasses and the glint of silver, internationally acclaimed standards are jealously maintained.

Each of the 16 bedrooms has its own character and highly individual furnishings; common to all are immaculate housekeeping and lovely displays of fresh flowers.

There is no reason to ever feel bored or to suffer from lack of exercise.

For the very energetic there are watersports at the pier with water-skiing and windsurfing, tennis on the En Tous Cas all-weather court or clay pigeon shooting.

Those who have experience are welcome to trek over the island on the sure-footing Icelandic ponies. By far the most popular of all activities, however, is exploring this magical island on foot.

Ledaig, Oban, Argyll PA37 1SD, Tel: (063172) 371, Fax: (063172) 531

The Isles Of Glencoe Hotel

This outstanding new hotel juts out into the serene Loch Leven and is a centre for all kinds of activities set amid this most beautiful landscape. The hotel is situated in a highland estate with two loch-side harbours and three kilometres of water frontage, which play host to local craft and watersports.

Glencoe itself provides stunning terrain for walking and climbing. In the winter months, Glencoe and the new ski resort of Nevis Range make the area one of the best ski centres in Britain. Guests also have full access to the recently completed, fully equipped Leisure centre with its swimming pool, sauna and gymnasium. For the less athletic, there are a multiplicity of things to see and do in the area such as catch

a steam train down the West Highland Line, from Fort William to Mallaig, or indulge in a cruise up Lochs Leven, Linnhe, Etive or Shiel. Pony trekking at Appin and Torlundy and of course fishing and golf is available locally too.

The hotel is modern, plush and comfortable. The 39 bedrooms are spacious and well equipped to cater for the needs of any guest, including those with disabilities. Many feature glorious views of the surrounding mountains.

A delicious three-course dinner is served in the Restaurant, or guests may wish to try the similarly mouth watering range of food in the warm and lively surroundings of the Bistro Bar. The hotel runs special festive house parties that provide an ideal and memorable evening's entertainment.

Ballachulish, Argyll PA39 4JY, Tel: (08552) 603, Fax: (08552) 629

Glenfeochan Gardens

Glenfeochan House is a listed, turreted, Victorian Country Mansion at the head of Loch Feochan, built in 1875 and set amidst a 350 acre Estate of Hills, Lochs, Rivers and Pasture. The House is surrounded by a mature 6 acre Garden (open to the Public) with a 1½ acre Walled Garden with herbaceous borders, vegetables fruit and Herb beds.

The house has recently been carefully restored with family antiques and beautiful fabrics. All the main rooms have high ceilings with original ornate plasterwork. The intricately carved American Pine staircase with beautifully Pargeted canopy lead Guests to three large comfortable bedrooms with ensuite bathrooms. The views over the Garden and Parkland through to Loch Feochan are spectacular. This is a really peaceful setting for a holiday.

The Victorian Arboretum is "One of the Great Gardens of the Highlands". Many rare shrubs and trees, some planted in 1840, make a wonderful canopy for the tender Rhododendrons and other rare shrubs including a large Embothrium and Davidia which abounds with "White Handkerchiefs" in the Summer.

Carpets of Snowdrops, Daffodils and Bluebells herald the Spring. Many tender Acers love this sheltered garden. The Herbaceous Borders are a blaze of colour in the summer and provide many of the flowers for the house. The walled garden has one of the old Victorian heated walls. This gives shelter to a huge Magnolia, Eucryphia and a Ginkgo. All the vegetables for the house are grown here. There is a large greenhouse entirely for white and yellow peaches and nectarines. Salmon and Sea Trout fishing on the River Nell and wonderful bird and otter watching make Glenfeochan a unique place to stay.

Kilmore, Oban, Argyllshire PA34 4QR, Tel: (063177) 273

The Invercreran is a stylish mansion house, now an outstanding small country house hotel. It rests in 25 acres of mature shrub gardens and woodlands beyond which, the view extends over the beautiful Glen Creran - its beautiful tree-lined meadows interspersed with walks to the River Creran surrounded by impressive mountains.

Viewed from the outside, it is difficult to imagine that the Invercreran has only 7 guest rooms. However, once one steps inside any of the bedrooms, bathrooms or public rooms it becomes easier to see why. With an unashamed emphasis on luxury the sheer spaciousness of the rooms is one of the most striking first impressions, on top of which the bedrooms all have en suite bathrooms and offer all the facilities the discerning guest would expect from such a hotel. They all enjoy commanding views too.

The lounge has been specially designed to curve to the contour of the hill. It boasts a freestanding marble fireplace, where the warm glow of logs under a copper canopy further enhances the relaxing, friendly atmosphere for which the hotel is especially renowned.

The hotel is run by the Kersley family and their sons. Tony is the chef, cooking exquisite Scottish fare to order. The menu is wide and varied, with the emphasis on local landed seafood, selection of finest Scottish meat, game and fresh vegetables. All complemented with an outstanding cellar of specially chosen wines.

Glen Creran, Appin, Argyll PA38 4BJ, Tel: (063173) 414 and 456, Fax: (063173) 532

Kinloch Lodge

Kinloch Lodge is an elegant white stone building situated at the head of Loch Na Dal in the South end of the Island of Skye. Originally built as a farm house, Kinloch Lodge is now the home of Lord and Lady Macdonald and their family, who several years ago turned their historic house into a small comfortable Hotel.

Lord and Lady Macdonald place particular emphasis on creating a relaxing and friendly atmosphere in their home. Guests are made to feel like family friends. Drinks are served in one of the two Drawing Rooms where there are open fires, panoramic views, books, magazines and peace. Here guests can enjoy the commanding views South across the Loch to the dramatic mountains of Knoydart on the mainland and West to Skye's famous jagged Cullin Ridge. The garden slopes down to the sea, which is on two sides, while on the other side the ground steeply rises to 1200ft. The Lodge is situated one mile from the main Broadford-Armadale road across a small river. It is a truly isolated spot. The Lodge now has ten bedrooms, eight have their own bathroom attached, and two have the exclusive use of a bathroom across the corridor. All the rooms are individually furnished and as little akin to hotel rooms as possible. Because the building was not designed as a hotel, the size of the rooms is variable.

Lady Macdonald, who is an award winning cookery writer, assisted by Peter Macpherson, produces the most innovative mouth-watering dishes. The whole emphasis is on fresh food. Skye abounds with the very best of meat, game and fish. Everything is homemade from the breakfast scones to the after dinner fudge.

Sleat, Isle of Skye IV43 8QY, Tel: (04713) 214/333, Fax: (04713) 277

Knipoch Hotel

Knipoch Hotel is eminently suitable for touring in Argyll and the Islands. It lies beside a quiet main road, the A816, six miles south of the main ferry terminal at Oban which crosses to Mull and Iona. The hotel is less than three hours drive from Glasgow and Edinburgh and is also charmingly accessible by rail. Knipoch is a luxury establishment with a country house atmosphere, which has been owned and run by the Craig family since 1981. Although parts of the building date back to 1592, the 17 bedrooms are modern and have all up to date facilities.

The food served in the restaurant varies according to what is freshly available. The wine list is comprehensive and includes modestly priced house wines. The hotel annually produces a small helpful brochure with advice on what can be done in the area; riding, fishing, golf, walking, places worth visiting, etc.

by Oban, Argyll PA34 4XG, Tel:(085 26) 251, Fax:(08526) 249

A mortified appetite is never a wise companion

Robert Louis Stevenson

One of Scotland's most remarkable hotels, Kinloch Castle, is situated on an island nature reserve of spectacular wildness and beauty. The hotel offers guests the opportunity to experience living history in the Edwardian castle rooms, whose character and contents have altered little since the turn of the century.

Kinloch Castle was built in 1901 as a sumptuous shooting lodge for Sir George Bullough, a wealthy Lancashire industrialist who used Rum as a sporting estate. No expense or extravagance was spared in either the building or furnishing of the castle, which was sold to the nation along with the island in 1957.

The castle is now owned by Scottish Natural Heritage and is run as a unique hotel with the majority of the original fittings and furnishings intact.

Guests are invited to step back in time to savour a luxurious Edwardian lifestyle. Highlights of an invariably memorable stay include the wonderful reception rooms, with their evocative period detail, and baths equipped with seven controls, ranging from wave, plunge and sitz to the startling jet.

Meals at Kinloch Castle are no less impressive, with breakfast

and dinner served at the original dining table from the Bulloughs' ocean-going yacht 'Rhouma'. After dinner drinks can be savoured whilst listening to the sounds of the orchestrion, a mechanical organ reputedly built for Queen Victoria.

There can be few better settings for a hotel of distinction than the Isle of Rum. A private sporting estate for many years, it is now owned and managed by Scottish Natural Heritage as a National Nature Reserve which the public are welcome to visit. The island is roughly diamond shaped and is about 8 miles in length and breadth. It is renowned for its wild flowers, birds, red deer, wild goats, Rum ponies and highland cattle, with nature trails laid out in the area around Loch Scresort and Kinloch Glen. Angling can also be arranged for sea trout through the Reserve Office.

Visitors to Rum and this outstanding hotel should make their way by car or train to Mallaig, from where the Small Isles Ferry service runs throughout the year. The journey to reach Kinloch Castle is matched in its magnificence only by the quality of the hotel itself and its magical setting. Visitors to one of the country's most sumptuous and unique retreats are inevitably entranced and vow to return, time and time again.

Isle of Rum PH43 4RR, Tel: (0687) 2037

This delightful old country house is set in 30 acres of secluded grounds on the shores of Loch Sunart and is strategically placed in some of the very best scenery in Scotland. The hotel faces south across the Loch to the remote and beautiful Mavern Hills.

The road passes behind the hotel and beyond the woods ensuring perfect peace, quiet and privacy.

The hotel is situated in Strontian which is a small and attractive village.

There are 10 comfortable rooms all with their own private bathroom or shower room and there is central heating throughout. The Blakeway family maintain very high standards and many personal touches are evident.

The food is of excellent quality and all home-cooked, taking full advantage of the very best of local foods. Many of the vegetables are grown organically by the Blakeways whose aim is to give a quality meal you will remember.

Kilcamb Lodge Hotel is perfectly situated for guests who wish to explore the surrounding area. A good road leads to Lochaline from where the ferry to Mull departs. A short trip of 15 minutes then makes a day trip to Mull easy and enjoyable. Mallaig is only 30 miles away and here you can take the ferry to the Isle of Skye.

Sailing trips on Loch Sunart can be arranged in the hotel's 37 foot yacht and fishing rods and picnic hampers are all available from the hotel.

A stroll along the shores of the Loch will reveal an area of outstanding natural beauty and this private shoreline is a haven for wildlife - Red Deer, Hawks, Eagles, Otters and Seals.

Strontian, Argyll PH36 4HY Tel: (0967) 2257.

The Kilfinan Hotel has been welcoming travellers since the 18th century. The spectacular Highland scenery on the eastern shores of Loch Fyne and the peaceful, unhurried lifestyle of the area make it a perfect year round retreat.

Owners Nicholas Wills, the Laird of Kilfinan, and his wife have extensively refurbished this old coaching inn to provide high quality accommodation, without losing any of its original character.

The hotel has 11 bedrooms, all centrally heated, with en suite bathroom, colour TV and direct dial telephone. Some have a magnificent view over St Finnan's cemetery.

All public rooms are beautifully finished, cosy and comfortable with blazing log fires.

Chef/Patron Rolf Mueller is a member of the Master Chefs of Great Britain. Trained in Switzerland, he brings an international touch to the best of local produce. Salmon, Trout, Venison, Pheasant and Wild Duck from Kilfinan Estate are often on the menu along with Scottish lamb, beef and dairy produce - giving a true taste of Scotland.

Good walking country begins at the hotel door. Short walks to Kilfinan Bay or long hikes on the hills - both provide rewarding wildlife sightings and spectacular views. Fishing of every variety is nearby, from Salmon and Trout on Kilfinan Burn to sea angling on Loch Fyne.

Discovering this remote Highland inn is a delightful experience.

Kilfinan, Nr Tighnabruaich, Argyll PA21 2EP, Tel: (070 082) 201, Fax: (070 082) 205

Loch Melfort Hotel

Loch Melfort Hotel is marvellously situated in thirty acres of Scottish magic with views of the islands of Shuna, Scarba and Jura. In addition, Arduaine Gardens and more than twenty other gardens are readily accessible from the hotel.

In the area, riding, fishing, golf at two local courses, scuba diving and sailing can be enjoyed, as well as much local walking, for which maps are available from the hotel. If you wish to venture further afield there are ferries to the islands of Islay or Jura or Ghiga.

All the 27 bedrooms in the hotel have modern facilities; those on the ground floor have a patio and those on the first floor have a balcony.

The Cedar Wing is joined to the Main House by a covered walkway.

Philip Lewis is the chef and proprietor and with his team specialises in home cooking, with seafood a speciality. The beef understandably comes from Aberdeen. Special Spring Breaks and Easter Breaks are available. Children under 12 can be accommodated in their parents' room at a reduced rate.

Arduaine, by Oban, Argyll PA34 4XG, Tel:(08522) 233, Fax:(08522) 214

The Lodge On The Loch

This delightful hotel is set in five acres of grounds on the edge of the broad, serene Loch Linnhe, at the foot of the beautiful and haunting Pass of Glencoe. The area, characterised by soaring mountains and bubbling brooks, is engulfed in legend, folklore and an intriguing and tragic history.

The hotel lies within easy range of some of the Highland's most famous sights - the mighty Ben Nevis dominates the northward view and lies just twelve miles away with Fort William nestled at its foot. Loch Ness lies a little further on and Oban, gateway to Mull and the Hebrides, is just an hour's drive away. Guests at the Lodge are granted 'Freedom of the Glen', which entitles them to use the facilities of two other hotels on Leven - Ballachulish and the Isles of Glencoe, including 'Dining around the Loch' and relaxing in the Isles' warm swimming pool.

The Lodge, formerly the country home of Sir John and Lady MacPherson, is enticingly furnished with gentle colours and soft woven fabrics. Wide bay windows offer views of the breathtaking scenery. The gracious Victorian cocktail bar serves an array of malts and real ales, while the Dining Room features a la carte and table d'hote menus offering 'Taste of Scotland' dishes, made only from fresh, wholesome ingredients, such as local salmon, trout, seafood and venison. Guests may also wish to try the Crofter's Lunches which are served at the bar, dining room and in the garden. A range of health and vegetarian foods is also available. The eighteen well-appointed bedrooms have individually controlled heating, colour television and a range of other facilities.

Onich, nr Fort William, Inverness-shire PH33 6RY, Tel: (08553) 237, Fax: (08553) 463

And now I am come,
with this lost love of mine,
To lead but one measure,
drink one cup of wine.

Marmion

The Machrie Hotel enjoys a superb position on the enchanting Isle of Islay, the most southerly island of the Hebrides. It is very peaceful, providing an ideal escape for those seeking a holiday in totally tranquil surroundings. Islay is famous for malt whiskies and the industry still thrives here although there are now only half a dozen distilleries left on the island. Visitors can spend an enjoyable day going around one of them. The Hotel is a marvelously relaxing place to stay. The proprietors are Murdo and Kathleen Macpherson. Mr Macpherson's grandfather was in the same line of business, so all guests can be sure they will be very comfortable indeed.

In the cocktail bar visitors have the chance of trying eighty different malt whiskies before enjoying a suberb dinner in the Byre restaurant, once the old byre of the farm, which concentrates on using local produce such as fish and game and serves sumptious shellfish. Conference facilities are also available at The Machrie.

The hotel has a large number of extremely comfortable bedrooms, with private bathroom, television, radio and tea and coffee making facilities and hairdryer.

For those who like to come and go as they please, 15 de lux self-contained cottage suites have been created, complimenting the hotel's facilities. Each suite is well appointed with independent central heating, full bathroom and shower, colour television and kitchen. Each cottage has been furnished to an exceptionally high standard.

The hotel is alongside the 18-hole golf courses and golf is free for those staying at the hotel. However, golf is not the only enjoyable sport on offer. There is also clay pigeon shooting, and a stretch of the river to try casting a fly for salmon or trout, which Mr Cassidy the chef will be only too pleased to cook. Windsurfing, tennis and riding are available nearby.

Port Ellen, Isle of Islay, Argyll PA42 7AN, Tel: (0496) 2310

Onich Hotel

Onich is situated between Ben Nevis and Glencoe and is ideal for touring or activity holidays. Onich Hotel prides itself on the enjoyment it can offer all the year round. In the immediate neighbourhood you can enjoy mountaineering, riding, golf and many other activities. The hotel is helpful in informing guests of what is available and is an excellent base for hill walking for which the area is famed. There is a spa bath and a solarium. The hotel faces south and has fine views across Loch Linnhe to Glencoe and the Ardnamurchan peninsula with landscaped gardens which extend to the lochside. Ski hire facilities are adjacent to the hotel and the Watersports Centre on the foreshore offers reduced rates to hotel guests.

All 27 bedrooms have private facilities and there are play areas, cots and high chairs available for children who are welcome. The hotel prides itself on its freshly prepared food. Autumn, winter and spring bargain breaks are available.

Onich, Inverness-shire PH33 6RY, Tel: (08553) 214/266, Fax: (08553) 484

Port Askaig Hotel

Port Askaig Hotel is a picturesque Highland Inn on the shores of the Sound of Islay. The sea laps on the rocky shores of the hotel grounds and the views across the Sound to the Paps of Jura, southward to Kintyre, or northwards to the Island of Mull, some 35 miles away, are truly magnificent. There was an Inn at Port Askaig 400 years ago and this is now incorporated in the hotel as the Public Bar. The rest of the building dates back to the 18th century. Although now adapted to provide a high standard of comfort with modern kitchens and equipment, great care has been taken to preserve the character and peace of a bygone age. The bedrooms are on the first floor and some have private bathrooms. All rooms are fully heated with colour TV, radio, electric blankets and tea/coffee making facilities. The varied menus offer a good selection of traditional fare, making use of fresh local produce. Coffee is served in the Residents Lounge or Snug Bar.

Car ferries from the mainland berth at Port Askaig daily. High above the village is Dunlossit Estate and the beautiful lochs of Ballygrant, Lossit and Allan. All are easily approached by road and are well stocked with excellent trout. There is an excellent natural Golf course, and to the birdwatcher, naturalist, photographer and artist the Isle of Islay is an endless joy

Isle of Islay, Argyll PA46 7RD, Tel: (049 684) 245, Fax: (049 684) 295

Skeabost House Hotel

The Skeabost hotel was originally built in 1870 as a hunting lodge at the north end of the Isle of Skye. It stands in its untarnished Victorian splendour amid 12 acres of secluded woodlands and gardens, looking out across the serene Loch Snizort. It is a comfortable, relaxing hotel, with a beckoning log fire in the main lounge. There are three lounges, as well as a billiard room and a cocktail bar and the young staff are eager to make their guests feel at home. There are twenty-one rooms and sixteen of these include private en suite bathrooms.

In a picturesque clearing in the garden, there is the 'Garden House' and this contains six more bedrooms, three with en suite bathrooms. The attractive restaurant specialises in local dishes such as such as fresh salmon, venison and Skye lamb. Guests are offered a range of activities during the day. The hotel owns an eight mile tract of the River Snizort for fishing and when in flood this is teaming with sea trout and salmon; they also have a boat for trout fishing at Storr Lochs and during the summer organise fishing trips to the Ascrib Islands in a 31-foot sea angler. There is also an attractive nine-hole golf course in the grounds, while pony trekking expeditions can also be arranged by the hotel. The beautiful Skye terrain is ideal for walks, while the more adventurous may wish to try their hand at climbing the Cuillins.

Skeabost Bridge, Isle of Skye IV51 9NP, Tel: (047) 032 202, Fax: (047) 032 454

The recently opened Strongarbh House was built in 1865 and it retains much of the Victorian character and appearance of the original building. This fine-looking house is beautifully situated in its own extensive gardens overlooking Tobermory Bay and is sumptuously furnished and spacious throughout, with four rooms, all with private bathrooms, colour television and other facilities. The comfortable lounge is open all day, a place to relax with a drink from the house's fine collection.

Strongarbh's Seafood Restaurant and Grill uses a variety of local produce, such as jumbo prawns, clams, mussels and white fish from local boats, locally caught salmon and venison, and even vegetables from the hotel garden. The Charcoal Grill gives further range to the menu with mouthwatering dishes such as sauteed Mull Scallops and char-grilled Lamb with Rosemary.

The house is ideally placed to explore the delightful island of Mull - its stunning landscapes populated by roaming herds of deer in the glens and darting otters in the streams. Visitors can indulge in a host of activities - golf, fishing, bird-watching and visit local attractions such as Fingal's Cave, Duart and Torosay Castle and Mull's Little Railway, or, depending on the time of year, enjoy events such as the Car Rally and the Music Festival. Ferry trips are also available to the nearby islands of Staffa and Iona. Strongarbh offers several packages to ensure guests make the most of their stay on the island.

Tobermory, Isle of Mull PA75 6PR, Tel: (0688) 2328, Fax: (0688) 2142

Situated right on the shores of Loch Awe, the longest freshwater loch in Scotland, Taychreggan is steeped in history - the site itself dates back over 300 years. The old stone house, which is more than 100 years old, was originally a cattle drovers Inn, where the drovers would spend the night before swimming their cattle across the loch on their way to the Falkirk Tryst. Sympathetic building around the original house has enabled Taychreggan to become a superb hotel with 25 acres of both cultivated and wild private grounds.

Most of Taychreggan's 15 bedrooms, including the wonderful four-poster suite, overlook the beautiful loch and all have private facilities. Guests can also relax in the main residents' lounge, or there is a comfortable TV lounge if preferred. The cobbled courtyard makes a pleasant place to enjoy a cool drink.

A varied menu of freshly prepared and well-presented cuisine is available in the well laid out restaurant. Taychreggfan's chef, Hugh Cocker, offers only the finest food available, much of which is produced or caught locally. Even the cheeseboard has a definite Scottish theme to it. Meals are complemented by a comprehensive wine list, including some half bottles, and there is an extensive range of malts. The bar is also open at lunch time (non residents are welcome) serving a range of fresh and interesting bar snacks.

Taychreggan is perfectly situated for guests to make the most of a variety of activities. Walkers, ramblers and wildlife enthusiasts can enjoy the numerous forest trails and the angler is spoilt for choice as a number of nearby lochs and rivers are famed for their excellent trout and salmon sport.

Well-behaved dogs are welcome at Taychreggan given advance notice. There is also the opportunity to arrive in real style - by sea plane!

Kilchrenan, By Taynuilt, Argyll PA35 1HQ, Tel: (08663) 211, Fax: (08663) 244

Tiroran House

Mull is an island in the Inner Hebrides, seven miles west of Oban and separated from the mainland by the firth of Lorne and the Sound of Mull. Tobermory is its main town. Forty minutes drive away from the ferry terminal at Craignure, (or Fishnish) travelling west towards the Isle of Iona you will come, via the A849 and the B8035, to Tiroran.

Tiroran House itself, is a remote and charming country house and well worth the travelling and the search. It is set in 15 acres of beautiful woodland gardens, on the shores of Loch Scridain, with rhododendrons and many flowering shrubs. Fantails, duck, geese, golden pheasants are everwhere.

Tiroran House is run more as a family home than as an hotel. The resident proprietors, Robin and Sue Blockley, converted their sporting lodge back in 1977 and it is their particular pride that guests return again and again to enjoy their hospitality.

The house is furnished with antiques and has eight double bedrooms and one single and all have private facilities. The central heating throughout the hotel can be supplemented by homely log fires in the evenings. Meals are a special occasion at Tiroran House and much of the food is local. The beef and lamb are from the estate and venison, fish and seafood are all gathered from the island. Drinks are served in the drawing room and the wines are carefully chosen. Both the bread and gravadlax are home made.

There is much to be explored on Mull; Tobermory, Torosay Castle with its Italian terraced gardens and Duart Castle, the home of the Chief of the Clan Maclean. There is safe swimming from a choice of sandy beaches. There is the famed Mull Little Theatre and the Old Byre Museum. There is much to discover archaeologically. Fishing and stalking can be organised in season.

Packed lunches can be arranged for hotel guests if they are required. Consult Wing Commander or Mrs Blockley for details.

They will be happy to tell you also about the landing craft which plies half hourly to Iona and about Fingal's Cave. Be ready for relaxation and peace if you travel and stay at Tiroran. There is no television.

Tiroran, Isle of Mull, Argyll PA69 6ES, Tel: (068 15) 232, Fax: (068 15) 232

The Tobermory Hotel

Tobermory, the capital of Mull, is a busy seaside fishing town with many interesting shops.

The family-run Tobermory Hotel was once a row of fishermen's cottages and is set on the waterfront. The hotel has 17 bedrooms, most with a view of the Bay and many have private facilities. There are Superior Rooms which are larger and of a higher standard than others. One smaller, single, Superior Room on the ground floor could be used for the disabled or elderly.

There are two lounges and an attractive dining room with views towards the Bay. The menu offers such tempting products as wild salmon, venison and Scottish beef and lamb. A selection of vegetarian dishes is always available and special diets can be catered for if the hotel is notified in advance. There is a good range of wines and a wide selection of single malt whiskies.

On Mull one can walk, study wildlife, pony trek, fish, play golf or go to the theatre.

53 Main Street, Tobermory, Isle of Mull PA75 6NT Tel: (0688) 2091, Fax: (0688) 2140

Uig Hotel

This delightful old coaching inn stands in three acres of grounds on a hillside overlooking Uig Bay on the mystical Isle of Skye.

Established in 1946, the hotel is today pleasantly furnished with comfortable lounges and a glass-fronted sunlounge which boasts a breathtaking view of the bay. Grace Graham is responsible for the tasteful decor which includes watercolours and etchings by well known artists. Her son, David Taylor, is responsible for the day to day running of the hotel. Coal and wood fires give a warm welcome.

All bedrooms have private facilities and are equipped with direct dial telephones, T V and tea/coffee making facilities. Sohhraig House, a converted steading, stands just above the hotel in the grounds. There are six bedrooms furnished and equipped to a very high standard. The view is particularly attractive and many returning guests request to stay here.

The hotel has a full licence and is open for morning coffee, light lunches and afternoon tea. Tables for dinner should be reserved to avoid disappointment.

The hotel organises pony trekking, and Uig is an ideal centre from which to explore an island remaining largely unspoilt. The lighthouse keepers are often happy to show visitors around and with spectacular scenery and rare wildlife there is much to see.

The Museum of Island Life, the Clan Donald Centre and Dunvegan Castle all offer an insight into Skye's rich history. Portree, the small central town, has a heated indoor swimming pool, squash court and tennis court. There is a nine hole golf course at Sconcer.

With the continually improving road network Skye is a comfortable days drive from Glasgow and Edinburgh and just half a day from Inverness.

Uig, Isle of Skye, Highland IV51 9YE, Tel: (047042) 205, Fax: (047042) 308

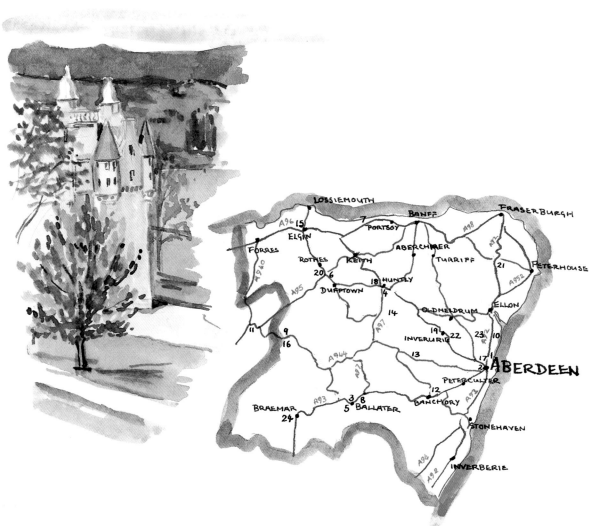

1 Aberdeen Marriott Hotel	13 Kildrummy Castle
2 Ardoe House	14 Leslie Castle
3 Balgonie Country House	15 Mansion House
4 Castle Hotel	16 Minmore House
5 Craigendarroch Hotel	17 New Marcliff
6 Craigellachie Hotel	18 Old Manse of Marnoch
7 Cullen Bay Hotel	19 Pittodrie House
8 Darroch Learg Hotel	20 Rothes Glen Hotel
9 Delnashaugh Inn	21 Saplinbrae House Hotel
10 Foveran House Hotel	22 Thainstone House Hotel
11 Garth Hotel	23 Udny Arms Hotel
12 Invery House	24 Invercauln Arms

The Grampian region captures the whole essence of Scotland in breathtaking vistas and spectacular scenery. The dense pine forest that once covered this north eastern shoulder of Scotland may have given way over the centuries to the farmer's plough, but the soaring granite peaks of the Grampian mountain range bear testimony to more turbulent times. A legacy carved in the very rocks of the region as pagan man left his mark in the shape of standing stones, stone circles and hill forts. Here too, can be traced the development of the Christian faith in Scotland, grand cathedrals reflecting the wealth of the Scottish church and the depth of faith.

Amidst spectacular scenery of river, loch and glen the Grampians also offer a unique malt whisky trail, a castle trail and much besides.

Aberdeen, the Flower of Scotland, is the region's principal conurbation. Throughout the seasons the Grampians and Highlands are ablaze with colour and Aberdeen is no exception. Floral displays are commonplace from town to town, delighting the many visitors to the area. This is particularly so in Moray where floral sculptures, herb gardens, and walled gardens are a feature of almost every town and village. The more formal Great Garden of Pitmedden, Crathes Castle, a magnificent walled garden of historic roses at Drum Castle and the water gardens at Kildrummy are not to be missed. This wonderful array of floral extravagance is capitalised in style in Aberdeen, ten times the winner of 'Beautiful Britain in Bloom'.

The Grampian Highlands are also blessed with some spectacular houses and castles of interest. Quiet country roads will almost invariably lead to a fascinating monument to the area's past. Some are mysterious, haunting ruins, while others have been restored. Some are hotels where the comforts of modern living may be enjoyed in the style and elegance of a bygone era. You may see Slains Castle, allegedly the inspiration for Bram Stoker's Dracula novel, or Delgate, the oldest inhabited castle in Scotland. Braemar Castle and Brodie adorned with spectacular daffodils in spring are others of note. The Castle Trail marks nine of the most outstanding properties and needless to say these tend to be the most popular. However the National Trust of Scotland has also created some woodland trails and picnic areas en route, so crowds never seem to be a problem.

When you've taken in the Castle Trail, a light refreshment or two may well be in order and there are plenty of watering holes from which to choose. If you are a whisky lover then this is the place for you as more than half of Scotland's whisky distilleries are located in the Grampian Highlands, from Fettercairn in the south to Forres in the north west. Not all distilleries welcome visitors but a good number do. Guides are on hand to explain the tricks of the trade which have been passed down through many generations. They will explain how pure water from the tumbling rivers and springs continues to give each malt its own distinctive flavour. Although the fundamental process and ingredients are similar, each whisky has its own individuality and fascinating history. At Cardhu the story of illicit distillery is told and Glenfiddich, Glendonach, Strathisla and Glenlivet all have an original tale to tell. The Malt Whisky Trail, a unique journey of unparalleled delight will take you through the thick of this bonny trade to the celebrated names of Cardhu, Glenfiddich, Glen Grant, Glenfarclas, the Glenlivet, Strathisla and Tamnavillin.

As so often in Scotland not only has the natural heritage been lovingly preserved for all to see with museums giving a fascinating insight into times gone by, but nature itself remains essentially unspoilt with abundant wildlife in the rugged mountains, misty glens and crystal clear rivers that are home to herds of red deer, thriving bird communities, and not least of all the trout and salmon.

Many have fallen for this beautiful area and Queen Victoria was one such enthusiast. Balmoral Castle was designed and built for the Queen and it remains a favoured holiday retreat for the Royal Family. Parts of the house and grounds are open in May, June and July and the Victorian Trail marks some of the spots particularly cherished by the monarch. The Braemar gathering, traditionally held on the first Saturday in September, is usually attended by the Royal Family and is a splendid day out steeped in Highland tradition.

Finally, there is the Coastal Trail. Here you find cliff tops which play host to masses of seabirds such as puffins, kittiwakes and guillemots, while Arctic terns and eider ducks are to be found in sand dunes of immense proportions. Johnshaven, Gourdon and Cruden Bay are but three charming villages to explore in a world far removed from 20th century hustle and bustle. There are others, some in splendid isolation at the foot of fortress cliffs, best discovered not named.

Golfers may set their sights on better known links than those of Grampian but this would be a mistake. There are over fifty courses in the area and they offer huge variety in the way of challenge. What is more they are rarely too busy to make the casual visitor feel anything other than an honoured guest. Cruden Bay and Royal Aberdeen are acknowledged as championship courses, while Braemar boasts the highest 18 holes in Britain.

The Grampian region has activities and trails to cater for all ages and interest groups, and with some of the finest watering holes in Scotland located here, we can safely say whatever your taste you'll also find it catered for amongst the splendid flora and fauna. Enjoy.

Inspiring, bold John Barley corn,
What dangers that canst make us scorn!

Burns

Aberdeen Marriott

The Aberdeen Marriott is conveniently located close to Aberdeen airport and is a short distance by car from the City of Aberdeen. The hotel makes an excellent base from which to explore the many attractions of the Grampian Mountains, the dramatic Aberdeenshire coastline and the 'Granite City' itself.

All 134 spacious bedrooms feature a lounge area, remote control colour TV with satellite and video channels, trouser press, hairdryer, tea/coffee making facilities and direct-dial telephone.

Peppers Restaurant is locally renowned for its fine cuisine and offers a superb a la carte menu, including Scottish speciality dishes. Relax before, or after, your meal with a leisurely 'dram' in the bar.

The Aberdeen Marriott hotel offers excellent, fully-equipped conference and banqueting facilities which can accommodate everything from a small boardroom style meeting to a dinner-dance or banquet for up to 350 guests.

After a busy day take time to relax in the delightful Leisure Area which features a pool, whirlpool, fitness equipment, sauna and solaria.

Riverview Drive, Fairburn, Dyce, Aberdeenshire AB2 0AZ, Tel: (0224) 770011, Fax: (0224) 772977/722347

Ardoe House

The magnificent Ardoe House stands, enclosed by trees and rich foliage, amid the commanding heights overlooking the river Dee and some spectacular countryside. Built in 1878, Ardoe is moulded in Scottish Baronial style, with lofty turrets and inscriptions of heraldry and is similar to Balmoral House, the Royal retreat, which lies about forty miles further up the Dee. With Aberdeen just four miles away and a number of golf courses nearby and some stunning scenery, the house is ideally placed whether visitors are here for business or for pleasure.

The house is no less spectacular inside, with its huge and decorative Grand Hall that has pillars and stained glass windows on the stairway. The other public rooms are similarly impressive, with their wonderful carved wood panelling and magnificent fireplaces. There are also a number of newer parts to the house, such as the Garden Room, an ideal venue for a small party or a private lunch; the elegant Ogston Suite, which is one of the most sought after venues in the area and 'Soapies', a warm and friendly family room next to the Laird's Bar. The Restaurant also has elegance and atmosphere. Here, a delicious range of dishes are served using a wide selection of fresh local ingredients. Vegetarians are imaginatively catered for and the house takes great pride in its wine list.

A word of advice - when it's in season don't leave without trying the fresh salmon!

South Deeside Road, Blairs, Aberdeen AB1 5YP, Tel: (0224) 867355, Fax: (0224) 861283

Balgonie Country House

Built in the early 1900's, Balgonie House lies on the outskirts of the village of Ballater, in the heart of one of the most beautiful and unspoilt areas of Scotland. Unsurpassed for privacy, with no passing traffic, this Edwardian style Country House is a haven for those who enjoy peace and tranquillity in a traditional setting.

With its four acres of mature gardens, Balgonie commands truly superb views overlooking Ballater Golf Course towards the hills of Glen Muick beyond.

The village of Ballater, a five minute walk away, is a thriving community, many of its shops sporting Royal Warranty shields as suppliers to the Queen. There is much to appeal to visitors. Set on the banks of the River Dee, the village makes an ideal centre for golf, hill-walking, sight-seeing and touring, the Malt Whisky Trail and Castle Trail both within easy reach.

Balgonie has nine bedrooms, each named after a fishing pool on the river Dee. The rooms are individually decorated and furnished, equipped with private bathroom, colour TV and direct dial telephone.

The dining room provides excellent Scottish cuisine using only the best of local produce. Fresh salmon from the River Dee, marvellous local game, traditionally high-quality Aberdeen Angus beef and excellent seafood fresh from the East Coast are complemented by a carefully selected wine list. The menus are balanced and interesting; a Fan of Chilled Melon and Kiwi Fruit, Fillet of Turbot topped with a Basil Crust, Roast Local Wood Pigeon, Hot Grand Marnier Souffle. Friendly staff offer attentive, yet unobtrusive service.

Balgonie House is personally supervised by John and Priscilla Finnie, the resident proprietors, whose aim is to make your stay, however long or short, both enjoyable and memorable.

Braemar Place, Ballater, Royal Deeside AB35 5RQ, Tel: (03397) 55482, Fax: (03397) 55482

The Castle Hotel

The Castle Hotel is a magnificent 18th century stone building, standing in its own grounds above the ruins of Huntly Castle, on the banks of the river Deveron. Sandstone as it was originally known was built as a family home to the Dukes of Gordon

Run by a keen hotel family, the Castle Hotel has recently been refurbished providing good comfortable accommodation with en suite facilities. Good traditional food using local fresh produce is served in our spacious Dining Room, complemented by a selection form the well stocked wine cellar.

Only 40 minutes drive away from the Royal Aberdeen and Cruden Bay Golf courses (listed in the U.K. top 50 courses) the hotel ideally situated for your golfing holiday. Closer to home the Royal Tarlour, Duff House Royal and Elgin courses can be found. Huntly's own attractive and well laid out 18 hole course, Cooper Park, lies at the bottom of the hotel's drive adjacent to the river Deveron.

The town lies in Scotland's famous Castle Country and provides an abundance of leisure and sporting activities. Not to be missed are the many famous distilleries which make up the Whisky Trail.

The hotel's aim is to make your stay an enjoyable and memorable one. Situated on the main A96 between Aberdeen (45 minutes away) and Inverness the hotel is easily reached by road, rail and air.

Huntly, Aberdeenshire AB54 4SH, Tel: (0466) 792696), Fax: (0466 792641)

Craigendarroch Hotel

The Craigendarroch Hotel is situated on the slopes of Craigendarroch Hill above the village of Ballater and a few miles down river from Balmoral. The city of Aberdeen is just over 40 miles away.

Although converted into a luxurious hotel, all the charm of an old country home has been retained. Old fashioned standards of service are combined with the very latest in leisure facilities.

Craigendarroch's bedrooms are individually and elegantly furnished, the style is unashamedly luxurious. Room service is available around the clock and each room features telephone, radio, remote control television, hairdryer, tea/coffee making facilities and trouser press.

Dining at one of the three excellent restaurants is a delight. The Oaks Restaurant serves cuisine modern, together with traditional Scottish dishes using only the finest, fresh local produce. The country house splendour is enhanced by the fine china, silver and crystal on every table.

The Lochnagar Restaurant offers marvellous local game and superb seafood. Alternatively, the elegant Cafe Jardin offers everything from delicious light snacks to substantial three course meals.

The adjoining Country Club provides full sport and leisure facilities. There are two indoor pools, two squash courts, a sauna, steam room, trimnasium, solarium and luxurious health and beauty salon.

Braemar Road, Ballater, Royal Deeside AB35 5XA, Tel: (03397) 55858, Fax: (03397) 55447

One of the most beautiful villages in Moray, Craigellachie, lies at the confluence of the Fiddich and Spey rivers in a picturesque setting equal only to the sumptuous and elegant Victorian hotel itself. Only one hour's drive from the airports of Aberdeen and Inverness, the Craigellachie is a haven of highland hospitality set in a spectacular countryside - unspoilt, wild and beautiful and ideal for all kinds of modern sporting activities.

According to the season you can play tennis, ski, ride horseback or mountain bike along forest and mountain trails and fish for salmon or brown trout.

And then there's the golf. The Craigellachie offers a unique opportunity to enjoy a holiday in the land where golf was born, with a choice of links, moor or parkland courses all within a short drive of the hotel. whatever your handicap, there's a course her to challenge your skill. We can arrange golf club hire and private tuition by professionals at selected clubs.

After sampling the variety of outdoor pursuits or one of the many golf courses in this beautiful part of Scotland, it's always a pleasure to return to the Craigellachie and sit beside the glowing embers of a real log fire in the hall or one of the comfortable lounges. An equally warm welcome will await you in the Quaich cocktail bar and when it's time to dine, the Ben Aigan Restaurant offers a tempting menu in the hearty tradition of the finest Scottish cuisine. Here, you can savour the delights of our culinary excellence (which, according to season, feature prime local produce from sea and countryside) and then linger over coffee in the drawing room before retiring to the comfort and luxury of one of 30 splendidly appointed bedrooms. Each has its own en suite bath/shower, direct-dial telephone, radio remote-control colour television and special hospitality features. And for your further enjoyment you can make use of our library, billiards room, exercise room, sauna, solarium and rod room.

Here, at the Craigellachie, all the amenities of an international class hotel have been tastefully incorporated to retain all the original charm of a delightful Scottish country house.

Craigellachie, Speyside, Banffshire AB38 9SR, Tel: (07213) 233, Fax: (07213) 244

Cullen Bay

Set in its own grounds, the Cullen Bay Hotel has magnificent views of Cullen Bay itself, with its long sweep of white sand and Cullen Golf Course.

Within easy reach are numerous other golf courses and there are opportunities for bowling, fishing, pony trekking, cycling and bird watching. Other attractions close by include the world's only Malt Whisky Trail, Scotland's Fishing Heritage Trail and the Castle Trail, taking in Fyvie, Cawdor and Brodie. There are many gardens and pretty villages to explore as well as coastal and woodland walks and places of interest such as Baxters of Speyside.

All 14 bedrooms have been upgraded and refurbished and now have en suite bathrooms with power showers, individually controlled central heating, remote control colour television, radio, direct-dial telephone and tea and coffee making facilities.

The hotel's other facilities include the Cullen Bay Restaurant overlooking the bay, the newly refurbished Verandah Restaurant and Bar with garden patio in the summer, a Lounge with a log fire and garden with a children's play area. For conferences, dinner dances or weddings the hotel can cater for up to 150 guests in the Farskane Function Suite.

At the Cullen Bay you will enjoy good food using local produce and can choose from an informal bar meal or high tea to a three course dinner from the a la carte menu. All this, amidst a friendly atmosphere, adds up to an unforgettable stay

Cullen, Buckie, Banffshire AB56 2XA, Tel: (0542) 40432, Fax: (0542) 40900

Darroch Learg Hotel

Built in 1888 as a country residence on fashionable Royal Deeside, this family owned hotel stands in four acres of wooded grounds on the side of the Craigendarroch, the rocky hill which dominates Ballater.

From this fine vantage point there are panoramic views over the golf course, River Dee and Balmoral Estate to the Grampian Hills.

Formerly a shooting lodge, the house was converted into a hotel fifty years ago. The Darroch Learg has 15 bedrooms. A further five bedrooms are to be found in Oakhall, a second mansion standing adjacent to Darroch Learg. Both buildings are built in traditional local pink and grey granite and are listed for their architectural features.

The polished natural pine and good quality furniture assure guests of the high standards throughout the hotel. There are open log fires in the drawing room and adjoining smoking room, where pre-dinner drinks can be enjoyed in a relaxed atmosphere of elegance.

The dining room and spacious conservatory allow diners to enjoy the outlook south towards the hills of Glen Muick. In the evening, tables are individually lit and enhanced by fine crockery, cutlery and linen. The dinner menu changes daily and is created using the best, fresh ingredients; Aberdeen Angus beef, Scottish lamb, game from the surrounding estates, fresh fish and seafood and free-range eggs from local farms. Fine Scottish cheeses complete the menu.

A great deal of care and imagination goes into the preparation of the food which is best described as modern, and in the Scottish style.

Bedrooms are individually decorated and furnished to give each its own character, All rooms have en suite bathrooms with bath/shower and each is equipped with colour TV, direct-dial telephone, trouser press, hair drier, hospitality tray and other extras.

Darroch Learg is a delightful centre for an active holiday, for motoring or just relaxing. The area is full of places of interest and justly famous for its castles and its Highland Games.

At the end of he day, the hotel will provide a rod box for fishers, a drying room, log fires on a cold day, comfortable rooms and good food.

Braemar Road, Ballater, Aberdeenshire AB35 5UX, Tel:(03397) 55443, Fax: (03397) 55443

The Delnashaugh Inn

The Delnashaugh Inn enjoys a beautiful setting in the heart of the Highlands. Formerly the Drovers Inn, it has been refurbished by the proprietors David and Marion Ogden and yet it has lost none of its original charm. The hotel provides 9 bedrooms, all en suite with colour television and tea & coffee making facilities. The restaurant boasts a different dinner menu every night and all meals are created using local fresh produce.

The bar also stocks many local malts as here, the visitor is in the heart of one of Scotland's oldest industries. The Whisky Trail is open between April and October for those wanting to learn more about the making of Whisky and the opportunity is there to take a 'dram'.

As the Delnashaugh is part of the Ballindalloch estate, there are plenty of opportunities for sportsmen in the area. The estate provides sea trout and salmon fishing on the Avon and shooting for 8 guns can be arranged, as can roe buck stalking.

For the Winter visitor, Aviemore and Tominton are within easy reach for ski-ing.

Grantown-on-Spey, Elgin and Boat-of-Garten all have golf courses and with the beautiful walks around the area there really is something for everyone.

The area itself is peaceful and yet Inverness and Nairn are not too far away and access to the hotel is reasonably easy. This is a beautiful part of Scotland where visitors are guaranteed the peace and quiet that many of us are so eager for.

Ballindalloch, Banffshire AB37 9AS, Tel:(0807) 500255

The well that once watered the garrison of the medieval Foveran Castle still refreshes the guests of this now converted Georgian Mansion. Its name is derived from the Gaelic 'Fobhar', meaning 'Well', and the ancient traditions are continued in this historic house. The ancient castle is long gone, lost to the ravages of war and time, but the stones from its legendary Turin Tower were used in the foundations of the present house. During the past 250 years the House and surrounding estate have been home to a number of prosperous merchants, all have left their mark, leaving a long tradition to enhance this unique Scottish house.

Scotland has a long history of hospitality and Foveran is no exception. Open fires add warmth and a general feeling of welcome and well being. The hotel has many fascinating aspects, not least of which is the McBey Lounge with its permanent exhibition of etchings by the local, and now world famous, artist, James McBey. Its relaxed atmosphere is the perfect place to enjoy a pre-dinner drink, or a comforting nightcap.

The restaurant itself is the setting for the delicious preparations of the chef, who applies his long experience to mouth-watering traditional dishes, such as prime Aberdeen Angus beef, succulent game, seafood and crisp vegetables, all made with the choicest of local ingredients to ensure a full, fresh flavour.

The leisure facilities available in Scotland as a whole are quite astonishing, and the Foveran itself is no exception. For the fisherman it is ideal, being less than five minutes drive from the river Ythan, recognised as some of the finest trout and salmon fishing in the country. This stunning body of water also provides the opportunity for a variety of water sports; windsurfing and sailing in particular are popular. Golf is almost a way of life here and there are many local courses to choose from for the serious sportsman. Of course the scenery of Scotland is renowned throughout the world and there is no better way to explore than walking, the Sands of Forvie Nature Reserve - a paradise for walkers and naturalists alike - are nearby. Without even leaving the grounds of the hotel you can try your hand at clay pigeon shooting, with expert tuition available, and if the urge for the more demanding challenge of game shooting and stalking begins to grow, the hotel can easily arrange it a little further afield. Most of all for those interested in the country's heritage, this is an ideal base from which to explore the famous Whisky, Fishing and Castle Trails.

At the end of a long day there can be nothing better than slipping into one of the deliciously comfortable beds in one the individually furnished rooms. All, naturally, have private facilities.

There can be no doubt that the tradition and hospitality that form the backbone of Scotland and Foveran House will not fail to please.

Newburgh, Aberdeenshire AB4 0AP, Tel: (035 86) 89398, Fax: (035 86) 89398 ext. 20

The Garth Hotel

The Garth Hotel is set amongst four acres of landscaped gardens with a picturesque location overlooking the historic square of Grantown-on-Spey in the heart of the Scottish Highlands.

Whilst you are offered olde worlde charm, your hosts ensure you enjoy every modern comfort and convenience. The Scottish Tourist Board's four crowns dates back to the seventeenth century, so they have something to be very proud of.

The bedrooms are all individually furnished in a tasteful manner and are equipped with en suite bathrooms, telephone, colour television and tea and coffee making facilities.

The warm and friendly atmosphere of The Garth extends to the dinning room where you can sample 'Taste of Scotland' dishes, enjoying fresh local produce from the hills and glens of the Highlands which include salmon, trout, venison and game. The wine list is imaginative, complementing the cuisine.

Visitors can enjoy the splendid gardens and look out over Grantown-on-Spey which provides an unrivalled centre for relaxation or excursions to every part of the Central Highlands. It is within easy reach of the West Coast, Romantic Skye, the world renowned Malt Whisky Trail, the busy shops of Inverness, Aviemore, Loch Ness and much more.

With the Garth Hotel open all year round it is ideal for the skier and winter sports enthusiast. Whatever your reason for staying here you will be well looked after in the intimacy of this historic hotel.

The Square, Grantown On Spey, Moray PH26 3HN, Tel: (0479) 2836, Fax: (0479) 2116

Invery House

Invery House is a country house hotel of great charm and character. It is a Georgian mansion set on the west bank of the river Feugh in 40 acres of magnificent grounds which include a croquet lawn and walled garden. Although Invery House has had many owners it still retains a great many of its original architectural features and character.

The well known writer Sir Walter Scott visited Invery House frequently during the early Eighteen Hundreds and it is after the famous visitor's novels the bedrooms are named; Marmion, Lady of the Lake, Ivanhoe and the Red Gauntlet to name just a few.

The culinary skills at Invery House are certainly not to be missed. Here you can sample Scottish Country House cuisine enjoying Scotland's finest fish, meat and game. The wine cellar boasts over 400 international wines, catering for all tastes. After dinner drinks can be savoured in the warm atmosphere of the drawing room

If you require a business meeting or discreet dinner party, Invery has the answer in its Garden Room which has excellent facilities and is decorated in style, as the rest of the house.

For those of you who enjoy fishing, there is no better place for you to stay. Invery House has fishing rights on several beats of the River Dee.

Pheasant and grouse shoots and deer stalking can all be arranged.

In such wonderful surroundings you can enjoy anything from walking and golf to visiting historical monuments or just taking in the peace and solitude this exceptional hotel has to offer.

Bridge of Feugh, Banchory, Royal Deeside AB31 3NJ, Tel:(033 02) 4782, Fax:(033 02) 4712

The Invercauld Arms

There was an Inn at Braemar long before the Jacobite Standard was raised on the mound where the hotel now stands. It was in the nineteenth century, though, when the young Queen Victoria and her Prince Albert discovered the Highlands and the area became famous as `Royal Deeside', that this fine Victorian mansion was built. Recent refurbishment has detracted not one ounce of its original charm.

Each of the elegant 68 bedrooms is brightly decorated and furnished to the highest standard, with bath and shower, tea/coffee making facilities, colour television, direct dial telephone and hairdryer.

Whisky is very much the theme in the cocktail bar, making it an ideal setting for entertaining or for that longed for pre-dinner drink. The Public Bar has a wide range of beers and is open seven nights a week and from lunchtime at weekends.

The Castleview Restaurant serves the best of local produce, and offers both traditional Scottish fayre and international cuisine.

All around are magnificent pine-clad hills and lush farmland. The River Dee winds it way down from the Cairngorms, and salmon leap up the rapids at Banchory. Glenshee, a 15 minute drive from the hotel, rivals traditional Continental skiing resorts. There is an 18-hole golf course in Braemar, and hill walking, pony trekking and even a hang-gliding school nearby.

Braemar, Aberdeenshire AB35 3YR, Tel:03397 41605, Fax: 03397 41428

Set in the heart of Donside amidst acres of planted gardens specialising in rare shrubs, specimen trees and Alpine plants, and overlooking the ruins of the original 13th century castle, Kildrummy Castle Hotel offers a rare opportunity to relax and enjoy the style and elegance of a bygone era combined with the comforts and service of a first class hotel.

At Kildrummy history is always to hand and with over 70 castles to visit in the Grampian region this is rightly called 'Castle Country'. Within 30 minutes drive can be found the unique Scotch Whisky Trail. The Lonach Highland games in Strathdon are held on the last Saturday in August, followed by the Braemar Gathering during the first week in September.

Built in 1900, the hotel itself is a grand castellated country house. Inside, two carved lions guard the ornate staircase leading to the 17 bedrooms. Charming attic rooms have sloping ceilings. All bedrooms are fitted with television, radio, tea-maker, telephone, trouser press, hairdryer and have a private bathroom.

The long time owner, Thomas Hanna, strongly motivates his staff who are outgoing and friendly.

The restaurant enjoys an excellent reputation for the standard of its food and service. Both table d'hote and a la carte menus specialise in the prime beef, game and fish to be found in Aberdeenshire.

Located off the A97 Huntly to Ballater road, 35 miles west of Aberdeen, Kildrummy Castle offers the ideal location from which to explore Donside, Royal Deeside, Aberdeen, Inverness and the Spey valley.

Those keen on sport will find much to offer with a choice of over 20 golf courses within 1 hours drive, trout and salmon fishing on a 3 mile private stretch of the River Don, clay pigeon shooting by arrangement, pony-trekking and horse-riding, and the Lecht ski slopes just 30 minutes away.

Kildrummy, By Alford, Aberdeenshire A33 8RA, Tel: (09755) 71288, Fax: (09755) 71345

Wee Willie Winkie rins through the town,
Up stairs and down stairs in his night gown,
Tirling at the window, crying at the lock,
Are the weans in their bed, for it's now ten o'clock

In the fertile valley of the Gadie Burn, 30 miles north west of the City of Aberdeen and at the west end of the Bennachie Range, stand the 17th century turrets of Leslie Castle. The original seat of Clan Leslie and the caput of the Barony of Leslie, the castle is the third fortified building on the site since 1070. The present Baron and Baroness, David and Leslie Leslie, are also the owners and hosts.

Accommodation available includes two four-poster bedrooms, one double bedroom and one twin bedroom, all en suite with colour television, telephone, trouser press, alarm clock/radio, courtesy tray facilities, fresh fruit and flowers. Furnished in the Jacobean style, all the rooms are comfortable, spacious and afford fine views of the surrounding countryside. Special rates are available for children sharing a room with parents.

The Baroness personally prepares splendid Scottish and International cuisine. Local produce features prominently and specialities include, according to season, smoked and fresh fish, game, lamb and Aberdeenshire beef, all served with fresh vegetables. A wide selection of wines, beers and spirits are on offer.

Many sporting activities can be incorporated into a holiday or short break at Leslie Castle, yet the ultimate attraction is the building itself. The Baronial Hall with its timber beamed ceiling, open fireplace and stone flagged floor creates a magnificent atmosphere to be relished by up to 24 guests and the Withdrawing Room is a perfect place to relax after dinner. A more private atmosphere in which to enjoy a meal is to be found in the barrel vaulted Kitchen Dining Room.

Ten years ago Leslie Castle was a roofless ruin. Painstakingly restored it is now no less than a fairy-tale castle. A magical transformation indeed!

Leslie, By Insch, Aberdeenshire AB52 6NX, Tel: (0464) 20869, Fax: (0464) 21076

Already firmly established as the leading hotel in Elgin, this 19th century mansion has been newly refurbished and extended to include a quite remarkable range of indoor leisure facilities.

The surrounding area of Moray is well known for the Whisky Trail and the Mansion House provides the ideal base from which to embark on such a challenging adventure.

For the sports enthusiast there are ten golf courses within ten miles, fishing on the Spey, several stables and unlimited watersports in Findhorn Bay.

Although almost in the centre of town, the hotel is set in private woodland overlooking the River Lossie to the west and expansive lawns dotted with mature trees to the south. The chandeliered entrance hall makes a fine impression with its oak-panelled walls, and plethora of antique curiosities. The majestic staircase leads to 23 excitingly diversified bedrooms all complementing period furnishings with modern comforts such as mini-bar and trouser press.

The Piano Lounge is a favourite pre-dinner gathering point. The restaurant is elegant and the menu well compiled and balanced - ideal for those who enjoy the simple yet delicious things in life. The Still-Room, so called because of its unique collection of whiskies, is a private area often available to residents. The 'Wee Bar' serves as a watering point in the centre of the House, just next to the Snooker Room and its patio is a bonus on fine summer days. Even when the weather is not so fine all is not lost.

The Country Club with its warm, inviting pool complemented by a spa, sauna, steam room and sunbed is sure to provide the answer for cold or rainy days. A computerised gymnasium for those with an eye on their figures is as is always the way at the Mansion House complemented perfectly. In this instance the Dip Inn all-day snack bar is where lost calories can be replenished.

The Haugh, Elgin, Morayshire IV30 1AN, Tel: (0343) 548811, Fax: (0343) 547916

Minmore House was originally the home of George Smith, the famous founder of Glenlivet whisky and the memory of his trade is kept alive in the hotel with each of the ten individual rooms named after a local Speyside malt, not to mention the impressive range of single malt whiskies available and proudly displayed in the beautiful oak-panelled bar.

The Minmore is a family run hotel and the atmosphere is relaxed. Set in four acres of its own, the secluded gardens that surround the house make it a haven of peace and quiet. Log fires and an abundance of fresh flowers add to the homeliness.

The food is Highland and hearty with five course meals ranging from salmon to venison as well as local, organically grown vegetables.

The hotel is ideally placed for a wonderful array of pastimes: exploring, walking, bird watching, horse riding and for those with an interest in Scottish heritage, a grand variety of castles, art galleries, local museums and crafts and, of course, the famous Whisky Trail are all at your disposal.

Within the grounds there is a hard tennis court, croquet lawn, an outdoor pool for those long summer days and plenty of space and tranquillity in which to totally relax.

Glenlivet, Banffshire AB3 9DB, Tel: (08073) 378

Fair fa' your honest, sousie face,
Great Chieftain o'the puddin-race.
Aboon them a'ye tak your place,
Painch, tripe, or thairm:
Weel are ye wordy o'a grace
As lang's my arm.

To a Haggis   Robert Burns

The New Marcliffe in Aberdeen offers guests the highest standards of service to ensure that their visit will be an enjoyable one. The hotel offers a number of suites catering for all occasions.

The 27 bedrooms are all en suite and have cable television, coffee making facilities and telephone.

The restaurant provides an excellent menu with a wine list to match.

Aberdeen is a major city and provides all the facilities expected. There is a theatre, art galleries and museums as well as a wide range of sporting facilities. The hotel can arrange golf at numerous local courses and for the keen fisherman beats can be obtained.

For those less keen on sport there is the Malt Whisky Trail; numerous distilleries are open to the public and are well worth visiting.

Aberdeen is the gateway to Royal Deeside. The scenery is beautiful and there are numerous historical landmarks and beauty spots well worth a visit.

The New Marcliffe is an ideal base for either business or pleasure. Whether guests seek the bustle of this commercial centre or the tranquillity of the countryside, The New Marcliffe's staff will do everything possible to make your stay an enjoyable one.

51-53 Queens Road, Aberdeen AB9 2BE, Tel: (0224) 321371, Fax: (0224) 311162

The Old Manse Of Marnoch

The Old Manse is a fine Georgian country house set amid three acres of attractive gardens on the banks of the River Deveron. The house was built in 1805 and retains its Georgian feel throughout although its amenities are modern. There are five spacious and well-appointed bedrooms - each with their own tea/coffee-making facilities, radio and individually controlled central heating - guest lounges and an elegant dining room.

Much pride is taken in the food at The Old Manse with an award-winning breakfast menu which includes three different sausages, devilled ham, Scotch woodcock, and an array of homemade bakery and preserves prepared in the kitchen. Dinner consists of four set courses which change each day, and the staff are more than happy to prepare imaginative dishes for vegetarians and those on special diets, making full use of organic produce from the kitchen garden. The kitchen is also happy to provide packed lunches and afternoon teas to order.

Situated less than a mile from the main A97 Huntly/Banff route, the Old Manse is ideally placed to explore the North-East of Scotland: the Castle Trail, the Whisky Trail and Fishing Heritage Trail all lie within a ten-mile radius. The golfer can choose from several parkland or links courses, whilst sea and river fishing and a wide range of country pastimes can be pursued locally. Guests are welcome to explore the garden which abound with unusual plants and old-fashioned roses and features a herb parterre and a walled kitchen nursery garden.

Bridge of Marnoch, Huntly, Aberdeenshire AB54 5RS, Tel: (0466) 780873

Pittodrie House dates back to 1490 when it was originally owned by the Erskine Family. The house and estate was originally bought by the Grandfather of the present owner in 1895 and was converted by his Grandson Theo Smith to a Hotel in 1977.

The house was extensively modernised internally to bring it up to a high standard of comfort. A lot of time has been spent trying to retain the atmosphere of a Country House. All the rooms abound in antiques, paintings and family portraits.

A five course dinner is served nightly in the restaurants with the emphasis on fresh local produce. The menu changes daily. We have an impressive wine list with over 200 wines from 19 different countries. The bar is also well stocked with over 80 different malt whiskies and over 50 liqueurs.

We offer people at Pittodrie a chance to relax in comfortable surroundings. It is possible to take leisurely strolls in the 5 acre walled garden or a more energetic walk up Bennachie - the hill behind the house. There are also 2 squash courts, tennis court, snooker table, croquet, table tennis and clay-pigeon shooting.

Pitcaple, Aberdeenshire AB5 9HS, Tel: (046768) 444, Fax: (046768) 648

Surveying the Terrain – *Elizabeth Halstead. Courtesy of Rosentiel's.*

Rothes Glen Hotel

Situated at the head of the Glen of Rothes this Victorian mansion enjoys spectacular views over the Spey Valley to the distant heather-clad Banffshire hills. Fully modernised, the Rothes Glen has retained many original features. The elegant lounge for instance, with its ribbed ceiling and white marble fireplace, exudes the antique charm this relaxed country house is famous for.

Every bedroom is equipped to the highest standard with direct-dial telephone, remote control television, trouser presses, tea/coffee making facilities, hair dryer, radio, child listening service and mini-bar. All have en suite facilities.

The best of Scottish beef and venison features prominently on the menus, as does fresh fish and shellfish from the Moray Firth. An extensive cellar provides an impressive selection of vintage wines and the Cocktail Bar gives guests the opportunity to choose from a range of mellow Speyside Malts. On summer evenings the Fountain Patio is a favourite spot for pre-dinner drinks.

The Birchfield Room caters for private dinner parties or mini conferences for up to 20 people.

In the 40 acres of wood and parkland surrounding the hotel are a nine hole putting green and croquet pitch. A burn runs through the garden to a quarter acre loch stocked with Rainbow trout. A small, pedigree herd of long-haired Highland Cattle graze in the grounds.

Eight golf courses are within 20 miles of the hotel - some inland, others by the sandy shores of the Moray Firth. For guests who wish to see the surrounding countryside the hotel makes an excellent base.

Whatever your preference a warm welcome awaits you and the caring and attentive staff will do their utmost to ensure that your stay at Rothes Glen is a happy one.

Rothes, Nr Elgin, Moray AB38 7AH, Tel: (03403) 254/255, Fax: (03403) 566

Saplinbrae House Hotel

The Saplinbrae House Hotel, set in the heart of the Buchan countryside, was built in 1756 as a Dower House for the Pitfour Estate. Combining the resplendent character of the past with the highest standard of sumptuous modern day comforts, the hotel will inspire you to return time and time again.

Saplinbrae, a popular meeting place for friends and business associates, provides the very best in private and corporate hospitality with the facilities to cater for the most sumptuous wedding or business conference.

Enjoy a meal with family or friends in the warm and relaxed atmospheres of either Stag Restaurant. Alternatively, should you be in a more informal mood you may wish to try The Bistro. Both offer excellent cuisine chosen, wherever possible, from local produce and both have superb wine lists.

All of the 14 bedrooms have been lovingly furnished with complementary decor. Rooms have en-suite facilities, all have colour TV, radio alarm, tea and coffee-making facilities and direct dial telephone.

A firm favourite with the country sportsman, corporate party or family group, Saplinbrae Estate provides clay pigeon shooting and excellent trout fishing by boat on the well-stocked 37 acre lake. The area is famous for its beautiful countryside and inspirational coastal scenery. You could follow the famed castle or malt whiskey trails or should you feel more energetic you may wish to test your handicap on one of the eight championship golf courses that are all within easy reach.

The Saplinbrae House Hotel is situated approximately 33 miles north of Aberdeen on the A950, midway between Peterhead and Fraserburgh.

Old Deer, Nr Peterhead AB42 8LP, Tel: (0771) 23515, Fax: (0771) 22320

Thainstone House Hotel and Country Club

This palladian mansion, set in 40 acres of meadowland, offers guests the highest standards of luxury accommodation and service.

The public rooms are elegant and the 48 bedrooms have all been furnished with the comfort of the guests in mind. Several rooms have original four poster beds and all have satellite television, tea/coffee making facilities and direct dial telephone. On arrival, guests receive a fresh flower for their buttonhole and a decanter of sherry awaits them in their room.

Simpson's restaurant has a sumptuous Georgian setting and the menu is varied and exciting. For those wishing to dine less formally Cammie's grill is available.

Thainstone House is not simply a hotel. It provides a wide range of leisure facilities. As well as a swimming pool and jacuzzi there is a fully equipped gymnasium and a splendid snooker room. For those wanting more outdoor pursuits there is a golf course, clay pigeon shooting, fishing and falconry.

This is not just a place for a holiday. The hotel offers full conference facilities and private function suites with the necessary back up service required by guests.

For those wishing to explore the region the hotel is located at the start of the Grampian Castle and Whisky Trails. Aberdeen is only 14 miles away and it has all the amenities you would expect of a large commercial centre.

Your stay at Thainstone House is guaranteed to be a pleasure however you choose to spend your time.

Inverurie, Aberdeenshire, AB51 9NT, Tel: (0467) 21643 Fax: (0467) 25084

The Udny Arms

Whatever the reason for your visit, whether it's for a holiday, sporting weekend, business trip or simply for a meal, you can be assured of a warm welcome from the Craig family and

their staff, whose main aim is to ensure you have a pleasant stay at the Udny Arms Hotel, on the beautiful Aberdeenshire coast.

The Victorian charm, friendly atmosphere and excellent facilities of the hotel have drawn visitors to Newburgh for over 100 years. The elegant Dining Room offers an a la carte menu renowned throughout Scotland while the less formal Bistro places special emphasis on local produce. And although the menu changes daily, sticky toffee pudding is always available.

The Cafe Bar is an informal, self service bar with an emphasis on wholesome food. Soups, salads, quiches and hot meals are all available from noon until late. Least formal of all the hotel's public rooms is the country style Bar, a favourite with residents and locals alike. Here there is an excellent choice of malt whiskies, real ales and wines from all over the world.

The bedrooms are comfortable and individually styled, many with antiques. All 26 have private bathroom, telephone, television, tea/coffee making facilities, hair dryers and trouser presses, though naturally, room service is available.

There are three championship golf courses within ten minutes drive of the hotel or alternatively you'll find one of the finest 9-hole links courses in Scotland just at the bottom of the garden. Overlooking the peaceful Ythan Estuary which is famed for its trout fishing the Udny Arms is the ideal base for a sporting holiday second to none.

Newburgh, Ellon, Aberdeenshire AB4 OBL, Tel: (03586) 8944, Fax: (03586) 89012

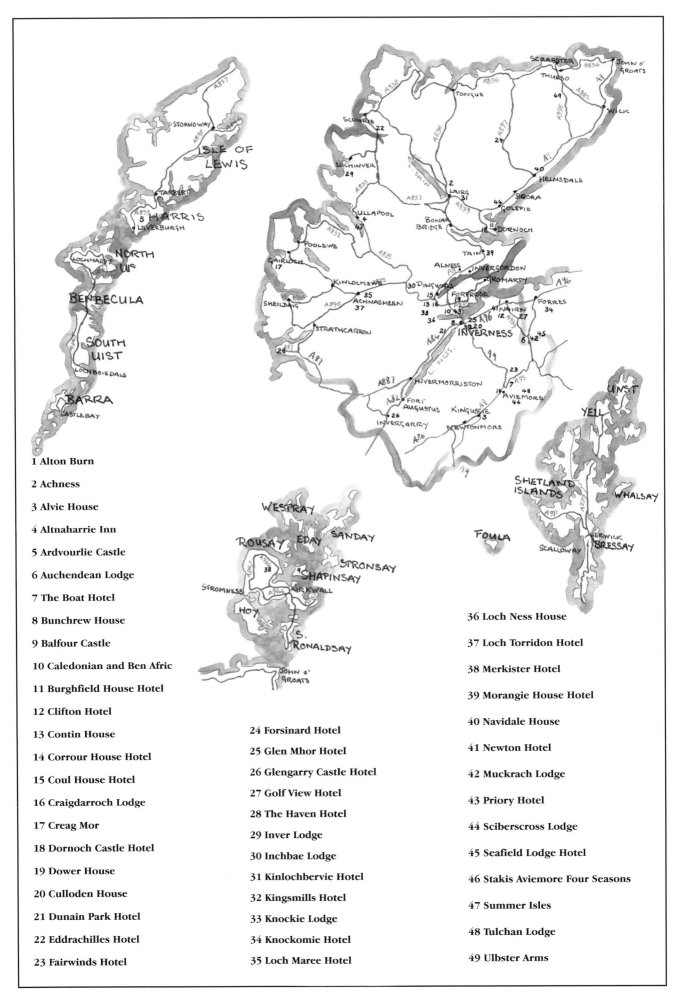

1 Alton Burn

2 Achness

3 Alvie House

4 Altnaharrie Inn

5 Ardvourlie Castle

6 Auchendean Lodge

7 The Boat Hotel

8 Bunchrew House

9 Balfour Castle

10 Caledonian and Ben Afric

11 Burghfield House Hotel

12 Clifton Hotel

13 Contin House

14 Corrour House Hotel

15 Coul House Hotel

16 Craigdarroch Lodge

17 Creag Mor

18 Dornoch Castle Hotel

19 Dower House

20 Culloden House

21 Dunain Park Hotel

22 Eddrachilles Hotel

23 Fairwinds Hotel

24 Forsinard Hotel

25 Glen Mhor Hotel

26 Glengarry Castle Hotel

27 Golf View Hotel

28 The Haven Hotel

29 Inver Lodge

30 Inchbae Lodge

31 Kinlochbervie Hotel

32 Kingsmills Hotel

33 Knockie Lodge

34 Knockomie Hotel

35 Loch Maree Hotel

36 Loch Ness House

37 Loch Torridon Hotel

38 Merkister Hotel

39 Morangie House Hotel

40 Navidale House

41 Newton Hotel

42 Muckrach Lodge

43 Priory Hotel

44 Sciberscross Lodge

45 Seafield Lodge Hotel

46 Stakis Aviemore Four Seasons

47 Summer Isles

48 Tulchan Lodge

49 Ulbster Arms

Although Shetland was in the news for all the wrong reasons recently, it would thankfully take more than an oil spillage to shake the resolve of these tenacious island folk.

The Shetland Islands are a world apart, snared between the sea and endless sky on Britain's northernmost horizon. Nowhere in Shetland is more than three miles from the sea and its coast provides some of the most spectacular shoreline in Britain. Despite the fact that the islanders are outnumbered by sheep in the ratio of fifteen to one, visitors should not consider Shetland underpopulated for there are literally thousands of tourists during the summer months, flying in from many parts of the world. The seabirds and seals that frequent the islands are perhaps more welcome guests than the two legged visitor who thankfully remains a less common sight, though no less cordially welcomed. As well as the sheep there are, as may be expected, many Shetland ponies on the islands whilst out to sea the seals are often kept company by dolphins.

Should you visit during the month of June, the period of Simmer Dim, you can play golf, go walking, fishing and even read your book all day - and night!

The history and heritage of the islands is fascinating. Iron Age buildings have withstood the test of time and weather and Viking memorabilia is there for all to see. Modern souvenirs are found in the shape of the famous Shetland jersey and other handcrafted goods made by the islanders.

Game fishermen have ample opportunity to fish for trout and sea anglers will find the sport here outstanding. Food is fresh and many malt whiskies are there to be tested. Above all, a sense of peace pervades these islands and all who visit them.

The Orknies are also spectacular. The Old Man Of Hoy, which bravely weathers storm after storm, is probably the best known face on the map but there are many more equally as memorable. The peace once again is all pervading, despite a sense of intrigue and mystery. Who were the people who built the Ring of Brodgar some 5,000 years ago? The wildlife of the Orknies is fascinating and sport, particularly brown trout fishing on Loch Harray, is excellent.

Lewis, Harris and the Western Isles are also worth a visit. The islands, which have been inhabited for over 6,000 years, remain remarkably well preserved and immune from modern day influences. Nature is at one with the visitor to the Outer Hebrides.

Returning to the mainland, we find further isolated areas of great natural beauty. Caithness combines mountains with 'flow country' in the interior. Spectacular cliffs, unspoilt beaches and a wide range of cultural, natural and sporting attractions make the area an ideal one for any visitor to Scotland.

John O'Groats, a popular tourist haunt, is the furthest point from Lands End on the British mainland. A full 876 miles separate the two points. There are a number of towns and villages of interest nearby including Halkirk, a pleasant village on the River Thurso where in 1222 Adam, Bishop of Caithness, was roasted alive by the local folk who had become exasperated by the severe taxes imposed. Mr Lamont please note.

There are a number of sporting opportunities with some excellent salmon rivers and sea fishing. The golf courses of Brora, Nairn and Royal Dornoch make a memorable trio but there are, however, many more in the vicinity none of which will disappoint the discerning golfer looking to uncover a well-kept secret.

Dunrobin Castle, seat of the Earls and Dukes of Sutherland, dates from the 13th century although much was recrafted in the 19th century. The castle is open throughout the summer and is one of the most fascinating in the country.

Although no part of this area could be described as overcrowded, the true isolation of the North East coast is hard to beat. The beaches are beautiful and countryside delightfully remote, Lochinver, Scourie, Cape Wrath and Altnaharra are just a number of the villages to enjoy on the way. This is an area of tranquillity and an ideal place for recharging your batteries.

Those who decide to make the journey north by car should also consider breaking their journey in Brora, where the Clynelish Distillery and Hunter's Woollen Mill are well worth a visit. Inverness and Nairn provide the two centres with the largest concentration of fine watering holes for the visitor whose palate seeks the same pleasure afforded his eyes and ears. The haunting scene of Loch Ness is enough to intrigue the most sceptical of visitors and always remember the auld saying 'many a fine man has been hung on less evidence than of the Loch Ness monster'.

Although the tourist authorities in the region are at pains to point out that the Highlands and Islands are within easy reach for the modern traveller they remain, in spite of this, essentially unspoilt. For those who are seeking a bit of peace and quiet, some fine sport and good fayre, the Highlands and Islands await.

Behold her, single in the field,
You solitary Highland Lass

The Solitary Reaper William Wordsworth

The hotel resides in picturesque countryside, close to the banks of the river Cassley, in the centre of southern Sutherland. It has well appointed accommodation including seven double rooms with private bath and is renowned for its friendly atmosphere and excellent cuisine.

The area has some of the finest salmon fishing in Scotland with the rivers that flow into the Kyle of Sutherland such as the Oykel, Cassley, Shin and Carron, all having a world wide reputation.

Brown trout fishing in some of the local hill lochs is also of a very high standard, but there are also many others that are well populated with smaller trout. These offer excellent sport for both children and the inexperienced. Sea trout fishing both in Kyle and elsewhere in the locality can also provide good sport. Salmon fishing on the Cassley begins on 11th January and closes on 30th September and is by fly only. Catches on the Rosehall beat average over 300 fish per annum. Although most of this fishing is let on a weekly basis from year to year, it is possible from time to time to obtain rods through the hotel.

Trout and seatrout fishing can also be arranged on request.

For the non fisher there are many other varied activities to partake in, such as hill walking, bird watching, pony trekking and claypigeon shooting all in peaceful surroundings. Expert tuition can be arranged for the latter two sports if required. Photographers and painters alike, will find a wide and challenging range of subjects to test their skills. The hotel is also ideally placed for excursions, with the North, West and East coast all less than an hours drive away. Due to its central situation it is possible to chose differing routes daily thereby cutting down repetition to a minimum. Dunrobin Castle and Inverewe Gardens are amongst many other interesting attractions that appeal to many. Visits to local industries such as the Woollen Mills at Brora, the Caithness Glass factory, potteries or distilleries can also be arranged. For the golfing enthusiast famous courses such as Royal Dornoch, Tain, Brora and Golspie are all within easy reach, whilst the nine hole course at Bonar Bridge is even closer. Those interested in either archaeology or botany will find plenty to explore in the local glens and surrounding mountains.

Rosehall By Lairg, Sutherland IV27 4BD, Tel: (054984) 239, Fax: (054984) 324

Alton Burn Hotel is an imposing building, originally constructed as a Preparatory School in 1901. It stands in it's own grounds overlooking the 17th Tee of the Nairn Golf Club, with glorious views across the course, Moray Firth with the Sutherland Hills in the background. The hotel has been owned and run by the MacDonald family since 1956, and is geared to the needs of the golfer and families in particular.

There are 25 rooms all with Private facilities, Colour T.V., Radio, Baby Listening and Tea & Coffee Makers.

Recreational facilities abound and one can have a relaxing round of putting on the green, or an exacting game of Tennis, followed by a session on the Practice Golf Area, finished off by a swim in the Heated Out-door Swimming Pool. There is also a Games Room with Pool Table and Table Tennis.

Nairn has a very fine Indoor Deck Level Swimming Pool, and Squash can be arranged from the Hotel, for the very energetic guest.

There are many fine courses in the area, and one cannot fail to mention Nairn Dunbar Golf Course – very popular venue for this year's Northern Open and only 2 miles from the Hotel. Forres, Grantown on Spey, Boat of Garten, Elgin, Lossiemouth, Inverness and Dornoch are all within easy driving distance of the Hotel. Inverness Airport is 8 miles from the Hotel and with prior notice, transport to the Hotel is easily arranged. It is possible therefore to be on the Nairn Courses within 2 hours of leaving Heathrow or Gatwick.

The A9 North now makes Nairn very accessible by car, with Edinburgh and Glasgow a comfortable 3 hours driving time. Within the surrounding area Cawdor and Brodie Castles, Loch Ness and the elusive Monster, Culloden Battlefield, Clava Stones are just a few of things to see. If you feel you are 'Over-golfed,' the Whisky Trail is also easily found and never forgotten!

So if you want to get away from it all, and enjoy good golf, good food and good company, there can be no better choice than Alton Burn Hotel, where we can cater for groups of up to 40.

Nairn. Tel: (0667) 53325

Alvie House is an unspoilt Victorian/Edwardian Shooting Lodge situated in its own grounds on Alvie Estate (13,000) acres in Strathspey. It maintains a dual role of family home and place of gracious entertainment. Past owners include Lady Caernarvon, widow of the ill-fated discoverer of Tutenkamhun's tomb, who modernised the house in the late 1920s. The present Laird, Jamie Williamson and his family are resident all year round and retire to private quarters within the house to make room for their guests.

The house itself enjoys a secluded setting, overlooking a small trout loch, surrounded by pine woodland with views of the Cairngorm Mountains beyond.

Alvie House retains the traditional character of a Highland Shooting Lodge while still providing its guests with the modern facilities they require. Stags heads adorn the walls, there are large fire places, enormous baths and a full size billiard table.

The spacious bedrooms accommodate up to 14 guests on the first floor with additional comfortable accommodation on the second floor to cater for larger groups. Alvie House is available for groups only (6-20 persons) although special arrangements can be made to accommodate larger numbers in the estate cottages.

Sporting facilities on the Estate and in the surrounding country-side are almost endless; fishing, shooting, falconry, clay pigeon shooting, archery, stalking and tennis are all laid on either in the grounds or on the Estate. Nearby there are skiing and ice climbing on Cairngorm (heli-skiing can be arranged) during the season plus curling, skating and husky races. The area is also famous for its hill-walking and bird watching and there are six golf courses within a 20 mile radius of Alvie.

Alvie fishing is particularly varied; Brown Trout from Lochs Alvie and Beag, Brown Trout, Arctic Char, Salmon, Sea Trout and Pike from Loch Insh or Brown Trout, Sea Trout and Salmon from the Rivers Spey and Feshie. There is also a two acre loch stocked with Rainbow Trout for beginners or those less successful days on the river or loch.

The lawn in front of Alvie House leads down to Loch Bourne which is stocked with large Trout exclusively for the entertainment of the keen anglers amongst the house guests.

Alvie Estate, Kincraig, Kingussie, Inverness-shire PH21 1NE, Tel: (0540) 651255/249, Fax: (0540) 651380

Originally the home of Lord Rothermere and now commended by the Scottish Tourist board, Burghfield House has been run by the Currie family as a hotel since 1946. This welcoming family atmosphere is well in evidence and the hotel is relaxed and friendly. Standing in over five acres of beautiful gardens it overlooks the city of Dornoch with its fascinating 13th century cathedral.

The elegant restaurant can seat 120 people, this is particularly useful as the hotel is renowned for its superb food and great pride is taken in the preparation and serving of the extensive menu which boasts classical dishes to mouth-watering Highland fare, which makes good use of the very best of the fresh, local produce including prime beef, game, salmon and shellfish. Vegetables and flowers are grown in the hotel's own greenhouses and gardens. There is an excellent wine list available to complement the menu.

For the serious golfer, the Burghfield is only a few minutes drive from the renowned Royal Dornoch Golf Course. Ranked as the 10th greatest course in the world by an international panel of golf architects, professionals and journalists, it is a wonderful course to play. It is also a fabulously historic course indeed golf has been played on these links since 1616. The 14th, Foxy, is considered by many to be the finest natural hole in the game. As one would expect, the hotel has had a long association with the course and can arrange bookings, teetimes etc. For a change of scenery the courses of Tain, Golspie and Brora are also close by.

For a break from the golf, this is an excellent centre for exploring the beauty of the North, with miles of sandy beaches nearby and a number of stunning lochs available for fishing.

All of the 38 bedrooms have private facilities and colour television; all have radio, direct-dial telephones, baby listening and tea/coffee making facilities.

Following extensive re-furbishment during 1991 the hotel boasts two lounges, two cocktail bars, a TV room, games room and more than enough space for energetic children and energetic golfers.

Dornoch, Sutherland IV25 3HN, Tel: (0862) 810 212, Fax: (0862) 810 981

Altnaharrie Inn

Altnaharrie lies on the southern shores of Loch Broom on the North West coast of Scotland, just opposite the fishing village of Ullapool. The house was originally built as a stop-over point for drovers on their way to sell their cattle in the south.

There is no road by which to reach the Inn but the ten minute boat journey adds greatly to the charm and atmosphere, providing a taste of the tranquillity of island life. Your car will be parked in Ullapool, in a private car park belonging to another hotel, and the Inn's own launch runs at least five times daily.

The waves lap at the edge of the garden, and the surrounding heather-clad hills offer magnificent walks and the chance of spotting a variety of wild life, including golden eagles, seals and otters.

Inside Altnaharrie the atmosphere is relaxed and informal. All of the eight bedrooms have their own bath or shower room and lovely views. Some of these rooms are in separate buildings. There are two lounges with open fires and lots of books for the 'stay at home' days. The dining room has a red-pine scrubbed floor, a few rugs, weavings on the walls and an easy, friendly air. There is a list of over one hundred and fifty carefully chosen wines.

The food is freshly produced and of the very highest quality, much of it grown or caught locally. Gunn Erikson's skill and artistry in the kitchen has earned her a world-wide reputation.

There is no mains electricity supply, and the Inn's own generator is switched off when everyone has gone to bed - hence the torch and candle by the bedside

Ullapool, Wester Ross, Tel: (085 483) 230

Ardvourlie Castle

Ardvourlie Castle stands on the shores of Loch Seaforth, under the crags of the Clisham. The Isle of Harris is a wild and lovely place. Otters swim in the bay, seals come in to fish, golden eagles soar above the hills. In contrast to the ruggedly beautiful landscape, the castle is elegant and comfortable, offering tranquillity and the warmth of well-being.

Built in 1863 by the Earl of Dunmore as a hunting lodge and now owned by Paul and Derek Martin, Ardvourlie is an ideal centre for exploring the mountains and lochs of North Harris on foot.

Freshwater fishing can be arranged and naturalists will find a wealth of interest, whether amongst the wild flowers of the machair or the birds of the sea and mountains. Car hire is available on the island.

Lovingly restored, the castle is furnished in keeping with the Victorian period. The ceilings have elaborate cornices, the furnishings incorporate many fine Victorian pieces and antiques. Gas and oil lighting in the four bedrooms and fires in Victorian grates enhance the sense of times gone by. A private bathroom can be reserved subject to availability. The mahogany panelled baths have elaborate brass faucets and are tiled in Victorian designs.

The food is a blend of the traditional and the imaginative, based on good natural ingredients and avoiding factory farmed and factory processed produce wherever possible. There is delicious home-made bread, and Ardvourlie now has a resident's licence.

Relax on a chaise-longue in the well stocked library and appreciate the unusual distinction of this fine guest house.

Aird a' Mhulaidh, Isle of Harris PA85 3AB, Tel: (0859) 2307

Auchendean Lodge

Set above the confluence of the Dunlain and Spey rivers, Auchendean Lodge was built just after the turn of the century as an Edwardian hunting and fishing lodge for the largest estate in Morayshire.

The lodge's architecture shows some influence of the Scottish Arts and Crafts style, considered one of the high points of the Art Nouveau movement. The present owners - Eric Hart and Ian Kirk have incorporated modern comforts whilst keeping the period features and maintaining the traditional style of furnishings.

In the drawing room you can relax in front of a log fire and enjoy stunning views down Scotland's finest salmon river, across the Abernethy Forest to the Cairngorn Mountains.

The Dining Room faces out across fields to the mountains and antique furniture and fine paintings give an added elegance. The best use is made of fresh produce from the hotel garden, local farms, rivers, forests and moors. The cuisine is based on Continental methods incorporating traditional Scottish recipes. Cheeses are a speciality - Scottish varieties and the best from France.

The cellar, with over 100 wines, represents many years of laying down and more than 30 whiskies include the famous local Spey malts.

The seven bedrooms are comfortably furnished with period furniture. Most have private toilets and bath or shower, all have central heating, heated towel rails, tea/coffee making facilities, radio, colour TV, handbasins and shaver sockets.

For lodge residents, fishing for salmon, sea and brown trout is available at low cost. There are six golf courses nearby, canoes pass along the Spey below the hotel, and in winter there is downhill skiing just 30 minutes' drive away.

One and a half acres of garden backs onto Broomhill, covered in matured pines and carpeted with moss, blueberry and heather. Dogs and their owners are spoilt for choice!

Dulnain Bridge, Grantwon-on-Spey, Morayshire PH26 3LU, Tel: (047 985) 347

The Boat Hotel

The Boat Hotel is run by the Wilson familly and has been described by former guests as 'a real country house hotel'. Ideally situated in the picturesque village of Boat of Garten five miles from Aviemore, and two miles off the Perth to Inverness trunk road, the Boat Hotel is the perfect base for a holiday in the Scottish Highlands. Direct air links connect London, Glasgow and Edinburgh to Inverness which is only 30 miles away. A courtesy car will pick you up from Aviemore station should you choose to travel by rail.

Each of the Hotel's 34 bedrooms have en suite bathrooms, colour televisions, radios, hairdryers, and a telephone.

The restaurant has built up an excellent reputation for the high quality of its cuisine making use of the superb Highland produce available locally and complementing it with friendly and efficient, yet discreet service.

The hotel is ideally placed for the golfing enthusiast. There are six courses within 30 minutes easy drive. In the Spring, Summer and Autumn, the hotel organises special golf weeks with their own visiting professional, Alex Fox based at the hotel. The list six comprises: Abernethy, Carrbridge, Grantown-on-Spey, Kingossie, Newtonmore and of course, Boat of Garten.

All golfing groups of twelve or more will receive a bottle of Speyside whisky as a prize.

Groups of sixteen or more will be offered an organisers discount of one free place. For the non-golfer, the area is rich with many treasures: fishing, climbing, hill walking and skiing are all possible here.

Bruce and Jean Wilson look forward to welcoming you to The Boat Hotel.

Boat of Garten, Invernesshire, Tel: (047983) 258, Fax: (047983) 414

Bunchrew House

Set amidst 15 acres of beautifully landscaped gardens and woodland on the shores of the Beauly Firth, Bunchrew House is a 17th Century Scottish mansion steeped in history and tradition.

With the sea lapping the garden wall only yards from the house, guests can enjoy the breathtaking views of Ben Wyvis and the Black Isle and relax in a rare sense of timelessness and tranquillity.

Bunchrew has been lovingly restored to preserve its heritage whilst affording guests high standards of luxury and modern day amenities. Whether relaxing in the charming panelled drawing room (with its roaring log fires in winter), resting peacefully in one of the exquisitely decorated suites, or dining in the candlelit restaurant you will enjoy the warm hospitality and informal ambience of a Scottish country house.

The traditional cuisine includes prime Scottish beef, fresh lobster and langoustines, locally caught game and venison and freshly grown vegetables. We take special pride in our wine list which has been designed to perfectly complement your choice of menu.

Guest accommodation comprises eleven luxury suites. The Lovat and Cedar, for example, feature magnificent fully canopied four poster beds, the Wyvis suite a sumptuous half tester and jacuzzi. Each is furnished to extremely high standards and is individually decorated to enhance its natural features. All suites include bathroom, shower, colour television and telephone.

For those with an eye for places of local interest, there is an abundance of possibilities, including Cawdor Castle, Loch Ness, Castle Urquhart, and the beautiful glens such as Affric, Strathglass and Strathconon.

Further afield are the famed sub-tropical gardens at Inverewe, the fishing port of Ullapool, the Cairngorns and the Hebrides. Those with sporting inclinations are well catered for, with sailing, fishing and golf all available locally.

Bunchrew, Inverness IV3 6TA, Tel: (0463) 234917, Fax: (0463) 710620

Balfour Castle, built in 1848, was purchased from the last of the Balfour line in 1961 by the Zawadski family. They opened the Castle to a limited number of paying guests some fifteen years ago. Set in an extensive acreage of wooded grounds and with panoramic views over the sea and neighbouring islands, the Castle remains very much as it was in its Victorian heyday and contains its original furnishings.

The woods, an unusual feature for Orkney, are a naturalist's paradise, from the bluebells in springtime to the bird life which abounds. The two acres of walled gardens are still traditionally cultivated, providing fruit and vegetables which are picked daily throughout the year. Milk, butter, cream, cheese, eggs, poultry and pork are all home produced. With the finest of fresh ingredients, the traditional menu is outstanding - complemented by scallops, crab, salmon and game from the Island.

Household arrangements are very informal and a family atmosphere prevails. Guests' bedrooms are individual in character, with canopy and four poster beds, all with modern en suite bathrooms. A family room is available.

Our guests have full use of the oak panelled library, the drawing room with its relief plaster-guilded ceilings and adjoining conservatory and snooker room.

The island of Shapinsay is tranquil and beautiful with clean sandy beaches, wild flowers and dramatic coastal walks. Our speciality is wildlife excursions in our speed boat to the seabird cliffs, seal colonies and uninhabited islands. Orkney's wild life has to be seen to be believed!

Additionally, Shapinsay is only a 20 minute boat ride from Kirkwall, from where numerous archaeological sites can be visited.

There is also an inter-island ferry service.

Shapinsay, Orkney Islands KW17 2DX, Tel: (085671) 282

Clifton House

Built in 1874, the elegant theatrical Clifton House is run by the owner, J.Gordon Macintyre, who has lived in the house all his life. Many things go towards making the unique atmosphere of this charming very personal establishment: a Victorian house, which has been most decoratively revived and carefully restored, abounding with flowers, paintings and colour. The restaurant is the cornerstone of this establishment and although the wine list is probably the longest in the North of Scotland, there are still a hundred odd at under £15.00.

The hotel has twelve individually decorated bedrooms on two floors. The public rooms include The Yellow Sitting Room, with a blocked paper from Temple Newsham, The Green Room and The Drawing Room, where a log fire is always burning except in warmest weather. The blocked paper in this room was designed by Pugin and was used for the Robing Room in the Palace of Westminster in 1849. For the use of colour in a traditional building, Clifton won a Design Award of Distinction in 1988 among the British Tourist Authority Commended Hotels.

The cooking is very traditional, bringing together only basic raw materials, the best of Scottish produce and cooked using classic techniques...Mallard, Guinea Fowl, Wild salmon, Lamb, Brill, Turbot, Wolf Fish and Halibut.

Viewfield Street, Nairn, Highland IV12 4HW, Tel (0667) 53119, Fax (0667) 52836

Contin House

Set in the midst of some of the finest scenery, wildlife and sporting opportunities in the Highlands, Contin House is ideally placed as a central point from which to explore. The West Coast is only 40 minutes away and Inverness is within a 20 minute drive. The house is situated in its own garden, surrounded by pasture land, on a peaceful island in the River Blackwater. The two world famous golf courses, Royal Dornoch and Nairn, are within easy reach.

Now a traditional Highland lodge, Contin House was formerly a Church of Scotland manse and was built in 1794. Tasteful refurbishment has achieved a very high standard of accommodation and David and Daphne DuBouby are excellent hosts who provide good food great comfort and individual attention.

There are two double and three twin bedrooms. All rooms have bathrooms en suite, radio alarms and direct dial telephones. Colour televisions are provided on request. The drawing room and sitting room both have log fires creating a very cosy and relaxed atmosphere. Dinner, by candlelight, is served at a prearranged time to suit the days activities and the menu is created from home-cooked, seasonal country dishes with fresh vegetables from the walled garden.

There are many peaceful, scenic walks nearby and within a comfortable day's drive are the Isle of Skye, Loch Ness, the Speyside Distilleries and the Castles of Cawdor and Brodie. Salmon fishing and grouse shooting can be arranged, given notice, and when conditions are right salmon can be seen making their spectacular leap up Rogie Falls.

Contin, By Strathpeffer, Ross-Shire IV14 9EB, Tel: (0997) 421920, Fax: (0997) 421 841

The Corrour House is a wonderful Victorian country house set in four acres of secluded garden and woodland where Roe Deer, Red Squirrel and a variety of bird life abound. The house looks out over Rothiemurchus Forest and enjoys spectacular views of the Lairig Ghru Pass and the Cairngorm Mountains.

There is a wealth of activities to enjoy in the area. This is walking country and walks can vary from a quiet stroll through Rothiemurchus, or a stiff climb to the Cairngorm Plateau, the highest range of mountains in Britain. Birdwatching on Speyside is very rewarding - with rare species such as Ospreys, Golden Eagles, Crossbills, Goldcrests and Crested Tits to be seen. The hotel has a small reference library to help with bird identification. Trout fishing is possible on the Spey and in local lochs. Fishing, shooting and stalking are activities which can be arranged through Rothiemarch Estate. The area is noted for its ski-ing in season and at the nearby Cairngorm slopes there are chairlifts, restaurants, bars, shops and equipment hire. Corrour in conjunction with leading ski schools, offers Ski Holiday packages and can arrange equipment hire and instruction.

The hotel is full of charm and character and combines the elegance of days gone-by with the practicality and facilities modern travellers have come to expect. The ten comfortable bedrooms have private bathrooms, tea/coffee trays, colour television, telephone and radio. After a hard day on the piste guests can retire in the relaxing surroundings of the drawing room, with its log fire, library and selection of games, or in the cocktail lounge and bar. The restaurant offers a table d'hote menu which changes daily and emphasises fresh produce such as prime Scottish beef, locally caught game and venison, salmon and trout and is complemented by a fine wine list.

Inverdruie, Aviemore PH22 1QH, Tel: (0479) 810220, Fax: (0479) 811500

This secluded mansion has an incomparable Highland setting with views of forest and mountains. The ancient Mackenzies of Coul certainly chose a wonderful place for their home.

Coul House is now run by Martyn and Ann Hill who provide a warm welcome and a friendly, personal service. The hotel is a favourite with both golfers and salmon fishermen and is a first class holiday hotel.

It also caters well for all manner of business meetings and conferences.

The restaurant, supervised by chef Chris Bentley is excellent providing an a la carte menu. The cellar is also well stocked and with the Mackenzie Cocktail Bar provides numerous malts for those wishing to sample them.

The bedrooms are of a similarly high standard all 21 being individually designed and especially well equipped. All rooms are en suite and contain a colour teletext television, direct dial telephone and beverage maker.

During the Summer months a piper plays on Friday evenings. For those wishing to explore this beautiful region there is the 'Highland Passport' which can be used to cruise Loch Ness, and who knows, discover the truth about the monster. Visitors can also explore the Summer Isles or visit Cawdor Castle.

Coul House provides the ideal venue either for a relaxing break or a successful conference. Whatever the reason for staying there, guests can be certain of the highest standards and of seeing a magnificent part of Scotland.

Coul House Hotel, Contin, By Strathpeffer, Ross-shire IV14 9EY, Tel: (0997) 21487, Fax: (0997) 21945

Creag Mor Hotel

Amidst the spectacular scenery of Wester Ross and set in its own landscaped gardens stands the Creag Mor Hotel. From this wonderful location you can enjoy outstanding views over Old Gairloch Harbour and over the sea to Skye.

The resident proprietors, Larry and Betty Nieto, offer a warm, friendly and relaxed atmosphere in this luxurious, family run hotel. Highland hospitality is extended all year round. All 16 bedrooms have recently been refurbished to the highest standards of comfort and are designed to offer a distinctive ambience. There is a 24 hour room service and all bedrooms have en suite facilities, colour TV with in house video facility, direct dial telephone, tea/coffee making facilities, trouser press and electric blankets. The elegant gallery lounge has been beautifully redesigned and enjoys superb views of Skye and the Outer Isles.

Dining at Creag Mor is something of a treat. The delightful Mackenzie room specialises in salmon, trout, venison, prime highland beef and locally landed seafood. Alternatively the Buttery's less formal surroundings provides a varied and interesting all-day menu. After dining a visit to the popular 'Bothan Bar' is a delight. With over 100 different brands of malt and blended Whisky to choose from it offers many qualities of a traditional Highland Inn.

Close by the Creag Mor is a 9-hole golf course, pony-trekking, river, loch and sea-fishing, sailing, para-gliding, windsurfing, canoeing, abseiling, and guests also have the opportunity to go on 'safari' over the surrounding hills in a four wheel drive all-terrain vehicle.

For the less energetic there are many safe, sandy beaches and relaxing hill walks. Fly fishing, tackle and tuition can be arranged locally and permits for salmon and trout fishing are available from reception.

Charleston, Gairloch, Ross-Shire IV21 2AH, Tel: (0445) 2068, Fax: (0445) 2044.

Dornoch Castle Hotel

Formerly the Palace of the Bishop of Caithness, Dornoch Castle is thought to have been built in the late 15th or early 16th century on the site of an earlier palace. The views across the Dornoch Firth to the hills of Ross and Cromarty are simply breathtaking.

Dornoch, the county town of Sutherland has below average rainfall throughout the year and above average sunshine during the summer months making it an ideal place to visit when embarking on activities such as golf. The Royal Dornoch Golf Club hosted the 1980 Home International Championships and the 18 hole links course is said to be one of the finest in the world as well as being the third oldest in Scotland.

The long golden sandy beach which is about 10 minutes walk from Dornoch Castle definitely warrants a leisurely stroll. Other facilities at Dornoch include tennis, bowling and a few miles away pony trekking and bird watching can be enjoyed.

The bedrooms as one would expect in this lovely old castle are decorated with style and sophistication with all the amenities you require. They mostly overlook the well tended garden which is a joy to see. All the reception rooms are tastefully furnished and decorated in different styles ranging from the wood panelled cocktail bar to the Green Lounge in the new wing. The restaurant overlooks Dornoch Cathedral and is charmingly located in what was the kitchen of the Old Bishops Palace.

Dornoch Castle is run on a personal level with great attention being given to your needs to ensure a wonderful stay in such splendid historic surroundings.

Castle Street, Dornoch IV25 3SD, Tel: (0862) 810216, Fax: (0862) 810981

The Dower House

Standing in three acres of mature grounds between the rivers Beauly and Conon the Dower House is an attractive and intimate hotel.

This is more of a home than a hotel and the proprietors Robyn and Mena Aitchison provide a relaxed and informal atmosphere both for individual guests or for private house parties.

The Dower House was converted around 1800 and is traditionally furnished. All 5 bedrooms are en suite and the bathrooms have traditional cast iron baths and brass fittings. One of the rooms also has its own sitting room.

Dinner is taken in the ornate dining room where guests are requested not to smoke, and the 5 courses are prepared by Robyn. The menu provides an excellent and varied choice.

Highfield, Muir of Ord, Highland IV6 7XN, Tel: (0463) 870096, Fax: (0463) 870090

Beauly is pretty much mainstream when it comes to fishing. When the Picts lived in vitrified forts at Dunmore and Plaicho above the village they guarded their fish traps from 'Crannogen', or man-made islands, in the estuary. The remains of these structures can still be seen today. Ptolemy, the Cartographer of Alexandria, shows the Estuary of the Farrar on his map of Britain, pre-dating the Roman occupation. That most ancient of all our place names is still used for the headwaters of the Beauly in Glenstrathfarrar.

More recently the river served as the march between the Viking Kingdom of the North and the Celtic kingdom of Caledonia, from which the hotel takes its name, in the South. The river quietly looked on as the blend of poverty and patriotism led to Simon, the Lord Lovat of the '45, to his death and a place in history as the last peer of the realm to lose his head. Boats of over 100 tonnes would come up on the tide from the Low Countries and the silver bars taken from the 'Cruives', another ingenious salmon trap, would ensure, much to neighbouring chief's envy, that the Lord Lovat's coffers were well endowed. This lasted until June when the last of the winter's ice could be stored in the 'Corff House'. At this time one of the conditions of employment on the estate was that workers would not be asked to eat salmon more than three times a week.

Today when most rivers have 'gone back' the Beauly is showing the best, if not the biggest, returns for forty years, and the hotel would be pleased to arrange a package for you. By way of an alternative, the 'Caley' has been lucky to let from the Forestry Commission three readily accessible Hill Lochs in Glen Affric, in a SSSI designated area of breathtaking natural beauty. Each loch has a boat, with ghillie if needed, and several fish approaching two pounds have been landed in 1992. Other rivers within easy reach include the Ness, the Onon, and the Blackwater. The latter yielding 20 fish to one hotel party on one day in 1990. The Beauly Angling Association issues tickets and a day on this beat offers good prospects at a modest cost.

Included in our package is a birdwatching trip down the estuary. The mud flats, practically inaccessible from the bank, are home to an ever-increasing variety of ducks, waders, and geese, both European and Arctic migrants as well as the native population.

And finally the 'Caley' itself. Run by fishermen for fishermen and other kindred spirits this home-from-home of nearly 300 years standing truly has a life of its own. It offers home cooking with friendly service, and welcome to stranger and regular alike. Its ten rooms are mostly ensuite and the genuine original atmosphere leaves the plastic plushness of modern hotels green with envy and gawking in the wake.

Send for brochure and full particulars of our package.

With the Glen Affric Hotel we are glad to say:

'Fish a loch a day for your stay'

The Caledonian Hotel, Beauly, Inverness-shire IV4 7BY, Tel: (0463) 782278
The Glen Affric Hotel, Cannich, Beauly, Inverness-shire IV4 7LW, Tel: (04565) 214

In a glorious setting at the foot of the mountains midway between the two jewels of highland golf, Royal Dornoch and Nairn what better 19th than CRAIGDARROCH LODGE HOTEL.

After an exhilarating days golf played against an ever changing backdrop of mountain, loch, forest and seascapes come home to CRAIGDARROCH, relax and unwind with good food, good wines and good company.

Once the dower house of the clan McKenzie, CRAIGDARROCH is now a comfortable traditional country house hotel in 8 acres of lawns and woodland with plenty of space to practise your swing. Alternatively you can swim in our new indoor pool, try the sauna and solarium, or enjoy a game of croquet on the lawn. We can also arrange clayshooting, fishing, horse riding, and sailing for you, so there's plenty for the non golfer too.

We offer 3 and 7 night golf packages inclusive of green fees on a selection of 18 hole courses. Tee times are prearranged to avoid disappointment and green fees are paid. All you have to do is play. Alternatively we are happy to tailor a golf holiday to your exact requirements, any number of nights and any of the courses within reasonable travelling distance of the hotel

from Golspie and Brora in the North to Boat of Garten in the South and from Gairloch in the West to Elgin in the East.

If your holiday dates are flexible you may be able to take advantage of the special FREE GOLF deals that we run from time to time.

Away from the courses you will something to see or do around every corner. Visit Macbeths castle at Cawdor. Learn how whisky is made and sample a dram at the local distillery. Bask in the sun on an uncrowded beach and swim in the clean warm waters of the Gulf Stream. Cruise around the Summer Isles, and photograph the seals or look for dolphins in the Moray Firth. Explore wild Strathconon and keep an eye on the skyline for eagles, or sit by the falls at Rogie to watch the salmon leap. Climb Ben Wyvis for a view from the North Sea to the Atlantic. Listen to the Strathpeffer pipe band and watch the Highland dancers in the village square on Saturdays.

For the best of golf holidays it has to be Scotland, the home of golf and for the best value in Scotland it has to be CRAIGDARROCH, so let Julia and Mark Garrison and their attentive staff provide for you a most memorable holiday.

Contin, Ross-shire IV14 9EH, Tel: (0997) 421265

Culloden House is a handsome Georgian mansion with a tradition of lavish hospitality stretching back hundreds of years. Among its famous visitors was Bonnie Prince Charlie who fought his last battles by the park walls. The house stands in forty acres of elegant lawns and parkland, enhanced by stately oaks and beech trees.

The resident proprietors, Ian and Marjory McKenzie, extend a warm welcome to all visitors to their hotel. Culloden House is decorated to the highest standard, particulary the comfortable drawing room, which is decorated with magnificent Adam-style plaster work.

Every bedroom is individually decorated and has redirect dial telephone, television, trouser press, bath and shower. Guests can chose from four-poster bedrooms, standard rooms, or rooms with a jacuzzi. The garden mansion also has non-smoking garden suites for those who wish. Dining is also a memorable experience at Culloden House; the emphasis in the Adam Dining room is on friendly and unobtrusive service, matched by the highest standards of cuisine. The wine cellars hold a superb range of wines from the great vineyards of the world, and there is a wide selection of aged malt whiskies.

Leisure facilities include a hard tennis court, sauna and solarium. There is much to visit in the area - golfing, fishing and shooting can be arranged and the Highlands, Loch Ness and Inverness are just waiting to be explored. Also nearby are Cawdor Castle, the Clava Cairns and Culloden Battlefield.

Situated three miles from the centre of Inverness, off the A96, Inverness - Nairn Road, Culloden House extends the best of Scottish hospitality to all its guests.

Inverness IV1 2NZ, Tel: (0463) 790461, Fax: (0463) 792181

Salmon Fishing....

The Hotel has two salmon rivers for guests to fish, the River Halladale and the River Strathy. The Halladale rises on the north slopes of the Helmsdale watershed and empties into the sea at Melvich bay, with good salmon fishing from mid April to September.

The hotel beat starts at Forsinain Bridge and flows north for 2 1\2 miles to the junction with the river dyke. There are nine named pools. Best catch 6 Salmon and 1 Seatrout on a July spate.

The river Strathy rises on the Creag Anh-Lolaire Hills and flows north to Strathy Bay, this is a spate river and can give good summer sport. All Salmon fishing is by Fly only.

Trout Lochs....

The Hotel has 5 lochs exclusively for guests and 24 lochs open to non hotel guests, Loch Sletill is quoted as one of the best lochs in the north of Scotland. It lies to the east of the Hotel, 4 miles off the A897 road. There is a 3 mile drive on forestry roads and a 10 minute walk. Sletill is remote, beautiful and full of excellent trout. The average weight of 12oz and catches of 12 trout are common and fish of over 2lb are produced each season. All fishing is by boat and bank.

Loch Garbh, Loch Talaheel, Loch Leir, Loch Caise, The Cross Lochs, and Slethill are reserved for Hotel guests only.

Best Flies

Ke-He Black Pennell, Soldier Palmer, Worm fly, Greenwells, and Dapping Flys.

Loch An-Ruathair - This Loch is on the Achentoul Estate, and lies on the side of the A897 road 4 miles from the Hotel. Day permits are available to non guests. Worms and spinners can be used on Loch An-Rauthair ONLY. There is a fishing tackle and gift shop in the Hotel.

Forsinard, Sutherland KW13 6YT, Tel: (06417) 221, Fax: (06417) 259

Dunain Park

This secluded Georgian country house, in six acres of gardens and woodlands, offers high standards of comfort and service. The dining room overlooks two acres of walled garden supplying herbs, soft fruit and vegetables. The cuisine, imaginatively prepared by Anne Nicoll, is Scottish with a French influence. Home-baking, home-made jams and fresh local produce such as wild salmon and seafood, according to season are a special delight. A separate menu of fillet and sirloin Highland beef steaks served plain or with a variety of sauces is always available.

Log fires, antiques and oil paintings enhance the elegance of the hotel interior. All 14 bedrooms have private facilities, and four-poster bed and half-tester bed are available in rooms in the original house. Accommodation has been extended in Georgian style to include six suites with double or twin rooms, lounges and Italian marble-lined bathrooms, each with bath shower and bidet. The Coach-house in the grounds has been converted into two family suites, each with their own lounge.

The hotel has an indoor heated swimming pool and sauna in a log cabin in the grounds. Dunain makes an ideal centre for touring the Highlands situated as it is close to its capital of Inverness, with its many shops offering Scottish woollens, crafts and products.

Inverness IV3 6JN, Tel: (0463) 230512, Fax: (0463) 224532

The Eddrachilles Hotel

Situated on the north west coast of Scotland, the Eddrachilles Hotel stands at the head of Badcall Bay in its own 320 acre estate. The building itself is 200 years old and although it has been refurbished to provide guests with modern bedrooms it has lost none of its charm. The Dining Rooms are stone flags and have stone walls giving them a very distinctive character.

The bedrooms all have either private baths or showers and other facilities include direct dial telephone, colour television and ironing facilities. The restaurant has an a la carte as well as a table d'hote menu and provides a good wine list to accompany these.

From the Eddrachillies Hotel, visitors can explore this beautiful region. Trips can be made from the hotel to Eddrachilles Bay with its many islands. Guests can do some sea-fishing or even just take a picnic. For those wanting to do a day's fishing on one of the nearby lochs it should be noted that the hotel is not a fishing hotel. however, membership of an angling club for brown trout is available at Scourie.

The hotel is not far from the Handa Island Bird Sanctuary and trips to the island may be made from Tarbet.

Much of this area with its rugged scenery has remained largely unspoiled by man and is ideal for walkers. To the north there are miles of sandy beaches which, in this somewhat remote area, are deserted. The best of these is the haunted Sandwood bay where ships wrecked off Cape Wrath finally came to rest. To the south are the tallest waterfalls in Britain and for climbers there are mountains within reach of Scourie.

Badcall Bay, Scourie, Sutherland IV27 4TH, Tel: (0971) 502080/502211

Fairwinds Hotel

The Fairwinds is an attractive early Victorian manse set among grounds of seven acres, including mature pine woodland and a small loch and located at the heart of the small Highland village of Carrbridge. Being six miles north of Aviemore, it lies within easy reach of the Cairngorm mountains which, in season, offers some of the best skiing in Britain, weather permitting, as well as some challenging climbs and walks.

The area is full of sports facilities. There are seven golf courses within thirty minutes' drive, there are water sports at Loch Morlich, pony trekking and sea and loch fishing. The stunning scenery boasts 92 different species of bird, including ospreys at Loch Garten, to excite ornithologists. The less active visitor has a wide range of places of interest to visit, such as the Highland Wildlife Park, Waltzing Waters, several Clan Museums, the Carrbridge Landmark Visitors Centre, as well as a number of castles and distilleries.

Fairwinds' guests are also permitted to use the local Woodland Club's facilities, including swimming pool, sauna, steam room, dry ski slope and tennis courts.

An open log fire in the main lounge gives the hotel a warm and beckoning atmosphere. The restaurant offers a varied menu, including traditional Scottish dishes such as Speyside trout, salmon and venison and vegetarians are well catered for. The hotel contains five tastefully decorated bedrooms and all are equipped with facilities such as en suite bath or shower rooms, tea/coffee facilities, colour television, clock radios and hairdriers. In the main building there is also a twin-bed studio apartment with fully equipped kitchen and bathroom. There are six two to three bedroomed chalets set behind the main house overlooking the loch, complete with squirrels, deer and ducks. The chalets are centrally heated and equipped with fridge, electric cooker, washing machine, colour television, cutlery and crockery.

Carrbridge, Inverness-shire PH23 3AA, Tel/fax: (0479) 84240

The Glen Mhor Hotel

The magnificent Glen Mhor is situated on the banks of the River Ness, overlooking the town's two main historic buildings, the Castle and the Cathedral. It is ideally situated for the sportsman with no fewer than 25 golf courses within an hour's drive and Inverness district boasts some of the finest salmon and trout fishing in the country. As a result, the hotel lays on special sporting breaks for golfers and fishermen, and for those who like shooting. The shoot includes two days clay pigeon shooting at the Dan'l Fraser Shooting Centre, as well as game shooting.

The hotel has thirty attractively furnished rooms, mainly with en suite bathroom facilities. There are also De Luxe rooms including 'The Prince of Wales Suite' so-called because the Prince once stayed here. Every bedroom has individually controlled heating, telephone, colour television, baby listening service and tea/coffee facilities. Eleven of these rooms are in the adjacent cottage. The beautifully appointed restaurant has always enjoyed an excellent reputation; it serves fresh local produce such as salmon, seafood, lamb and game in both modern and traditional 'Taste of Scotland' dishes. This is complemented by a fine range of wines, from the 'House Selection' to the First Growth Claret and Burgundy.

There is a choice of three bars. The cocktail bar offers peace and relaxation and an extensive selection of malts. Nico's, one of Inverness's foremost bistro bars is one of the town's most popular nightspots and has a late licence on most evenings. Nicky Tam's is a stable bar with a lively atmosphere and offers a number of pub games, snacks and real ale.

9-12 Ness Bank, Inverness, IV2 4SG, Tel: (0463) 234308, Fax: (04653 713170

Glengarry Castle

Set at the very heart of the Highland's spectacular Great Glen, Glengarry lies on the shores of the serene Loch Oich, a stretch of water sandwiched between the better known Loch Ness and Loch Lochy. The Victorian building is attractively furnished, with a distinctive pine-panelled reception hall, and a lounge adorned with mellow oil paintings reflecting the glow of a welcoming log fire. There are 27 well-appointed bedrooms, all with splendid views, most with private bathrooms and some with four-poster beds and colour television. Much pride is taken in the traditional Scottish dinners, made with fresh local produce in season, and good old-fashioned highland afternoon teas are offered as well.

This attractive hotel lies within the sixty acres of its tranquil woodland grounds, including the ruins of Invergarry Castle, the clan seat of the MacDonnells of Glengarry and Bonnie Prince Charlie's refuge in the disastrous wake of Culloden. Loch Oich is open to guests to try a spot of trout fishing in one of the hotel's rowing boats, and there is a tennis court for the more athletically inclined. The legendary Loch Ness and its discreet occupant are just seven miles away, while the region's two key towns, Fort William and Inverness are both less than an hour's drive through a breathtaking landscape. Among the region's other attractions are Britain's highest mountain, Ben Nevis, and for the more sedate sightseer, the Abbey of Fort Augustus and the Parallel Roads of Glen Roy.

Invergarry, Inverness-shire PH35 4HW, Tel: (08093) 254, Fax (08093) 207

Golf View Hotel

The Golf View Hotel can be found in the most delightful setting on the sheltered shores of the Moray Firth, overlooking the magical black isle. Built at the end of the last century this imposing hotel commands spectacular views and is ideally situated in the Scottish Highlands.

The 48 bedrooms all have en suite facilities, colour television, radio, telephone and trouser press. The decor is very tasteful and gives a feeling of comfort. The hotel has a number of facilities including heated outdoor swimming pool, tennis courts, putting green, hairdressing salon, satellite TV room and an excellent games room.

In-house entertainment plays a large part from mid-March until the end of October and includes dances, cabaret, film shows and much more.

The high standards of Golf View are continued in the dining room with guests able to choose from extensive table d'hote and a la carte menus. The grand buffet and regular Gourmet dinners are well worth sampling and the wine list provides excellent choice.

The cocktail bar provides guests with the ideal meeting place for a relaxing drink after all the fresh air enjoyed outdoors. Shooting and fishing can be arranged and the fantastic highland setting also enables you to enjoy some scenic trips . The Nairn Championship Golf Course is only a par four from the hotel gardens which extend down to the beach. There is also another 18 hole course nearby.

Golf View Hotel caters for weddings, private functions and parties for up to 140 guests. Whatever your reason for staying at this delightful hotel you can be sure you will have a pleasant and enjoyable stay.

Seabank Rd. Nairn IV12 4HG, Tel: (0667) 52301, Fax: (0667) 55267

The Haven Hotel

The Haven Hotel is a charming and intimate hotel set amid some of Scotland's most breathtaking scenery. It is situated at the heart of the beautiful lochside village of Plockton, 'the jewel of the Highlands'. Originally built as a home by a merchant in the last century, the Hotel has been carefully converted and extended, but retains much of its original character.

The hotel contains three lounges, including one with an open fire, a conservatory in which to relax after dinner and attractively furnished rooms. All have their own colour television, bathroom and numerous other facilities to make you feel at home. The spacious restaurant is ideal for candle-lit dinners, sampling local specialities such as fresh salmon and prawns caught in the local lochs, Highland venison, or a range of Scottish meats and home baking. The wine list is extensive and packed lunches are available for days out.

The village is ideally situated to experience Wester Ross - the mountains and glens, waterfalls and seascapes, lochs and castles. A car journey through such beautiful scenery can take you to Kintail, with its spectacular mountain backdrop and herds of red deer and wild goats, or Glenelg and the famed 2,000 year old Pictish Brochs of Dun Telve and Dun Trodden.

At Inverewe you will find the National Trust gardens, a sub-tropical garden of trees and flowers. The idyllic isle of Skye is just a five-minute ferry ride from nearby Kyle. Alternatively, you may wish to hire a boat and spend the day fishing on the tranquil Loch Carron.

Plockton, Ross-shire IV52 8TW, Tel: (059 984) 223

Inver Lodge Hotel

The small fishing village of Lochinver sits quietly at the head of Lochinver on the far north western shores of the Scottish Highlands. The Inver Lodge Hotel, built in 1988, has already been acclaimed by many of its clients as one of the best in the Highlands. Set high above the village, it looks out over the calm waters of the loch towards the distant outline of the Isle of Lewis.

Inside the hotel, modern comforts blend with traditional Highland hospitality. The cocktail bar has an impressive selection of Highland malt whiskies, including Inver Lodge's own blend. Huge windows in the dining room provide panoramic views across the loch and surrounding countryside. The cuisine is excellent and varied, often including locally caught fish and oysters and with a selection of fine wines. An open fire burns in the residents lounge, the games room has a full-size billiard table, and there is a sauna and solarium.

Each of the 20 bedrooms is named after a nearby mountain or loch and all are generously proportioned and tastefully furnished. Each room has its own private bathroom with a superior range of fittings and toiletries. There are two executive rooms - Suilven and Canisp - with dining table and chairs and sofa.

Inver Lodge makes an ideal base for bird-watching, hill walking and above all fishing.

The hotel offers 10 rods on the nearby Inver, Oykel and Kirkaig rivers, and a further 10 rods with boats on the lochs. There is a special drying room for wet clothes, a rod box and deep freeze in which - if you have any luck - your catch will be stored.

Lochinver, Sutherland IV27 4LU, Tel: (0571) 844496, Fax: (0571) 844395

Inchbae Lodge Hotel

Les and Charlotte Mitchell own and run this refreshingly unpretentious hotel - formerly a private shooting lodge - in what can truly be said to be the heart of the Highlands. Surrounded by pine-clad slopes with magnificent views of Ben Wyvis, Inchbae Lodge nestles on the banks of the River Blackwater six miles west of Garve, roughly mid-way between Inverness and the west coast fishing village of Ullapool. It has a superb setting which is secluded though not remote.

Having only twelve bedrooms, Inchbae has a warm and friendly atmosphere, intimate and informal. Six of the rooms are in the Lodge itself, four with private bathrooms. The other six rooms, all with private showers and toilet, are in the Red Cedar Chalet. All bedrooms are heated and equipped with tea and coffee making facilities and for the colder months there are electric blankets for all the beds. Pets are welcome by prior arrangement.

Inchbae Lodge is ideally located for exploring this beautiful unspoilt part of Scotland. North, East and West coasts are all within easy reach, though you need venture no farther than the bottom of the garden for free trout fishing.

After a day spent breathing the unpolluted air you will be ready for dinner. Les and Charlotte Mitchell love cooking and have built a reputation for inspired meals, concentrating on dishes prepared using only the freshest of local produce; salmon from the river, venison from the hill, scallops, prawns and fish from the West coast fishing villages. Service is relaxed and undemanding, children are genuinely welcome and Les and Charlotte are always happy to discuss special diets and create suitable menus accordingly.

By Garve, Ross-shire IV23 2PH, Tel: (09975) 269

The Kinlochbervie Hotel

Kinlochbervie is a small fishing port just south of Cape Wrath in the far north-west of Scotland, influenced by the Gulf Stream and where deep sea trawlers and seals call in from the Atlantic Ocean. The Kinlochbervie Hotel overlooks both village and surrounding lochs and has spectacular panoramic views towards the sea. The hotel is modern in design and its situation is unbelievably calm so one can enjoy total peace. For the more energetic there is pony trekking, fly fishing, golf and usually diving can be organised. Geologists will be able to indulge their interests wondering at the Lewisian Gneiss banded rocks of the pre-Cambrian Age which are over 1000 million years old. Those who study wild life will be happy for they can observe deer, pine martens, eagles and many other birds in the area. There is also a variety of wild flowers and much else of botanical interest. The hotel, which has 14 bedrooms with en suite bathrooms and modern facilities (but with varying views, so it would pay to enquire when booking) is renowned for its food and wine. It is open from 1 April to 31 October. There is bed and breakfast accommodation in the Annexe which is known as the Garbet Rooms. Between 1 November and 31 March only bistro meals are available.

by Lairg, Sutherland IV27 4RP, Tel: (0971) 521275, Fax: (0971) 521438

The Kingsmills Hotel, Inverness, is set in four acres of beautiful gardens, adjacent to Inverness Golf Club. It is one of the best known hotels in the Highlands and has recently been completely redeveloped and extended.

All 84 bedrooms, many of which overlook the gardens, have a private bathroom/shower, tea and coffee making facilities, satellite television, direct dial telephone and a minibar. In addition there are six luxury villas adjacent to the golf course and each with private bathroom, kitchen and sitting room - ideal for a self catering golfing holiday!

The Swallow Leisure Club has an extensive range of facilities. After a busy day on the golf course you can enjoy a leisurely swim in the pool, relax in a sauna, work out in the mini gym or try the three hole pitch and putt course.

The hotel itself is spacious and elegant with large public lounge areas and a new conservatory which overlooks the gardens and makes pleasant setting for morning coffee or afternoon tea.

As well as being situated next to Inverness Golf Course, other courses within easy reach are the Championship Links Course at Nairn West, with the 14th green being reputedly the most undulating in Europe. The picturesque Boat of Garten Course is only 20 miles from Inverness and slightly further afield is the Royal Dornoch Course which is a true Scottish Links Course and has been voted by many professionals as one of the best ten courses in the world.

The Kingsmills Hotel, Inverness, provides an unbeatable combination - superb facilities for leisure and entertainment plus a spectacular location with so many fine courses on the doorstep.

Culcabock Road, Inverness IV2 3LP, Tel: (0463) 237166, Fax: (0463) 225208, Telex: 75566

Loch Maree Hotel was built in 1872 and has catered for fishermen ever since. It has been completely refurbished under the supervision of the new management. Mr Wilson and Mr Vincent have updated all the amenities to modern standards whilst maintaining the style of the original building.

The hotel is very comfortable with 22 double and twin bedded rooms, each with en suite facilities. The location of the hotel means that it can take advantage of the local produce, so the food is not only fresh but also of an exceptionally high standard.

For the fisherman the hotel excels; there is plenty of room for storage in the boat house with proper drying and boot room facilities. The hotel also boasts a small tackle shop, so it is very much self-contained. The guests of the hotel also enjoy preferential access to the fishing, although occasionally it can be arranged for non residents.

For the fisherman who enjoys his scenery as much as he enjoys his fishing, Loch Maree is legendary, offering the perfect combination, marvellous sea trout fishing in some of the best surroundings the Wester Islands can offer.

The sea trout fishing has been excellent for generations of fishermen and although current catches have been slightly down, an active restocking programme will ensure Loch Maree remains one of the best locations for sea trout fishing in the British Isles.

The first sea trout of the year enter the loch in mid June through the River Ewe, with the main runs being in July and August. Although the fishing tapers off towards the end of September, this is often when the largest fish are taken.

The guests of the hotel have eight boats at their disposal, each with a ghillie assigned to assist the fisherman in locating the best fishing available that particular day.

There are ten beats, which are operated on a rotational basis, allowing each fisherman to fish the best spots at least once during his stay.

They all have names which will be known to the avid sea trout fisherman: the Grudie, Weedy Bay, Ash Island, Pig's Bay and Fool's Rock, Hotel, North Shore, Steamer Channel, Back of Islands, Isle of Maree and Coree.

If you enjoy dapping, then this style of fishing was developed here in the 1930's, offers an interesting alternative for the fly fisherman and hopefully will prove successful.

Near Kinlochewe, Achnasheen, Wester Ross IV22 2HL, Tel: (044 584) 288, Fax: (044 584) 241

Knockie Lodge

In an unbelievably beautiful situation north east of Fort Augustus, just off the A82 on the B862 and due south of Drumnadrochit, lies the small town of Whitebridge. Inverness, the so-called 'capital of the Highlands' is 26 miles to the north. This means that Knockie Lodge, a splendid country house hotel, built in 1789 (the year of the French Revolution which helps to date it!) is near to that famous monster which they say resides in Loch Ness, although in fact the hotel is nearer to Loch Nan Lann. Knockie Lodge was formerly a shooting lodge but eleven years ago it was taken over by Ian and Brenda Milward and they have used their skills to convert it into a splendidly appointed hotel. You will find antique furniture there and family paintings. The accommodation includes three double bedrooms, five twin bedded rooms and two singles. There are no arrangements for children under ten. All ten bedrooms have the expected private facilities and are particularly well furnished so Knockie Lodge could be a good place to choose if you decide to settle in one place while you are touring in the area. The public rooms are well appointed and include a writing and reading and billiard room. Local food is a speciality and the menus in the restaurant are changed daily. Non-residents should note that dinner is by prior appointment and bar lunches are served to residents. Apart from snooker in the house, a well tended garden can be enjoyed and fishing can be arranged. Contact the Milward family for details of other pursuits you might wish to follow. Golf might be a possibility or there are many places of interest in the area. You might like to visit Cuill Barroch at Lochailort, from whose windows you can see the loch from where Bonnie Prince Charlie sailed; a long way but there are many other intriguing spots en route. There are half board terms only. The hotel is open between 2 May and 24 October.

Whitebridge, Inverness-shire IV2 2UP, Tel: (045 63) 276, Fax: (045 63) 389

Knockomie Hotel

Forres lies in a sheltered position at the foot of the Cluny Hills. It is readily reached from Dalcross Airport, Inverness and Forres railway station is on the main rail link between Aberdeen and Inverness.

The Knockomie Hotel lies well off any main road and has fine views over much of this impressive area but is well within visiting distance of Cawdor Castle and many other appealing places. Fishing, shooting, stalking, golf and riding can be arranged. The hotel restaurant specialises in using local produce, including shellfish from the Hebrides and game from nearby moors and glens. It prides itself on its selection of malt whiskies. All bedrooms have en suite and other anticipated facilities. The hotel recommends taking out travel insurance in case of enforced cancellation of bookings because the accommodation is much in demand.

Grantown Road, Forres, Moray IV36 0SG, Tel: (0309) 673146, Fax: (0309) 673290

Water, water, everywhere
and all the boards did shrink;
water, water, everywhere
nor any drop to drink.

The Rime Of The Ancient Mariner Coleridge

Loch Ness House Hotel

Lying only a mile from the Highland capital Inverness and all the amenities of a bustling country town, the Loch Ness House Hotel nevertheless offers all the traditional comforts of a Highland hotel. It stands within easy reach of the beautiful Loch Ness and there are cruises on both the Loch and Caledonian Canal.

Owned by the Milroy family, the Hotel has a friendly and relaxed atmosphere backed by professional service which has made it popular with locals and tourists alike. At weekends there is often a Ceilidh where guests can join with 'regulars' in a Highland concert of music and dancing.

The hotel has 23 bedrooms, all en suite. Two of the rooms have four poster beds and overlook the Tarvean Golf Course and Caledonian Canal. The restaurant is attractive, providing a menu including traditional as well as new Scottish dishes. Allister Milroy takes a close interest in the menus, ensuring that extensive use is made of local produce so that the dishes are both distinctive and tasty.

The hotel is an excellent base for those wishing to tour this beautiful region. Not only is Inverness itself an attractive town but whichever route you choose to take there are places worth seeing. If you simply want to fish or play a round of golf the Loch Ness House Hotel offers the opportunity for you to do so.

Whatever your pleasure, this hotel offers a cosy, pleasant place to come back to.

Glenurquhart Road, Inverness IV3 6JL, Tel: (0463) 231248, Fax: (0463) 239327

Loch Torridon Hotel

A family owned and run Country House Hotel, providing its guests with a Highland welcome, log fires, peace and seclusion, cordon bleu cuisine, and fine wines.

The hotel was a former shooting lodge built for the first Earl of Lovelace in 1887. The present owners are David and Geraldine Gregory. Set amidst some 58 acres of mature trees and parkland at the foot of majestic mountains on the shores of Loch Torridon.

This is the only hotel on the A896, do not turn off to Torridon Village.

The hotel has been recently refurbished. A lift has been installed between the floors, all bedrooms now have a bath and shower and the public rooms have been upgraded to provide some of the best facilities on the West Coast of Scotland.

The area is renowned for its beautiful scenery. There is excellent fishing on numerous hill lochs and rivers in the area and sea angling on Loch Torridon and along the coast. The restaurant menus make imaginative use of fresh local fish and seafood.

For the hill walker and mountaineer there are numerous climbs and, for the more sedate tourist, a number of nature trails laid out by the National Trust for Scotland on their land north of the Loch.

By Achnasheen, Wester-Ross IV22 2EY, Tel: (0445) 791242, Fax: (0445) 791296

Merkister Hotel

The celebrated Merkister Hotel is above all a fishing hotel, situated as it is on the island of Orkney, renowned as a fisherman's paradise. The hotel stands on the shores of Loch Harray with three lochs nearby. There are no fishing restrictions and the Merkister's proprietor is only too pleased to give guidance and advice. Boats, outboards and ghillies can be hired.

The hotel has freezing facilities and smoking of the day's catch can also be arranged.

If guests need a break from fishing, golf and squash is available and adventurous guests may wish to try rock-climbing or sub-aqua diving. Birdwatchers and archaeologists will find a great deal of interest on the island. There are numerous marine birds and ancient village sites.

The town of Kirkwall lies 11 miles away and provides all kinds of attractions, including a new discotheque development for the young at heart.

The Hotel stands in attractive grounds and contains seventeen comfortable bedrooms. All have colour television, electric blankets, tea/coffee facilities, telephones and most have en suite facilities. The Skerries Restaurant enjoys views of the hotel's spectacular surroundings and offers a varied cuisine to gourmet standard, complemented by the well-stocked wine and spirits cellar.

The Fishermen's Lounge and Bar provides a perfect venue to contemplate the day's catches and the ones that got away. The hotel also possesses the largest trout ever caught in Britain.

Harray Loch, Dounby, Orkney, Tel: (085) 677366

Morangie House Hotel

Morangie House Hotel, a fine old Victorian mansion, is set in its own grounds on the northern outskirts of the Highland town of Tain, one of Scotland's oldest Royal Burghs.

Built in 1903, Morangie House has been extensively modernised and tastefully decorated. The character of the building has not been lost and of particular interest are the superb Victorian stained glass windows illuminating the public rooms and hallway.

There are 11 bedrooms all individually decorated and furnished to the highest standards. All have en suite bathrooms, direct dial telephone, television, coffee making facilities, hair dryer and trouser press. The luxurious master bedroom has a large four poster bed while the bathroom boasts a whirlpool corner bath.

As a complement to the comfort and elegance of the bedrooms, the bar and dining room offer the best of Highland food and drink, with salmon, venison and game in season and a comprehensive selection of Highland malt whiskies.

The small Ross-shire town of Tain, close by the shores of the lovely Dornoch Firth, has much of interest for the visitor, with beach, bowling green, tennis courts and gardens. This ancient burgh was granted its Charter in 1066. It also has a fascinating museum and visitors are welcome at the famous Glenmorangie distillery.

There are several golf courses in the area. Tain itself has a first class course, while the world championship course at Dornoch is only half an hours drive away.

The area is excellent for the outdoor enthusiast. Whether it is fishing, shooting, hill walking or exploring the wonderful Northern Highlands you want, Morangie House Hotel is an ideal base for your Highland Holiday.

Morangie Rd, Tain, Ross-shire IV19 1PY, Tel: (0862) 892281

Navidale House Hotel

Situated on the coast of Sutherland, Helmsdale is ideally placed for touring in both Sutherland and Caithness. Navidale House Hotel, built as a hunting lodge for the Dukes of Sutherland, is spectacularly situated in six acres of woodland and garden which ramble down to the shore. The hotel is run in the manner of a country house, with log fires and attractive accommodation. In addition to the bedrooms in the hotel there is accommodation in the annex and in two chalets in the grounds which are suitable for families. Of the three resident proprietors, Marcus Blackwell, an internationally known chef, personally prepares the menus, which feature local fish, lobster, crab, in addition to Highland lamb, Caithness beef and game when in season.

The hotel will arrange fishing for its guests and will pack and freeze the catch to be taken home. Hind stalking and rough shooting can be organised if adequate notice is given. Squash and tennis can be played nearby and there is golf at Royal Dornoch, or closer at hand at Golspie, Brora and Helmsdale itself. The hotel is open from February to November.

Navidale, Helmsdale, Sutherland KW8 6JS, Tel: (04312) 258, Tel: (04312) 212

The Newton Hotel

The Newton Hotel, with its combination of Georgian and Scottish Baronial architecture, is one of the more distinctive houses in Scotland, It is situated amid 27 acres of secluded grounds overlooking the Moray Firth and the Ross-shire hills beyond, and provides an idyllic haven for peace and relaxation.

The 41 tastefully furnished bedrooms come with private bath and shower, telephone, colour television and tea/coffee facilities. There are also three private suites containing every modern facility anyone could need. The public rooms of the Newton are quite unique in their Victorian ambience, with elegant period furniture, subtly toned velvet upholstery and outstanding ceiling cornices. They are suitable for conferences, seminars and private dinner parties. Elsewhere, the hall is beautifully panelled and guests may wish to retire into the peaceful library and reading room. The Newton Court, nestling in the tall trees, has 14 contemporary bedrooms, similarly equipped to those in the main hotel. The restaurant offers a fine range of meals on its four course Table d'Hote menu and a la carte menu, the latter including a range of steaks charcoal grilled. There is also a great range of wines from the cellar.

The hotel lies about twenty minutes from Inverness and provides a wonderful base from which to explore places like Loch Ness, Glen Affric, Royal Deeside and the Central Highlands. Cawdor Castle and Culloden Battlefield are just a few minutes away. Nairn's championship golf course and the nine-hole Newton course are even closer. Stalking, fishing, squash and a range of other activities can be arranged locally and the hotel has its own tennis court and putting green.

Nairn IV12 4RX, Tel: (0667) 53144, Fax: (0667) 54026

'Oui, c'est un beau lieu', was how Mary queen of Scots described Beauly and gave the village its name in 1554.

Through the centuries Beauly has seen many changes. It has been variously, a place of great ecclesiastical learning and achievement centred on its 13th century Priory; a successful commercial township with its own markets and a prosperous export trade through the busy harbour and briefly at the end of the last century a spa dispensing cures from its own mineral wells.

Today Beauly is a bustling village with a reputation for good quality shops and services busy with the concerns of farming, fishing, shooting and many other outdoor activities for the tourist.

In the busy central square of the village stands The Priory Hotel, a comfortable establishment with an excellent reputation for good food. Bar meals and an a la carte menu are available, with steak, venison or chicken grilled on hot stones a speciality of the house.

First class accommodation with every modern facility, and friendly efficient service complete a combination which makes The Priory an ideal place to stay in the beautiful Scottish Highlands.

The Square, Beauly, Inverness-shire IV4 7BX, Tel: (0463) 782309, Fax: (0463) 782531

Scibercross Lodge

Six rivers and six lochs feed into the River Brora before it flows past the Scibercross Lodge, dissecting a breathtaking landscape of heathered hills, of random burns, of flourishing wildlife.

Visitors here may cross the path of red deer, otter, curlew, plover and golden eagle.

The Brora is also one of Scotland's finest fisheries, with brown trout and salmon in abundance and the lodge has become a classic fishing retreat. Guests are given access to several stretches of the Brora during season and can also fish on Loch Brora which offers excellent opportunities to expert and beginner alike.

The lodge also has its own small clay pigeon shoot and stalking and shooting in the nearby estates can be arranged.

For the non-sporting, there are castles, weavers, distilleries and glass engravers to visit and walks through the stunning Sutherland scenery.

The Scibercross Lodge was built in 1876 as a shooting lodge by the Duke of Sutherland. Today, Peter and Kate Hammond have turned it into an opulent retreat, with beautifully decorated drawing room, dining room and bedrooms. Stays are usually weekly and there are six single and twin rooms, all attractively furnished.

The guests are invited to discuss menus and wine for the five-course dinner, can serve themselves at breakfast and make up their own 'sporting' lunch, giving the lodge the cosy feel of a private house party rather than a hotel. All the food is made up from fresh local produce.

Strath Bora, Rogart, Sutherland IV28 3YQ, Tel: (04084) 246

Scots, wha hae wi' Wallace bled
Scots, wham Bruce has often led,
Welcome to your gory bed,
Or to victorie

Now's the day, and now's the hour;
See the front o' battle lour;
See the approach proud Edward's power,
Chains and slaverie.

Robert Burns

Seafield Lodge

Now under the personal management of experienced hoteliers, Alasdair and Kathleen Buchanan, assisted by Chef Alistair Garrow, the 'Lodge' has been restored to it's former glory.

Although the hotel has been open for visitors since 1881, recent major improvements to the public areas and bedrooms provide discriminating guests with the highest standard of modern comfort in elegant surroundings.

All bedrooms are en suite with direct dial telephone, television, hairdryer and hospitality tray. The Trout and Salmon Suites provide separate sitting room and bathroom with Spa bath.

Resident's lounges and the Lodge bar, with its fine array of malt whiskies, welcome you with open log fires and the barbecue and garden area is a popular venue in the summer months.

Chef Alistair Garrow uses all his culinary skills in creating an ever changing menu using the finest of local produce for which Speyside is famousfor its game, fresh Spey salmon in season, prime Aberdeen Angus beef, Moray lamb and West Coast scallops which all feature prominently on the tempting menus.

The Seafield Lodge is synonymous with Spey fishing and is the home of Britain's longest running angling courses under the personal supervision of renowned Chief Instructor Arthur Oglesby. However, other sports and activities are well catered for, including golf for which there are many challenging courses, hill walking, stalking, pony trekking, bird watching and in winter skiing on nearby Cairngorm and the Lecht. Grantown is at the start of the world famous Whisky Trail and no visit to Speyside would be complete without a Distillery tour.

The Buchanan family look forward to your visit to Grantown on Spey and their very special Seafield Lodge Hotel where discriminating travellers and sportsmen can be assured of a warm welcome and traditional Highland hospitality.

Grantown-on-Spey, Moray, Morayshire, Tel: (0479) 2152, Fax: (0479) 2340

The Stakis Four Seasons Hotel

The Stakis Four Seasons is a cosy, modern hotel set in attractive wooded grounds next to the Aviemore mountain resort. The surrounding countryside is famed for its beauty with the delightful River Spey running through the mighty Cairngorms which provide a magnificent backdrop for walkers, some challenging peaks for climbers to tackle and Britain's best pistes for the skiers in the winter months. Riding, golf, fishing and watersports are also available locally. The hotel also provides a host of exercise facilities in its Leisure Club which contains a swimming pool, Turkish steam room, sauna, whirlpool spa and gymnasium. Among the Activity breaks offered by the hotel are Hot Air Ballooning Weekends, for those looking for a peaceful break from terra firma.

The hotel takes great pride in the comfort and 'pampering' it offers its guests.

The 88 bedrooms, including five singles and six triples, are well furnished with en suite bathroom, satellite television, telephone and hospitality tray, while many feature stunning views of the Cairngorm mountains. A variety of drinks are served at the elegant cocktail bar and snacks and light meals at the coffee bar.

The Four Seasons Restaurant offers some spectacular views and has an extensive international menu to cater for all tastes, although its emphasis is 'Taste of Scotland' dishes, using fresh local produce. Entertainment is laid on most nights - usually a singer and pianist - and there is a dinner dance held every Saturday evening.

Aviemore, Inverness-shire PH22 1PF, Tel: (0479) 810681, Fax: (0479) 810534

Summer Isles Hotel

Ten miles north of Ullapool turn along the twisting single track road that skirts Lochs Lurgain, Badagyle and Oscaig under the eye of Stac Poly. Fifteen miles later you will come upon a straggle of white cottages gazing over the bay at the Summer Isles and beyond to the Hebrides. This is Achiltibuie. A few hundred yards past the post office you will find the hotel.

Mark and Geraldine Irvine run this individual but sophisticated hotel which has belonged to the family since the late 60's. Over the years the hotel has established itself as an oasis of civilisation hidden away in a stunningly beautiful, but still wild and untouched landscape. Mark and Geraldine will always be happy to give advice about fishing, walking, or bird watching.

The ambience of the hotel is undemanding. Although most guests like to change for dinner there is little formality. Chef Chris Firth-Bernard presents daily a single balanced menu, making fullest use of fresh home produced or locally caught produce. Scallops, lobsters, langoustines, crabs, halibut, turbot, salmon, venison, big brown eggs, wholesome brown bread fresh from the oven are among the seemingly endless list of gastronomic delights.

Eating well, sleeping well and moving about in beautiful surroundings is therapy for which many return year after year.

Guests should be able to make the most of this beautiful wilderness of islands and mountains. Those under eight and over eighty are not ideally suited. The gulf stream flows at the foot of the croft, but the weather can be anything from Arctic to Aegean inside a week.

Achiltibuie, Ross-shire IV26 2YG, Tel: (085 482) 282, Fax: (085 482) 251

Tulchan Lodge

Built in 1906, Tulchan Lodge is one of the finest examples of an Edwardian Sporting Lodge in the Highlands of Scotland. Constructed without regard to labour and cost, the Lodge was designed to provide every possible comfort and amenity to the owner, his family and friends.

The Lodge is a luxurious country house where guests are attended by a Butler, Housekeeper and full household staff, dedicated to providing those discreet standards of personal courtesy and service which are infrequently found elsewhere. The Lodge accommodates only twenty two guests in its well appointed bedrooms and large and well furnished public rooms.

Fresh local food and produce, much from the kitchen gardens and Estate, are used in the preparation of the excellent meals served to guests and the cellar is renowned for its carefully selected fine wines and spirits.

The public rooms include a drawing room, library, billiards room and two dining rooms. All these rooms are luxuriously appointed and hung with a collection of important paintings. There are ten double or twin bedrooms in Tulchan Lodge, all with private bathrooms and individually decorated and comfortably furnished in the traditional manner of a Scottish country house. There is also the Garden Cottage, offering accommodation for another two guests.

All bedrooms have direct dial telephones. Telex and Fax facilities are available by arrangement. There is a tennis court at the front of the Lodge for guests' use.

For those guests making a non-sporting visit, Tulchan Lodge makes an excellent base for visiting historic Scotland as Balmoral Castle, Craigievar Castle, Culloden Moor, Cawdor Castle, Loch Ness, Blair Castle and the cities of Aberdeen, Perth and Inverness are all within two hours driving time. Visits can also be made to the distilleries on the Speysdide Malt Whiskey Trail.

Nr Grantown-on-Spey, Morayshire PH26 3PW, Tel: (08075) 200 and 261, Fax: (08075) 234

There is nothing - absolutely nothing
half so much worth doing as simply
messing about in boats.

The Wind In The Willows Kenneth Grahame

This former Shooting Lodge set in 10 secluded acres overlooking the Dulnain River offers high standards of comfort and service. Privately owned and run by Captain Roy and Pat Watson they invite you to enjoy Highland hospitality, excellent cuisine in the Conservatory Restaurant and log fires in the Cocktail Bar and Lounge. The outstanding menus place a strong emphasis on a 'Taste of Scotland' using local produce wherever possible, with some European influence, complimented by a well balanced wine list featuring wines from around the globe. There are 8 en suite bedrooms individually furnished and 3 suites, 2 of which are in the Steading Annexe, just a short walk from the Hotel. The Dulnain Suite in the Steading is completely fitted out for the disabled.

Muchrach Lodge is ideally situated for all types of activities, including Cairngorm hillwalking, skiing, fishing on the River Spey or just complete relaxation. The Hotel has private fishing a short drive away on the River Findhorn.

The hotel is situated 12 miles north of Aviemore on the A938 between Dulnain Bridge and Carrbridge and is open all year except November.

Price Band: High Season £39 - £47. Low Season £30 - £40. Price per person in shared twin/double room with private facilities and full Scottish breakfast.

Dulnain Bridge, Grantown on Spey, Morayshire PH26 3LY, Tel: (047985) 257, Fax: (047985) 325

Anglers are beginning to re-discover the delights of brown trout fishing on the remote hill lochs of the northern Highlands. Apart from the natural beauty of their setting and the peace which surrounds them, they provide both fish and fishing of a quality far higher than many people today realise. Examples of the best of them are the hill lochs managed by Thurso Fisheries Limited for the Ulbster Arms Hotel, which has boats on these lochs and can arrange permits for others in the area.

The Hotel is the centre for fishing the River Thurso, one of Scotland's finest fly only salmon rivers, having both a Spring and Autumn run.

As well as fishing, many other outdoor pursuits can be undertaken using the hotel as a base; Birdwatching, Photography, Rambling, Painting and Geology, to name but a few, can all provide the visitor with the relaxation or stimulus that is desired.

The Hotel also arranges shooting and stalking over a wide variety of moors.

Caithness is renowned for its resident and visiting sea birds and waders, and fully equipped boats can be chartered for Sea Angling in the Pentland Firth. There are also many sites of archaeological interest in the area and exploring the castles, cairns, standing stones and old buildings can fill fascinating hours.

Halkirk, Caithness KW12 6XY, Tel/Fax: (084783) 206/641

Comlifoot Pool   (Ulbster Arms)

Scotland's Heritage

Scotland for Ever – Lady Butler. Courtesy of Rosentiel's.

The Lowlands are generally accepted as being that part of Scotland to the South of the Highland Boundary Fault, which runs diagonally across the country from the Firth of Clyde to Stonehaven on the east coast.

The dramatic rolling border hills, moorlands and forests of the Scottish Borders and Dumfries and Galloway are for many visitors, arriving from the south by road, their first and last sight of Scotland. Further north the Lowland corridor runs between the Firth of Clyde and the Firth of Forth and includes Scotland's capital, Edinburgh, and its largest city, Glasgow. This is the industrial heartland of the country and although much of the traditional industries such as shipbuilding, steel making and car manufacturing are in decline, they are being replaced by a new and cleaner working environment. North of the Forth, is the Kingdom of Fife and Angus, where the picturesque fishing villages and towns with their working harbours are dotted along this windy but sunny east coast. Historic Scotland maintain many properties throughout the Lowlands where visitors are made most welcome (featured later).

THE BORDERS

The Scottish Borders lie to the south east of Scotland, where the rolling hills of Lammermuir, Moorfoot and Pentland look out north towards the Forth Valley and the forests and woodlands of Ettrick, Eskdalemuir and Craik offer splendid walks. Testament to the area's bloody past are the sites of various battles with both the invading English and inter-family feuds; the now peaceful and impressive ruined Abbeys of Dryburgh, Jedburgh, Kelso and Melrose (where the heart of Robert the Bruce was buried) were looted and plundered by the English. Throughout the Borders there are examples of stately homes and castles designed by some of the best known architects of the time.

THE VALLEY OF THE TWEED

The River Tweed enters the North Sea at Berwick-upon-Tweed in England but for much of its length to a point west of Coldstream forms the natural border between Scotland and England. It is said that armies crossed the Tweed at Coldstream, which gave its name to the famous Guards founded in 1659, where the local museum preserves the regiment's treasures from various campaigns. Close by Coldstream is the Hirsel, the home of the Douglas-Homes; the Homestead Museum is housed in old farm buildings and the splendid rhododendron display should not be missed. This valley offers a wonderful array of churches, abbeys and chapels, castles and houses, towers, monuments and obelisks with spectacular views to the countryside beyond. The **Union Suspension Bridge**, the first of its type in Britain, built in 1820 by Samuel Brown, links Scotland with England two miles south of Paxton.

The fine Edwardian country house of **Manderston** is set in formal and woodland gardens. It was designed by John Kinross at the turn of the century for Sir James Miller, the wealthy racehorse owner, whose horses won the Derby and lived a pampered life in the luxurious stables. An enormous amount of money was spent on the construction of this Georgian style mansion and much of the lavish interiors are modelled on Lady Miller's family home in Derbyshire, Kedleston Hall by Robert Adam. The grand ballroom ceiling is decorated in Sir James' racing colours of primrose and white.

Duns Castle is the private family home of Alexander Hay and is not open to the public except by special arrangement. The castle was built in 1696 by the Earl of Tweedale for his son William Hay and the Hays have lived here ever since. The castle has been remodelled over the years but still retains detailed panelling, plasterwork and fireplaces. The trophies of the world champion racing car driver Jim Clark, who was killed in 1968 and buried nearby at Chirnside, can be seen in the market town of Duns.

Thirlestane Castle near Lauder is one of Scotland's oldest and finest castles. Built originally in the 13th century as a fort, it was rebuilt in the 16th century to defend the main approaches to Edinburgh from the south. The seat of the Earls and Duke of Lauderdale, it remains the home of the Maitland family to this day. The richly decorated rooms contain many treasures including some superb plaster ceilings which were added to the State Rooms in the 17th century. Children are able to entertain themselves browsing through the enormous toy collection now housed in the old nurseries, and a tour of the castle ends with the Exhibition of Border Country Life.

Mellerstain House, home of the Earl of Haddington, is set in magnificent grounds and is a fine example of Adam family architecture, as both father and son were involved. The beautiful decoration and plasterwork together with the unique collections of 18th century furniture and Old Masters make it perhaps one of the best Georgian houses in Scotland. The splendid library is possibly Robert Adam's masterpiece of interior design.

Close by is the isolated **Smailholm Tower** with spectacular views to a loch below and countryside beyond. The tower now exhibits the costumes and tapestries of the characters in Scott's 'Minstrelsy of the Scottish Border'.

Standing on John Rennie's bridge (built in 1803) over the Tweed at Kelso affords a magnificent view of **Floors Castle**. Built in the early 18th century Floors Castle, the family seat of the Dukes of Roxburghe, commands spectacular views over the castle ruins of old Roxburgh to Kelso, the River Tweed and the Cheviot Hills beyond (featured later).

There are fine Georgian buildings in Kelso, in addition to the ruined Abbey ravaged in 1545 by the English.

THE CHEVIOT FOOTHILLS

Jedburgh Abbey, by Jed Water, also plundered by the English in the 1540s, stands complete, except for its roof. The imposing red sandstone abbey with its Norman Tower houses a museum containing medieval treasures and a history of the Augustinian Canons from France who founded the monastery in the 12th century. In the town a Museum of Methods of 19th Century Imprisonment is housed in what was the county prison. This Georgian building built in 1823 stands on the site of the old Jedburgh Castle, built in the 12th century as a home for Scotland's kings, but later demolished by the Scottish parliament as it was too difficult to defend from attack by the English. Visit the tragic Mary, Queen of Scots' House which stands in gardens and contains mementoes from the Queen's life.

Travel north to Dryburgh on the A68, a scenic tourist route

from the south past the Waterloo Monument and site of An-crum Moor Battlefield, to visit **Dryburgh Abbey**. Once a holy place for Premonstratensian Order or White Canons, large parts of the Abbey still stand including the 13th century portal and cloister buildings. Sir Walter Scott is buried in the abbey grounds. The ruins of the famous **Melrose Abbey** suggest a fine 15th century building with detailed stonework and features, which was the inspiration to many of Sir Walter Scott's romantic works.

Bowhill, the Borders home of the Duke of Buccleuch and Queensberry, K.T., dates from the early part of the 19th century and is set in extensive grounds with lochs, rivers and woodlands and a wonderful adventure playground. Its lovely setting makes Bowhill the ideal venue for cultural and educational meetings, art courses and conferences, fully equipped with its own Little Theatre and restaurant. In the fine rooms, world famous collections of furniture, porcelain and paintings, including works by Canaletto, Claude, Gains-borough and Holbein can be found. An interesting feature is the portraits and manuscripts of Sir Walter Scott, who lived nearby on a farm on the bank of the Tweed in the early part of the 19th century. Scott created the romantic image of Scot-land and had **Abbotsford House** built at this place, west of Melrose which now houses many personal mementoes and treasures. Beyond Selkirk stands his statue in the market place.

Over one thousand years old **Traquair House** on the bank of the Tweed is said to be the oldest, continuously inhabited, family home in Scotland. It has been visited by twenty seven monarchs of Scotland and England and has associations with Mary, Queen of Scots and the Jacobites (featured later). Close

by is Innerleithen, which became a wealthy spa town in the last century (the Well on the hillside above the town can be visited and the health giving waters can still be taken) and is remembered in Sir Walter Scott's novel 'St Ronan's Well'. This is Sir Walter Scott's country for all visitors to enjoy.

One mile west of Peebles is **Neidpath Castle**, dramatically situated on a bluff above the River Tweed. This 14th century castle with its 11 foot thick walls contain a pit prison, a well hewn out of solid rock. The castle was remodelled in the 17th century to a more gracious style of living and contains an interesting mix of 14th and 17th century architecture. Neid-path Castle has been the home to the Fraser, Hay and Douglas families and since 1810 to the Earl of Wemyss and March. The scenic nature of the castle's setting in a wooded gorge of the River Tweed attracts artists and photographers alike, others just enjoy the fine views from the parapets and the walks around the castle.

DUMFRIES AND GALLOWAY

In the south west of the country the peaceful Dumfries and Galloway has dramatic south facing coastline overlooking the Solway Firth. From Gretna Green, where eloping couples from England were married by local blacksmiths until 1940, to the birthplace of Scottish Christianity at Whithorn, at pre-sent an archaelogical dig, there is much to see and do. Inland, visit the **Scottish Leadmining Museum** at Wanlockhead, Scotland's highest village, where in nearby Leadhills the source of the River Clyde rises, before descending past **Drumlanrig Castle** to Dumfries.

Neidpath Castle

Drumlanrig Castle built in the late 17th century is the Dumfriesshire home of the Duke of Buccleuch and Queensberry, K.T., set in fine grounds on the site of a medieval Douglas fortress (featured later).

Dumfries 'the Queen of the South' sits on the River Nith, and was home to Robert Burns for the last 5 years of his life. Both he and his wife are buried in a Mausoleum behind St Michael's Church. Eight miles south of Dumfries is **Caerlaverock Castle** which, with its moat, turrets and towers, is probably what is expected of a medieval fortress. The marshland and mudflats of the National Nature Reserve is home to breeding toads and flocks of geese and wildfowl. Close by is the delightful New Abbey Corn Mill and the ancient Sweetheart Abbey.

THE GARDEN OF SCOTLAND

The mild south westerly winds allow exotic plants and wildlife to grow and inhabit interesting gardens and nature reserves throughout the region.

The daunting **Threave Castle** ruins, set on an island in the River Dee (ring a bell and the keeper will row you across!), give some indication of the development of Scottish secular architecture in the later medieval and early modern period. 'The Tall Forbidding Tower House' was built in the latter part of the 14th century by Archibald The Grim, for the 'Black Douglases', one of Scotland's most powerful families.

Over the last thirty years the National Trust for Scotland has developed the 60 acre **Threave Gardens**, one mile away. Renowned for its plant collection and interesting layout, it has, in addition to the traditional walled garden, greenhouses and vegetable collection, magnificent seasonal displays of daffodils – some 200 varieties in a spectacular springtime display – roses, heathers and conifers. Nearby on the Dee, ducks and geese flock to the **Threave Wildfowl Refuge** in the winter months (open November/March).

The home of the present Earl and Countess of Stair is Lochinch Castle built in 1867 to replace **Castle Kennedy** which was razed to the ground in 1716, although it had been in existence since before 1482. The internationally famous gardens around the ruins are set between two lochs in 35 hectares featuring beautiful rhododendrons, azaleas, magnolias and monkey puzzle trees.

Almost surrounded by the sea and benefiting from the warm breezes of the Gulf Stream **Logan Botanic Garden** capitalises on its unique location by nurturing the growth of plants not normally associated with this part of the world. Originating from the turn of the century, it is now owned by the Royal Botanic Garden in Edinburgh. Further south at Logan Bay, a tidal fish pool 10 metres deep was constructed in 1788 to supply the Lairds of Logan with cod; the fish can be fed by hand today.

Back inland, north of Moffat, near the Borders is the National Trust owned Grey Mares Tail Waterfalls. The spectacular waterfalls are set in over 2000 acres in which herds of wild goats roam amongst interesting wild flowers.

The coastline, inland walks and pleasant climate make Dumfries and Galloway a varied and interesting place to visit.

LOTHIAN

Lothian is made up of the Forth Valley with its impressive bridges across the Forth; the birthplace of Mary, Queen of Scots at the **Linlithgow Palace** and canals, mines and railways from the industrial past; West and Mid Lothian bounded to the south by the Border hills; east Lothian with its sandy beaches and unspoilt coastline; and Edinburgh.

Gosford House between Longniddry and Aberlady, stands in a spectacular seaside location overlooking the Firth of Forth with distant views of the Forth Rail and Road Bridges and Edinburgh Castle. Francis Charteris, who was to become the 7th Earl of Wemyss, bought the Estate in 1781 in order to play golf on the sandy shores nearby and avoid travelling from his then home at Amisfield near Haddington.

The Classical Roman house, designed by Robert Adam, was finished in 1800, eight years after Adam's death. The founder's grandson, also Francis, 8th Earl of Wemyss, demolished the Wings, whilst adding to the 'old house' which was joined to the Adam Stables. Towards the end of the 19th century another Francis, 10th Earl of Wemyss, re-established the house with new wings designed by William Young, and it became the family home in 1890.

Haddington was the birthplace of the main founder of the Scottish Protestant Church, John Knox, who spent much of his life in Europe, before returning to Edinburgh to establish the Reformed religion with the blessing of the Scottish parliament.

EDINBURGH – THE ROYAL MILE

The architectural quality of the elegant Georgian New Town with its wide streets, crescents and circuses, contrasts with the Old Town crammed around the Royal Mile and together with the historical monuments and statues gave rise to Edinburgh's nickname 'the Athens of the North'. Probably Scotland's best known landmark, **Edinburgh Castle** stands on what was an extinct volcano and the fortress provides a spectacular setting for the annual military tattoo, part of the annual festival of arts (featured later). From the castle the Royal Mile leads to the **Palace of Holyroodhouse and the Abbey Ruins**, founded by King David I in 1128. One hundred and eleven portraits of Scottish Kings hang in the splendid picture gallery in the Palace of Holyroodhouse, built for Charles II in 1671, which is still used by members of the Royal Family today. Mary, Queen of Scots lived here for six years during her reign and witnessed the murder of her secretary David Rizzio, by her over protective husband.

Along **the Royal Mile**, where some of the buildings were built before the 1700s, the visitor can find St Giles Cathedral dating from the 14th century; Lady Stairs House containing original works by Robert Burns, Sir Walter Scott and Robert Louis Stevenson, possibly the oldest house in Edinburgh, built in 1490 where the reformer John Knox lived in the 16th century; the noisy Museum of Childhood; and The Canongate Tollbooth which now houses the Dunbar collection of Highland dress and tartans.

James Playfair's mid 19th century building in Princes Gardens houses **The National Gallery of Scotland** with its fine collection of paintings, including distinguished works by Scottish artists. Close by, the enormous **Scott Monument**, built in 1840 has a statue of Sir Walter Scott below its arches. **Princes Street** opposite is the only 'one sided' shopping street in the country.

To the north is the **Royal Botanic Gardens** famed for its rhododendron collection. **The National Gallery of Modern Art**, with its works by Henry Moore and Barbara Hepworth, is housed in Inverleigh House set in the Garden and surrounded by the spectacular landscaping and Heath, Peat Woodland and Rock Gardens.

At Edinburgh University, Arthur Conan Doyle studied medicine in the 1880s before becoming a novelist and Alexander Graham Bell, who later invented the telephone in America, studied sciences.

The Drum is Edinburgh's largest private house with over 60 rooms and has been the home of the More Nisbetts for over 130 years. Set in 500 acres of wooded parkland but only 20 minutes from Princes Street, the main house was built by William Adam in 1715, and adjoins an earlier 15th century keep where the family now live. The splendid Entrance Hall has the only known example of William Adam's plastering and this splendour is maintained in the plasterwork in the State Apartments. The 400 year old avenues of cedars point north, south, east and west – the summer solstice sets down the north avenue and is directly in line with the Dining Room. The 18th century garden has been recreated by the More Nisbetts with splendid walks through azaleas and rhododendrons. There is a troop of polo ponies, Highland cows, Charolais cattle and ponies for disabled riders.

THE FORTH VALLEY

To the east of the Forth Bridges stands the present **Dalmeny House,** built in 1815 by William Wilkins. It is Scotland's first Tudor Gothic Revival house and the Primrose family, the Earls of Roseberry, have lived here for over 300 years. Inside the house the Rothschild Collection was brought from Mentmore in Buckinghamshire, the home of the present Earl's grandmother and includes magnificent French 18th century furniture, tapestries and other works of art. The contents of the Napoleon Room, collected by the 5th Earl, includes period furniture used by him at the height of his glory and the basics he used when exiled to St Helena – the Duke of Wellington's campaign chair adds a touch of irony to the situation. Scottish portraits, 17th century furniture, 18th century portraits by Reynolds, Gainsborough, Raeburn and Lawrence and racing objects from the Mentmore stud, which produced seven Derby winners, make up the Roseberry collection.

Outside, the landscaped garden and shoreline walk offer fantastic views across the mud flats and sandy beaches, where many varieties of sea birds can be seen, to the Forth Road and Rail Bridges beyond. On an island in the Firth of Forth opposite Aberdour stands Incholm Abbey.

Hopetoun House is Scotland's greatest Adam mansion, standing on the shores of the Forth, to the west of the Forth Bridges. Originally designed by Sir William Bruce (architect of Holyrood Palace) for the 1st Earl of Hopetoun, it was enlarged some 20 years later in 1721. There is a superb nature trail

Edinburgh Castle

through part of the 100 acre woodlands, where fallow and red deer roam and St Kilda sheep (with 4 horns) can be seen (featured later).

Linlithgow Palace is best known as the birth place of Mary Queen of Scots, born on the 8th of December 1542. The magnificent ruins of the Palace stand proudly by the shore of the Loch and replaced an older castle razed to the ground in 1424. The splendid quadrangle with its finely detailed 16th century ornamental fountain is a beautiful setting for the late 15th century Great Hall and Chapel.

Harburn House is a splendid Georgian house built in 1807 after the original mansion was blown up by Oliver Cromwell, with only the stables from the old house remaining and in use today. The estate extends to some 3000 acres of woodland and farmland. The house is hidden away in parkland with views over lakes to the Pentland hills beyond. This country residence offers total seclusion for private use for business entertaining, yet is only a few minutes from the M8 motorway and easy access to both Edinburgh and Glasgow. Visitors to the Lothians should try to visit Edinburgh during 'The Festival' to enhance an already enthralling experience into Scotland's past.

FIFE

Scotland's ancient Capital **Dunfermline** is situated just to the north of the Forth Road Bridge. Here in the town centre is the **Andrew Carnegie Birthplace Museum** which comprises the original weaver's cottage and the adjoining Memorial Hall which tells the fascinating story of Mr Carnegie's early life and his later achievements. In his lifetime (1835 to 1919) he gave away $350,000,000 by way of public benefactions and even now, two generations after his death, his Trust are spending $4 per second.

For golf fanatics and even those who do not play this religion, the clubhouse on the **Old Course, St Andrews**, is one of the most famous sights in the world. Whilst an exact date for the birth of golf still causes a certain amount of controversy, golf was played here in the 15th century. In 1754 the Society of St Andrew's Golfers was founded by 22 diehards and in 1834 King William 1V allowed the society to become **the Royal**

Dalmeny House

184

and Ancient Golf Club, now the game's governing body. A walk along 'The Scores' overlooking the seafront takes the visitor to **St Andrews Castle**, built in 1200 to repel raiders and home of the Bishop of St Andrew's. The unpleasant 24 feet deep bottle dungeon and secret passage are well worth a visit. Once an important religious town, the Cathedral built in 1160 and consecrated in 1318, welcomed medieval pilgrims to pray at the 31 altars and shrine of St Andrew in the sanctuary. Close by are the ruins of the 12th century Church of St Rule, who brought St Andrew's relics to this place and there is a spectacular view from the church tower (108 feet high) which takes in the town and the harbour to the east. The Scottish flag (satire) comes from the cross of St Andrew, the patron saint of Scotland and dates from around the 13th century. St Andrew's is Scotland's oldest university founded in the 15th century and still an important seat of learning today, whose students can be seen attending church each Sunday in traditional red robes. In the 16th century John Napier, the mathematician who devised logarithms and the earliest calculator of ivory pieces, was a student here.

The National Trust for Scotland now administers on behalf of Her Royal Highness Queen Elizabeth II the **Royal Palace of Falkland**, the country residence of the Stuart kings and queens where wild boar and deer were hunted. The original castle and palace dates from the 12th century but the present palace was built between 1501 and 1541 by James IV and James V who was responsible for decorating the south and east ranges in the Renaissance style with medallions of figures from classical mythology. Restoration work to these ranges by the Marquess of Bute in the 19th century and more recent work by the Trust has allowed visitors to view the Chapel Royal, Library, Keeper's Apartments and the King's Bedchamber. The oldest Real (or Royal) Tennis Court in Britain, still playable to this day, built in 1539 is situated in the splendid gardens. The picturesque 17th to 19th century town of Falkland, with its cobbled streets, was Scotland's first conservation area in 1970.

THE WEST OF SCOTLAND

The West of Scotland comprises the southern part of the vast Strathclyde Region, the western part of the Lowland corridor and Glasgow.

Glasgow has come a long way since its 6th century beginnings by the missionary St Mungo, whose small timber church stood on the site of what is now the 12th century **Cathedral**

Carnegie Birthplace Museum

in St Mungo's memory. Close by the Cathedral, is the Necropolis with its fascinating array of statues, temples and monuments to the dead, where the important Victorian fathers of the city are buried. From this humble beginning much hard work has resulted in the successful Garden Festival in recent years and in 1990 the city was the 'European City of Culture'. The University was founded in 1451, the second oldest in Scotland, by Bishop William Turnbull and relocated from the High Street to Kelvingrove Park in 1870 to Victorian Gothic buildings designed by Sir Gilbert Scott.

Nearby is **The Hunterian Art Gallery** which houses a major collection of European Art, including paintings by Rembrandt, Stubbs, Chardin and Reynolds. There is also a fine collection of Scottish 19th and 20th century paintings, including works by McTaggart, Guthrie, Fergusson, Peploe and Eardley, and a group of works by French artists including Pissarro and Rodin. Contemporary sculpture is displayed in the Sculpture Courtyard. The outstanding Whistler Collection comprises 80 paintings; prints and drawings; and his furniture, silver and porcelain. Some 70 paintings and a selection of other items are on permanent display. The gallery also houses the largest collection of prints in Scotland. Changing selections are shown in the Print Gallery alongside a permanent display on Printmaking Techniques.

The Mackintosh House comprises the principal rooms from the home of C.R.Mackintosh, reconstructed as an integral part of the Gallery. The Mackintosh Collection contains over 60 pieces of furniture and nearly 800 drawings, watercolours and designs. Changing displays from the Mackintosh Collection of designs and watercolours are shown in the Mackintosh House Gallery.

At Kelvin Hill a fascinating collection of tramcars and other modes of transport is on display at the **Museum of Transport**. In the 17th century the Merchants of Glasgow were responsible for much of the new building of hospitals and public buildings. In the early part of the 19th century the architect David Hamilton designed various buildings including Hutcheson's Hospital in 1802 and part of Royal Exchange Square, including Stirling's Library in 1829. Alexander 'Greek' Thompson was the architect responsible for several churches; the Caledonian Road Church, built in 1857, and St Vincent Street Church built 2 years later, are both fine examples of the Grecian style. The School of Art, the Willow Tea Rooms in Sauchiehall Street and Hill House at Helensburgh were by the Scottish art nouveau architect and interior designer Charles Rennie Mackintosh, who is perhaps best remembered for his high backed chairs. **The Burrell Collection** is housed in a purpose built gallery in Pollok Country Park. Sir William Burrell, who died in 1958, collected magnificent 19th century French pictures, medieval art, Chinese ceramics, tapestries and stained glass, jades and bronze from his travels around the world.

Pollok House Mansion was built by William Adam in 1752, set in superb grounds overlooking the River White Cart. It houses the Stirling Maxwell Collection of Spanish and other European paintings, together with wonderful displays of furniture and decorative arts (featured later).

The Clyde Valley to the south east of Glasgow is steeped in history with a major Roman base near Crawford, where today their early work on the land allows soft fruit and tomatoes to be grown. William Wallace's statue at Lanark marks the spot where his men gathered before going into battle and close by is New Lanark, an important industrial archaeological site, founded by Robert Owen to give his cotton millworkers homes, a school, canteen and shops.

The David Livingstone Centre in Blantyre gives an insight into the missionary's work in Africa, where he died, whilst searching for the source of the Nile.

BURNS COUNTRY

Burns Country is centred around the county town of Ayr where the Bard Robert Burns was born on the 25th January 1759 in the nearby town of Alloway. To Scots all over the world his birthday is celebrated annually on 'Burns Night' with the traditional supper of tatties, neeps and haggis washed down with whisky, and reminiscing and recollecting the words of many of his 350 or so poems and songs. **Burns Cottage** was built by the poet's father in 1757 and is now open to visitors who come from all over the world to see the relics of his life. **The Burns Museum** is adjacent to the cottage and contains original manuscripts and books and close by is the **Burns Monument**, erected in 1820, where sculptures of characters from his poems stand in the grounds. The original Tam O'Shanter Inn in Ayr now houses a Burns Museum and is the starting point for the annual Tam's ride as depicted in the poem of the same name. His First Edition of poems was published chiefly in the Scottish dialect and made Burns

Hunterian Art Gallery

instantly famous. 'Auld Lang Syne', 'Tam O'Shanter' and 'My Love's Like a Red Red Rose' are perhaps the best known of his works. The village of Tarbolton became Burns' home for his late teens and early twenties after his father moved to the farm of Lochlea. With friends he founded a debating club in 1780, **the Bachelors Club**, now owned by the NTS and joined the Freemasons in 1781. At Leglen Wood it is said that his hero William Wallace, a Scottish nationalist and patriot, took refuge in the 13th century. Burns visited this area often and wrote a poem whose opening line is 'Scots wha hae wi Wallace bled', which is now a kind of rallying call to Scots.

Travel south from Ayr to **Blairquhan Castle**, built in 1820. The 3rd Baronet, Sir David Hunter Blair, commissioned William Burn to carry out the work to replace an earlier castle built in the 14th century. The Hunter Blairs still live here today, the building remains largely unaltered and many of the original fittings and fabrics are still in use. John Tweedie designed the gardens to compliment the 3rd Baronet's beautiful land-scaped grounds, which have a fine collection of mature trees. It is believed that the 4th Baronet planted a spectacular Sequoia Gigantea in 1860, from seeds brought on the SS 'Great Britain' from America. The visitor may be interested in Twee-die's Regency greenhouse, where it is possible to light fires in the specially designed chimneys to protect the fruit trees in cold weather.

The gardens and grounds of **Culzean Castle** are spectacular overlooking the Firth of Clyde (featured later). Close by at Turnberry, Prestwick and Troon there are some of the world famous golf courses where many Open Championships have been played.

The Lowlands covers a large part of the country where the vast majority of Scots live and offers the visitor varied excursions to enjoy fine country houses and parks, magnificent castles, superb gardens and the opportunity to enjoy some of the best golf and sailing in the world.

Culzean Castle

Overlooking the Tweed, one of Scotland's finest salmon rivers, Floors Castle occupies an outstandingly beautiful setting. Reputed to be the largest inhabited house in Scotland, it is home to the Duke of Roxburghe and his family.

When it was built for the 1st Duke in 1721 to a design by William Adam it bore little resemblance to the grand castle seen today. Adam's design was for a plain Georgian house. The 6th Duke called upon William Playfair to enlarge and embellish the castle in 1841 and he let his imagination and his talent run riot. The results are dramatic with two vast embracing wings and an exotic roofscape of pepper pot spires and domes.

There have been no external alterations since the 6th Duke's time of any note. Internally the story is quite different as many of the rooms were completely tranformed by the 8th Duke's American wife. The castle contains an outstanding collection of tapestries and French 17th and 18th century furniture, much of which were brought to Floors by the 8th Duchess.

She created the Drawing Room in Louis XV style to accommodate the magnificent set of late 17th Century Brussels tapestries brought from her family's Long Island mansion. The Louis XV gilt suite of eight chairs is covered in Beauvais tapestry.

The Needle Room, said to be a copy of a room at Versailles, was decorated by Duchess May in the style Louis XVI and the French furniture includes several important pieces of this period. The walls are hung with the Duchess' collection of modern post-impressionist paintings including works by Henri Matisse, Pierre Bonnard, Odilon Redon, Augustus John and Sir Matthew Smith.

The Ballroom, one of Playfair's additions, was also modified by Duchess May for more of her wonderful tapestries, in this case a set of 17th Century Gobelins. Besides fine paintings and an impressive collection of English, French and Italian furniture this room contains a spectacular collection of Chinese porcelain.

The gardens at Floors are informal with extensive herbaceous borders and rose beds. For many years the castle has been famous for the quality of its carnations; several new varieties have been propagated here.

Floors Castle provides an unrivalled location for corporate entertaining, offering exclusive style, service and privacy in elegant surroundings.

Almost a thousand years old, Traquair is the oldest inhabited house in Scotland. The River Tweed, famous for its salmon fishing, runs at the back of the house, and the wooded hills of the Border landscape provide the perfect peaceful setting for this romantic house. Traquair was originally used as a hunting lodge for Scottish monarchs who took part in their favourite pastimes of hunting, hawking and fishing. Then the forests abounded in game, small and large.

In 1478 the Earl of Buchan, an uncle of the King, bought the house for the paltry sum of £3.15s and in 1491 he bestowed it to his son, James Stuart, who became the first Laird of Traquair. James had plans for extending his house, but before this could be done he fell alongside his King, James IV, at Flodden Field in 1513. During the 16th century, Traquair began a gradual process of transformation under successive generations to the stately mansion seen today, practically untouched since the end of the 17th century.

Traquair became one of the great bastions of the Catholic faith, and at the top of the house in a room commanding a view of the approaches Mass was celebrated in secret. The concealed staircase at the back of a cupboard, connecting with one from the Museum Room was constructed at this time as Traquair became a refuge for Catholic Priests in times of terror. The Stuarts of Traquair suffered for their religion and their Jacobite sympathies without counting the cost. Imprisoned, fined and isolated for their beliefs, Traquair became the Jacobite centre of the South.

When the 5th Earl of Traquair bade farewell to this guest, Prince Chalres Edward Stuart, on his long march south to claim the throne, the famous Bear Gates were closed behind him. The Earl promised that the gates would not be reopened until a Stuart King was returned to the throne. The gates have remained shut ever since.

Besides the fine furniture and paintings, the house contains collections of manuscripts, books, letters, silver and needlework. A particularly fine collection of Jacobite drinking glasses includes the famous Traquair 'amen' glass engraved with a Jacobite verse and a portrait glass showing the head of Bonnie Prince Charlie.

In the peaceful grounds an active craft centre flourishes, there is a maze to wander through and enchanted woods to explore. Ale has been brewed at Traquair since Mary Queen of Scots visited in 1566, and no doubt fortified Prince Charles Edward Stuart before he left on his long journey. Visitors may once again sip Traquair Ale, brewed in the old brewhouse, with a light lunch.

After 19 Lairds and 8 Earls, the present owner is Catherine Maxwell Stuart, 21st Lady of Traquair.

Drumlanrig Castle is the ancient stronghold of the Douglas family and Dumfriesshire home of the Duke of Buccleuch and Queensberry. The castle, of local pink sandstone, is set on a hill at the end of a long ridge with beautiful views across Nithsdale to rolling hills and woodlands. William Douglas, 1st Duke of Queensberry, began to build in 1679 around an open court-yard, with a circular staircase tower in each corner. Four square towers with twelve turrets form the outside angles. Drumlanrig is one of the first and most important renaissance buildings in the grand manner in Scottish domestic architecture.

Almost 700 years ago the Douglases were staunch supporters of Robert Bruce, King of Scotland. When he died in 1329 his heart was entrusted to Sir James Douglas, or 'Black Douglas', who would take it on the next crusade and thus fulfill his King's ambition. While fighting in Spain he fell mortally wounded and hurled the heart in its silver casket with the cry 'Forward, brave heart'. To this day the Douglas motto is 'Forward' and their striking crest, a winged heart surmounted by Bruce's crown is emblazoned all over Drumlanrig in stone, lead, iron, wood and even woven into the carpeting.

The graceful curves of the horseshoe staircase and the arches of the lower colonnade contrast with the hard straight lines of the main structure; the rich carvings over the windows and the charm of the little cupolas further help to soften the sense of fortress-like severity. Drumlanrig is steeped in history and filled with treasures, greatly enriched by the merger of the three families Montagu, Douglas and Scott in the 18th century.

Within the entrance hall there is an immediate sense of civilised living - fine oil paintings, a magnificent French longcase clock, a rare Italian statuette and 17th century chairs all set against a wall covering of Douglas hearts stamped on gilded leather. A fine piece of needlework is believed to be the work of Mary Queen of Scots and her ladies.

The oak staircase and balustrade is one of the first of its kind in Scotland. The oak panelling is adorned by eight curved giltwood sconces in the style of Thomas Chippendale and some out-standing paintings. The most notable are Holbein's 'Sir Nicholas Carew', Leonardo da Vinci's 'Madonna with the Yarnwinder' and Rembrandt's 'Old Woman Reading'. The mgnificent silver chandelier in the staircase gallery has sixteen branches in the form of dolphins and mermaids and was made in about 1670.

The well proportioned drawing room with its fine Grinling Gibbons carvings contains some magnificent works of art. They include two French cabinets of outstanding merit, believed to have been presented by King Louis XIV to King Charles II. Both were made for Versailles c. 1675. The Boulle table with red tortoiseshell and brass inlay is also of the Louis XIV period, as are the pair of kneehole writing tables. Above these are a mag-nificent pair of late 17th Century mirrors.

Drumlanrig's builder, the 1st Duke of Queensberry, was a little concerned at the cost he incurred. He might well have felt happier about his investment had he been able to see for him-self the contribution his castle now makes in our history.

Edinburgh Castle rises majestically from its rocky cliff high above the Firth of Forth, dominating the beautiful town which sprawls around its feet. The Castle, an active army garrison until 1923, is approached across an open, sloping parade ground known as the Esplanade which terminates at the Gatehouse and drawbridge. Here the impressive spectacle of the Edinburgh Military Tattoo is held against the backdrop of the flood-lit castle, when the parade ground echoes once more to the sound of marching feet and the skirl of the pipes.

This side of the Castle is fortified by gun emplacements or batteries, the most impressive of which is the Half Moon Battery, built in 1574 and jutting out over the easterly quarter above the town below. Within the Castle walls are barracks, the 18th century Governor's House and a military hospital which now houses the Scottish United Services Museum. Most of the older buildings are found in an area known as the Citadel. Grouped around Crown Square at its southern end are the Palace, the Great Hall and the Scottish National War Memorial.

By far the oldest building in the Citadel, indeed it is the oldest in Edinburgh, is the tiny St Margaret's Chapel dating from the 12th century. Its main features, the rounded interior within rectangular walls and the carved chancel arch, are characteristically Norman.

Within the wall of the Half Moon Battery are the remains of David's Tower, a great square Keep which dominated the Castle until it was destroyed during the 'Long Siege' of 1571-1573. The Castle was bombarded and besieged many times during the

centuries when England was at war with Scotland and changed hands on more than one occasion.

The Great Hall, with its splendid hammer beam roof, was built by James 1V and extensively restored in the 1880s and now displays a fine collection of weaponry. The Palace, also built in the 15th century but greatly remodelled in 1617, was the royal residence of the Stuart monarchs and the royal arms and ciphers can be seen in several places. Mary Queen of Scots gave birth to her son, the future James V1 in a small chamber of the royal apartments in 1566. It was he who united the two warring factions in 1603 when he became King James I of England.

The last great siege of the castle took place in 1659 when it was held for the deposed James II against William and Mary; the last defence of all was in 1745 when Bonnie Prince Charlie and his Jacobite supporters ineffectively blockaded the castle.

For over a hundred years after the Act of Union in 1707 the Honours of Scotland had disappeared. They were discovered in 1818 hidden in a chest in the Crown Chamber and are now on display. Part of the crown, the oldest in the United Kingdom c1540, is said to date from the time of Robert the Bruce. The jewels include pearls fished from the River Tay. The sword and sceptre were both gifts to James 1V, while the sword belt, lost in the 17th century when the Honours were being hidden from Cromwell was found in a wall and finally restored to the castle in 1893. The Honours were last used during the Queen's visit after her Coronation in 1953.

191

The site for Hopetoun House was well chosen, affording fine views over the deer park to the shores of the Firth of Forth and the hills of Fife beyond. The house was designed for Charles Hope, 1st Earl of Hopetoun, by Sir William Bruce and built between 1699 and 1707. Enlargements were made by William Adam and completed by his three sons after his death in 1748. The interior decoration was completed largely under John Adam's supervision between 1752 and 1767 and much of the original decorations and furniture survives today. In effect Hopetoun House is two buildings in contrasting styles, one designed by Sir William Bruce and the other by William Adam, linked by the Entrance Hall.

The front staircase is one of the outstanding decorative features of the Bruce house. The pine-panelled walls, frieze, cornice and panel borders are carved with flowers, fruit, wheatears and peapods. The murals within these framed panels are modern, painted in 1967 by William McLaren as a memorial to the wife of the 3rd Marquess. The Cupola painting depicts angels and cherubs supporting the Hope crest and coat-of-arms and although painted early in the 18th century is perfectly in harmony with the modern panels.

The Bruce Bedchamber, designed for the young 1st Earl contains a magnificent gilt four-poster bed hung with red damask and a unique Pattern Chair. This was made to display various forms of carving to enable the 2nd Earl to select which style he preferred for the State Apartments. The panelled Garden Parlour has a portrait of the 4th Earl wearing the uniform of the Company of Archers of which he was Captain-General in 1822, when he entertained George IV at Hopetoun. He had had a distinguished military career and was responsible for the completion of the State Dining Room, and for the purchase of several important pictures.

The State Apartments were created by William Adam and executed by his eldest son, John. The Yellow Drawing Room, its walls hung with glowing yellow silk damask, was originally the dining room. The magnificent furniture was made by the noted rococo cabinet maker and upholsterer James Cullen, a contemporary of Thomas Chippendale.

The Red Drawing Room has a beautiful coved ceiling with an enriched cornice and frieze which is one of the finest examples of rococo decoration in Scotland. The furniture, again by James Cullen, is arranged in the 18th century manner known as 'Parade' style, with all the furniture placed around the walls.

The State Dining Room was created from two rooms in the early 19th century and represents a fine example of a Regency room as practically everything in it dates from that period, including the cornice, chimneypiece, elaborate curtains and golden wallpaper. This room contains a wonderful collection of family portraits and exquisite Meissen and Dresden porcelain. To ensure that food arrived from the distant kitchens piping hot it was packed in a steam-heated container and trundled along a railway track and up in a lift to a warming oven in the specially created Serving Room, and the waiting footmen. In the South Pavilion the elegant Ballroom is hung with eight late 17th century Aubusson tapestries. Nowadays the Ballroom provides an impressive setting for special functions including gala dinners, concerts and balls.

From the roof-top viewing platform the gardens and grounds can be fully appreciated. In the 18th century formal gardens were laid out on the west lawn, and although the Parterre is no longer there, the intricate outlines are still visible some 250 years later, and the 'large bason of water' (the Round Pond) still remains. The 'Terras' is now the Bastion or Sea Walk and a walled kitchen garden occupied the site of the present Garden Centre. It had an ingenious heated hollow 'firewall' against which were grown the luscious peaches and nectarines for this grand household.

In early spring drifts of daffodils flutter on the slopes above the Bowling Green; primroses, bluebells and many other wild flowers carpet the lovely woodland walks. In early summer the soft shades of spring give way to iridescent azaleas and rhododendrons; later still berries of all kinds and many types of fungi may be seen. The large lawned areas are excellent for a host of outdoor events, and everywhere the views are spectacular.

Only 12 miles from Edinburgh on the A904, Hopetoun has excellent facilities for both business and private entertaining. The Scottish Gala Evening in particular provides a taste of the finest entertainment 'north of the border', and can be rounded off by the stirring ceremony of Beating the Retreat.

Standing proudly on the Ayrshire coast overlooking Arran, the Mull of Kintyre and Ailsa Craig, Culzean Castle is one of Robert Adam's most spectacular achievements. Built between 1772 and 1792, its Gothic style is less familiar than Adam's more usual Classicism.

Robert Adam was commissioned by the 10th Earl of Cassilis and began to remodel the south front to incorporate an older mansion. Work on the north front followed and then the impressive round tower, which was linked to the south front by Adam's imaginative oval staircase, was completed. In the 19th century an entrance hall was added, but most of the lovely Adam interiors are relatively unchanged.

The splendid Round Drawing Room and Oval Staircase are lavishly furnished and decorated with ornate plasterwork friezes,

fireplaces and finely moulded ceilings. As was his practice, much of the fine furniture was designed by Adam himself to complement a particular room and the carpets were often made to echo the design of the ceiling. The house also contains some very fine family portraits, silver and porcelain.

The magnificent Country Park extends to some 560 acres including the Swan Pond, formal walled gardens, quiet woodlands and 2½ miles of picturesque coastline. The walled garden is entered through a Victorian camellia house which is a wonderful sight in summer filled with exotic blooms. Inside the walled garden is the grotto and the formal fountain garden has terraces and herbaceous borders planted with an ever changing show of colour as the summer days lengthen. There is a varied programme of guided walks along the coast. There are excellent facilities for conferences and seminars.

The Highlands and Islands are located to the north of the Highland Boundary Fault Line and normally divided to comprise the Central Highlands and the Northern Highlands and Islands. The Central Highlands stretch from the Trossachs and Loch Lomond west to Argyll and its Islands, north to Inverness, Fort William and Aberdeen. Caithness, Sutherland, Ross and Cromarty, Skye, Western Isles, Orkney and Shetland form the Northern Highlands and Islands.

From the large and small islands in the Firth of Clyde and the west beyond, the Central Highlands include the most westerly point on the British mainland at Ardnamurchan. With the magnificent splendour and history of Stirling and Perth, the Great Glen to the north and the fishing ports of Fraserburgh and Peterhead on the shoulder of Scotland, this is perhaps a region that has everything. Historic Scotland looks after many historic properties throughout the area where visitors are most welcome.

ARGYLL

North and west of the Firth of Clyde sits Argyll, with its lush green hills descending to hundreds of miles of rugged coastline. No matter where the visitor travels in this area superb scenery is assured from Campbelltown on the south tip of the Kintyre peninsula (Scotland's longest); to the Isles of Arran and Bute in the Firth of Clyde (reached by ferry from Ardrossan or Wemyss Bay); the Atlantic coast islands of Islay, Jura and Gigha; and Mid-Argyll and the Cowal Peninsula (reached by ferry from Gourock) with Loch Fyne between.

LOCH FYNE

Near the head of the loch is **Inveraray Castle** built in the latter half of the 18th century, the home of the Duke and Duchess of Argyll. Designed by Roger Morris and decorated by Robert Mylne, the style of Robert Adam is to be seen in his role as clerk of works. The turreted Gothic revival exterior gives way to a splendid decorative interior which now houses the family's magnificent collection of pictures and tapestries, over 1300 pieces of armour, French 18th century furniture and Continental china. Numerous walks in the woodlands offer spectacular views, none better than from the top of the Inveraray Bell Tower, some 126 feet high.

Inveraray Jail in the town centre is worth a visit to get some idea of the conditions prisoners were kept in during the last century. The 18th century courtroom is of architectural and

Glenfeochan Gardens

historical interest and in addition has a real life period trial with jury on display.

Further south on the north bank of the loch is **Crarae Forest and Lodge Gardens** with its splendid displays of azaleas, rhododendrons and exotic shrubs, set in a beautiful glen. Driving south through Lochgilphead and Ardrushaig, the pretty fishing village of Tarbert not only lands the famous Loch Fyne herring but also plays host to a tremendous variety of sailing events, with yachts from all over the world enjoying the local hospitality.

The Isle of Arran can be reached by ferry from Claonaig to Lochranza, where the ruins of Lochranza Castle is said to be the landing point for Robert the Bruce on his return from Ireland. This is splendid walking and climbing country, particularly high above Brodick Bay and **Brodick Castle, Garden and Country Park** with fine views from Goat Fell to the mainland. The Dukes of Hamilton owned the castle, built in the 13th century, which now houses fine paintings, silver and porcelain. North from Inveraray lies Oban, where a regular ferry service sails to the Western Isles and Iona, where St Columba landed from Ireland in 563. The original monastery has been destroyed but remains of the later 13th century nunnery and monastery, from where followers were sent to convert Scotland to Christianity, survive today. Sitting by the bustling harbour with its pleasure and fishing boats and commercial ferries there are splendid views of the Island and Sound of Mull.

Not far from Oban, is Kilmore and **Glenfeochan Gardens**, the Victorian Arboretum is 'One of the Great gardens of the Highlands'. Many rare shrubs and trees, some planted in 1840, make a wonderful canopy for the tender rhododendrons and other rare shrubs including a large embothrium and davidia which abounds with 'white handkerchiefs' in the summer. The walled garden has one of the old Victorian heated walls giving shelter to a huge magnolia, eucryphia and a ginkgo.

CENTRAL AND TAYSIDE

The Heartlands of Scotland consist of Loch Lomond, Stirlingshire, Perthshire and the Trossachs leading to the Gateway to the Highlands. This is the land of Sir Walter Scott and Rob Roy MacGregor with castle strongholds shrouded in mystery, and breathtaking scenery over hills and lochs.

Stirling, the Gateway to the Highlands, is so called due to its central location in the country. It sits by the River Forth, overlooked by the Ochil Hills and has in the past been the scene of many battles, including Bannockburn where Robert the Bruce defeated the English in 1314. **Stirling Castle**, standing high above the town, was the scene of much fighting between the Scots and the English until it became the home of the Scottish kings from 1370 to 1603. Both Mary Queen of Scots and James VI (James I of England) lived here and James II and James V were born in the Castle.

A short drive from Glasgow is Britain's largest lake, Loch Lomond, 24 miles long and in the shadow of the majestic Ben Lomond, 3194 feet high, which the healthy visitor can climb from the 'bonnie bonnie banks' of the loch. From Balloch in the south, the traditional cruise ship 'Countess Fiona' sails to Inversnaid and around the islands of Inchmurrin and Inchcailloch where the ruins of a castle and nunnery can be seen. On Loch Katrine steamer trips are available on the SS 'Sir Walter Scott'. Scott's poem 'The Lady of the Lake' is said to be set in the lochs and hills of this area of outstanding natural beauty. North at Balquhidder, is the grave of Rob Roy MacGregor, who died in 1734, near his house at Inverlochlarig. At Lochearnhead the A85 west to Crieff passes the Melville Monument, set 859 feet above sea level from where there are breathtaking views of the countryside. In nearby Comrie is the **Museum of Scottish Tartans**, where the history of every tartan, clan and surname can be traced.

Drummond Castle, south of Crieff, dates from the 15th century although Cromwell attacked and destroyed most of this structure in 1745. A well tended formal Italian garden is set in the grounds with a multiple sundial dating from 1630.

THE FINEST SALMON WATERS IN THE WORLD

Beyond the region's highest mountain Ben Lawers (3984 feet), with views to both the North Sea and the Atlantic is Loch Tay, 14 miles long and reputedly the finest salmon waters in the world.

From the Firth of Tay east of Perth the River Tay can be traced to Scone, Regorton and Almondmouth, to Stanley with its craggy glen, by the River Isla, to Dunkeld where sea trout have improved in recent years. Here in the 9th century the Scots and the Picts came together in what was then the religious centre of Scotland at the Cathedral of Columba. Part of Shakespeare's Macbeth is set in Birnham Woods to the south of the town. The River Lyon enters the Tay downstream from Kenmore where the autumn scenery is spectacular in this stretch to Aberfeldy.

Castle Menzies, west of Aberfeldy, has recently been restored by the Menzies Clan Society, and houses the Clan's Museum. The turrets and finely detailed dormers were added in 1577 to this magnificent early 16th century fortress after the original castle was burnt to the ground by the Wolf of Badenoch.

From Ben Lui the clear streams collect at Fillan Water, near Crianlarich, then to Loch Dochart with its ruined castle, to Glen Dochart and its river where the Lochay joins at Killin, at the west end of Loch Tay. From its source in these high, deserted mountains of Perthshire to the Firth these majestic waters travel over 100 miles to provide spectacular – and frustrating – fishing.

Blair Castle, north of Perth, was built in the 13th century and since the mid-19th century has been home to the Earls and Dukes of Atholl (featured later). South of Blair Castle, through the Pass of Killiecrankie, where in 1689 the Jacobites defeated the Government's army, there are some fine walks through woodlands following the Tunnell Nature Trail. Here the Pitlochry Power Station and Dam, part of the hydro electric system, allows visitors to view salmon through windows in the fish ladder.

Glamis Castle, west of Forfar, has been the home of the Lyons family since the 14th century; Princess Margaret was born here in 1930 (featured later). Further east beyond Brechin to the north is **Edzell Castle and Garden**, an early 16th century tower house and late 16th century castle, with an

unusual walled garden in the Renaissance style, designed in 1604 by Sir David Lindsay. The recesses in the walls are filled with flowers and highlight the sculptures of The Planetary Deities, Liberal Arts and Cardinal Virtues.

Scone Palace was built in 1803 on the site of an ancient church dating back to the 6th century and earliest days of Scottish history (featured later). The Fair City of Perth, with its Georgian houses on both banks of the Tay and colourful past, was once Scotland's capital. The famous Black Watch has its museum containing regimental honours in Balhousie Castle and the tiny Branklyn Gardens, at less than two acres, has been described as the finest private garden in the country.

GRAMPIAN AND THE HIGHLANDS

The Grampian Region in the north east of the country stretches from a point east of Nairn on the Moray coast, with its sandy beaches and picturesque fishing villages; around the shoulder of Scotland, where the Moray Firth meets the North Sea, with its breathtaking views out over rugged cliffs, natural wildlife, and historic castles; beyond Aberdeen to Deeside, where the Dee provides some of the best salmon fishing in the country. Inland, there is good farmland, spectacular views to the Cairngorm Mountains, the River Spey, the ruins of Elgin Cathedral and, believe it or not, a Scotch Whisky Trail. The City of Aberdeen, Scotland's third largest, is an important staging post for the worlds oil companies and their offshore operations in the North Sea – but there is much more to this granite city and its 'northern lights'. William the Lion granted Aberdeen the royal charters in the 12th century and it has been an important sea port ever since, first trading tea with China, then in the 19th century, trawling fish. The 18th century chapel, at the Kings College University buildings built in 1494, is a particularly important example of a medieval college church. The Art Gallery and Maritime Museum contain some interesting paintings and models depicting the city's traditions with the sea, as does the early morning daily auction at the local fishmarket.

THE MALT WHISKY TRAIL

Travel north from Aberdeen to **Fyvie Castle**, some 25 miles away, a fine example of Scottish baronial architecture dating from the 13th century. Each of the five towers is named after one of the five families who have owned the Castle through the centuries. Recently refurbished to the Edwardian style, created by the first Lord Leith of Fyvie, the great wheel stair, panelling and plaster ceiling in the 17th century Morning Room are of particular interest. Fine portraits by Raeburn, Romney, Gainsborough and others hang in the principal rooms. There are interesting walks through the landscaped woodlands around Loch Fyvie. Fyvie Castle is part of Scotland's only Castle Trail, which includes eight other interesting castles in the Grampian Region, but for those more inclined to have 'a wee dram', then head for Dufftown. Here in beautiful Speyside are eight distilleries where the visitor can learn more of the skills and mysteries behind the making of malt whisky. Smoking peat fires dry locally harvested barley, water is added then distilled in copper stills and left to mature in oak casks – simple isn't it! The Malt Whisky Trail allows visits to the distilleries making Glenfiddich (Dufftown), Strathisia (Keith), Glenfarclas, Cragganmore, the Glenlivet and Tamnavulin (Tomintoul). From here head south through the Lecht Ski Area to Balmoral and Braemar.

The Waterfall – *Elizabeth Halstead. Courtesy of Rosentiel's.*

196

Balmoral Castle has been used as a summer holiday residence of the Royal Family since purchased by Prince Albert in 1852, and is the private residence of the Queen. Queen Victoria's consort had much of the castle rebuilt in a Scottish baronial style in white granite with its 100 foot tower, turrets and battlements. When the Royals are not in residence visitors can walk through the garden, designed by Prince Albert, with its rare conifers and trees. Also on view is Queen Mary's sunken garden and Queen Victoria's garden cottage. Close by is Crathie Church, where the Royals worship when in residence.

Braemar Castle, an impressive fortress built in 1628 by the Earl of Mar as a bulwark against the rising power of the Farquharsons, was destroyed in 1689 by the Black Colonel, John Farquharson of Inverey. The castle remained an uninhabited ruin for 60 years until after the defeat of Bonnie Prince Charlie at Culloden in 1746, when the English troops, with the help of John Adam, made good the earlier damage and used the castle as a garrison. Later, the Farquharsons of Invercauld, who had purchased the castle as a ruin in 1732, transformed it into a private residence of unusual charm still in use today. The iron 'yett', newel staircase and the Lairds Pit – an underground dungeon – together with the daunting fortification and central round tower allow the visitor to imagine the past mystery and intrigue of the castle. The famous Braemar Highland Gathering is held annually at the nearby village where, at a cottage in Castleton Terrace, Robert Louis Stevenson wrote 'Treasure Island'.

Crathes Castle near Banchory, was built in the later half of the 16th century in Scottish baronial style, although it was extended during Queen Anne's reign and later in Victorian times. It was the home of the Burnett family for 370 years. After negotiating the 16th century vaulted kitchen and other service rooms, a turnpike staircase leads the visitor to the impressive Great Hall in which hangs the Horn of Leys, a hunting horn said to have been given to the family by King Robert the Bruce in 1323. Further up the tower there are three rooms with beautiful ceilings painted around 1600. However, those of a nervous disposition may wish to avoid one of them, the Green Lady's Room, with its biblical inscriptions on the cross-beams – it is said to be haunted! At the top of the house is the Long Gallery used for the Laird's Court and remarkable for its oak-panelled ceiling.

The spectacular walled garden extends to over three and a half acres and contains eight different sections each with its own theme. One of these, the Upper Pool Garden, includes purple foliage with red and yellow flowers. Thick yew hedges, interesting examples of the art of topiary, divide some of the gardens and were planted in the early 18th century. Many unusual trees grow in the 600-acre estate and energetic visitors will enjoy six well-marked trails, the longest being 7 miles in length.

THE CAIRNGORM MOUNTAINS

The Cairngorm Mountains lie to the east of the Grampians and straddle the boundary with the Highland Region. Here in this rugged but beautiful part of the country are some of Britain's highest mountains with Ben Macdui 4296 feet and Cairn Gorm 4084 feet. There are numerous fascinating walks and climbs for the visitor of every ability, although, as always on mountains care should be taken, as the weather can change quite suddenly. In the Cairngorms National Nature Reserve, the country's largest eagles and stags can be seen in their natural habitat, whilst to the north at the Glen More Forest Park, now owned by the Forestry Commission, the visitor should be on the lookout for eagles and ospreys, and reindeer brought from Scandinavia 30 years ago. Travelling south from Scotland's premier ski resort of Aviemore – the skiing actually takes place on the northern slopes of Cairn Gorm – is the Highland Wildlife Park in the Spey valley where wild horses and goats, red deer, bison, grouse and many other animals can be seen. Nearby at Loch Insh, eagles, ospreys and other rare birds are protected by the RSPB ownership.

Heading north towards Inverness, there stands the ruins of a medieval castle on Loch Moy. Taking the road to Newlands, the exposed moorland is the place where the last battle on mainland Britain, in 1746, was fought at Culloden between Bonnie Prince Charlie and the Duke of Cumberland. The Scots were outnumbered two to one and suffered appalling casualties and 1200 deaths both during and after the surrender, earning the Duke his nickname 'Butcher' Cumberland. Old Leanach Cottage, at the centre of the battlefield, now houses a museum run by the National Trust for Scotland. In 1881 a cairn to the dead was erected by the side of the road and across the road are scattered stones marking the names of the clans involved in the fighting. The Cumberland Stone in the adjacent Field of the English, where only 76 of the Dukes troops perished, is said to mark the spot from where the Duke orchestrated the slaughter. The circular burial chambers and upright stones of the Clava Cairns are about 3500 years old and are an important prehistoric monument to Scotland's past. After Culloden, **Fort George** was built to ensure that there was never another Highland uprising.

Continue on to Cawdor to find **Cawdor Castle** made famous by Shakespeare with its Macbeth overtures (featured later). In Inverness, only Cromwell's Clock Tower remains of the large monument built by his army, the remainder was destroyed when Charles II regained the throne. Standing on the banks of the River Ness, the town has been the capital of the highland region for many a day, its Castle dating back to the 12th century. In front of the present Castle, built in 1834, is a statue of Flora Macdonald, who assisted Bonnie Prince Charlie to escape from Cromwell's army.

THE GREAT GLEN

Running from Inverness to Fort William is Glen Albyn or Glen Mor, a natural fault often referred to as The Great Glen. From Fort Augustus look across to **Castle Urquhart** standing on the bank of Loch Ness overlooking Urquhart Bay. Although a ruin today, the visitor is able to imagine the mystery and romance of this beautiful location. Keep an eye out for 'Nessy' the Loch Ness Monster as you travel the 24 mile length of the loch and if unsuccessful take a trip to the Drumnadrochit Monster Centre – unfortunately on the other side of the loch! Fort William stands in the shadow of Britain's tallest mountain, Ben Nevis, although not visible from the town, some 4406 feet above sea level, where on good days the visitor can walk the well worn paths to the summit. The **West Highland Museum** contains many items belonging to Bonnie Prince Charlie and Flora Macdonald and is an interesting visit for those now coming to terms with this period of Scotland's history.

The route south to Ballachulish takes the visitor to Glencoe country, a spectacular skiing, walking and climbing destination for people from all over the world. With the bleak Rannoch Moor to the south and isolated Rannoch railway station accessible only from the east by road, the area gives a fabulous insight into the past. It was here in the winter of 1692 that the tragic massacre of Glencoe took place, when the visiting Campbells turned on their hosts, the Macdonalds, to murder men, women and children. Many of those who fled died in the cold February weather. On the old road, near the Clachaig Inn, stands a memorial to the Macdonalds and the Signal Rock where, it is said, the word was given by King William III to the Campbells to proceed with the massacre – the Clachaig is to be recommended for the thirsty traveller!

THE NORTH

If the first stop for visitors travelling from Inverness is to be the spectacular Rogie Waterfalls, near Contin, by the Victorian Spa town of Strathpeffer, then the Black Isle has been bypassed. This quiet peninsula with its attractive villages and gently sloping hills is worth discovering, as is the 18th century geologist Hugh Miller's cottage in Cromarty. Macbeth is said to have been born in the country town of Dingwall on the Cromarty Firth, where a journey along the A862 reveals an extraordinary scene of huge oil rigs moored in the Firth for repairs against the rolling hills behind. Beyond the Clan Ross Museum in Tain and the Cathedral in Dornoch is **Dunrobin Castle,** by Golspie. The seat of the Countess of Sutherland, one of the seven ancient Earldoms of Scotland, it was built around the early 1300s, overlooking the Moray Firth, but with various extensions in 1650, 1780 and 1845, the latter by Barry, who designed the Houses of Parliament. The house has been continuously inhabited since then. In 1915 Sir Robert Lorimer redesigned the main Barry rooms which were destroyed by fire. The contents of the Castle have been collected by the owners over six centuries and provide an important insight into the life of the Dukes of Sutherland. The magnificent display of furniture, pictures, china and ceremonial costumes can be seen by visitors in the Library, Drawing Room, Queen Victoria's Room, where she slept during her stay in 1872, and other State Rooms. The original Summer House was converted and extended to a Museum which now houses hunting trophies and other mementoes of the Sutherland family and their friends. Charles Barry also designed the splendid gardens in 1848, with terraces and fountains modelled on Versailles.

Inverewe Gardens, north of Poolewe by Gairloch, were created in 1862 by Osgood Mackenzie who began to plant a garden in the grounds of his house overlooking Loch Ewe. However, before a proper start could be made he had to establish the right conditions by importing soil and by planting tree breaks to provide shelter from the salt winds from the Atlantic. The warm air of the Gulf Stream allowed rare and precious exotic plants from all over the world to flourish. Of particular interest to the many visitors nowadays are the giant ferns and eucalyptus, the quaint forget-me-nots and colourful rhododendrons.

The lush green hills, rugged coastline, deserted beaches and single track roads with passing places make this part of the country a delight for the visitor. The castle ruins at Strome and the scenic harbour at Plockton, with its warm Gulf breezes and palm trees are magnificent. Set by lochs Duich, Long and Alsh is **Eilean Donan Castle**. The causeway approach to the islet where Eilean Donan Castle stands is somewhat oversha-

dowed today by the construction of a second bridge across Loch Long. Built in 1220 by Alexander II of Scotland to prevent attacks by invading Danes, it was captured by Spanish Jacobites from Clan MacKenzie in 1719 and subsequently shelled by the English battleship Worcester. It has recently been rebuilt after 200 years of neglect and contains many interesting treasures.

THE ISLANDS

The Isle of Skye can be reached by ferry from the Kyle of Lochalsh and Mallaig. With over 900 miles of craggy coastline, the spectacular Cullin Hills rising to a ridge over 3000 feet high and picturesque villages such as Portree, the visitor, like Bonnie Prince Charlie who fled to this place, will not be disappointed.

Dunvegan Castle, set in a magnificent location on the Isle of Skye has been the home of the Clan Macleod chiefs since 1200; the present owner is the 29th Macleod to inhabit the castle in almost 800 years (featured later).

The Western Isles or Outer Hebrides, made up of five main islands of Lewis and Harris, North Uist, Benbecula, South Uist and Barra, are unbelievably beautiful and peaceful. Separated from the mainland by up to a six hour ferry trip, their Gaelic character and culture has been preserved to provide the visitor with unspoilt sandy beaches on the west and craggy cliffs and inlets on the east. The standing stones at Callanish, Lewis, west of the main town of Stornoway and nearby Giarynahime, are said to date from 2000 BC and are to this day surrounded with mystery and legend.

St Kilda, being 60 miles west of Harris is a National Nature Reserve with puffins, fulmars and gannets inhabiting this remote, picturesque outcrop in the Atlantic.

The enormous natural harbour of Scapa Flow protected by the mainland, Hoy and South Ronaldsay, in the Orkney Islands provided the Royal Navy with natural shelter in both world wars. Only a few miles north of the mainland, the numerous islands are linked by car and passenger ferries. Here visitors are impressed by the solitude and scenic beauty and over one million seabirds in nine RSPB reserves. The prehistoric village of Skara Brae, the Stones of Stenness and the burial ground at Maes Howe, dating from around 2000 BC are some of the most historically important sites in Europe. At one time ruled by the King of Norway's representative, it has since the 15th century been part of Scotland.

Lying almost as close to Norway as to Scotland, the Shetland Islands are made up of over 100 separate islands. The Viking heritage has been retained in language and culture, and can be studied at the **Shetland Museum** in Lerwick. The giant Sullom Voe oil terminal has been constructed in the last 20 years to take advantage of the Islands' proximity to the North Sea oil industry. Here, like Orkney, there are numerous nature reserves for thousands of birds around cliff tops and solitary islands, sea trout in clear lochs and seals and otters along the magnificent coastline.

The Highlands and Islands of Scotland are probably the least populated areas in Britain offering the visitor peace and tranquillity with beautiful scenery, breathtaking views and interesting treasures into the area's heritage.

Glamis Castle, framed by the majestic Grampian Mountains, is one of the most beautiful and historic of Scotland's great castles. It is the family home of the Earls of Strathmore and Kinghorne and has been a royal residence since 1372. It is also the childhood home of Her Majesty Queen Elizabeth The Queen Mother, the birthplace of Her Royal Highness The Princess Margaret and the legendary setting of Shakespeare's Macbeth.

The thaneage of Glamis was granted to Sir John Lyon in 1372 by King Robert II of Scotland. Four years later Sir John married the King's daughter and founded a line of feudal barons, and later earls, which still flourishes and dwells at Glamis. The King made his son-in-law Chamberlain of Scotland and Sir John began to construct a new house befitting a great officer of state and a royal princess. Much of what he built is incorporated in the present castle, a five-storey 'L' shaped tower block of sandstone not dissimilar in colour to the heather-covered mountains beyond. Sir John's castle was a simple tall, narrow building, with an entrance hall on the first floor reached by outer stairs with the Great Hall above it and bedchambers above that. Although never intended as a fortress, it would have been fairly impregnable to attack.

Patrick Lyon was created Earl of Kinghorne in 1606 and in 1677 the 3rd Earl added Strathmore to the title, and continued the extension and improvement of the castle begun by his grandfather. This was an amazing achievement by the young Earl since, when he came into his inheritance, he found debts totalling £400,000 - a monumental sum in those days. It took 40 years of determination and strict economies, but he restored the estate to solvency.

He added two wings to the castle, remodelled the Great Hall and decorated the chapel. During this period the castle assumed its present fairy-castle appearance with turrets, towers and spires everywhere, causing Daniel Defoe to liken it to a city.

The Crypt and the eerie Duncan's Hall are little changed since medieval times. The Crypt contains numerous big game heads and arms and armour, some of which dates from the 15th century. A secret chamber is thought to be located within the massive thickness of the walls. Here, it is said, one Lord of Glamis and the Earl of Crawford played cards with the Devil on the Sabbath. So great were the resulting disturbances that the room was permanently sealed. Duncan's Hall is by tradition where Macbeth murdered his cousin King Duncan.

The Chapel was richly decorated by the 3rd Earl who commissioned Jacob de Wet to paint the beautiful panels on the walls and ceiling, making this one of the finest small chapels in Europe.

The Great Hall was transformed into an elegant Drawing Room. The bare stone walls were plastered, the ceiling was stuccoed in the Italian manner and a frieze was added. The soft pink wash on the walls makes a perfect background for the many family portraits, notably the enormous painting of the 3rd Earl and his sons, who looks down on his favourite room in the castle.

King Malcolm's Room is not the actual room where the King died in 1034, but is close to where it was in the original hunting lodge. The glory of this room is its plasterwork ceiling, and the arms of the 2nd Earl picked out in full heraldic colours.

Following Lady Elizabeth Bowes Lyon's marriage into the Royal Family in 1923, her mother, the Countess of Strathmore, arranged the Royal Apartments for the couple whenever they visited Glamis. The suite of three rooms is comfortable rather than grand and filled with family portraits, photographs and personal mementoes. The bedhangings in the Queen Mother's Bedroom bear the embroidered names of the children of the 14th Earl and Countess including 'Elizabeth 1900'. Also in this room is a copy of the lovely portrait by de Laszlo of the Queen Mother when she was Duchess of York.

A grand tree-lined drive leads down through the lush Angus landscape to the castle and its gardens. The Dutch garden was laid out in the 1890s in the form of low box hedges containing a profusion of roses. The Queen Mother's parents adapted part of the shrubberies to form the Italian Garden, two acres enclosed within high yew hedges, with herbaceous borders, a fountain and two attractive 17th century style gazebos.

A 21 foot high 17th century sundial dominates one of the castle lawns. Placed three degrees west of the Greenwich Meridian by the 3rd Earl, it was extremely accurate. There are lovely woodland walks among the massive Douglas firs where the peace of Glamis can be enjoyed to the full. A licensed Restaurant provides light lunches and teas, there are Gift Shops and a Picnic Area and the picturesque village of Glamis lies 5 miles west of Forfar on the A94. Glamis Castle is available for a variety of social and sporting functions from cocktail parties and champagne receptions to archery and clay pigeon shooting. The magnificent setting, excellent food and wines and resident piper make dinner parties at Glamis very special.

Scone is at the very centre of Scotland, both geographically and historically. It is the ancient crowning place of Scottish kings, including the legendary Macbeth and Robert the Bruce, and one time home of the Stone of Scone. The chroniclers tell us of Druids, of fantastic glimpses of kings and king-making and of the high kings of the Picts in the 'Kingdom of Scone'. In 1296 the Stone was removed by King Edward I and placed beneath the Coronation Chair in Westminster Abbey, upon which Queen Elizabeth II was crowned in 1953.

Without the Stone the Royal City of Scone began to lose prestige and in 1559 the Abbey of Scone was destroyed and what remained of the Palace was given to the Gowrie family. Their part in the 'Gowrie Conspiracy', when the life of King James VI was threatened but saved by Sir David Murray, led to their downfall. Thus, in 1604, Sir David was rewarded with the Palace and lands of Scone. He was also created Lord Scone and later Viscount Stormont. In 1776 William Murray, son of the 5th Viscount was created Earl of Mansfield, whose descendants continue to live at Scone.

The Palace, as we see it today, was adapted and enlarged for the 3rd Earl by the architect William Atkinson in 1802. The restrained Gothic style is well suited to the monastic history of Scone. Throughout the house there are fine collections of furniture and works of art, porcelain and needlework.

The beautiful Drawing Room, whose walls are hung with Lyons silk, contains some excellent pieces of French boulle furniture, together with an important set of French armchairs covered in superb needlework. An exquisite little writing table was made for Marie Antoinette and bears her cypher. A portrait of the 1st Earl of Mansfield by Reynolds shows him in the robes and wig of Lord Chief Justice of England - a position he held for over 32 years. He was instrumental in the beginning of the Abolition of Slavery and respected as the greatest lawyer of all time.

In the Dining Room the fabulous Ivories, collected mostly by

the 4th Earl, are displayed. Carved in elephant and walrus tusk, they came from Bavaria, Flanders, Italy and France.

The enchantingly pretty Ante-Room, painted in white, gold and silver is the perfect setting for a set of Chinese Chippendale chairs and a portrait of Sir David Murray, first Lord Scone.

The Library bookcases have been taken over by the exceptional collection of fine and rare Meissen, Sevres, Ludwigsburg, Chelsea, Derby and Worcester porcelain. From the windows may be seen the mighty oak planted by James VI before 1603 and, across the silver ribbon of the Tay, the distant mountains around Ben Vorlich.

The Long Gallery, hung with many family portraits is of an unusual length for a Scottish home. Its magnificent floor is of Scottish oak inset with bog oak and has been trodden by many kingly feet. Here the comprehensive and unique collection of Vernis Martin is displayed.

The Duke of Lennox's Room contains very fine examples of needlework including a magnificent set of bed hangings worked by Mary Queen of Scots, mother of King James VI, and her ladies.

The beautiful grounds at Scone Palace are peaceful and informal. The Pinetum was first planted in 1848 with exotic coniferous trees, including a vast and very special fir. This was raised from seed sent to Scone by David Douglas in 1826. Douglas was born at Scone in 1798 and worked as an under-gardener until he joined the Botanical Gardens in Glasgow. During a trip to America he discovered the 'Douglas Fir' for which he is now famous.

Scone Palace, just outside Perth on the A93 Braemar road, provides a grand and historic setting for business and private functions, including Scone Palace Grand Dinners when Roast Palace Peacock may appear on the menu.

The ancient fortress home of the Earls and Dukes of Atholl, situated in the wide Strath of Garry, commands a strategic position on the main route through the central Highlands, in a wild and rugged setting of wooded mountains and picturesque rivers. About a mile to the east the Tilt joins the Garry on its course to the Pass of Killiecrankie three miles away. The Banvie burn, which runs in front of the castle, tumbles through its narrow glen among giant larches, Scots firs, beeches and rhododendrons.

During its almost 700 years of history the castle has seen splendid royal visits, occupation by enemy forces on four occasions, and has withstood siege and partial destruction.

The main tower, known as Cummings Tower, is part of the original 13th century building, but the main part of the castle owes much of its present appearance to the 2nd Duke who began an ambitious scheme of alterations. He was interrupted by the Jacobite revolt in 1745, but in the more peaceful times that followed he remodelled the castle in the style of a grand Georgian house. There are now thirty two rooms of infinite variety displaying beautiful furniture, fine collections of paintings, arms and armour, china, costumes, lace and embroidery, masonic regalia and a host of other treasures from the 16th century to the present day.

The Picture Staircase, made in 1756, and the Dining Room are notable examples of the extensive work carried out for the 2nd Duke. Both have particularly fine stuccoed ceilings, and the striking overmantel in the Dining Room is in the form of a trophy of arms of all periods - a fitting subject for Blair Castle.

The magnificent Drawing Room, its walls hung with crimson damask, has perhaps the most beautiful ceiling and above the white marble fireplace the charming portrait of the 3rd Duke and Duchess with their seven children by Zoffany. Amongst the wealth of furniture are two gilt settees and twelve chairs, their covers finely worked by Lady Charlotte, the pretty girl holding the wreath in the Zoffany picture. For how many long hours she patiently stitched we do not know, but the castle is filled with the industry of many of the ladies who have lived here.

The Tapestry Room is hung with a fine set of Brussels Tapestries made for Charles I. The magnificent William and Mary bed, with rich silk hangings beneath great sprays of ostrich plumes belonged to the 1st Duke of Atholl.

In the Tullibardine Room a much simpler Tent Bed is covered with tartan over 200 years old, said to come from an earlier circular bed in which slept the seventeen sons of Sir David Murray of Tullibardine. Somewhat ahead of its time, it was presumably this shape to avoid small boys going bump in the night.

The China Room, Costume Room and Treasure Room contain many rare and beautiful things - fortunately generations at Blair did not discard items which became unfashionable.

Blair Castle is approached from the little village of Blair Atholl (off the A9 Perth - Inverness road) along a great avenue of limes which lead up to the castle through thickly wooded parkland. The 4th Duke was especially fond of trees, larch in particular, and planted great forests of them together with a wide variety of other trees, which provide a simple majestic setting for Blair - a setting which is perfect for special lunches, weddings, Highland Balls, equestrian events. The list if endless.

The magical name of Cawdor, romantically linked by Shakespeare with Macbeth, is steeped in the history and legend of the turbulent times of medieval Scotland. Periods of peace came and went, but to a family such as the Thanes of Cawdor, a stout defendable home meant survival itself. Quarrels and feuds were the rule, not the exception, and black and bloody deeds were not uncommon. During one such feud the infant daughter of the 8th Thane was kidnapped by the Earl of Argyll. For future recognition she was branded on the hip by her nurse with a red hot key, and the top joint of her left little finger was bitten off. In 1510, at the age of 12, she was married to the Earl's younger son, Sir John Campbell. The happy conclusion to this violent beginning was a union from which the present Campbells of Cawdor are descended.

The central 14th century tower, approached across a drawbridge, is the oldest part of the castle, which was protected on one side by the Cawdor Burn and on the others by a dry moat. During the 17th century this small defensive fort was transformed into a large family mansion. A massive building programme was carried out without the use of plans or drawings, the Thane of the day supervising the work as it proceeded. Amazingly they all seem to have favoured the same style - mellow sandstone with crow-stepped gables and slated roofs. In the 18th century a separate house was built and incorporated into the main building in the 19th century, again with no loss of harmony.

Whether Macbeth actually lived here or not, once over the drawbridge one can easily imagine that he did. The Tower Room, once the old entrance hall, is built around the ancient trunk of a thorn tree. The legend is that a certain Thane was told in a dream to build his new castle wherever a donkey laden with gold lay down to rest for the night. He would then prosper for evermore. The tree, and therefore the Tower, has been dated by modern scientific methods to 1372.

In the depths of the Tower is a small 'bottle' dungeon probably used to conceal ransomed prisoners - it boasts a privy - or for hiding women and children in times of danger. The only access was through a trap-door from the room above.

Cawdor is not simply a monument to the past, but a splendid house and a lived-in home filled with fine furniture and paintings, ceramics and beautiful tapestries. In the heart of the Tower is the cosy, flower-filled Yellow Sitting Room which is typically Jacobean in character. The Family Bedroom, with its Venetian bed draped in crimson velvet, is hung with Flemish tapestries made in 1682 specially for the room.

The elegant Drawing Room has a fine collection of family portraits including Sir Henry Campbell painted as a young man in the uniform of the Green Jackets. In later life he was advised by his doctor to drink a little brandy for his health, whereupon he told the poor man that every night on top of pints of champagne, claret and port, he was accustomed to drinking at least five large glasses of brandy. He was wise enough to employ a retired prostitute to guide him home in London, and to ward off the Ladies of the Night. Throughout their long history the Cawdor Campbells seem to have done nothing by halves.

There are three gardens to enjoy at Cawdor Castle, all of them beautiful in different ways and in different seasons. Hedges, fruit, flowers, shrubs and herbs framed by aged walls and mighty trees, which have been lovingly tended for thirty decades. And beyond the sweeping lawns and the babbling burn, the majestic Cawdor Wood.

There is a licensed restaurant and gift shop as well as a putting green and mini golf. As Shakespeare said 'This castle hath a pleasant seat; the air nimbly and sweetly recommends itself unto our gentle senses.'

Valley of the Stags – Elizabeth Halstead.

Food and Fayre for Thought

Dejeuner du Salon au Café la Cascade – Jean André. Courtesy of Rosentiel's.

Some love meat and cannot eat

Some cannot eat that want it

But we have meat and we can eat,

Sae let the Lord be thankit.

The Kircudbright Grace, Robert Burns

And thankful we should be for Scotland's fine natural fayre from the humble haggis or 'great chieftain o' the puddin race' to the venison, lamb, prime beef and salmon that is renowned the world over, and readily complimented by a host of fresh vegetables. Yet this is just a sample of the culinary delights awaiting visitors to Scotland as they munch their way from the Lowlands to the Highlands and Island to Island.

The West yet glimmers with some streaks of day

Now spurs the lated traveller apace

To gain the timely inn.

Macbeth

One thing the visitor can also be sure of is a more hospitable welcome than some of Macbeth's house guests, which is just as well as many of Scotland's finest restaurants are to be found in celebrated hotels. We have put together a listing of establishments some of which we feel fall into the outstanding category.

However, we make no apology for not highlighting our own particular favourites as we are confident that each restaurant is capable of satisfying the palate of the most demanding gastronome, depending on his/her preference. We also make no apologies for including restaurants that some may consider a trifle expensive. All our selections are based on the quality principle of value for money and will not disappoint.

Now good digestion wait on appetite

And health on both

Macbeth

The Borders, Lothian, and the Forth Valley

Champany Inn, *Champany*
Outstanding beef and seafood. Extraordinary and excellent wine list.   *Tel: (050683) 4532*

Greywalls, *Muirfield*
One of the finest 19th holes in the world. First class presentation and outstanding service.   *Tel: (0620) 842144*

Open Arms Hotel, *Newmill-On-Teviot*
Marvellous atmosphere, delightful cooking and good value.   *Tel: (0450) 85298*

La Potiniere, *Gullane*
Almost the best. A true delight from entrance to exit.   *Tel: (0620) 843214*

Sunlaws House, *Kelso*
Scottish fayre at its finest. Unimposing but stylish.   *Tel: (05735) 3312*

Edinburgh

L'Auberge, *Edinburgh* _____
Stylish French restaurant in Edinburgh's old town   *Tel: 031 556 5888*

Balmoral Hotel, *Edinburgh* _____
Magnificent dining room matched by fine cuisine and service   *Tel: 031 556 2414*

Caledonian Hotel, *Edinburgh* _____
Legends of the Scottish table combine heroically with modern French cuisine. A celebrated meeting place. *Tel: 031 225 2433*

Cosmo, *Edinburgh* _____
Cosmo by name, Cosmopolitan by nature.   *Tel: (031) 226 6743*

Indian Cavalry Club, *Edinburgh* _____
Elaborate Indian restaurant. Cooking in the modern style.   *Tel: 031 228 3282*

Keepers, *Edinburgh* _____
Imaginative Scottish fayre, atmospheric cellar restaurant.   *Tel: (031) 556 5707*

Kelly's, *Edinburgh* _____
Well managed, well priced, well served, well cooked, well.   *Tel: 031 668 3847*

Kweilin, *Edinburgh* _____
A fine place to enjoy the very best of eastern Cuisine.   *Tel: (031) 557 1875*

Martin's, *Edinburgh* _____
Charming atmosphere, imaginative cooking and good value wine list.   *Tel: 031 225 3106*

Raffaelli, *Edinburgh* _____
Italian cooking in sophisticated setting, excellent home-made pasta.   *Tel: 031 225 6060*

Vintner's Room, *Edinburgh* _____
A capital choice. Appealing menu with tremendous game, puddings, exceptional and not to be missed. *Tel: 031 554 6767*

The Witchery, *Edinburgh* _____
The Secret garden restaurant.   *Tel: (031) 225 5613*

Ayrshire, Dumfries, Galloway

Fouter's Bistro, *Ayr* _____
An extremely popular bistro which provides Scottish fayre cooked in French style at good value prices. *Tel: (0292) 261391*

Kirroughtree Hotel, *Newton Stewart* _____
A stylish house with an outstanding formal restaurant with an excellent wine list   *Tel: (0671) 2141*

Knockinaam Lodge, *Portpatrick* _____
An outstanding restaurant in every way. One of the finest establishments north of the border. *Tel: (077 681) 471*

Riverside Inn, *Canonbie* _____
A riverside setting is just one of many reasons for visiting this enjoyable, friendly restaurant. *Tel: (03873) 71512*

Glasgow, Loch Lomond and the Clyde Valley

Amber, *Glasgow* _____
Authentic Chinese cuisine served in style.   *Tel: 041 339 6121*

Buttery, *Glasgow* _____
Marvelously imaginative menu and easy going atmosphere.   *Tel: 041 221 8188*

Cameron House, *Alexandria* _____
Elegant and excellent quality throughout. Ideal for a celebration.   Tel: (0389) 55565

Gean House, *Alloa* _____
Limited choice menu, outstandingly prepared. Pleasant country house.   Tel: (0259) 219275

October Restaurant, *Bearsden* _____
Salmon features predominantly. Outstanding cuisine in relaxed atmosphere.   Tel: 041 942 7272

Rogano, *Glasgow* _____
Something of an institution amongst Glaswegians. Outstanding menu from top to toe.   Tel: 041 248 4055

Ubiquitous Chip, *Glasgow* _____
Scottish dishes, excellent international wine list. Whisky galore.   Tel: 041 334 5007

Westerwood Hotel, *Cumbernauld* _____
Elaborate dining room, ideal for gourmet golfers or golfing gourmets.   Tel: (0236) 457171

Perthshire, Angus and Fife

Auchterarder House, *Auchterarder* _____
Formal but friendly. Five course, fixed price menu. Fabulous fayre.   Tel: (0764) 63646

Castleton House, *Glamis* _____
Fish and meat, local produce galore in friendly Victorian hotel.   Tel: (030 784) 340

The Cellar, *Anstruther* _____
An elaborate predominantly fishy menu, charming character and excellent sophisticated wine list.   Tel: (0333) 310378

Cromlix House, *Dunblane* _____
Imaginative menu and excellent wine list served in historic hotel's formal dining room.   Tel: (0786) 822125

Farleyer House, *Aberfeldy* _____
Dinner only, Atkins matches any cooking in the land.   Tel: (0887) 820332

Kinnaird, *Dalguise* _____
Sporting estate, superbly renovated house with stylish, sophisticated cooking.   Tel: (0796) 482440

Murrayshall House, *Scone* _____
French and Scottish fayre, elegantly served, a distinguished 19th hole.   Tel: (0738) 51171

Number Thirty Three, *Perth* _____
An excellent fish restaurant with a pleasant relaxed aire.   Tel: (0738) 33771

Old Mansion House, *Auchterhouse* _____
A pleasant, beautifully situated house, restaurant offers first class cuisine with abundant local produce.   Tel: (082 626) 366

Ostlers Close, *Cupar* _____
An informal welcoming establishment with first class Scottish fodder.   Tel: (0334) 55574

Peat Inn, *Peat Inn* _____
Outstanding French fayre, an arena for eating which very few who can match.   Tel: (033 484) 206

Western Highlands and Islands

Airds Hotel, *Port Appin* _____
Lochside views, glorious wines and an extraordinarily fine cuisine.   Tel: (063 173) 236

Ardanaiseig, *Kilchrenan* —————————————————————————————
An awesome situation for a formal, often extravagant, ever changing menu.   *Tel: (08663) 333*

Crinan Hotel, *Crinan* ———————————————————————————————
The freshest of fresh fish, mussels, clams and salmon are part of the splendid array.   *Tel (054 683) 261*

Glenfeochan House, *Kilmore* —————————————————————————————
Excellent cooking, features local produce further enhanced by homely atmosphere.   *Tel: (063177) 273*

Inverlochy Castle, *Torlundy* ——————————————————————————————
Formal atmosphere, exquisite cuisine, first class service, a classic of its kind.   *Tel: (0397) 702177*

Isle Of Eriska, *Eriska* —————————————————————————————————
Relaxing, friendly and atmospheric restaurant, a fine all round menu.   *Tel: (063 172) 371*

Kilfinan Hotel, *Kilfinan* ———————————————————————————————
A first class restaurant in an old coaching inn.   *Tel: (070 082) 201*

Loch Fyne Oyster Bar, *Cairndow* ————————————————————————————
Excellent Scottish fayre with an emphasis on seafood.   *Tel: (04996) 264*

Three Chimneys Restaurant, *Colbost* ————————————————————————
Former crofters cottage now seafood restaurant of great quality and character.   *Tel: (047 081) 258*

Tiroran House, *Tiroran* ————————————————————————————————
House party atmosphere, superb views and cuisine to match.   *Tel: (068 15 232)*

Grampian

Gerard's, *Aberdeen* ——————————————————————————————————
Long established, French restaurant in central Aberdeen remains exceedingly popular.   *Tel: (0224) 639500*

Invery House, *Banchory* ————————————————————————————————
A charming restaurant in a delightful house, menu offers a variety of excellent game and fish.   *Tel: (03302) 4782*

Old Monastery, *Drybridge* ————————————————————————————————
*A marvellous setting for a restaurant which combines the best of Scottish fayre with a hint of
French flavour.*   *Tel: (0542) 32660*

Silver Darling, *Aberdeen* ————————————————————————————————
Seafood cookery with a French slant, wonderfully individual atmosphere.   *Tel: (0224) 596229*

Northern Highlands and Islands

Altnabarrie Inn, *Ullapool* ————————————————————————————————
*A celebrity among restaurants, beautiful setting for marvellous cuisine - worthy of the highest praise
and longest journey.*   *Tel: (085 483) 230*

Braeval Old Mill, *Aberfoyle* ————————————————————————————————
Old stone mill provides superb setting for fine cuisine with emphasis on local fayre.   *Tel: (08772) 711*

The Cross, *Kingussie* ——————————————————————————————————
Converted tweed mill houses a restaurant of real class, excellent menu and wine list.   *Tel: (0540) 661166*

Dower House, *Muir of Ord* ———————————————————————————————
A most appetising restaurant in which to enjoy well presented fayre.   *Tel: (0463) 870090*

Dunain Park Hotel, *Dunain Park, Inverness* ——————————————————————
Highland fayre featuring steaks and other local produce. Superbly presented in a pleasant dining room. *Tel: ((0463) 230512*

Knockie Lodge, *Whitebridge* ————————————————————————————————
A delightfully situated hotel with a restaurant of merit to please all residents.   *Tel: (0456) 486276*

Thistles, *Cromarty* ——————————————————————————————————
*An isolated but extremely popular restaurant, a fine varied menu combining traditional favourites
with imaginative individual recipes.*   *Tel: (03817) 471*

Complete Golf

King's Course, Gleneagles – Robert Turnbull.

Baberton G.C
031-453 4911
Baberton Avenue, Juniper Green, Edinburgh
W. of Edinburgh on the Lanark Road
(18) 6098 yards/*(intro by member)/F

Bathgate G.C
(0506) 630505
Edinburgh Road, Bathgate, West Lothian
400 yards E. of George Square
(18) 6328 yards/***/D

Braids United G.C
031-447 3327
22 Braids Hill Approach, Edinburgh
At Braids Hill, S. of Edinburgh
(18) 5731 yards/***/E
(18) 4832 yards/***/E

Broomieknowe G.C
031-663 9317
36 Golf Course Road, Bonnyrigg, Midlothian
S. of Edinburgh on the A6094 from Dalkeith
(18) 6046 yards/**/F

Bruntsfield Links G.C
031-336 1479
32 Barton Avenue, Davidsons Mains, Edinburgh
2-3 miles W. of Edinburgh on A90
(18) 6407 yards/**/F/H

Carrickvale G.C
031-337 1932
Glendevon Park, Edinburgh
Opposite Post House Hotel on Balgreen Road
(18) 6299 yards/***/F/H

Craigmillar Park G.C
031-667 2837
1 Observatory Road, Edinburgh
3 miles from City centre
(18) 5846 yards/***/D/H or M or L

Dalmahoy G.C
031-333 1845
Dalmahoy, Kirknewton, Midlothian 7 miles W.
of Edinburgh on the A71
(18) 6664 yards/***/F
(18) 5121 yards/***/F

Duddingston G.C
031-661 7688 4301
Duddingston Road, Edinburgh
E. of city centre, adjacent to the A1
(18) 6647 yards/**/D/H

Dunbar G.C
(0368) 62317
East Links, Dunbar
Half mile from Dunbar centre on sea side
(18) 6426 yards/***/C

Gifford G.C
(062 081) 267
Gifford
5 miles S. of Haddington off the A6137
(9) 5613 yards/***(not Tues, Wed, weekend
pm)/E

Glen G.C
(0620) 2221
Tantallon Terrace, North Berwick, East Lothian
22 miles N.E. of Edinburgh on the A198
(18) 6098 yards/***/E

Glencorse G.C
(0968) 77189
Milton Bridge, Penicuik, Midlothian
9 miles S. of Edinburgh on the A701
(18) 5205 yards/***/D/H

Greenburn G.C
(0501) 70292
Fauldhouse, West Lothian
Midway between Glasgow and Edinburgh
(18) 6210 yards/**/E/H

Gullane G.C
(0620) 842255
Gullane, East Lothian
Off the A1 on the A198 to Gullane
(18)6466 yards/**/F/H
(18)6127 yards/***/F/H
(18)5128 yards/***/F/H

Haddington G.C
(062 082) 3627
Amisfield Park, Haddington, East Lothian
17 miles E. of Edinburgh on the A1
(18) 6280 yards/**(not pm)/E

Harburn G.C
(0506) 871256
West Calder, West Lothian
S. off the A70, 2 miles S. of West Calder
(18) 5843 yards/***/E

Honourable Company Of
Edinburgh Golfers
(0620) 842123
Muirfield, Gullane, East Lothian
Off the A198 from Gullane to North Berwick
(18) 6601 yards/(Tues, Thurs, Fri am only)/A/H
(18)/M/L

Kilspindie G.C
(087 57) 358
Aberlady, East Lothian
On the South bank of the Forth Estuary
(18) 5410 yards/***/F

Kingsknowe G.C
031-441 4030
326 Lanark Road, Edinburgh
W. of Edinburgh on the A71
(18) 5979 yards/**/E/H

Liberton G.C
031-664 8580
297 Gilmerton Road, Edinburgh
S. of Edinburgh on the A7
(18) 5299 yards/***/F/H

Linlithgow G.C
(0506) 842585
Braehead, Linlithgow, West Lothian
20 miles from Edinburgh off the M9
(18) 5858 yards/***(not Wed, Sat)/E

Deer Park G.C
(0506) 38843
Carmondean, Livingston, West Lothian
Signposted from Knightsridge from the M8
(18) 6636 yards/***/D

Longniddry G.C
(0875) 52141
Links Road, Longniddry, East Lothian
(18) 6210 yards/***/F

Luffness New G.C
(0620) 843114
Aberlady, East Lothian E. of Edinburgh along the
A198
(18) 6122 yards/***/F/H

Merchants of Edinburgh G.C
031-447 219
10 Craighill Gardens, Edinburgh
South side of Edinburgh off the A701
(18) 4889 yards/(intro by member)/E

Mortonhall G.C
031-447 6974
231 Braid Road, Edinburgh
2 miles S. of city centre
(18) 6557 yards/***/F/M

Murrayfield G.C
031-337 3478
43 Murrayfield Road, Edinburgh
2 miles W. of the city centre
(18) 5727 yards/***/E/L/H

Musselburgh G.C
031-665 2005
Monktonhall, Musselburgh, Midlothian
1 mile S. of Musselburgh off the A1
(18) 6623 yards/***/F/H

Newbattle G.C
031-663 2123
Abbey Road, Dalkeith, Midlothian
7 miles S.W. of Edinburgh on the A7
(18) 6012 yards/**/D

North Berwick
(0620) 2135
West Links, Beach Road
North Berwick
(18) 6317 yards/***/D

Portobello G.C
031-669 4361
Stanley Road, Portobello, Edinburgh
(9) 2400 yards/***/E

Prestonfield G.C
031-667 1273
6 Prestonfield Road North, Edinburgh
Just off Dalkeith Road, nr Commonwealth Pool
(18) 6216 yards/*(+ Sat, Sun pm)/E

Pumpherston G.C
(0506) 32869
Drumshoreland Road, Pumpherston,
Livingston
1 mile S. of Uphall, off the A89(9) 5154 yards/
*(with member only)/F

Ratho Park G.C
031-333 1752
Ratho, Newbridge, Midlothian
8 miles W. of Edinburgh via A71 or A8
(18) 6028 yards/***/D

Ravelston G.C
031-315 2486
24 Ravelston Dykes Road, Blackhall, Edinburgh
Take A90 Queensferry Road to Blackhall
(9) 5200 yards/*(with member)/F

Royal Burgess G.C
031-339 2075
181 Whitehouse Road, Edinburgh
Take A90 to Queensferry, behind Barnton
Thistle Hotel
(18) 6604 yards/**/F/L

Royal Musselburgh G.C
(0875) 810276
Preston Grange House, Prestonpans, East
Lothian
(18) 6237 yards/***/D/H

Silverknowes G.C
031-336 5359
Siverknowes, Parkway, Edinburgh
On coast overlooking Firth of Forth
(18) 6210 yards/***/F

Swanston G.C
031-445 2239
111 Swanston Road, Edinburgh
5 miles from Edinburgh centre
(18) 5024 yards/**/F

Torphin Hill
031-441 1100
Torphin Road, Colinton, Edinburgh
On S.W side of Colinton
(18) 5024 yards/***/E

Turnhouse G.C
031-339 1014
154 Turnhouse Road, Edinburgh
(18) 6171 yards/**/D

Uphall G.C
(0506) 856404
Uphall, West Lothian
On outskirts of Uphall adjacent to the A8
(18)6250 yards/***/E

West Lothian G.C
(0506) 826030
Airngarth Hill, Linlithgow, West Lothian
On hill, marked by the Hope Monument
(18) 6578 yards/**/D

E.A. Pettitt   THE MARINE, NORTH BERWICK   Burlington Gallery

KEY

*** Visitors welcome at most times
** Visitors usually allowed on weekdays only
* Visitors not normally permitted (Mon, Wed) No visitors on specified days

APPROXIMATE GREEN FEES
A – £30 plus
B – £20 – £30
C – £15 – £25
D – £10 – £20
E – Under £10
F – Green fees on application

RESTRICTIONS
G – Guests only
H – Handicap certificate required
H(24) – Handicap of 24 or less required
L – Letter of introduction required
M – Visitor must be a member of another recognised club.

Airdrie G.C
(0236) 62195
Rochsoles, Airdrie
1 mile N. from Airdrie Cross (town centre)
(18) 6004 yards/***/F/L

Alexandra G.C
041-556 3711
Sannox Gardens, Alexandra Parade, Glasgow
Half mile E. of city centre
(9) 1968 yards/***/E

Annanhill G.C
(0563) 21644
Irvine Road, Kilmarnock
On the main Kilmarnock-Irvine Road
(18) 6270 yards/***(not Sat)/F

Ardeer G.C
(0294) 64542
Greenhead, Stevenston, Ayrshire
Turn into Kerelaw Road off the A78
(18) 6630 yards/***(not Sat)/E/H

Ayr Belleisle G.C
(0292) 41258
Belleisle Park, Doonfoot Road, Ayr
2 miles S.W of the town centre on the A719
(18) 6550 yards/***/F

Ayr Dalmilling G.C
(0292) 263893
Westwood Avenue, Ayr
2 miles from town centre, off the A77
(18) 5401 yards/***/E

Ayr Seafield G.C
(0292) 41258
Ayr
2 miles from town centre in Belleisle Park
on the A719
(18) 5244 yards/***/F/H

Ballochmyle G.C
(0290) 50469
Ballochmyle, Mauchline, Ayrshire
1 mile from Mauchline village
(18) 5952 yards/**/D/H

Balmore G.C
(0360) 2120240
2 miles N. of Glasgow, 7 miles from city centre
(18) 5736 yards/***/F

Barshaw G.C
041-889 2908
Barshaw Park, Glasgow Road, Paisley, Renfrewshire
Take A737 from Glasgow West to Paisley.
(18) 5673 yards/***/E

Bearsden G.C
041-942 2351
Thorn Road, Bearsden, Glasgow
1 mile from Bearsden Cross on Thorn Road
(9) 5569 yards/***/F/L

Beith G.C
(05055) 3166
Bigholm Road, Beith
1 mile E. of Beith
(9) 5600 yards/**/E/H

Bellshill G.C
(0698) 745124
Orbiston, Bellshill
10 miles S. of Glasgow on Bellshill to Motherwell road
(18) 6605 yards/**/D/H

Biggar G.C
(0899) 20618
The Park, Broughton Road, Biggar, Lanarkshire
1 mile E. of Biggar on the Broughton Road
(18) 5416 yards/***/E

Bishopbriggs G.C
041-772 1810
Brackanbrae Road, Bishopbriggs, Glasgow
Take A803 from Glasgow North for 4 miles to Bishopbriggs
(18) 6041 yards/*(intro only)/D/H

Blairbeth G.C
041-634 3355
Burnside, Rutherglen, Glasgow
1 mile S. of Rutherglen via Stonelaw Road, off the A749
(18) 5448 yards/*(with member)/F

Blairmore & Strone G.C
(036984) 217
Strone, By Dunoon, Argyll
9 miles N.W of Dunoon on the A880
(9) 2112 yards/***/E

Bonnyton G.C(035 53)2781
Eaglesham, Glasgow
(18) 6252 yards/**/E

Bothwell Castle G.C
(0698) 853177
Blantyre Road, Bothwell, Glasgow
Adjacent to the M74, 3 miles N. of Hamilton
(18) 6426 yards/***/D/H

Brodick G.C
(0770) 2349
Brodick, Isle of Arran
By ferry from Androssan
(18) 4404 yards/***/E

Calderbraes G.C
(0698) 813425
57 Roundknowe Road, Uddingston, Lanarkshire
At start of M74, 4 miles from Glasgow
(9) 5046 yards/*(intro by member)/F

Caldwell G.C
(050585) 616
Uplawmoor, Renfrewshire
15 miles from Glasgow off the A736
(18) 6102 yards/**/D

Cambuslang G.C
041-641 3130
30 Westburn Drive, Cambuslang, Glasgow
1 mile from the station in Cambuslang
(9) 6072 yards/*(intro by member)/E

Campsie G.C
(0360) 310244
Crow Road, Lennoxtown, Glasgow
N. of Lennoxtown on the B822
(18 5517 yards/**/E

Caprington G.C
(0563) 21915
Ayr Road, Kilmarnock
S. of Kilmarnock on the Ayr Road
(18) 5718 yards/***/F

Cardross G.C
(0389) 841754
Main Road, Cardross, Dumbarton
Between Dumbarton and Helensburgh on the A814
(18) 6466 yards/**/D

Carluke G.C
(0555) 71070Hallcraig, Mauldslie Road, Carluke
2 miles from town centre on the road to Hamilton
(18) 5805 yards/**(not Tues)/E/H

Carnwath G.C
(0555) 840251
Main Street, Carnwath
5 miles N.E of Lanark
(18) 5855 yards/***(not Tues, Thurs, Sat)/D/H

Carradale G.C
(05833) 387
Carradale, Campbeltown, Argyll
Off the B842 from Campbeltown to Carradale
(9) 2387 yards/**/E/H

Cathcart Castle G.C
041-638 9449
Mearns Road, Clarkston, Glasgow
7 miles from Glasgow on the A77
(18) 5832 yards/*(intro by member)/F/H

Cathkin Braes G.C
041-634 6605
Cathkin Road, Rutherglen, Glasgow
S.E of Glasgow on the road to East Kilbride
(18) 6266/**/D/H

Cawder G.C
041-772 5167
Cawder Road, Bishopbriggs, Glasgow
Half mile E. of Bishopbriggs off the A803
(18) 6229 yards/**(prior arrangement)/F/H
(18) 5877 yards/**(prior arrangement)/F/H

Clober G.C
041-956 1685
Craigton Road, Milngavie
7 miles N.W of Glasgow
(18) 5068 yards/**/E

Clydebank & District G.C
(0389) 73289
Hardgate, Clydebank, Dunbartonshire
8 miles N.W of Glasgow off Great Western Road
(18) 5825 yards/**/D/H

Clydebank Overtoun G.C
041-952 6372
Overtoun Road, Clydebank, Dunbartonshire
Turn right at Dalmuir station, 5 minutes from there
(18) 5643 yards/***/D(B on Sun)

Cochran Castle G.C(0505) 20146
Craigston, Scott Avenue, Johnstone
Quarter mile off the Johnstone-Beith Road, S. of the town
(18) 6226 yards/**/D/H

Colville Park G.C
(0698) 63017
Jerviston Estate, Motherwell
1 mile N. of Motherwell on the A723
(18) 6208 yards/**/D

Corrie G.C
(077081) 223
Sannox, Isle of Arran
By ferry to Brodick, then 7 miles N. on the A84
(9) 3896 yards/***/E/H

Cowal G.C
(0369) 5673
Ardenslate Road, Kirn, Dunoon
Quarter mile from A815 at Kirn
(18) 6250 yards/***/D

Cowglen G.C
041-632 0556
301 Barrhead Road, Glasgow
On S. side of Glasgow
(18) 6006 yards/**/E/L/H

Crow Wood G.C
041-779 1943
Garnkirk Estate, Muirhead, Chryston, Glasgow
1 mile N. of Stepps on the A80
(18) 6209 yards/*(with member)/D/H

Cumbernauld G.C
(0236) 734969
Palacerigg Country Park, Cumbernauld
Take A80 to Cumbernauld, follow signs to Country park
(18) 6800 yards/**/E

Douglas Park G.C
041-942 2220
Hillfoot, Bearsden, Glasgow
Next to Hillfoot station on the east side of town
(18) 5957 yards/*(with member)/F

Douglas Water G.C
(0555) 2295
Ayr Road, Rigside, Lanark
7 miles S.W of Lanark on A70
(9) 2947 yards/***/E

Douglaston G.C041-956 5750
Strathblane Road, Milngavie, Glasgow
7 miles N. of Glasgow on A81
(18) 6683 yards/***/E

Drumpellier G.C
(0236) 24139
Drumpellier Avenue, Coatbridge
1 mile from Coatbridge off A89
(18) 6227 yards/**/D

Dullatur G.C
(023 67) 27847
Dullatur, Glasgow
12 miles E. of Glasgow on Kilsyth road
(18) 6195 yards/**/F

Dumbarton G.C
(0389) 32830
Broadmeadows, Dumbarton, Dunbartonshire
Quarter mile N. of Dumbarton off A814
(18) 5654 yards/**/D

Dunaverty G.C
Southend, Campbeltown, Argyll
10 miles S. of Campbeltown on B842
(18)4597 yards/***/F

Easter Moffat G.C
(0236) 842289
Mansion House, Plains, By Airdrie, Lanarkshire
(18) 6221 yards/***/D/H

East Kilbride G.C
(035 52) 20913
Chapelside Road, Nerston, East Kilbride
Leave Glasgow by A7 and turn off at Nerston village
(18) 6419 yards/*(with member)/F

East Renfrewshire G.C
(035 55) 206
Loganswell, Pilmuir, Newton Mearns, Glasgow
1 mile from Mearns Cross off the A77
(18) 6100 yards/***/C

Eastwood G.C
(035 55)261
Muirshield, Loganswell, Newton Mearns, Glasgow
3 miles S. of Newton Mearns Cross on A77 from Glasgow
(18) 5886 yards/***/D

Elderslie G.C
(0505) 22835
63 Main Road, Elderslie, Renfrewshire
Leave M8 for Linwood road to traffic lights
(18) 6004 yards/**/D

Erskine G.C
(0505) 863327
Bishopston, Renfrewshire
Leave M8 for B815 for 1 mile
(18) 6287 yards/*(with member)/F

Girvan G.C
(0465) 4346
Girvan, Ayrshire
Off the A77 from Glasgow to Ayr
(18) 5078 yards/***/E

Glasgow (Gailes) G.C
(0294) 311347
Gailes, By Irvine, Ayrshire
2 miles S. of Irvine on the road to Troon
(18) 6500 yards/***(on application)/B/H

Glasgow (Killermont) G.C
041-942 2340
Killermont, Bearsden, Glasgow
6 miles N.W of Glasgow off the A81
(18) 5968 yards/***(on application)/C/H

Gleddoch G.& C.C
(047554) 711
Langbank, Renfrewshire
Langbank signposted on M8 W. of Glasgow
(18) 6333 yards/***(by arrangement)/C

Glencruitten G.C
(0631) 62868
Glencruitten Road, Oban
1 mile from town centre off the A816
(18) 4452 yards/***/F/M

Gourock G.C
(0475) 31001
Cowal View, Gourock, Renfrewshire
2 miles W. of Gourock Station via Victoria Road
(18) 6492 yards/**/E/H

Greenock G.C
(0475) 20793
Forsyth Street, Greenock, Renfrewshire
1 mile S.W of the town on the main road to Gourock
(18) 5838 yards/***(not Sat)/F/H

Haggs Castle G.C
041-427 1157
70 Drumbreck Road, GlasgowS.W of Glasgow nr Ibrox Stadium
(18) 6464 yards/*/F

Hamilton G.C
(0698) 282872
Riccarton, Ferniegair, Hamilton, Lanarkshire
2 miles up Larkhall Road off the M74
(18) 6264 yards/*(with member)/F

Hayston G.C
041-776 1244
Campsie Road, Kirkintilloch, Glasgow
10 miles N.E of Glasgow off the A803
(18) 6042 yards/**/D

Helensburgh G.C
(0436) 74173
15 Abercromby Street, Helensburgh, Dunbartonshire
Off Sinclair Street on N.E side of town
(18) 6053 yards/**/D/H

Hollandbush G.C
(0555) 893484
Acretophead, Lesmahagow
Leave M74 or A74 between Lesmahagow and Coalburn
(18) 6100 yards/***/E

Innellan G.C
(0369) 3546
Knockamillie Road, Innellan, Argyll
4 miles from Dunoon
(9) 4878 yards/***/E

Irvine G.C
(0294) 75626
Bogside, Irvine
Through Irvine to Kilwinning and Ravenspark Academy
(18) 6434 yards/***(not Sat)/F

Irvine Ravenspark G.C
(0294) 76983
Kidsneuk, Irvine, Ayrshire
On the A78 between Irvine and Kilwinning
(18) 6429 yards/***/F

Kilbirnie Place G.C
(0505) 683398
Largs Road, Kilbirnie, Ayrshire
On the outskirts of Kilbirnie
(18) 5411 yards/***(not Sat)/F

Kilmalcolm G.C
(050587) 2139
Porterfield Road, Kilmalcolm,
RenfrewshireTake A740 to Linwood, then A761
to Bridge of weir
(18) 5890 yards/**/D

Kilmarnock (Barassie) G.C
(0292) 311077
29 Hillhouse Road, Barassie, Troon, Ayrshire
(18) 6473 yards/**(not Wed)/B

Kilsyth Lennox G.C
(0236) 822190
Tak-Ma-Doon Road, Kilsyth, Glasgow
12 N.E of Glasgow on the A80
(9) 5944 yards/***(not weekend am)/E/H

Kirkhill G.C
041-641 3083
Greenless Road, Cambuslang, Glasgow
Take the East Kilbride Road from Burnside
(18) 5862 yards/***/F

Kirkintilloch G.C
041-776 1256
Todhill, Campsie Road, Kirkintilloch, Glasgow
1 mile from Kirkintilloch on road to
Lennoxtown
(18) 5269 yards/*(with member)/F/H

Knightswood G.C
041-959 2131
Lincoln Avenue, Knightswood, Glasgow
Off Dumbarton Road from city centre
(9) 2717 yards/***/E

Kyles of Bute G.C
(0700) 811355
Tighnabruaich, Argyll
Take A885 from Dunoon, then B836 to
Tighnabruaich
(9) 2389 yards/***(not Sun am)/E

Lamlash G.C
(07706) 296
Lamlash, Brodick, Isle of Arran
On A841, 3 miles S. of ferry terminal
(18) 4681 yards/***/F

Lanark G.C
(0555) 3219
The Moor, Whitelees Road, Lanark
Leave A73 or A72 at Lanark, take Whitelees Road
(18) 6423 yards/**/F/H

Largs G.C
(0475) 673594
Irvine Road, Largs, Ayrshire
1 mile S. of Largs on the A78
(18) 6220 yards/***/D/H

Larkhall G.C
(0698) 88113
Burnhead Road, Larkhall, Lanarkshire
On east side of town, on B7019
(9) 6236 yards/***/F

Leadhills G.C
(0659) 74222
Leadhills, Biggar, Lanarkshire
Within the village, 6 miles from A74 at Abington
(9) 2400 yards/***/E

Lenzie G.C
041-776 1535
19 Crosshill Road, Lenzie, Glasgow
Take A80 to Stepps and into Lenzie Road
(18) 5982 yards/*(with member)/F

Lethamhill G.C
041-770 6220
Cumbernauld Road, Glasgow
On A80 adjacent to Hogganfield Loch
(18) 6073 yards/***/E

Linn Park G.C
041-637 5871
Simshill Road, Glasgow
Off the B766, 5 miles S. of Glasgow
(18) 4848 yards/***/F/H

Littlehill G.C
041-772 1916
Auchinairn Road, Bishopbriggs, Glasgow
3 miles N. of city centre
(18) 6228 yards/***/E

Lochranza G.C
(077 083) 273
Lochranza, Isle of Arran
(9) 1815 yards/***/E

Lochwinnoch G.C
Burnfoot Road, Lochwinnoch, Renfrewshire
On A760, 10 miles W. of Paisley
(18) 6202 yards/**/E/H

Loudoun G.C
(0563) 821993
Galston, Ayrshire
From Kilmarnock, take A71 towards Galston
(18) 5854 yards/**/F

Machrie G.C
(0496) 2310
Machrie Hotel, Port Ellen, Isle of Islay, Argyll
On A846 adjacent to airport
(18) 6226 yards/***/D/H

Machrie Bay G.C
(077084) 267
Machrie, by Brodick, Isle of Arran
Take ferry to Brodick, take String Road to
Machrie
(9) 2123 yards/***/E

Machrihanish G.C
(058 681) 213
Machrihanish, Campbeltown, Argyll
5 miles W. of Campbeltown on the B843
(18) 6228 yards/***/D/H
(9) 2395 yards/***/D/H

Millport G.C
(0475) 530311
Golf Road, Millport, Isle of Cumbrae
Take McBrayne ferry from Largs to Cumbrae
(18) 5831 yards/***/F/H

Milngavie G.C
041-956 1619
Laighpark, Milngavie, Glasgow
Off the A809, N.W of Glasgow
(18) 5818 yards/*(with member)/D

Mount Ellen G.C
(0236) 872277
Johnston House, Johnston Road, Gartcosh,
Glasgow
1 mile S. of the A80
(18) 5526 yards/***/E

Old Ranfurly G.C
(0505) 613612
Ranfurly Place, Bridge of Weir, Renfrewshire
7 miles W. of Paisley
(18) 6266 yards/**/D/L/H

Paisley G.C
041-884 3903
Brachead, Paisley
From Glasgow take the A737 to Paisley
(18) 6424 yards/***/D/L

Pollok G.C
041-632 1080
90 Barrhead Road, Glasgow
On A762, 4 miles S. of Glasgow
(18) 6257 yards/**(male only)/C/H

Port Bannatyne G.C
(0700) 2009
Bannatyne Mains Road, Port Bannatyne,
Isle of Bute
2 miles N. of Rothesay ferry terminal
(13) 4654 yards/***/E

Port Glasgow G.C
(0475) 704181
Devol Farm Industrial Estate, Port Glasgow,
Renfrewshire
(18) 5712 yards/**/E

Prestwick G.C
(0292) 77404
2 Links Road, Prestwick, Ayrshire
1 mile from Prestwick airport
(18) 6544 yards/***/F/M/L

Prestwick St Cuthbert G.C
(0292) 77101
East Road, Prestwick, Ayrshire
Off the A77, nr the irport
(18) 6470 yards/**/E

Prestwick St Nicholas G.C
(0292) 77608
Grangemuir Road, Prestwick, Ayrshire
On the seafront, off the A79
(18) 5926 yards/**/D/H

Ralston G.C
041-882 1349
Strathmore Avenue, Ralston, Paisley
To the E. of Paisley, off main road
(18) 6100 yards/*(by arrangement)/F

Ranfurly Castle G.C
(0505) 612609
Golf Road, Bridge of Weir, Renfrewshire
Leave M8 ta junction 29, take A240 and A761
(18) 6284 yards/**/F/L

Renfrew G.C
041-886 6692
Blythswood Estate, Inchinnan Road, Renfrew
Take A8 to Renfrew
(18) 6818 yards/*(with member)/D/H

Rothesay G.C
(0700) 2244
Canada Hill, Rothesay, Isle of Bute
Take hourly steamer from Wemyss Bay
(18) 5440 yards/***/E/H

Routenburn G.C
(0475) 673230
Largs, Ayrshire
1 mile N. of Largs off A78
(18) 5650 yards/**/E/H

Royal Troon G.C
(0292) 311555
Craigend Road, Troon, Ayrshire
3 miles from Prestwick airport on B749
(18) 6641 yards/**/A/H (18 max)
(18) 6274 yards/**/B/H

Sandyhills G.C
041-778 1179
223 Sandyhills Road, Glasgow
Sandyhills Rd on E. of city
(18) 6253 yards/***/E/H

Shiskine G.C
(077086) 293
Blackwaterfoot, Isle of Arran
(12) 3000 yards/***/E

Shotts G.C
(0501) 20431
Blairhead, Shotts
Between Edinburgh and Glasgow, 2 miles off
M8
(18) 6125 yards/***/E

Skelmorlie G.C
(0475) 520152
Skelmorlie, Ayrshire
5 miles N. of Largs
(13) 5104 yards/***(not Sat)/E

Strathaven G.C
(0357) 20421
Overton Avenue, Glasgow Road, Strathaven
On outskirts of town, on A726
(18) 6226 yards/**/F

Tarbert G.C
(088 02) 565
Kilberry Road, Tarbert, Argyll
Leave A83 from Tarbert for B8024
(9) 2230 yards/***/E

Torrance House G.C
(035 52) 33451
Strathaven Road, East Kilbride, Glasgow
(18) 6640 yards/***/F/H

Troon Municipal G.C(0292) 312464
Harling Drive, Troon, Ayrshire
Take A77 from Glasgow, follow signs for Troon
(18) 6687 yards/***/E
(18) 6327 yards/***/E
(18) 4784 yards/***/E

Turnberry Hotel G.C
(0655) 31000
Turnberry Hotel, Turnberry, Ayrshire
Off A77 from Glasgow
(18) 6950 yards/***/A/H
(18) 6276 yards/***/B/H
(less for Hotel guests)

Vale of Leven G.C
(0389) 52351
Northfield Course, Bonfield, Alexandria,
Dunbartonshire
Leave A82 at Bonhill
(18) 5156 yards/**/E

Vaul G.C
(087 92) 566
Scarinish, Isle of Tiree, Argyll
(9) 6246 yards/***/E

Westerwood Hotel & G.C
(0236) 725281
St Andrews Drive, Cumbernauld
(18) 6800 yards/***/F

Western Gailes G.C
(0294) 311649
Gailes, By Irvine, Ayrshire
5 miles N. of Troon on A78
(18) 6664 yards/***(not Thurs or Sat)/F/H

West Kilbride G.C
(0294) 823911
33-35 Fullerton Drive, Seamill, West Kilbride,
Ayrshire
Leave A78 at Seamill
6247 yards/**/F/L/H

Whitecraigs G.C
041-639 4530
72 Ayr Road, Giffnock, Glasgow
7 miles S. of Glasgow on the A77
(18) 6230 yards/*(intro only)/F

Williamwood G.C
041-637 2715
Clarkston Road, Netherlee, Glasgow
5 miles S. of city centre on the B767
(18) 5808 yards/***/F/H

Windyhill G.C
041-942 7157
Bal Jaffray Road, Bearsden, Glasgow
Take A809 for 1 mile to A810 to club
(18) 6254 yards/**/F

Wishaw G.C
(0698) 372869
55 Cleland Road, Wishaw, Lanarkshire
In centre of town, 3 miles S. of Motherwell
(18) 6160 yards/***(not Sat)/D

Arthur Weaver   YOUNG TOM MORRIS
Burlington Gallery

KEY

*** Visitors welcome at most times
** Visitors usually allowed on
weekdays only
* Visitors not normally permitted
(Mon, Wed) No visitors on
specified days

APPROXIMATE GREEN FEES
A – £30 plus
B – £20 – £30
C – £15 – £25
D – £10 – £20
E – Under £10
F – Green fees on application

RESTRICTIONS
G – Guests only
H – Handicap certificate required
H(24) – Handicap of 24 or less
required
L – Letter of introduction required
M – Visitor must be a member of
another recognised club.

Aberdour G.C
(0383) 860256
Seaside Place, Aberdour
From Inverkeithing, turn off A92 to Aberdour
village
(18) 5469 yards/**/E

Anstruther G.C
(0333) 312055
Marsfield, Shore Road, Anstruther
4 miles S. of St Andrews
(9) 4120 yards/***/E

Auchterderran G.C
(0592) 721579
Woodend Road, Cardenden
On the Glenrothes-Cardenden road
(9) 5400 yards/***/F

Burntisland G.C
(0592) 874093
Dodhead, Burntisland
1 miles N.E of town on the B923
(18) 5871 yards/***/F/H

Canmore G.C
(0383) 724969
Venturefair Avenue, Dunfermline
1 mile N. of Dunfermline on the A823
(18) 5474 yards/**/C

Crail G.S
(0333) 50960
Balcomie Clubhouse, Fifeness, Crail
2 miles E. of Crail
(18) 5720 yards/***/D/H

Cupar G.C
(0334) 53549
Hilltarvit, Cupar
10 miles from St Andrew off the A91
(9) 5300 yards/***(not Sat)/F/H

Dunfermline G.C
(0383) 723534
Pitfirrane, Crossford, Dunfermline
4 miles W. of town on Kincardine Bridge road
(18) 6244 yards/**/D

Dunnikier Park G.C
(0592) 261599
Dunnikier Way, Kirkcaldy
(18) 6601 yards/***/D/H

Elie G.C
(0333) 330301
Golf Club House, Elie, Leven
6 miles from Leven on the A917
(18) 6241 yards/***/F

Glenrothes G.C
(0592) 754561
Golf Course Road, Glenrothes
At W. of town, 8 miles from M90
(18) 6449 yards/***/E

Kinghorn G.C
(0592) 890345
Macduff Crescent, Kinghorn
3 miles W. of Kircaldy, off the A92
(18) 5246 yards/***/E

Kirkcaldy G.C
(0592) 260370
Balwearie Road, Kirkcaldy
W. of town on the A907
(18) 6004 yards/***(not Sat)/D

Ladybank G.C
(0337) 30814
Annsmuir, Ladybank
6 miles S. of Cupar on Edinburgh-Dunbar road
(18) 6617 yards/***/C

Leslie G.C
(0592) 741 449
Balsillie, Leslie
W. of Glenrothes on the A911
(9) 4940 yards/***/E

Leven Thistle G.C
(0333) 26397
Balfourst, Leven
In Links Road, off Church Road from the
Promenade
(18) 6434 yards/***/D

Lochgelly G.C
(0592) 80174
Cartmore Road, Lochgelly
W. of town, off the A910
(18) 5491 yards/***/F

Lundin Links G.C
(0333) 320202Golf Road, Lundin Links
3 miles E. of Leven on the A915
(18) 6377 yards/**(+ Sat pm)/F/H

Pitreavie (Dunfermline) G.C
(0383) 722591
Queensferry Road, Dunfermline
Leave A90 for the A823 to Dunfermline
(18) 6086 yards/***/D

St Andrews
(0334) 75757
St Andrews
(9) 1754 yards/***/F (Balgove)
(18) 5971 yards/***/F (Eden)
(18) 6284 yards/***/F (Jubilee)
(18) 6500 yards/***/F (Strathyrum)
(18) 6604 yards/***/F (New)
(18) 6933 yards/**(not Sun)/F/H/L (Old)

St Michaels G.C
(033 483) 365
Leuchars, St Andrews
200 yards W. of the village on the A919
(9) 5510 yards/***(not Sun am)/E

Saline G.C
(0383) 852591
Kinneddar Hill, Saline
5 miles N.W of Dunfermline, off the A907
(9) 5302 yards/***(not Sat)/E

Scoonie G.C
(033) 27057
North Links, Leven
10 miles S.W of St Andrews
(18) 5500 yards/***/F

Scotscraig G.C
(0382) 552515
Golf Road, Tayport
S. of the Tay Bridge, off the B946
(18) 6496 yards/***/F/M

Thornton G.C
(0592) 77111
Station Road, Thornton
In centre of village, 1 mile E. of A92
(18) 6177 yards/***/F

Arthur Weaver   **TEEING OFF**   *Burlington Gallery*

KEY

*** Visitors welcome at most times
** Visitors usually allowed on weekdays only
* Visitors not normally permitted (Mon, Wed) No visitors on " specified days

APPROXIMATE GREEN FEES
A – £30 plus
B – £20 – £30
C – £15 – £25
D – £10 – £20
E – Under £10
F – Green fees on application

RESTRICTIONS
G – Guests only
H – Handicap certificate required
H(24) – Handicap of 24 or less required
L – Letter of introduction required
M – Visitor must be a member of another recognised club.

TAYSIDE

Aberfeldy G.C
(0887) 20535
Taybridge Road, Aberfeldy, Perthshire
10 miles from Ballinluig off the A827
(9) 2733 yards/***/F

Alyth G.C
(08283) 2268
Pitcrocknie, Alyth, Perthshire
Off the B954 road, off the A926
(18) 6226 yards/***/F

Arbroath G.C
(0241) 72666
Elliot, Arbroath, Angus
2 miles S. of Arbroath on A92
(18) 6078 yards/***/F

Auchterarder G.C
(0764) 62804
Orchil Road, Auchterarder, Perthshire
S.W of town, off the A9
(18) 5737 yards/***/F

Blair Atholl G.C
(079681) 274
Blair Atholl, Perthshire
6 miles N. of Pitochry on the A9
(9) 5710 yards/***/F

Blairgowrie G.C
(0250) 873116
Rosemount, Blairgowrie, Perthshire
Take A923 from Perth and turn off to Rosemount
(18) 6588 yards/***/F/H
(18) 6895 yards/***/F/H

Brechin G.C
(03562) 2383
Trinity, by Brechin, Angus
In Trinity village, 1 mile N. of Brechin on B966
(18) 5267 yards/***/D

Caird Park G.C
(0382) 453606
Mains Loan, Dundee
N. of city, just off Kingsway
(18) 6303 yards/***/F

Callander G.C
(0877) 30090
Aveland Road, Callander, Perthshire
Signposted off the A84
(18) 5125 yards/***/D

Camperdown G.C
(0382) 623398
Camperdown Park, Dundee
In Coupar Angus Road, off Kingsway
(18) 6561 yards/***/E

Carnoustie
(0241) 53789
Links Parade, Carnoustie, Angus
12 miles E of Dundee, off the A630
(18) 6020 yards/***/F/H
(18) 5732 yards/***/F/H
(18) 6931 yards/***/F/H

Comrie G.C
(0764) 70544
c/o Sec, Donald C McGlashan
10 Polinard, Comrie, Perthshire
6 miles W. of Crieff on the A85
(9) 5966/***/F

Craigie Hill G.C
(0783) 22644
Cherrybank, Perth
1 mile W. of Perth
(18) 5739 yards/***/E

Crieff G.C
(0764) 2397
Perth Road, Crieff, Perthshire
18 miles along the A85, Perth-Crieff Road
(18) 6402 yards/***/F
(9) 4772 yards/***/F

Dalmunzie Hotel & G.C
(025085) 226
Spittal of Glenshee, Blairgowrie, Perthshire
22 miles N. of Blairgowrie on the A93
(9) 2035/***/E

Downfield G.C
(0382) 825595
Turnberry Avenue, Dundee
Leave Dundee by Kingsway and take A923
(18) 6804 yards/***/F

Dunblane New G.C
(0786) 823711
Perth Road, Dunblane, Perthshire
6 miles N. of Stirling on A9
(18) 6876 yards/**/D

Dunkeld and Birnam G.C
(035 02) 524
Fungarth, Dunkeld, Perthshire
1 mile N. of Dunkeld off the A9
(9) 5264 yards/***/E

Dunning G.C
(076484) 398
Rollo Park, Dunning, Perth
9 miles S.W of Perth off the A9
(9) 4836 yards/***/F/H

Edzell G.C
(03564) 7283
High Street, Edzell, By Brechin, Angus
Leave the A94 for the B966 at by-pass
(18) 6299 yards/***/F

Forfar G.C
(0307) 62120
Cunninghill, Arbroath Road, By Forfar, Angus
1 mile from town on road to Angus
(18) 6255 yards/***/C

Gleneagles Hotel & G.C
(0764) 62231
Auchterarder, Perthshire
Take A9 from Perth S.W for 16 miles
(18) 6471 yards/*/F
(18) 5964 yards/*/F

Killin G.C
(056 72) 312
Killin, Perthshire
On outskirts of village
(9) 2508 yards/***/E/H

King James VI G.C
(0738) 32460
Moncreiffe Island, Perth
By footbridge over River Tay
(18) 6026 yards/***(not Sat)/D

Green Hotel G.C
(0577) 63467
Beeches Park, Kinross, Perthshire
17 miles S. of Perth
(18) 6111 yards/***/D

Kirriemuir G.C
(0575) 72729
Kirriemuir, Angus
1 mile N. of town centre
(18) 5591 yards/**/E

Letham Grange G.C
(024 189) 373
Letham Grange, Colliston, By Arbroath, Angus
Take the A933 for 4 miles
(18) 6789 yards/***/F/H

Milnathort G.C
(0577) 64069
South Street, Milnathort
2 miles N. of Kinross, off the M90
(9) 5411 yards/***/E

Monifieth Links G.C
(0382) 532767
Dundee, Angus
Just outside Monifieth on the A930
(18) 6657 yards/***(not Sat)/D/H
(18) 5123 yards/***(not Sat)/E/H

Montrose Links Trust
(0674) 72932
Trail Drive, Montrose, Angus
1 mile from town centre off the A92
(18) 6451 yards/***/F/H
(18) 4815 yards/***/F/H

Murrayshall Hotel & G.C
(0738) 52784
Murrayshall, by Scone, Perthshire
On the A94 from Perth
(18) 6416 yards/***/F/H

Muthill G.C
(0764) 81523
Peat Road, Muthill, Crieff
Signposted off the A822
(9) 2371 yards/***/E

North Inch G.C
Near centre of Perth off the A9
(18) 4736 yards/***/E

Panmure G.C
(0241) 53120
Barry, Angus
Take A930 to Barry
(18) 6317 yards/***(not Sat)/D/H

Pitlochry G.C
(0796) 2796
Golf Course Road, Pitlochry
Half mile from Pitlochry on A9
(18) 5811 yards/***/F/H

St Fillans G.C
(0764) 85312
St Fillans, Perthshire
On A85 between Crieff and Lochearnhead
(9) 5268 yards/***/E

Strathtay G.C
(08874) 367
Tighanoisinn, Grandtully, Perthshire
4 miles W. of Ballinkrig
(9) 4980 yards/***/E

Taymouth Castle G.C
(088 73) 228
Kenmore, by Aberfeldy, Tayside
6 miles W. of Aberfeldy
(18) 6066 yards/***/D/H

CENTRAL

Aberfoyle G.C
(08772) 441
Braeval, Aberfoyle, Stirlingshire
1 mile from Aberfoyle on the A81
(18) 5205 yards/***/D

Alloa G.C
(0259) 722745
Schawpark, Sauchie, Clackmannanshire
On A908 between Alloa and Tillicoultry
(18) 6230 yards/***/E

Alva G.C
(0259) 60431
Beauclerc Street, Alva, Clackmannanshire
3 miles N. of Alloa on the A91
(9) 2407 yards/***/F

Bonnybridge G.C
(0259) 722078
Larbert Road, Bonnybridge, Stirlingshire
3 miles W. of Falkirk on the B816
(9) 6060 yards/*(with member only)/F

Brachead G.C
(0259) 722078
Cambus, By Alloa, Clackmannanshire
1 mile W. of Alloa on the A907
(18) 6013 yards/***/E/H

Bridge of Allan G.C
(0786) 832332
Sunlaw, Bridge of Allan, Stirling
Over the River Allan off Stirling Road
(9) 4932 yards/***(not Sat)/E

Dollar G.C
(02594) 2400
Brewlands House, Dollar, Clackmannanshire
(18) 5144 yards/**/F

Falkirk G.C
(0324) 611061
Stirling Road, Cumlins, Falkirk
2 miles W. of Falkirk centre on A9
(18) 6202 yards/**/E

Falkirk Tryst G.C
(0324) 562091
Burnhead Rd, Larbert
1/4 mile from Larbert Station
(18) 6053 yards/***/D

Glenbervie G.C
(0324) 562605
Stirling Road, Larbert, Stirlingshire
1 mile N. of Larbert on the A9
(18) 6469 yards/*(by intro only)/C

Grangemouth Municipal G.C
(0324) 714355
Polmont Hill, Polmont, Falkirk, Stirlingshire
Leave M9 at junction 4 and follow signs to Hill
(18) 6314 yards/***/F/H

Muckhart G.C
(025 981) 423
Drumburn Road, Muckhart, Dollar, Clackmannanshire
Signposted off the A91 and A823 S. of Muckhart
(18) 6115 yards/***/E

Polmont G.C
(0324) 711277
Maddiston, by Falkirk, Stirlingshire
4 miles S. of Falkirk
(9) 3044 yards/**/E

Stirling G.C
(0786) 64098
Queens Road, Stirling
Half mile W. of town centre on A811
(18) 5976 yards/**/D

Tillicoultry G.C
(0259) 50124
Alva Road, Tiilicoultry
(9) 2528 yards/***/E

Tulliallan G.C
(0259) 30897
Alloa Road, Kincardine on Forth, By Alloa
2 miles N. of Kincardine Bridge on Alloa Road
(18) 5982 yards/***/F

KEY

*** Visitors welcome at most times
** Visitors usually allowed on weekdays only
* Visitors not normally permitted
(Mon, Wed) No visitors on specified days

APPROXIMATE GREEN FEES
A – £30 plus
B – £20 – £30
C – £15 – £25
D – £10 – £20
E – Under £10
F – Green fees on application

RESTRICTIONS
G – Guests only
H – Handicap certificate required
H(24) – Handicap of 24 or less required
L – Letter of introduction required
M – Visitor must be a member of another recognised club.

GRAMPIAN

Aboyne G.C
(03398) 86328
Formaston Park, Aboyne, Aberdeenshire
Signposted on the A93 from Aberdeen
(18) 5330 yards/***/F

Auchenblae G.C
(05612) 407
Auchenblae, Laurencekirk
5 miles N. of Laurencekirk
(9) 2174 yards/***/E

Auchmill G.C
(0224) 642121
Auchmill, Aberdeen
(9) 2538 yards/***/E

Ballater G.C
(03397) 55567
Ballater, Aberdeenshire
40 miles W. of Aberdeen on A93
(18) 5704 yards/***/D

Banchory G.C
(03302) 2365
Kinneskie, Banchory, Kincardineshire
18 miles W. of Aberdeen
(18) 5305 yards/***/F

Balnagask G.C
(0224) 876407
St Fitticks Road, Aberdeen
2 miles S.E of the city centre
(18) 5468 yards/***/E

Bon-Accord G.C
(0224) 633464
19 Golf Course Road, Aberdeen
Beside Pittodrie Stadium near the beach
(18) 6384 yards/***/F

Braemar G.C
(03397) 41618
Cluniebank, Braemar, Aberdeenshire
Half mile from the village centre
(18) 4916 yards/***/E

Buckpool G.C
(0542) 32236
Barhill Road, Buckie, Banffshire
At end of A98 to Buckpool
(18) 6259 yards/***/E

Caledonian G.C
(0224) 632 443
20 Golf Road, Aberdeen
Adjacent to the Pittodrie Stadium
(18) 6384 yards/***/F

Cruden Bay G.C
(0779) 812285
Aulton Road, Cruden Bay, Peterhead, Aberdeenshire
7 miles S. of Peterhead
(9) 4710 yards/***/E
(18) 6370 yards/***/F

Cullen G.C
(0542) 40585
The Links, Cullen, Buckie, Banffshire
W. of Cullen off the A98
(18) 4610 yards/***/E

Deeside G.C
(0224) 867697
Bieldside, Aberdeen
3 miles W. of Aberdeen on the A93
(18) 6332 yards/***/D/H or M or L

Duff House Royal G.C
(02612) 2062
Barnyards, Banff, Banffshire
2 minutes from town centre off A97 and A98
(18) 6161 yards/***/F/H

Elgin G.C
(0343) 54238
Hardhillock, Elgin, Morayshire
Signposted off the A91
(18) 6401 yards/***/D

Forres G.C
(0309) 72949
Muiryshade, Forres
1 mile S. from town centre
(18) 5615 yards/***/E/H

Fraserburgh G.C
(0346) 28287
Philorth, Fraserburgh, Aberdeenshire
1 mile S.E of Fraserburgh on the A92
(18) 6217 yards/***/E

Garmouth and Kingston G.C
(034 387) 388
Garmouth, Fochabers, Moray
(18) 5649 yards/***/E

Hazelhead G.C
(0224) 321830
Hazelhead Park, Aberdeen
4 miles W. of the city centre
(18) 5303 yards/***/E
(18) 5673 yards/***/E

Hopeman G.C
(0343) 830578
Hopeman, Moray
(18) 5439 yards/***/E

Huntly G.C
(0466) 2643
Cooper Park, Huntly, Aberdeenshire
Half mile from town centre on the A96
(18) 5399 yards/***(not Wed or Thur)/F/H

Inverallochy G.C
(03465) 2324
Inverallochy, Nr Fraserburgh, Aberdeenshire
3 miles S. of Fraserburgh on the B9033
(18) 5137 yards/***/E

Inverurie G.C
(0467) 24080
Blackhall Road, Inverurie, Aberdeenshire
On the A96 Aberdeen-Inverness Road
(18) 5096 yards/***/E

Keith G.C
(05422) 2469
Fife Park, Keith, Banffshire
Half mile off the A96
(18) 5811 yards/***/F

Kings Links G.C
(0224) 632269
Golf Road, Kings Links, Aberdeen
E. of city, near Pittodrie Stadium
(18) 5838 metres/***/E

Kintore G.C
(0467) 32631
Balbithan Road, Kintore, Inverurie, Aberdeenshire
12 miles N.W. of Aberdeen off the A96
(9) 2650 yards/***/E

Macdonald G.C
(0358) 20576
Hospital Road, Ellon, Aberdeenshire
Leave Ellon on A948 for Auchnagatt
(18) 5986 yards/***/E

Moray G.C
(034 381) 2018
Stotfield Road, Lossiemouth, Moray
6 miles N. of Elgin off the A941
(18)6643 yards/***/F/H
(18)6005 yards/***/F/H

Murcar G.C
(0224) 704354
Bridge of Don, Aberdeen
3 miles N.E of Aberdeen on the A92
(18) 6240 yards/**/F

Newburgh-On-Ythan G.C
Newburgh, Aberdeenshire
14 miles N. of Aberdeen on the Peterhead Road
(9) 6404 yards/***(not Tues pm)/F

Nigg Bay G.C
(0224) 871286
St Fitticks Road, Balnagask, Aberdeen
S.E of the city centre
(18) 5984 yards/***/E

Peterhead G.C
(0779) 72149
Craigewan Links, Peterhead, Aberdeenshire
30 miles from Aberdeen, between A92 and A975
(18) 6182 yards/***/D
(9) 2950 yards/***/E

Royal Aberdeen G.C
(0224) 702571
Balgownie, Bridge of Don, Aberdeen
Over River Don, 2 miles N. of Aberdeen on A92
(18) 4033 yards/**/F/H
(18) 6372 yards/**/F/H

Royal Tarlair G.C
(0261) 32897
Buchan Street, Macduff
48 miles from Aberdeen on the A98
(18) 5866 yards/***/D

Spey Bay G.C
(0343) 820424
Spey Bay, Fochabers, Moray
Follow the B9104 Spey Bay road to the coast
(18) 6059 yards/***/F/H

Stonehaven G.C
(0569) 62124
Cowie, Stonehaven
N. of the town on the A92
(18) 5103 yards/***(not Sat/Sun am)/F

Strathlene G.C
(0542) 31798
Portessie, Buckie, Banffshire
Take A942 to Buckie and to Strathlene
(18) 6180 yards/***/E

Tarland G.C
(033981) 81413
Tarland, Aboyne, Aberdeenshire
3 miles W. of Aberdeen on the A93
(9) 5812 yards/***/E

Torphins G.C
(033982) 493
Golf Road, Torphins, Banchory, Aberdeenshire
6 miles W. of Banchory on A980
(9) 2330 yards/***/E

Turriff G.C
(0888) 62745
Rosehall, Turriff, Aberdeenshire
Signposted off the B9024
(18) 6105 yards/***/E

Westhill G.C
(0224) 740159
Westhill Heights, Westhill, Skene, Aberdeenshire
6 miles from Aberdeen on the A944
(18) 5866 yards/***(not Sat/Sun pm)/E/H

HIGHLAND

Abernethy G.C
(0479 82) 637
Nethybridge, Inverness-shire
N. of Nethybridge on the B970
(9) 2484 yards/***/F

Alness G.C
(0349) 883877
Ardross Road, Alness, Ross-shire
10 miles N.E. of Dingwall on the A9
(9) 4718 yards/***/E

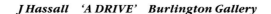

J Hassall 'A DRIVE' Burlington Gallery

Askernish G.C
Askernish, Lochboisdale, South Uist,
Western Isles
Take ferry from Oban to S.Uist
(9) 5114 yards/***/F

Boat of Garten G.C
(0479 83) 282
Boat of Garten, Inverness-shire
Take the A9 to the B970
(18) 5720 yards/***/E

Brora G.C
(0408) 21417
Golf Road, Brora, Sutherland
65 miles N. of Inverness on the A9
(18) 6110 yards/***/F

Carrbridge G.C
(047984) 674
Carrbridge, Inverness-shire
200 yards from the village on the A938
(9) 2623 yards/***/F

Fort Augustus G.C
(0320) 6460
Markethill, Fort Augustus, Inverness-shire
Entrance is just off the A82
(9) 5454 yards/***/E

Fortrose and Rosemarkie G.C
(0381) 20529
Ness Road East, Fortrose, Ross-shire
Take A9 from Inverness and follow signs to
Fortrose
(18) 5973 yards/***/F

Fort William G.C
(0397) 4464
North Road, Turlundy, Fort Wiiliam
2 miles N. of Fort William off the A82
(18) 5686 yards/***/E

Gairloch G.C
(0455) 2407
Gairloch, Ross-shire
S. of the town, on the A832
(9) 2093 yards/***(not Sun)/E

Golspie G.C
(04083) 3266
Ferry Road, Golspie, Sutherland
Take A9 from Inverness to Golspie
(18) 5900 yards/***/F

Grantown-On-Spey G.C
(0479) 2079
Golf Course Road, Grantown-On-Spey
N. of town off the A939
(18) 5745 yards/***/E

Invergordon G.C
(0349) 852116
Cromlet Drive, Invergordon, Ross and
Cromarty
The club house is in King Geoge Street
(9) 6028 yards/***/E

Inverness G.C
(0463) 239882
Culcabock Road, Inverness
1 mile from town centre on S. of River Ness
(18) 6226 yards/***/D/H

Kingussie G.C
(054 02) 600
Gynack Road, Kingussie, Inverness-shire
Take A9 to village and follow signs
(18) 5504 yards/***/E

Lybster G.C
Main Street, Lybster, Caithness
13 miles S. of Wick on the A9
(9) 1898 yards/***/E

Muir of Ord G.C
(0463) 870825
Great Northern Road, Muir of Ord, Ross and
Cromarty
12 miles N. of Inverness on the A862
(18) 5129 yards/***/E

Nairn G.C
(0667) 53208
Seabank Road, Nairn
1 mile N. of the A96, near Nairn
(18) 6556 yards/***/F/H

Nairn Dunbar G.C
(0667) 52741
Lochloy Road, Nairn
Half mile E. of town on the A96
(18) 6431 yards/***/D

Newtonmore G.C
(05403) 328
Golf Course Road, Newtonmore, Inverness-
shire
Near centre of village off the A9
(18) 5890 yards/***/E

Reay G.C
(084 781) 288
By Thurso, Caithness
11 miles W. of Thurso towards Bettyhill
(18) 5865 yards/***/E

Royal Dornoch G.C
(0862) 810219
Golf Road, Dornoch, Sutherland
Take A949 for Dornoch and follow signs
(18) 6577 yards/***/F/H
(9)***/F

Sconser G.C
(0478) 2277
Sconser, Isle of Skye, Inverness-shire
Between Broadford and Portree on the
main road
(9) 4796 yards/***/E

Stornoway G.C
(0851) 2240
Castle Grounds, Stornoway, Isle of Lewis
Near town centre, in castle grounds
(18) 5119 yards/***(not Sun)/E/H

Strathpeffer Spa G.C
(0997) 21219
Strathpeffer, Ross-shire
5 miles W. of Dingwall on the A834
(18) 4792 yards/***/E

Tain G.C
(0862) 2314
Tain, Ross-shire
Half mile from town centre off A9 N.
(18) 6222 yards/***/F

Tarbat G.C
(086287) 236
Portmahomack, Ross-shire
7 miles E. of Tain on the B9165 off A9
(9) 2329 yards***(not Sun)/E

Thurso G.C
(0847) 63807
Newlands of Geise, Thurso, Caithness
2 miles S.W of Thurso station on B870
(18) 5818 yards/***/E

Torvean G.C
(0463) 237543
Glenurquhart Road, Inverness, Inverness-shire
1 mile W. of city on the A82
(18) 4308 yards/***/F

Wick G.C
(0955) 2726
Reiss, Wick, Caithness
3 miles N. of Wick on the A9
(18) 5976 yards/***/E

ORKNEY AND SHETLAND

Orkney G.C
(0856) 2457
Grainbank, St Ola, by Kirkwall, Orkney
Half mile W. of Kirkwall
(18) 5406 yards/***/E

Shetland G.C
(059584) 369
Dale, P.O Box 18, Lerwick, Shetland
3 miles N. of Lerwick on the main road
(18) 5776 yards/***/F

Stromness G.C
(0856) 850772
Ness, Stromness, Orkney
(18) 4600 yards/***/E

Shortspoon   *IN THE BURN*   *Burlington Gallery*

KEY

*** Visitors welcome at most times
** Visitors usually allowed on weekdays only
* Visitors not normally permitted (Mon, Wed) No visitors on specified days

APPROXIMATE GREEN FEES

A – £30 plus
B – £20 – £30
C – £15 – £25
D – £10 – £20
E – Under £10
F – Green fees on application

RESTRICTIONS

G – Guests only
H – Handicap certificate required
H(24) – Handicap of 24 or less required
L – Letter of introduction required
M – Visitor must be a member of another recognised club.

BORDERS

Duns G.C
(0361) 83327
Hardens Road, Duns, Berwickshire
1 mile W. of Duns on A6105
(9) 5754 yards/***/E

Eyemouth G.C
(08907) 50551
Gunsgreen House, Eyemouth
3 miles N. of Burnmouth on A1107
(9) 5446 yards/***/E

Galashiels G.C
(0896) 3724
Ladhope Recreation Ground, Galashiels, Selkirkshire
N.E of town, off A7
(18) 5309 yards/***/E

Gatehouse G.C
(055 74) 654
Laurieston Road, Gatehouse
Quarter of a mile off A75
(9) 4796 yards/***/E

Hawick G.C
(0450) 72293
Vertish Hill, Hawick, Roxburghshire
S. of Hawick on A7
(18) 5929 yards/***/E

Hirsel G.C
(0890) 2678
Kelso Road, Coldstream
At west end of Coldstream on A697
(9) 2828 yards/***/E

Jedburgh G.C
(0835) 63587
Dunion Road, Jedburgh, Roxburghshire
Half mile out of town
(9) 5522 yards/***/F

Kelso G.C
(0573) 23009
Racecourse Road, Kelso, Roxburghshire
1 mile from town centre within National Hunt Racecourse
(18) 6066 yards/***/F

Lauder G.C
(057) 82409
Galashiels Road, Lauder
Half mile from Lauder off A68
(9) 6003 yards/***/F

Melrose G.C
(089682) 2855
Dingleton, Melrose, Roxburghshire
Half mile S. of Melrose town centre
(9) 5464 yards/**/F

Minto G.C
(0450) 87220
Minto Village, by Denholme, Hawick, Roxburghshire
5 miles N.E. of Hawick off A698
(18) 5460 yards/***/E

Peebles G.C
(0721) 20197
Kirkland Street, Peebles
N.W. of town off the A72
(18) 6137 yards/***/E

St. Boswells G.C
(0835) 22359
St Boswells, Roxburghshire
At junction of A68 and B6404
(9) 2625 yards/***/E

Selkirk G.C
(0750) 20621
The Hill, Selkirk
1 mile S. of Selkirk on the A7 to Hawick
(9) 5640 yards/***/E

Torwoodlee G.C
(0896) 2260
Edinburgh Road, Galashiels, Selkirkshire
1 mile from Galashiels on A7 to Edinburgh
(9) 5800 yards/***(not Sat)/F

West Linton G.C
(0968) 60256
West Linton, Peebleshire
17 miles S.W. of Edinburgh on the A702
(18) 6024 yards/***/D

DUMFRIES & GALLOWAY

Castle Douglas G.C
(0556) 2801Abercromby Road, Castle Douglas, Kirkcudbrightshire
In the centre of the town
(9) 5400 yards/***(not Thurs pm)/F

Colvend G.C
(055663) 398
Sandyhills, By Dalbeattie, Kirkcudbrightshire
6 miles from Dalbeattie on A710
(9) 2322 yards/***/F

Dumfries & County G.C
(0387) 53585
Edinburgh Road, Dumfries
1 mile N. of Dumfries on the A701
(18) 5928 yards/***(not Sat)/D

Dumfries & Galloway G.C
(0387) 63582
Laurieston Avenue, Dumfries
W. of Dumfries on the A75
(18) 5782 yards/***/D

Kircudbright G.C
(0567) 30542
Stirling Crescent, Kirkcudbright
Near centre of town, off B727
(18) 5598 yards/***/F

Langholm G.C
(0541) 80559
Langholm, Dumfriesshire
Between Carlisle and Hawick on the A7
(9) 5246 yards/***/E

Lochmaben G.C
(0387) 810552
Castlehill Gate, Lochmaben, Dumfriesshire
Leave A74 at Lockerbie for A709 for Dumfries
(9) 5304 yards/***/F

Lockerbie
(05762) 3363
Currie Road, Lockerbie, Dumfriesshir
Take A74 to Lockerbie
(18) 5228 yards/***(not Sat)/F

Moffat G.C
(0683) 20020
Coatshill, Moffat
Take A701 for 1 mile off the A74
(18) 5218 yards/***(not Wed pm)/D

New Galloway G.C
(06442) 239Castle Douglas, Kirkcudbrightshire
Just out of Village on the A762
(9) 5058 yards/***/E

Newton Stewart G.C
(0671) 2172
Kirroughtree Avenue, Minnigaff, Newton Stewart
Leave the A75 at sign for Minnigaff Village
(9) 5500 yards/***/E

Portpatrick (Dunskey) G.C
(077681) 273
Portpatrick, Stranraer, Wigtownshire
Signposted on the A77 to Portpatrick
(18) 5644 yards/***/D/H

Powfoot G.C
(04612) 2866
Cummertrees, Annan, Dumfriesshire
3 miles from Annan on the B724
(18) 6266 yards/**/F

St Medan G.C
(098 87) 358
Monreith, Port William, Wigtownshire
3 miles S. of Port William on the A747
(9) 4454 yards/***/E

Sanquhar G.C
(0659) 50577
Old Barr Road, Sanquhar, Dumfriesshire
mile from Sanquhar off the A76
(9) 2572 yards/***/E

Southerness G.C
(038 788) 677
Southerness, Dumfries
16 miles S.W of Dumfries off the A710
(18) 6554 yards/***/D

Stranraer G.C
(0776) 3539
Crechmore, Stranraer
Take the A718 from Stranraer towards Leswalt
(18) 6300 yards/***/D

Thornhill G.C
(0848) 30546
Blacknest, Thornhill, Dumfries
14 miles N. of Dumfries on the A76 to Thornhill
(18) 6011 yards/***/E

Wigtown and Bladnoch
(098 84) 3354Lightlands Avenue, Wigtown, Wigtownshire
Right at town square, left at Agnew Crescent
(9) 2732 yards/***/F

Wigtownshire County G.C
(05813)420
Mains of Park, Glenluce, Newton Stewart, Wigtownshire
8 miles E. of Stranraer on the A75
(18) 5715 yards/***/D

Rich or Poor, on expenses or on holiday, one way or another few travellers fail to budget their journey. It is, therefore, without any undue apologies that we present the following price guide to the accommodation available at our selected watering holes. We would, however recommend particularly in this day and age of the special break a phone call in advance to check room rates as well as availability.

It cannot be stressed enough that each establishment has been included on merit and the guide was not compiled with any preconceived notions of suiting each and every pocket. One thing our Watering Holes do have in common is that, whatever the price, they provide the quality every discerning traveller recognises. If for any reason you do have cause for complaint or compliment please do let us know.

Key to Price Guide.

£	*Prices from less than*	*£40 room and breakfast*
££	*Prices from between*	*£40 - £60*
£££	*Prices from between*	*£60 - £80*
££££	*Prices from between*	*£80 - £100*
£££££	*Prices from between*	*£100 - £150*
*	*Prices from*	*£150*

221

King's course, Gleneagles - Robert Turnbull:
Image size 28ins x 21 3\4ins

St Andrews - Robert Turnbull: Image size 28ins x 21 3/4ins

Crofters Cottage - David Dane:
Image size - 10 x 13ins 25 x 33cms

Highland Cattle - David Dane:
Image size 10 x 13ins 25 x 33cms

Scotland for Ever! - Lady Butler: Image size 15 x 29ins 38 x 74 cm

Highland River - Wendy Reeves 24ins x 36ins

The Waterfall - Elizabeth Halstead
30ins x 20ins

An Early Start - Wendy Reeves 43ins x 53ins

Peaceful Moments - Don Vaughan
24ins x 36ins

Fishing in Calm Waters - George Cammidge 40ins x 16ins

Valley of the Stags - Elizabeth Halstead 20ins x 30ins

Order Form

Prints	Artist	Size	Price not including VAT	Qty.	Cost
Kings Course Gleneagles	Robert Turnbull	28" x 21¾"	£35		
St. Andrews	Robert Turnbull	28" x 21¾"	£35		
Highland Cattle	David Dane	38" x 45"	£23		
Fishing in Calm Waters	George Cammidge	40" x 16"	£13		
The Scotch Gamekeeper	Richard Ansdell	76" x 64"	£65		
Highland Rivers	Wendy Reeves	60" x 90"	£13		
Crofter Cottage	David Dane	38" x 45"	£23		
The Last Drive	Robert Wade	36" x 53"	£65		
Surveying the Terrain	Elizabeth Halstead	70" x 56"	£13		
Scotland for Ever	Lady Butler	38" x 74"	£17		
Dejeuner du Salon	Jean André	46" x 66"	£17		
The Waterfall	Elizabeth Halstead	76" x 50"	£13		
Valley of the Stags	Elizabeth Halstead	50" x 76"	£13		
An Early Start	Wendy Reeves	43" x 53"	£23		
Peaceful Moments	Don Vaughan	60" x 90"	£13		
The Kensington Collection					
Holiday Golf Guide 1994			£14.95		
Ping Women's Golf Year 1992-1993			£12.95		
Following the Fairways			£15.95		
Travelling the Turf 1994			£15.95		
Fishing Forays 1994			£15.95		
Postage and Packing					£3.50
				TOTAL	

I enclose a cheque for the sum of £................... payable to Kensington West Productions.

Please debit my: Access / Visa / Amex / Diners Card by the sum of £.................................

No.

Name ....

Address ....

Tel. No ....Signature ....

All orders should be sent to:
Kensington West Productions Ltd, 5 Cattle Market, Hexham, Northumberland NE46 1NJ.
Telephone your order on 0434 609933